DATE DUE

DEMCO 38-296

Peggy Glanville-Hicks

Peggy Glanville-Hicks. Music Division, The New York Public Library at Lincoln Center, Astor, Lenox and Tilden Foundations.

PEGGY GLANVILLE-HICKS

A Bio-Bibliography

Deborah Hayes

Bio-Bibliographies in Music, Number 27
Donald L. Hixon, Series Adviser

GREENWOOD PRESS
New York • Westport, Connecticut • London

Riverside Community College
Library
4800 Magnolia Avenue
Riverside, CA 92506

ML 134 .G52 H4 1990

Hayes, Deborah, 1939-

Peggy Glanville-Hicks

Library of Congress Cataloging-in-Publication Data

Hayes, Deborah.
 Peggy Glanville-Hicks : a bio-bibliography / Deborah Hayes.
  p. cm.—(Bio-bibliographies in music, ISSN 0742-6968 ; no.
27)
 Includes bibliographical references.
 ISBN 0-313-26422-8 (lib. bdg. : alk. paper)
 1. Glanville-Hicks, Peggy—Bibliography. 2. Glanville-Hicks,
Peggy—Discography. I. Title. II. Series.
 ML134.G52H4 1990
 016.78'092—dc20   90-34140

British Library Cataloguing in Publication Data is available.

Copyright © 1990 by Deborah Hayes

All rights reserved. No portion of this book may be
reproduced, by any process or technique, without the
express written consent of the publisher.

Library of Congress Catalog Card Number: 90-34140
ISBN: 0-313-26422-8
ISSN: 0742-6968

First published in 1990

Greenwood Press, 88 Post Road West, Westport, CT 06881
An imprint of Greenwood Publishing Group, Inc.

Printed in the United States of America

The paper used in this book complies with the
Permanent Paper Standard issued by the National
Information Standards Organization (Z39.48-1984).

10 9 8 7 6 5 4 3 2 1

Contents

Preface

This bio-bibliography is the first book on Peggy Glanville-Hicks (1912-), Australian-born composer and critic. It is the work of an "outsider," a music historian, drawing on the writings and recollections of many "insiders," the composer's close friends and colleagues. It documents the music, performances, and critical writings of the composer herself, and the work of previous biographers, bibliographers, and interviewers. While information has come from many parts of the world, most of the sources are in Australia, where Glanville-Hicks now lives, and in the United States, where she established her reputation in the late 1940s and 1950s.

The biography chapter, a chronological account of Glanville-Hicks's life, examines certain constant themes in her work: her search for authentic historical and spiritual sources of musical inspiration and technique, her enthusiasm for American music in the mid-twentieth century, and her speculations on music's future path. This chapter uses the sources listed in later chapters: "Works and Performances" (**W** numbers), "Discography" (**D** numbers), "Bibliography by Glanville-Hicks" (**G** numbers), "Bibliography About Glanville-Hicks" (**B** numbers), and "Archival Resources" (**A** numbers).

The second chapter, "Works and Performances," with the mnemonic **W** before each catalog number, lists her compositions, **W1** through **W70**, in chronological order by year of composition, 1931-1989, including information on publisher, date of publication, duration, and instrumentation. Chronological order seemed most appropriate here, for Glanville-Hicks has been concerned with working out, over time, certain styles, forms, and textures. In this chapter, premiere and other selected performances are indicated by lower-case letters after the work's number (**W46a**) and listed below each title. References are given to recordings (**D** numbers) and to bibliographical items (**G**, **B**, and **A** numbers). A publishers directory, an alphabetical list of her compositions, and a classified list conclude the chapter.

The third chapter, with the mnemonic **D**, is a "Discography" of the commercial recordings of Glanville-Hicks's works, both in and out of print, in alphabetical order, **D1** to **D21**. References are given to the work's main listing in the previous chapter (**W** numbers) and to bibliographical items (**G**, **B**, and **A** numbers).

The fourth chapter, "Bibliography by Glanville-Hicks," with the mnemonic **G**, lists her writings in chronological order 1945-1989, numbered **G1** to **G699**. For each of the years 1947-1955, her reviews for the *New York Herald Tribune* are grouped separately from longer items, as are her *Musical America* reviews for January-May 1950, and her composer entries for *Grove's Dictionary* in 1954. Each item in the chapter is annotated. This is the first attempt at a complete listing of the writings of Peggy Glanville-Hicks. Besides showing the scope of her own interests, it provides a record of this period in American music history in the words of a perceptive, articulate listener and active participant.

The fifth chapter, "Bibliography About Glanville-Hicks," with the mnemonic **B** before the catalog number, lists music reviews, performance reviews, feature articles, publicity items, and press announcements about her life and works. This chapter lists items from all previous Glanville-Hicks bibliographies and from library clipping files and indexes (*Music Index, RILM, ARTSDOC, Bibliography Master Index,* etc.), no matter how brief the reference to her compositional and critical ideas. Each item is annotated. This listing is alphabetical by author and title, an arrangement that may seem at odds with the chronological order of the biography, **W** listings, and **G** listings. The **B** listings, though, taken as a whole, have an un-chronological quality. Some reviewers use information from earlier times to explain the work they are hearing, and some encyclopedia entries are very out of date by the time they are published. The **B** listings can be read separately, or they can be read in the groupings by chronology and subject in which they appear, as *see* references, in the chapters of biography and works.

The sixth chapter, "Archival Resources," with the mnemonic **A** before the catalog number, lists materials by library; libraries are in alphabetical order by country and name (with international library sigla in parentheses). For large collections, such as the Peggy Glanville-Hicks Collection in Melbourne (**A3**), categories of material are indicated by lower-case letters (**A3a**).

The "Index" lists authors and composers, titles of Glanville-Hicks's compositions and longer articles, and other significant categories. References to the "Biography" are indicated by the actual page number, while items located in the other chapters are identified with the relevant mnemonic (**W, D, G, B, A**) and catalog number.

Readers able to supply information not included in this volume, or wishing further information, are encouraged to contact the author through Greenwood Press.

Acknowledgments

My deepest gratitude to Peggy Glanville-Hicks for her hospitality in Sydney in July 1988 and for granting permission to obtain copies of her correspondence from American libraries.

Several other individuals in Australia were invaluable to the project. In Sydney, Angela Gaffikin at the Australian Music Centre went out of her way to find information even beyond the extensive files available at the Centre. My thanks go to the entire Centre staff, including director Richard Leets and information specialist Angela Lenahan.

In Melbourne, Joyce McGrath, Arts Librarian at the State Library of Victoria which houses the Glanville-Hicks collection, and a close friend of the composer as well, was able to answer my numerous questions. Joel Crotty, also of Melbourne, author of a bibliographic study of Glanville-Hicks that includes the Melbourne library collection, was also able to answer my questions and continued to send me materials after I returned to Colorado, including things published in Australia that I would not have known about.

Many others in Australia provided information, encouragement and support, foremost among them Alison Alsop, Fraser Fair, and Frederick Fair in Melbourne, and Margaret Fair in Braidwood. From Melbourne, Thérèse Radic, Roger Glanville-Hicks, and Kay Dreyfus provided information and documentation. In Sydney, my search for materials was aided by Andrea Stanberg, Leonard Burtenshaw, James Murdoch, Peter Sculthorpe, Adrienne Askill, Catherine Adamson of the University of Sydney News Service, Frances Love of the Australia Council, and the staffs of the State Library of New South Wales and the Dennis Wolanski Library of the Performing Arts at the Sydney Opera House. At the beginning of the project, while I was still in Colorado, James Murdoch sent copies of the two invaluable "Peggy Glanville-Hicks" brochures produced in 1969, when she was living in Athens, which are difficult if not impossible to find in the United States. In Canberra, the National Film and Sound Archive staff were exceedingly helpful, as were Pru Neidorf, Music Librarian at the National Library of Australia, and staff members Georgina Binns of music, and Jennifer Gall of oral history.

My thanks go also to Margarita M. Hanson of Éditions de L'Oiseau-lyre in Monaco for information on materials in the L'Oiseau-lyre Library.

x Acknowledgments

In the United States, my very special thanks go to Virginia Boucher and her staff, especially Regina Ahram and Anne McCollum, at the University of Colorado Interlibrary Loan department in Boulder, who managed to fill my seemingly endless orders for the *New York Herald Tribune* on microfilm and for books and periodicals from all over the world, while remaining calm, efficient, and optimistic. Thanks go also to Margaret Howell, Special Collections librarian at the University of Missouri, who helped in my further searches through the *Herald Tribune* microfilms, as did staff members in the microfilm departments of the libraries at Stanford University and the University of California at Berkeley.

Many librarians provided bibliographic assistance. Wayne Shirley, music specialist at the Library of Congress, provided detailed information on several of the library's holdings, as did Kendall L. Crilly at the Yale University Music Library, and Richard Jackson and the staff (who request anonymity) of the New York Public Library. Additional bibliographic assistance was provided by several other librarians: Marion Korda at the University of Louisville Music Library; William McClellan at the University of Illinois Music Library; Fred Blum at the Eastern Michigan University Library; Barbara Jeskalian at San Jose State University; Ralph Hartsock at the University of North Texas; Suzanne Moulton at the University of Denver; Barbara B. Rhyne at the Multnomah County Library in Portland, Oregon; Michael Meckna at Ball State University; the reference staff of the *St. Louis Post-Dispatch*; and Karl Kroeger, Leah Middlemiss, and Anita Cochran of the University of Colorado Music Library. My searches were also aided by Tom Dickinson, Allen Hughes, and Jane Weiner LePage. Alastair Reid graciously shared reminiscences. Theresa Bogard provided reviews and translations from the Amsterdam press. Information on performances came from: Nan Washburn at the Bay Area Women's Philharmonic in San Francisco; Scott Stacey of the Albany Symphony Orchestra; and Virginia J. Frey at CBS Entertainment in New York.

Concerning Glanville-Hicks's music, several individuals have been helpful. Melanie N. Williams of Illinois Wesleyan University in Bloomington, Indiana, provided tapes of performances of the songs, and Peter Garland of Soundings Press in Santa Fe, New Mexico, provided invaluable information on recordings and scores. At the University of Colorado, graduate students Deborah Miller and Lisa Steinbrink aided in the initial bibliographic search, and members of my graduate seminar on Glanville-Hicks in 1988 performed several of her unrecorded works and assessed her musical style and critical writings.

I am grateful to my friends and family for their patience while I have been enthralled by this project. My mother in California, a discerning listener to new music and reader of music criticism, has provided a needed perspective from the "real" world of professional music today; her informative reports have also served to remind me that there is indeed (musical) life after word processing.

Generous financial assistance was provided by the University of Colorado in 1988 and 1989. Special thanks go to Don Hixon, series adviser, and Marilyn Brownstein and Mary Blair, editors at Greenwood Press.

Peggy Glanville-Hicks

Biography

Peggy Glanville-Hicks, Australian-born composer and critic of international renown, was a major figure in New York musical life in the late 1940s, 1950s and 1960s. Documenting her work are the items listed in the other chapters of this bio-bibliography: her scores and recordings, her critical writings, reviews of her published works and performances, encyclopedia articles and other studies published at all stages of her career, interviews published since her return to Australia in the 1970s, and unpublished correspondence and other materials in several archival collections. References to items with a **W** are to entries in "Works and Performances," with a **D** to entries in the "Discography," with a **G** or **B** to entries in the "Bibliography" chapters, and with an **A** to entries in "Archival Resources."

From the abundance of detail this volume contains, and its sometimes confusing mixture of fact, insight, opinion, and misconception, certain observations about Glanville-Hicks emerge concerning the nature of her work and her place in twentieth-century music. She is principally a composer for theatre: she has written five operas and several ballets, and at this writing (in 1989) she is working on a sixth opera. Likewise, most of her other music is inspired by a text, an image, an artifact, a location, or some other extra-musical association. In New York at mid-century she viewed herself as part of the American *avant garde*. As a critic for the *New York Herald Tribune* and writer for journals, magazines, and *Grove's Dictionary of Music and Musicians*, she explained and promoted the work of composers, mostly Americans, and other important musicians. As a composer trained principally in Melbourne and London, she maintained her independence from atonalism and neo-classicism, two European techniques embraced by so many Americans, and looked instead to ancient sources and to Asian and African musical cultures for inspiration. Recent performances of her music by major Australian and American artists have displayed the attractiveness and power of the music itself and its stylistic resonance with much that is current today.

Her music is dramatic and so is she. Her own accounts of her life often take the form of stories and recollections of dramatic scenes, always entertaining and enlightening though sometimes hyperbolic in comparison to other accounts of the same events. This chapter is a chronological account of the musical and spiritual journey which has taken her from Melbourne to London, Europe, the United States, Athens, and back to Sydney where she now lives.

AUSTRALIA TO 1932

Peggy Glanville-Hicks was born in Melbourne, Victoria, on 29 December 1912, the daughter of Ernest and Myrtle (Bailey) Glanville-Hicks (**B22, B279, B400**). In an article published in New York in 1977 (**B403**) the composer was quoted concerning her childhood piano playing and writing of music: "mother thought it quite the right thing for little girls to develop their talents" at age seven, but later on "mother began to feel that it was more alarming than charming." In more recent interviews in Australia (**B183, B184, B367**) Glanville-Hicks has continued to emphasize the young age at which she was fascinated with music: her feet barely reached the piano pedals, so her compositions "were rather staccato," she says. "I didn't know a treble clef from a golf-club so my piano teacher would write down my music."

She was educated at the Clyde School, a girls' boarding school in Woodend, Victoria. (The school is now part of Geelong Grammar School, a Church of England school for boys and girls). She then attended the Albert Street Conservatorium in Melbourne, studying piano with Waldemar Seidel and composition with Fritz Hart (1874-1949), conductor of the Melbourne Symphony Orchestra and composer of over twenty operas and numerous other works. Her lifelong interest in opera composition and all aspects of music theatre production can be seen to date from her study with Hart, whom she has called a "master of setting words in a natural way" (**A1**) and "the best teacher in the world of vocal music" (**B120**). Hart, born and trained in England, was interested in the movement to restore traditional English and Welsh folk materials, the so-called "Celtic revival" in literature, and used the contours, rhythms, and melodic shapes of English folksong in his music. The Conservatorium was also famous for its women's voices--many young Australian singers had come there to study with soprano Nellie Melba.

The first composition by Peggy Glanville-Hicks to be reviewed in the press was a choral piece, *Ireland*, performed by the Ladies' Choir at the Conservatorium (**W1a** [the **W** numbers are chronological]); the reviewer for *The Australian Musical News* on 1 July 1931 (**B244**) commented on the "good writing." In December 1931 the *News* reported (**B252**) that she was runner-up in a scholarship competition at the Conservatorium. Her address was given as "Muritai," Barker's Road, Auburn, just outside Melbourne. (The next occupant of the house [it is now numbered 442 Barker's Road], interviewed there in August 1988, remembers seeing Peggy Glanville-Hicks's piano in the large front room.)

At this time Australian musicians (like American musicians) typically studied in England or Europe, and Glanville-Hicks decided to go to the Royal College of Music in London. At a "Complimentary Farewell Concert to Miss Peggy Glanville-Hicks, the Young Composer-Pianiste" on 2 June 1932 (a poster announcing the concert is in **A3**) she performed a Mozart piano concerto movement and some of her own compositions (**W2**). The concert was reviewed the next day in the Melbourne newspapers *The Argus* (**B75**) and *The Age* (**B76**); she "met with every encouragement from the friendly audience," *The Age* reported. She sailed for London with her mother on 13 June, arriving on 21 July. While her recent recollection (**B184**) that she arrived "penniless" is probably inaccurate, perhaps she did continue to wear her Melbourne "school uniform."

LONDON AND THE CONTINENT--THE 1930S

Reports of her activities from 1932 to 1938 continued to be published back home. In October 1932 the *News* reported (**B408**) that she had won a highly competitive scholarship at the Royal College, the Carlotta Rowe scholarship, competing against aspiring musicians throughout the United Kingdom. The *News* also reported that efforts by Mrs. James Dyer, Acting Lady Mayoress of Melbourne, to obtain financial aid for Glanville-Hicks by sending her compositions on ahead had proved fruitless. (Later in 1932 Mrs. Dyer, as Louise Hanson-Dyer, founded Éditions de l'Oiseau-lyre or Lyrebird Press in Paris [the lyrebird is one of Australia's unique fauna], and in 1938 Oiseau-lyre became the young composer's first publisher.) In 1932 Glanville-Hicks, aged nineteen, "felt herself in a complete daze" in London at the overwhelming experience of meeting so many famous musicians. She attributed her success to the training of Seidel and Hart.

Her teachers in London (listed in **B408** in 1932, **B405** in 1980, and almost every other biographical article) did include famous musicians: Arthur Benjamin (piano), Constant Lambert and Sir Malcolm Sargent (conducting), R. O. Morris and C. Kitson (harmony and counterpoint), Gordon Jacob (orchestration), and Ralph Vaughan Williams (composition). Sargent had her play percussion because, according to a 1982 report (**B120**), "he said she was the only one in the class who could come in on the beat," and thus she began a lifelong interest in percussion and rhythm. She copied music for Vaughan Williams and was given the original of the *Fantasia on a Theme of Thomas Tallis*, which she later donated to the Library of Congress, she has recalled (**A1, B120**). Vaughan Williams, leading exponent of the Celtic revival in music, believed that his music lived because of its folkloric root, and that all folk music was originally written by women, Glanville-Hicks told an interviewer in 1985 (**B260**).

Four years after her arrival in London, in August 1936 (**B407**), the *News* reported that she had won her fifth scholarship from the Royal College, an Octavia travelling scholarship, which would take her to the Continent (Budapest and Vienna were mentioned) beginning in October for advanced composition study. After over a year, in February 1938 (**B194**) she was reported to be back in London, having studied in Vienna, Milan, and Florence and with Nadia Boulanger in Paris. The *Choral Suite* (**W19**), an important early work, is inscribed at the end "Paris, September 1937."

In Europe she studied with Egon Wellesz in Vienna who taught the twelve-tone and "atonal" techniques of Arnold Schoenberg, but she had little liking for atonalism and the "Schoenberg school." Her training with Hart and Vaughan Williams had developed her affinity for the English choral sound, for consonant, often non-diatonic harmonies, for modal melodies, especially traditional or folk melodies, and for continued investigation of music's traditional sources, both spiritual and historical. Atonalism's melodic and harmonic dissonances and chromaticism she found particularly unattractive, and she could not accept the idea that increasing dissonance, indeed "obligatory" dissonance, was the way of the future.

With Boulanger in Paris she studied "neo-classicism" or the techniques of the "Stravinsky school." She has recalled (B346, A2b) that Boulanger let her students find their own direction, perhaps, Glanville-Hicks has speculated, because Boulanger was a woman. As time went on, Glanville-Hicks came to view neo-classicism, with atonalism, as merely reactions against nineteenth-century romantic tonality rather than promising directions for the future. She continued to search the world for more ancient, more authentic materials that might infuse new life into twentieth-century music.

By 1939 she had written twenty-six more works (W3-W28), including her first opera, Caedmon (W5), the genre of major interest to her. Seven of these works were published, and six of those seven (all but the Trio for Pipes, W11) continued to be performed in the 1970s and 1980s: the four songs Be Still You Little Leaves, Come Sleep, Frolic, and Rest (W7-W10) and the Choral Suite (W19), all published by Oiseau-lyre, and the Sonatina for Recorder and Piano (W27) published by Schott. The others are in several genres: further works for chorus and instruments (W3, W6, W15), orchestral pieces (W4, W12, W23), concertos for piano (W17) and flute (W20), music for short films (W18, W24, W25), ballets (W16, W26), and chamber music (W13, W22, W28). While most of the nineteen unpublished titles appear on her early work lists (B36 in 1946, B11 in 1954), they do not appear on the later ones (B81 in 1967, B297 in 1969). She recalled later, in the 1950s (A13a), that in the 1930s she toured her first opera, presumably Caedmon, with London students as cast and orchestra; the opera was not published, however, and is evidently no longer extant. More recently, she has said she made "bonfires" of her earlier music (B120), or "tore it up" (B205); whether or not these statements are to be taken literally, they dramatize her waning interest in the earlier works as she continued to compose and to develop her ideas.

Her first major performance took place in London in June 1938 when two movements of the Choral Suite (W19a) were performed at the festival of the International Society for Contemporary Music (ISCM), conducted by Sir Adrian Boult at the BBC concert hall; a recording of the two movements (D1) was issued by Oiseau-lyre, publisher of the score. Her early works, no matter what she was to think of them later, seemed significant enough then so that Eric Blom included an article about her in his Everyman's Dictionary of Music (B36), the first article about her in a music dictionary. While it was not published until after the war, in 1946, in London (after she had come to the United States), it names only her early works to 1939. In London in the 1930s she also met her husband, English pianist and composer Stanley Bate (1911-1959); she competed with him for scholarships and prizes, shared scholarships and prizes with him (**B26, B102**), and married him on 7 November 1938 (**B22, B133**).

CONCERT TOURS

Concerning musical life in England in the 1930s, Glanville-Hicks recalled some years later (**G683**) that the musical establishment (the publishing firm of Boosey and Hawkes, the British Council, the Arts Council) sponsored Benjamin Britten, to the exclusion of other composers, until the war years; presumably she was including Stanley Bate in the category of the neglected. In London, therefore, Bate and Glanville-Hicks organized their own musical activities. At the beginning of the 1939-1945 war they produced "blackout" concerts (in Underground train stations, she has recalled, **B367**). They also founded and co-directed a theatre arts performing company called Les Trois Arts which commissioned and performed ballets of Bate, Elizabeth Lutyens, and other young composers. She has other recollections of wartime London: during the "Blitz" some of her scores were destroyed (**G594**), and her piano fell three floors but survived (**B184**).

Soon after the beginning of the war, Glanville-Hicks and Bate left London, first on an Australian concert and lecture tour for Bate funded by the British Council, and then going to America. Glanville-Hicks has said that they came first to Boston in 1940 and that because they were given a "quota visa" by mistake, they were allowed to stay on (**B183, B205**). She has said she felt at home in America from the beginning: many American composers had been, like Glanville-Hicks and Bate, part of the "Boulangerie" in Paris (**A2b, A8**). For her, "it was the land of the present and of the future and was, besides, survival" (**B264**). By 1942 Glanville-Hicks and Bate were residents of New York City.

Glanville-Hicks's marriage has been described as "uneasy" (**B120**). The couple's New York neighbor, composer and writer Paul Bowles, has written of Bate's mistreatment of his wife, including drunken beatings (**B40**). Composer and critic Virgil Thomson (**B383**) has written of Bate's drinking and quarrelling and envy of Britten's successes, in spite of loyal support from Glanville-Hicks. The marriage lasted, she tells interviewers, about eight years. Eventually, in 1949 (after ten-and-a-half years), Glanville-Hicks travelled to Reno, established the six weeks' residency required for a Nevada divorce, and was granted the divorce on 8 June 1949. Bate left the country in July (Glanville-Hicks borrowed money for him for the trip [**A13a**]), while she, a U. S. citizen since 1948, stayed on. Bate remarried (**B166, B383**), turned from composing to painting, and died a few years later at the age of forty-six. Glanville-Hicks still occasionally called herself Peggy Bate, as for her "802" (musicians union) membership into the 1950s. She has continued to extol Bate's music and to recall fondly his beautiful face and his lovable helplessness in practical matters. Earlier she had copied his scores and put them in order, and in the 1970s she began investigating setting up an archival collection of his work (according to letters in **A11**). She has also talked about her use of Bate's royalties for a scholarship for young composers (**A1, B120**). In 1988 she mentioned to an interviewer for the first time that Bate was homosexual (**B26**).

In New York, as in London, Glanville-Hicks was active in producing concerts and supporting other musicians (**B37, B405**). She joined the League of Composers, an American organization supporting new music by American and expatriate European composers. In 1943-44 she was a member of a League of Composers committee producing concerts of modern music in Central Park. She collaborated with Carleton Sprague Smith, music librarian at the New York Public Library, in founding the International Music Fund which operated through UNESCO to assist European artists in postwar reestablishment. She also began work in support of American composers. In 1946 she financed the recording of an album of "New American Songs" by creating a subscription to the project.

By the mid-1940s she had resumed composing. In 1944 she completed *Five Songs* (**W29**) on poems of A. E. Housman, and then began to set American texts. She completed *Ballade* (**W31**) on three poems by Paul Bowles, and *Profiles from China* (**W32**) in 1945, the *Concertino da Camera* (**W33**) in 1946, *Thirteen Ways of Looking at a Blackbird* (**W37**) on the poem of Wallace Stevens in 1948, and in 1949 *Thomsoniana* (**W38**), settings of excerpts from five of Virgil Thomson's *New York Herald Tribune* concert reviews in the respective styles of the people being reviewed. These six works were later published and have continued to be performed. Besides these she composed: an *Aria Concertante* (**W30**); another ballet (**W34**); a large *Dance Cantata* (**W35**) to a Navaho text for tenor, narrator, speaking chorus, and orchestra; settings of three more Bowles poems (**W36**); two more film scores, one of them for the U. S. Department of State (**W39**) and the other for a cartoon (**W41**); and a *Sonata for Harp, Flute, and Horn* (**W40**). She continued to develop her ability to create effective musical settings for text, simplify texture, and distill structural principles, searching for her own idiom, her own direction.

She supported herself in New York by copying scores for other composers, in particular Bowles [*see* **B40**] and Thomson (according to letters in **A11**), and by writing about music. In 1945 her first major article, a study of Bowles, appeared in the English journal *Music and Letters* (**G1** [the G numbers are chronological]). Two years later, in June 1947 she attended the ISCM festival in Copenhagen and published reviews in two New York periodicals, the *Musical Courier* (**G2**) and the League of Composers journal *The Composer's News-Record* (**G3**). At the festival she heard music of India, an important style in her later works, played by the renowned Indian musician and author Marayana Menon, who was to become a longtime friend. Glanville-Hicks continued to work as a music critic, and soon became a regular "guest reviewer" for the *New York Herald Tribune*.

A second ISCM festival performance came in June 1948 in Amsterdam when the *Concertino da Camera* (**W33a**) was performed as an independent Australian entry. Glanville-Hicks also reviewed the festival, apart from her own piece, for the New York magazine *Musical America* (**G28**) and for the *Herald Tribune* (**G72**). The American works by Roger Sessions and Walter Piston, she reported, represented the "two main viewpoints still active in modern composition, the neo-classic and the atonal" (**G28**). The critic for the London *Times* (**B97**) found the *Concertino* "pleasant," while describing most of the other composers represented at the festival as "shipwrecked" in deep waters of stylistic "doubt and disillusionment" and clinging to "fragile rafts"-- twelve-tone, polytonal, polyphonic, neo-classic, expressionist. Another London critic (**B345**) commented on the piece's French "clarity, lightness, concision and simplicity" at a festival otherwise dominated by the "Teutonic tradition in decline." An Amsterdam critic (**B393**) judged the *Concertino* not "modern" enough for the festival, although noting that it was a "success" with the audience (always an important consideration for Glanville-Hicks). Peter Gradenwitz in the *New York Times* found the piece "entertaining" (**B162**). H. H. Stuckenschmidt in *Musical America* (**B365**) thought it reflected the weaknesses of the Boulanger school and a misunderstanding of Stravinsky. Later, in her liner notes (**G675**) for the 1955 Columbia recording (**D2**), Glanville-Hicks was to describe the *Concertino* as her 1946 "swan-song" for the "Paris neo-classic schoolroom."

Her first public concert in New York took place in October 1948 when her *Profiles from China* (**W32a**), *Concertino da Camera* (**W33b**), and *Thirteen Ways of Looking at a Blackbird* (**W37a**) were performed at a Composers Forum. Each of these Forums (around six per season) featured two composers, some of them fairly untried (with Glanville-Hicks was Irwin A. Bazelon); performances were followed by audience questions and discussion. This particular Forum concert was reviewed by two fellow composers, Carter Harman in the *New York Times* (**B172**) and Arthur Berger, a colleague of Glanville-Hicks at the *Herald Tribune* (**B27**). Berger, his perceptions perhaps heightened by discussions with her, suggested that she was "in a transitional stage of reviewing the many directions open to one today in order to give greater depth to her creative approach." Thus in 1948, aged thirty-five, Glanville-Hicks was completing the first phase of her career as a composer. During the next phase, her "mature" phase, around 1950-54, she would establish an individual style influenced by ancient and non-Western traditions, and then, from 1955 on, her music would become more "romantic" or personally expressive.

"P. G.-H."

Beginning in October 1947 Glanville-Hicks developed her aesthetic ideas not only by composing, but also through reviewing hundreds of concerts for the *Herald Tribune*. Her concert reviews, signed P. G.-H., appeared almost exclusively during the seven months of the New York concert season, October through April, and she composed music between seasons, usually away from New York. On the average P. G.-H. published ten reviews a month for the *Herald Tribune*, or two to three a week. Most encyclopedia articles and other published sources about Glanville-Hicks say she began writing for the *Herald Tribune* in 1948 (too late), some say 1947, and a few 1946 (probably too early). Most say she continued for ten years, or nine (**A1**), which might be accurate, especially if reckoned from 1946.

In this volume, the *Herald Tribune* listings begin with 27 October 1947 (**G4**), which is almost certainly her first review: none earlier has been found, and it is the earliest one in her own scrapbook of reviews (in **A3**). The listings end on 31 January 1955 (**G674**); this, even though published after the latest review in the scrapbook, is probably not her last review, but is apparently close to it. For each of the years 1947-1955, the reviews are listed in chronological order separately from the other writings for that year; subheadings separate the January-April reviews from the October-December reviews. Of the 699 **G** listings, 513 are *Herald Tribune* reviews, or almost three-fourths (about seventy-three percent). There is no index for the newspaper, so a search through each issue has been almost the only source of information, and has still probably not uncovered everything.

P. G.-H. was one of several "stringers" identified only by initials at the end of the review, including A. B. (Arthur Berger), L. T. (Lester Trimble), A. H. (Allen Hughes), M. B. (Martin Bernheimer), and T. M. S (Theodore Strongin). Several reviews appeared each day, by different reviewers; typical length was 100-200 words each. Music staff members Jerome D. Bohm, Francis B. Perkins, and Jay S. Harrison, whose reviews sometimes had a full name by-line, sometimes just initials (J. D. B., F. D. P., J. S. H.), were responsible for music coverage the year round, including ads for performances and series, announcements of the day's musical events, schedules of classical music radio broadcasts, information about competitions and auditions, other news releases, and Sunday feature articles on musical topics, often written by a prominent composer or performer. "P. Glanville-Hicks" wrote three Sunday features over the years: in August 1948 on the ISCM festival in Amsterdam (**G74**), in February 1952 on new music recordings (**G351**), and in February 1953 on orchestras in Florida (**G444**).

Head of the music department was Virgil Thomson, who had been hired in 1940. Besides reviewing concerts during the season, he wrote a Sunday column almost all year, sending copy from Paris or elsewhere if necessary during May-September. His reviews (and only his) were under the title "Music" and had a by-line of his full name and a heading in large, bold type; they were of substantial length, 800-1000 words or more, and they were accompanied by an eye-catching close-up photo of a performer or composer he was discussing. (After Thomson's resignation in October 1954, this special treatment was given to Jay Harrison's reviews, and then to Paul Henry Lang's [as in **B212**] when he became the head critic.) Thomson hired only trained musicians as reviewers, demanded that they "express their honest opinion in correct English," and then stood by their work. If Peggy Glanville-Hicks's review [**G483**] of your piece was "a little severe," he wrote to composer Ernst Bacon (on 22 December 1953), at least "she did say that the audience liked it, thus attesting, as a good reporter, that the work was a success with the public" (**B382**).

THE 1947-1951 SEASONS

1947-48: The first concert review signed P. G.-H., published on Monday, 27 October 1947, was of the Composers Forum the previous Saturday night. Most of her *Herald Tribune* reviews appeared on Mondays, sometimes two or three on the same Monday and occasionally even four (**G385-388** on 21 April 1952). Her first review was about 400 words long. Though the usual length for initialed reviews was 100-200 words, Composers Forum reviews were typically longer than others, usually 300-500 words or more. Her next review (**G5**) was on the following Monday, 3 November, of the Philharmonic Orchestra's performance of another new work, Messaien's *L'Ascension*. P. G.-H. was especially interested in hearing, and discussing, new music: Composers Forums; League of Composers concerts; the "Music in the Making" series of new works; programs by the National Association of American Composers and Conductors (NAACC); radio station WNYC's annual American Music Festival held 12-22 February (between the two Presidents' birthdays); and solo recitals, whether debuts or appearances by major artists, when they included at least one new work.

Her next reviews in 1947, after the first two, were not of new music concerts but of performers interpreting well-known repertory. She reviewed a pianist on Wednesday, 12 November (**G6**), two singers in joint recital on Friday (**G7**), and another pianist the next Monday, 10 November (**G8**). That Wednesday she reviewed a performer "not quite up to the technical and emotional demands" of the music (**G9**); reviews like this, of performers not meeting New York recital standards, were short reports of 25-50 words (e. g., **G14**, **G75**, **G164**, **G602**). On Friday, 14 November, P. G.-H. reported (**G10**) that violinist Paul Makovsky's playing, mostly of standard repertory, demonstrated his highly sensitive musicianship, as did his placement of a "major modern work," the Stravinsky *Duo Concertant*, at a "major position" on the program. Her next review (**G11**, of a Saturday night concert) appeared in Sunday morning's paper, not in the "Music" section, which would have been prepared before Saturday night, but towards the end of the first, news section, near the weather report, the bridge column, society news, and obituaries. On Monday, 17 November, reviews by P. G.-H. of two more weekend concerts appeared (**G12-13**). Reviews of weekend concerts on Sunday as well as Monday were almost as typical a pattern as the concentration of P. G.-H. reviews on Monday alone.

From 27 October 1947 through April 1948 she (apparently) published sixty-six reviews (**G4-G27** and **G30-G71**), plus one in May of a Composers Forum (**B72**). She attended the ISCM festival in Amsterdam in June, and when she returned to New York she reviewed a Lewisohn Stadium concert in August (**G73**), and the ISCM festival (**G74**). She also published in *Musical America*, besides the ISCM festival review in August (**G28**), an important essay on composer John Cage (**G29**). During the 1947-48 season she heard at least twenty singers, twenty pianists, ten violinists, six orchestras, six instrumental chamber music concerts (including four Composers Forums), five choral concerts, two operas, one violist, one cellist, and (quite unusual) one thereminist.

Her story about the theremin recital, reviewed on 1 March 1948 (**G54**), is among her favorite recollections of her years at the paper. The theremin, invented by electrical engineer Leon Theremin in the 1920s, produced any pitch; movement of the player's hand altered the frequency of vibration by changing the resistance of the rheostatic environment. The tones were not precise as to pitch, however, and change of pitch brought an unwelcome glissando. Glanville-Hicks recently recalled that the instrument looked "rather like a central-heating unit with two wires going up into space," and that in her review she pronounced the theremin "untameable" and also commented on the player's appearance: "even her hair looked as if it had been wired for sound " (**B346, A1**). Thomson had to fire her, and then rehired her the next week, she said. One finds that the actual review contains no such description and personal remark, although it does focus on the sound and the hearer's discomfort: when the performer "misses her point in space," she adjusts "with only the slightest of brooding glissandos," but in fast passages "precision departs entirely" and a "swooping sound reminiscent of an air-raid siren is the mournful result."

1948-49: During the 1948-49 season seventy-four of her reviews appeared in the *Herald Tribune* (**G74-G108** and **G116-G155**). She heard at least twenty-four singers, twenty pianists, nine new music concerts (only one of them a Composers Forum), eight violinists, three orchestras, two operas, two cellists, two instrumental chamber ensembles, two choirs, the Trapp Family singers, and one trumpet virtuoso (Edna White, **G139**). Her review of Britten's *The Rape of Lucretia* (**G117**) included comments on opera composition in general, a favorite topic; Britten's use of "musical instrumental caricature" underlining text and action is "a legitimate theatre practice," she noted, but it can not carry the text "to emotional heights inaccessible to plain speech." In early 1949 her review of Thomson's score for the opera *Four Saints in Three Acts* appeared in the journal *Music Library Association Notes* (**G109**), and a long article about Thomson in *The Musical Quarterly* (**G110**). At the end of the season she travelled to Reno, Nevada, as mentioned earlier, and points west.

1949-50: She returned to New York and published a review of another Lewisohn Stadium concert in the *Herald Tribune* on 1 August (**G155**). During the 1949-50 season she published forty-seven reviews in the paper, twenty in October-December 1949 (**G156-G175**) and twenty-seven in January-April 1950 (**G209-G235**), or slightly fewer than usual. She also published two reviews in *Musical America* in September and December 1949 (**G111, G115**), and then twenty-nine more in January-May 1950 (**G180-G208**), bringing her total to seventy-eight reviews in the two publications combined, or slightly more reviews than usual. There were only four concerts that she reviewed for both the *Herald Tribune* and *Musical America*.

In December 1949 (**G172**) she reported that a sonata by Eusebia Simpkins Hunkins (b. 1902) "does not inspire too much confidence in the fair sex as exponents of the art of composition," but, in spite of the shortcomings of the other two works on the program, both by men, she expressed no lack of confidence in *all* men. It was unusual in those years for any of the *Herald Tribune* critics to attribute music's quality to the gender of the composer, and

Glanville-Hicks apparently did so nowhere else in the newspaper. Over the years she reviewed many concerts that included new works by women: Lutyens (**G28**), Miriam Gideon (**G87, G289**), Louise Talma (**G90, G276**), Julia Smith (**G158**), Germaine Tailleferre (**G128**), Gena Branscombe (**G139**), Beatrice Laufer (**G162**), Ludmila Ulehla (**G221**), Priaulx Rainier (**G265**), Marga Richter (**G269**), Judith Dvorkin (**G274**), Beatrice McLaughlin (**G456**), Grazyna Bacewicz (**G605**), and Marion Bauer (**G20, G26, G129, G234, G413, G443, G614, G682**).

In November 1949 *Musical America* published Glanville-Hicks's second essay on Bowles (**G112**). She also wrote five short features for *Cue, The Weekly Magazine of New York Living,* but apparently quit shortly after her submission "New Trends in Opera" was retitled "Opera Made Painless," almost totally rewritten, and published without her authorization (**G177, A3b(3)**). That article focused on the work of Thomson, Marc Blitzstein, Gian-Carlo Menotti, and six other men; her other *Cue* articles dealt with the Little Orchestra's children's concerts for 1949-50 (**G113**), music in New York 1900-1950 (**G114**), the Metropolitan Opera's new manager Rudolf Bing (**G176**), and the WNYC American music festival (**G178**). In 1949 her *Ballade* (**W31**) was published by Hargail, and reviewed in *MLA Notes* (**B23**). In 1950, Oiseau-lyre published the *Concertino da Camera;* in 1982, an Australian interviewer observed (**B367**) that the beautiful edition still had "pride of place on her piano."

At the end of the concert season she left New York, perhaps (as suggested by letters in **A11**) spending June and July in Jamaica in the British West Indies. In August 1950 she travelled to Colorado for a performance of her *Thomsoniana* (**W38b**) at the Colorado College music festival, that year featuring works by and about Thomson, who attended as well. The Colorado Springs *Gazette Telegraph* (**B96**) called her piece the "biggest surprise of the evening" and described the "hilarious" spoof of "Schoenberg." Thomson, in the *Herald Tribune* (**B378**), called *Thomsoniana* "a skit pulled off with no mean skill," but with "more character and musical power in it than one might expect of a good joke." Glanville-Hicks published a review of the festival in the September issue of *Musical America* (**G208**); an accompanying photo shows her with Thomson and five other composers.

In November, *Vogue* magazine in New York published her article "Musical Explorers" (**G179**) on the work of Cage, Alan Hovhaness, Colin McPhee, Bowles, Lou Harrison, and Edgard Varése; these six composers, she explained, were discovering new sound materials and exploring new musical paths. She speculated that they, not the atonalists and neo-classicists, might well turn out to be the real *avant garde*. She felt part of this "avant-garde spearhead," which she described in 1986 (**B200**) as the "unpaying aspect" of music; these are the musicians who "don't know where they're going," go "by intuition," and "turn up the furrows that will produce the crops of tomorrow."

In the 1950s, having become increasingly interested in the Composers Forum series, she became its concert manager or executive director, working from offices in the New York Public Library provided by Carleton Sprague Smith. Most sources date her work 1950-60, though the beginning date is not firm and her correspondence (**A11, A13a**) indicates that she considered a new contract with the Forum in 1961. She raised funds, including her own salary, worked with the composers, organized scores and parts, hired the performers (her work as a critic enabled her to be a superb talent scout), booked the hall, saw to the printing of the programs, and in later years also produced a radio program using tapes of Forum performances. This work, plus her reviews, allowed her to subsist in New York.

1950-51: At the beginning of the 1950-51 season (and the American academic year) she went on a seven-week lecture tour to universities and colleges in Minnesota and the Dakotas, travelling by bus (according to Thomson, **B383**). This tour was about her only direct contact with music in the schools. Although the apparent security of a salaried academic position may have intrigued her (according to letters in **A11**, when Berger left the *Herald Tribune* in 1953 to teach at Brandeis University), she evidently did not pursue further the possibility of teaching. As a critic, she endorsed the musical education provided by children's and young people's concerts by orchestras and other groups, especially when they included new music (**G238**, **G382**, etc.).

Though her first *Herald Tribune* review for the 1950-51 season did not appear until 17 November, due to her lecture tour of the northern states, she published about sixty-one reviews that season (**G236-G296**), her usual number. The *Pastoral* (**W3**) for chorus, a work from the early 1930s, was published by Weintraub. Two of the song cycles from the 1940s, *Profiles from China* (**W32**) and *Thirteen Ways of Looking at a Blackbird* (**W37**), were also published in 1951 and reviewed in *MLA Notes* (**B340**) and in *Repertoire* (**B312**), adding to her recognition as a composer. *Thirteen Ways* had a second performance in February 1951 (**W37b**), during the WNYC American music festival, at a concert of music by three *Herald Tribune* critics, Glanville-Hicks, Thomson, and Berger, reviewed by Jay Harrison at the *Herald Tribune* (**B174**) and Ross Parmenter at the *Times* (**B291**). At the close of the season she travelled to California (**A13a**), returning to New York in October 1951.

MATURE WORKS: 1950-1954

In the early 1950s Glanville-Hicks established an individual style as a composer in the seven "mature" works **W42-W48**: *Sonata for Harp* (1950-51); *Sonata for Piano and Percussion* (1951) for piano and four percussionists; *Letters from Morocco* for tenor and small orchestra (1953); *Sinfonia da Pacifica* (1952-53); the opera *The Transposed Heads* (1952-53); *Three Gymnopédies* (1953) for small instrumental ensembles; and *Etruscan Concerto* 1954) for piano and chamber orchestra. In the *Sonata for Harp* (**W42**), written for famed Spanish harpist Nicanor Zabaleta, she set out to recapture the "curious grace" of harp music up to the eighteenth century (its "golden age") and to restore the instrument's natural capacities and attributes (**G684**). The first movement is titled *Saeta*, a traditional Spanish genre, and Spanish rhythms and guitar effects are reflected in all three movements. The *Sonata* is part of the standard repertory: all harpists know it, Zabaleta himself recorded it on several labels (**D12-15**), and in 1988, aged eighty-one, he was still performing it in concert (**W42o**).

In the next six works, beginning with the *Sonata for Piano and Percussion* (**W43**), Glanville-Hicks wrote for instrumental ensemble, with and without voice. Investigation of folk music and its ancient roots had showed her that melody and rhythm are universal principles of music, while harmony, so long developed by Western European musicians, was apparently only incidental in music's historical development. She began to compose according to what she called a "melody-rhythm structure," featuring melody supported by rhythm, not the traditional harmonic or "figured bass" structure of Western music.

In the architectural metaphor of her later writings, the tonal system was like the *arch* of classical architecture, as in the medieval European cathedral, resting firmly on the ground. Then Schoenberg abandoned verticality and "the principle of the arch" and "put music on the principle of horizontality, no matter how dreadful it sounded" (**B346**). Although atonalism at first seemed the way out of the "collapsing building" of tonality, it turned out to be, for composers, a "cement building with no doors or windows" and "blank walls" (**B346, A1**). Neo-classicism, for its part, consisted of "pasting bits of glass and steel on the front of a good old brownstone bulding to make it look more odd." By contrast, the melody-rhythm principle is like the *cantilever* of modern American architecture (she often cites the work of Frank Lloyd Wright) which produces an *organic* structure that, while seemingly without support, rises into the air on its own energy (**G697**). The noted Australian musician and writer James Murdoch recently summarized Glanville-Hicks's position in the 1950s, without the architectural metaphor: she turned her back on the atonalists and neo-classicists, when she "jettisoned" harmony, and so became more *avant garde* than they (**B262**).

For the *Sonata for Piano and Percussion* she wanted to design an instrumental combination suitable for the melody-rhythm structure. For the melody, she used, not the traditional Western strings, winds, or brass, but more percussively rhythmic instruments. Xylophone and piano, she explained (**G675**), are melodic "partners" in the piece, while timpani, gongs, and tam tam sustain the sound (substituting for the sustained harmonies of figured-bass construction), and bass drum, tom tom, and suspended cymbal add "miscellaneous beats and accents." She continued to view percussion instruments as essential to new music. "A whole octave of timpani, bass marimbas, xylophones, and variously pitched drums is needed for the rapid articulation of the bass range, newly freed from its lugubrious ground-bass function," she wrote in 1964 (**G697**). The tune in the first movement of the *Sonata* comes, she said, from the "Watuzzi Africans;" its character--"fragmentary and highly restricted in scale"--seemed to suit "both the instrumental limitation and the esthetic of the work" (**G675**).

The instrumentation is similar to the Indonesian *gamelan* or gong-and-metallophone ensemble, and the layered textures of gamelan music are especially audible in the first movement. While she apparently never went to Indonesia, she probably heard Indonesian music at the 1948 ISCM festival in Amsterdam, where it was a notable concert offering, or in Australia or America or elsewhere. She may also have used other sources, such as recordings or transcriptions by Colin McPhee. She has not written of her affinity for Indonesian gamelan textures, although in 1988, questioned about Indonesian musical influences in her own work, she replied that she was the one who suggested to Lou Harrison that *he* write a Balinese piece.

Like the *Sonata*, the *Sinfonia da Pacifica* (**W44**) was also designed to "demote harmony" and "reassert the right of the melodic and rhythmic elements as the primary structural forces" (**G680**). The *Sinfonia* uses the same percussion ensemble as the *Sonata*, minus piano, plus single winds (flute, oboe, clarinet, bassoon), single brass (trumpet, horn, trombone), and orchestral strings. She used the *Sinfonia* instrumentation in the *Letters from Morocco* (**W45**), settings of Bowles's letters scored with suitably North African melodic and rhythmic colorings, then used it again in *The Transposed Heads* (**W46**), and in the *Etruscan Concerto* (**W48**) to accompany solo piano.

As announced in November 1953 (**B152**), *The Transposed Heads* was commissioned by the Louisville (Kentucky) Philharmonic Society under a grant from the Rockefeller Foundation, the first opera (though not the first work) so commissioned, and Glanville-Hicks's first important commission. She constructed the opera's libretto herself from the English translation of a novella by Thomas Mann based on a Hindu legend: a young woman, Sita, marries a young Brahmin, Shridaman, but finds she is really in love with his friend Nanda. Each of the two men beheads himself, Shridaman because Sita does not love only him and Nanda out of loyalty to Shridaman. The goddess Kali intervenes and tells Sita to restore life to the two men by replacing their heads, but Sita transposes them, putting husband's head on friend's body and vice versa. Eventually, all three realize the situation is still hopeless, and choose suicide as the "just solution to our problems."

Using Mann's dialogue, Glanville-Hicks condensed the story into six scenes, and, in keeping with the plot, used Indian themes in the composition of the music. Indian classical music now seemed to her to be among the most ancient musics still extant, and therefore an exceptionally authentic source of inspiration; the melody-rhythm structure was essentially a "raga-tala" structure, she pointed out. In the opera's third scene, the wedding vows are set to a motive that is almost the same as the main theme of the "Ansermet" movement of the *Thomsoniana*, where it depicts the noted conductor's beautifully serene blends of French orchestral sound. The lively melody of the wedding chorus "Lovely Sita" is also the main theme of the third movement of the *Sinfonia*, which she completed at the same time, and returns again with more extensive development in the third movement of the *Etruscan Concerto*, completed the following year in 1954.

Her intention in *The Transposed Heads* was to develop the melody-rhythm structure into an effective and expressive medium for opera. "It was my aim to create grand opera on a chamber music scale," she wrote. The "form and pacing" come from the "vocal element," just as the shape of a baroque concerto comes from the solo elaboration; rhythmic control, not harmonic and orchestral weight, nor even "literary development," functions as "crisis builder" (**G677**). In her remarks in the piano-vocal score, published in 1954, she advised against use of piano, an instrument "best suited to harmonic thought," and suggested electronic organ, for "sustained volume" in the "melodic element," plus three percussionists, for rhythmic accompaniment of "indefinite pitch."

THE 1951-1955 SEASONS

1951-52: From October 1951 through April 1952 she published ninety-four reviews in the *Herald Tribune,* thirty-five of them in October-December (**G297-G331**), her usual number, and fifty-nine of them in January-April (**G334-G392**), about twice her usual number (in fact **G359** covers two concerts). She also became active in the American Composers Alliance (ACA), an organization founded in 1938 to support American music, and owned and operated by its over one hundred composer-members. She began writing for the *ACA Bulletin* and organizing concerts for the ACA (as well as for the Composers Forum). She published an article in the *ACA Bulletin* in 1952 on recent developments in the Composers Forum (**G333**). In March 1952 she organized a concert at the Museum of Modern Art (she was a member of its "junior council") on the theme of Spanish influences on music, at which Zabaleta gave the U. S. premiere performance of her *Sonata for Harp* (**W42c**), which he had already premiered in Latin America and Europe (**W42a-b**). She began writing liner notes for a series of recordings by Zabaleta illustrating the history of harp music (**G332, G595, G672**).

In early May the *Sonata for Piano and Percussion* had its premiere performance (**W43a**) at a concert she organized at the Museum of Modern Art featuring new works for percussion. Her 1944 cycle *Five Songs* (**W29**) was published in 1952 and reviewed in *MLA Notes* (**B150**) and in *Musical America* (**B332**). At some point she also made a piano reduction of the orchestra part for Mendelssohn's *Violin Concerto*, published by C. F. Peters in New York in 1952 (**B104, A11**).

At the close of the New York season in mid-1952 she travelled to Australia to visit family in Melbourne. On board ship in the South Pacific, away from New York activity, she composed the *Letters from Morocco* and completed the *Sinfonia da Pacifica* and the libretto for *The Transposed Heads* (**G677, G680, B72**.) Interviewed in Melbourne (**B277**) she discussed her work as a critic. She said that out of thirty-two critics in New York she was the only woman, that she was attending at least four night concerts a week plus two on Saturday and sometimes three on Sunday (the previous months had indeed been busy) and that she wrote her *Herald Tribune* reviews with "one eye on my clock." She talked of her compositions and her work with the Composers Forum, and mentioned a "slight bias against employing women even in America."

1952-53: Back in New York for the 1952-53 season, she wrote sixty-four reviews for the *Herald Tribune,* thirty-one in October-December 1952 (**G388-G418**), and thirty-three in January-April 1953 (**G329-G387**), thus returning to her more usual number. She travelled to Florida in early February 1953 and published a Sunday feature on Florida's orchestras (**G444**). She also had many performances. The annual WNYC festival of American music in February included the second performance of the *Sonata for Piano and Percussion*

(**W43b**) and, on the last night of the festival, the premiere performance of her *Letters from Morocco* (**W44a**), conducted by Leopold Stokowski at the Museum of Modern Art on a "laboratory" program of *avant garde* American works (other composers were Halsey Stevens, Henry Brant, Lou Harrison, Jacob Avshalomov, and Charles Ives). Oliver Daniel, editor of the *ACA Bulletin*, reported that Bowles (whose letters Glanville-Hicks had set) attended the performance, "accompanied by one Moroccan in full burnoose" and a woman "in *purdah* by way of dark glasses, while numerous turbans and saris lent an additional dash of cosmopolitanism" (**B107**). Louis Biancolli in the *World-Telegram and Sun* (**B30**) called it a "brilliant" close to the festival, due to the "tireless godfather of new music," Stokowski. Olin Downes in the *Times* (**B118**) noted that the audience that packed the concert room, being "cordially disposed to all and sundry," applauded Glanville-Hicks's "conventionally oriental settings;" he wished the composers had learned their lessons in the laboratory before presenting their work to the public.

Glanville-Hicks herself reviewed the festival for the New York magazine *Musical Courier* (**G425**); as with the Colorado College performance of *Thomsoniana* in 1950, she had to review her own music. Lou Harrison's *Canticle for Percussion No. 3*, she reported, used only the "wearisome and external trappings of Asian style," whereas in her *Letters from Morocco* she had "eschewed" these trappings and used only the structural principle of a "melody-rhythm or raga-tala form." The next month, in March 1953, her *Sonata for Piano and Percussion* was performed again at a concert sponsored by the NAACC (**W43c**).

In early 1953 she published an article on the "Music in the Making" series in the *ACA Bulletin* and in *International Musician* (both **G424**). Here she singled out four "real repertory pieces for the general concert planner," by Hovhaness, Otto Luening, Roger Goeb, and Wallingford Riegger, and requested more of the "real repertory," the solid contemporary masterpieces, whether American or European. America's "Brave New Public," insulted for years by crass underestimation, she continued, deserves the best. She published an article about Arthur Berger in the *ACA Bulletin* (**G426**), and an article on "Tapesichord" music or *musique concrète* in *Vogue* magazine in July (**G427**). (The noted Australian conductor Sir Bernard Heinze said some years later [**B99, B315**] that Glanville-Hicks had explained *musique concrète* [not, however, her own favorite medium] to him in 1952.)

In May 1953 she retreated to Jamaica. She wrote the *Three Gymnopé-dies* (**W47**), scored for small instrumental ensembles, on "three consecutive Saturdays just before my departure to the Caribbean" as "fillers" for radio, in response to a remark by CBS (Columbia Broadcasting System) program director Oliver Daniel; the *gymnopédie,* she explained (**G594**), is a slow dance of ancient Greece used to instill grace in athletes. In Jamaica, she has recalled (**B205, B262**), she stayed at an establishment operated by Professor Theo Flynn, the Australian marine biologist (and father of actor Errol Flynn), and composed *The Transposed Heads*. She then sailed to Australia, as her mother was very ill. Although she said the next year that she had written the music for *The Transposed Heads* "in one long, unbroken period of work from May to September" of 1953 (**G677**), her letters to Thomson (**A11**) suggest that she suspended writing during the month in Australia. She arrived in Melbourne on 20 July, about a week after her mother's death, and had to deal with matters concerning her inheritance, a financial resource that eventually helped provide a measure of economic security beyond what she had known so far in New York. In late August she sailed for America.

1953-54: During the 1953-54 New York season, Glanville-Hicks published sixty-two reviews in the *Herald Tribune* (G462-G486, G597-G633). In early 1954 she published an article in the *ACA Bulletin* on jazz-classical cross-influences (G428). She had won a $1,000 award from the National Institute and American Academy of Arts and Letters in 1953, and a concert of works by the three award winners during the February 1954 WNYC festival included her *Letters of Morocco* in its second performance (W44b). In early April 1954 *The Transposed Heads* was premiered in Louisville by the Kentucky Opera Association (G46a); she evidently spent some time in Louisville before the premiere, because she published no reviews in March.

She wrote liner notes for a recording of works by Lou Harrison and Ben Weber (G486) issued in 1954. She attended the American music festival at the Eastman School of Music in Rochester, New York, in May 1954 and published an article on the festival in *Musical America* (G596). In Melbourne in June, Heinze conducted the *Sinfonia da Pacifica,* which was also broadcast on the radio (W45a). (A Barcelona performance was also mentioned at the time [B388], but has not been verified.) After the close of the concert season she completed the *Etruscan Concerto;* the end of the score is inscribed New York City, 13 July 1954.

Grove's Dictionary: During this period of the early 1950s, at the request of Eric Blom, general editor of *Grove's Dictionary of Music and Musicians,* 5th edition, she took charge of updating the American material. *Grove's Dictionary,* finally published in 1954, remained the major international encyclopedia of music for many years. While she assigned some topics (singers, instrumentalists, conductors, and others) to other writers, she wrote ninety-eight articles on current American composers herself (G487-G584). By now, having heard a great amount of American music and examined innumerable scores, she was eminently qualified to compile such an important survey, and her work received a favorable review from at least one American scholar (B186). She also wrote eight articles on Danish composers (G585-G592), the three that had so impressed her at the ISCM festival in Copenhagen in 1947 (G2) and five more.

Glanville-Hicks's work for *Grove's* helped confirm the importance of American music: inclusion in *Grove's* was a gauge of a musician's importance, and she greatly expanded the American coverage from previous editions, adding seventy-nine new composer entries and supplying additional material about the rest. Rather surprising, however, in view of her wide experience, is the meagre representation of women's names among the American composers. While she included Bauer (b. 1887) and Ruth Crawford Seeger (1901-53) she omitted many other important Americans: Gideon (b. 1906), Talma (b. 1906), and, from Glanville-Hicks's generation, Julia Smith (b. 1911), Vivian Fine (b. 1913), Esther Williamson Ballou (b. 1915), and others who, it could be argued, had by then acheived at least as much recognition as John Barrows (**G493**), Alvin Etler (**G524**), and Jerome Moross (**G562**).

1954-55: She published twenty-nine reviews in October-December 1954 (**G634-G662**) and twelve in January 1955 (**G663-G674**); statistics on the next months must await future searches. The 1954-55 season may even have been her last season at the *Herald Tribune*. Spot-checking in the 1955-56, 1956-57, and 1957-58 seasons, while admittedly not the most reliable method of investigation, has yielded no reviews. Further, the situation at the paper was not so attractive to her after Thomson's departure in October 1954 and the hiring of Paul Henry Lang (b. 1901), eminent Columbia University musicologist intensely loyal to the European tradition. Glanville-Hicks would have liked to succeed Thomson herself (**A13a**), or at least to have a salaried staff position to make her income more predictable. As a stringer, she felt, even during the last months of Thomson's tenure, that she was being assigned less interesting concerts than the men, and fewer concerts of new music than in her first few seasons, and she regretted no longer being able to publish any Sunday feature articles.

Discussing her *Herald Tribune* reviews in retrospect in the 1980s, Glanville-Hicks has sometimes referred to them simply as a means of supporting herself. She has said that she was subjected to standard repertory, pieces from the "box office years" (**G466**) of the eighteenth and nineteenth centuries, even the same "eighty pieces," Thomson called them, repeated over and over (**A8**). She has also said that she could not write "a note" of music in New York (**A1, A2b**); "you can't listen avidly *and* write [music]" (**B346**). Clearly she regretted the time taken away from composing, and she did complete most of her works between concert seasons, usually away from New York. At the same time, a glance through the hundreds of **G** listings and their annotations shows that she heard, not just the "eighty pieces," but much new music, as she confirmed in 1986 (ibid.): "I was sent to all the contemporary things; whenever there was a first performance, Virgil would send a critic," and "I enjoyed it very much." It is clear that her critical writing, especially about new music, even though it often necessitated postponing her own composition, nurtured the musical intelligence that enabled her to grow as a composer, learn to perceive and encourage musical growth in other musicians, and help listeners understand what the musicians were doing.

COMPOSER AND CRITIC

In 1953, the editor of *International Musician* noted that Glanville-Hicks was "at once a composer's critic, and a critic's critic. She is unbendable," he continued, "and her criticism is free from any touch of coteries, even of those to which she belongs" (**G424**). At the same time, Glanville-Hicks, like other composer-critics, reveals much about her own music in writing about other musicians. Her principal concerns were: the musician's integration of inspiration and technique, American composers and the *avant garde* of the mid-twentieth century, assimilation and synthesis of ancient and folk materials, and the creation of new forms from new materials.

Integration: Basic to Glanville-Hicks's thought is her concept of musical *integration*. This passage is from one of her earlier writings, her 1949 essay about Bowles:

> There is far too much thought about the technical aspects of music, the aspects subject to analysis; and there is far too little known or thought about the psychological, emotional, spiritual states of the artist, whose great force comes from his [her] need and ability to achieve and maintain a state of contact with his inspiration, a state produced by an unspecified emotional mood which is the wave length whereon he contacts his own point of integration.

A composer needs to "contact the original resources of his own nature," to "penetrate to the inner nature of his own impulse and discover the psychological and structural principle upon which he should build" before he can "emerge with a new and moving art form" (**G113**, p. 33).

In a later essay "Technique and Inspiration," published in 1958 in the *Juilliard Review* (**G690**), she defines terms she had been using for years. The composer has two areas of awareness: *technique,* which includes materials and analytical factors, and *inspiration,* which includes expression and instinctive factors. Only after a "journey inward," which requires both "silence" and "time," can the composer *integrate* the "emerged" and "submerged" sources and *synthesize* them into an *organic* form. (She herself found "silence" and "time" mainly between New York concert seasons.) When the technique used is appropriate to the inspiration received, then the form grows from the materials used, and the work is integrated or *organic* (again the terminology of Frank Lloyd Wright). The "composer-artist," who achieves such integration is distinct from the mere "craftsman" [or craftswoman--there is no inclusive language in her writings] who concentrates only on technique, and from the "talented amateur" who may have inner awareness but has not acquired technique or intellectual discipline.

In her *Herald Tribune* reviews, integration is an important criterion for judging performers as well as composers and works. Among composers, Leslie Bassett showed himself to be an integrated artist-craftsman (**G614**), but Carl Feurstner, Claus Adam, and George Rochberg only craftsmen (**G263**, **G431**). Dane Rudhyar (a composer with whom she shared an interest in astrology) expressed a "real artist nature" in his pieces of ca. 1925, heard on a 1950 Composers Forum (**G225**). Piston she described in 1952 as "a real master" in his integration of "personal and abstract" elements, classic architecture and romantic lyricism (**G352**); in *Grove's* she called him a "solid craftsman" and original in idiom (**G569**). Aaron Copland's *Piano Sonata* she judged in 1948 to be one of his most finely "integrated" works; its "crystallization point" is its "emotional content, rather than the terms of its expression" (**G38**). Among performers, Glenn Gould's strength in 1955 came from "complete integration of the component parts" of the pianist's art (**G665**). Gunnar Knudsen's playing in 1947 was able to "save" Grieg's third violin sonata, a piece that, in the view of Glanville-Hicks, "is not too well integrated formally" (**G24**).

Inspiration: For Glanville-Hicks, a composer's sources of inspiration are personal, cultural, and historical. Among American composers, Douglas Moore (b. 1893) was one who seemed to her to be in touch with both personal and historical musical sources. His music has an American folk sound to it, she observed in her *Grove's* article, as though he "had absorbed, digested and forgotten" the whole American folk music heritage, "or as though it had become a spring, deep underground" (**G561**). Later, describing his work *Farm Journal*, she defined his "melodic anchorage" as "Celtic-American folksong," lying "deep in the origin of his expressive impulse, not separate and acquired;" he uses American moods, color, and idiom but resorts to none of the typical phraseologies of standard "Americana" (**G682**). Similarly, Virgil Thomson (b. 1896) had successfully integrated the "substance" (i. e., inspiration) of Missouri church music and other sounds, with the "means" (i. e., technique) of French Dadaism, Boulanger's training, and dissonant neo-classicism (**G110**). Charles Ives (1874-1954), she explained in *Grove's*, used the "rugged and homely" elements of "Americana" as early as 1895, but many of his works are "without synthesis" (**G544**).

American composers: When Glanville-Hicks arrived in the U. S. in the 1940s, a strong "American school" existed among the generation of Thomson, Moore, Copland, Roy Harris, Piston, and Sessions. Atonalism and neo-classicism had their American followers, too, which evidently surprised her, coming to the U. S. from England as she did, with an English composer as a husband. Composers in England, she said later (**G668**), had not been so influenced; there, the most "organic modernism" was to be heard in Vaughan Williams's F-minor Symphony, which is "Medieval" in spirit, not a reaction against nineteenth-century tradition.

In the 1950s, when some young Americans seemed overly influenced by Europeans, including Schoenberg and Stravinsky, Glanville-Hicks saw a need to encourage the continued growth of American music and American audiences by describing and supporting the uniquely American, non-European stylistic ferment. Writer Nathan Broder, reviewing the Columbia series of recordings of American music which included the *Concertino da Camera* and *Sonata for Piano and Percussion*, similarly described in 1955 the "remarkable variety" of styles in the U. S.: the Schoenberg-Stravinsky-Hindemith-Bartók constellation was not a useful classification system, he observed, nor the chronological, nor the vague "conservative, conservative-advanced, advanced" division (**B46**).

In her *Grove's* articles, Glanville-Hicks recognized an American style in the work of composers of her own generation. She noted that Leonard Bernstein (b. 1918) used American elements such as cowboy songs, Mexican dances, and the "Negro jazz idiom," and that syncopation, rhythmic buoyancy, melodic freedom, and "a dissonant semi-jazz harmonic idiom" are disciplined in his music into a "compact and vivid expression" and a happy meeting of "ends and means" (**G500**). Berger's music likewise showed "assimilation and integration" of American elements to transform them "from a vernacular into an art expression" (**G498**).

Henry Brant (b. 1913) seemed to her the "catalyst" of a group of composers synthesizing jazz ("metropolitan folk-lore") with classical music

(**G428**). Jazz is a direct, almost collective expression of subconscious factors in music, she observed; a jazz tune is known to all, like the plot of a Greek drama, so the use of jazz gives music "real life." In 1947 (**G4**), she found in works of Lukas Foss (b. 1922) a synthesis of American folk elements and an atmosphere of tranquility; by the time of *Grove's* (**G529**), Foss, one of the youngest of the American composers she included, had also acquired more "stability" in his personal idiom or individual style. The youngest, the "neo-romantic" Peter Mennin (b. 1923), had achieved a rhythmic drive that is "integrated and structural rather than decorative" (**G558**).

She often commented on general traits of American music as well. American composers, she observed at one point, tend to use brass instruments thematically, while Europeans use the brass for harmonic underpinning (**G95**). Cage and many American composers, she wrote in 1948, were fascinated with percussion, and with "noises" (telephone bells, factory whistles) that Europeans take as ideology or proletarian utterance, but Americans take as technology or an offshoot of the percussion movement (**G29**). American performers have developed "electric" style and "technical streamlining," while Europeans have "thoughtfulness" and the "grand manner" (**G84, G329, G338**).

Technique: Of the two leading "modernisms," Glanville-Hicks continued to disparage atonalism more than neo-classicism. Atonal works were almost always "acid," "despairing," or "forbidding." Schoenberg's third string quartet was "difficult" for an audience (**G159**); his *Klavierstücke, Op. 23*, were surely among the world's most unattractive pieces (**G653**). Berg's *Chamber Concerto* was a "taxing" item for a fresh audience and an endurance test for a tired one (**G115**). She was dismayed by any young American composer's adoption of atonalism. In 1948, in the music of Miriam Gideon and Frank Wigglesworth (b. 1918) "notable craftsmanship and a real feeling" were unfortunately subdued by the "dreariness" of the atonal view of music (**G87**). Marga Richter in 1951 was in danger of "leaning on" formulas or systems such as "twelvetonism," thus "submerging" her natural "ability to make her own forms grow from the very nature of her materials and ideas" (**G269**).

At the same time Glanville-Hicks recognized the usefulness of some atonalist elements. Among American composers of her generation, she liked Ben Weber's rejection of the "pedagogic" row (**G192**), although atonalism could destroy even Weber's spontaneity and expressiveness (**G200**). Milton Babbitt's *The Widow's Lament in Springtime*, reviewed in 1951, showed fluent use of atonalism "to utter a poet thought poetically" (**G273**).

She reviewed music of several American neo-classicists, including John Lessard (**G46, G660**), Irving Fine, Harold Shapero (**G203**), and Elliot Carter (**G424**), and usually found some laudable features (having been a neo-classicist herself). She also liked Arthur Berger's synthesis of isolated elements of atonalism and neo-classicism (**G426**). Among the Europeans, she was especially admiring of Dallapiccola, who had "sloughed off the husk" of Europe's musi-cal cliques and schools of thought "and kept the precious grain from them all"--continuity devices from atonalism, atmospheric collages from impressionism, and formal charting and repose from tonality and consonance (**G251**). Glanville-Hicks herself, according to Edward Cole's liner notes for *Letters from Morocco* (**B67**), was similarly selective, using the "contrapuntal strength" of atonalism and the "formal projection" of neo-classicism, rejecting only the harmonic aspect of the two methods.

For her, any ready-made technique of composition was to be avoided if it prevented a composer from persuing personal inspiration and individual style. While she liked Hindemith's music, she disliked the "cramped diatonicism" and other "mannerisms" of Hindemith's system in the hands of his students Bernard Heiden (**G105, G310**), Remi Gassmann (**G150**), and Leonard Sarason (**G249**); Joseph Goodman had fortunately managed to absorb the principle without the mannerism (**G162**). (Stanley Bate had also been a Hindemith student, but by all reports an independent thinker like his wife.) Vaughan Williams could also produce students whose music reflected their teacher's "mannerism without strength," she observed (**G105**).

She was critical of composers whose modernism consisted in simply avoiding conventional consonances, as in the 1920s "modern" manner and "dissonant banalities" of Persichetti's *Poems* for piano (**G18**). In 1948 she reported that the music of Britten (her husband's nemesis) was without organic method, aesthetic selectivity or self-criticism (**G49**); in 1949 she described it as "English and conservative" with a decorative surface of dissonance (**G117**), and in 1984, as nineteenth-century music with an overlay of dissonance, much like glass on an old brownstone building (**B3**).

Among Americans, Julia Smith erred, in Glanville-Hicks's view, in using traditional tonal forms for non-traditional atonal materials (**G158**), as did many others. Cage (b. 1913), on the other hand, one of her "musical explorers," had invented new materials, so that he did not need to waste any energy avoiding traditional effects (as the atonalists avoided consonance). She was admiring of composers like the group around Howard Hanson at Eastman in 1954 who were practicing "sound, neutral techniques and a natural tonal idiom as a point of departure for the growth of a personal esthetic" (**G596**).

Assimilation and synthesis: Glanville-Hicks was interested in all kinds of folk and traditional music, both for its own sake and as a source of authentic musical materials. She reviewed Richard Dyer-Bennet (**G160**) and Virginia Davis (**G171, G258**) singing western European and American material, and Olga Coelho (**G440**) singing Latin American material. She noted, in reviewing a 1948 concert by the Vinaver Chorus, that the program, which included music "from Vaughan Williams to the music of the synagogue," demonstrated "a common bond of a modal structure and feeling," or the "skeletal remains of an ancient type" (**G42**). Folk art teaches the composer the importance of limits, she later explained (**B15, G697**), such as using only five- or six-note melodic modes, not all twelve chromatic pitches.

In new concert music she listened for the kind of synthesis and assimilation of folk material she heard in some American works (music of Moore, Thomson, Bernstein) but not others (Ives). Mordecai Sandberg attempted no "synthesis" in his oratorio *Ezkerah*, but combined quarter-tone melodies with "common chords and dominant sevenths of the squarest and most gauche kind" (**G389**). Works of Lorenzo Fernandez, heard in late 1949, used Brazilian folk material in a "cheap romantic-impressionism" that does not blend with the "primitive esthetic" (G174). Istanbul pianist Koharik Gazarossian, heard early in 1948, only "incompletely assimilated" Armenian and Middle Eastern elements such as "rhythm and scale limitation" in her own music (G39). Hovhaness, by contrast, assimilates these same Armenian elements into his "style, construction, and whole writing method" (ibid.); his whole expressive content is in fact Eastern (cumulative and hypnotic) rather than Western (climactic), she noted in her *Grove's* article (G542). His music is structured according to the "melody-rhythm form common in the Middle and Far East," she explained elsewhere (G424), and because "melodic and rhythmic elements are invariably more accessible to the public's ear and mind than are the harmonic," in particular "the vertically dissonant sounds of most modernism," she continued, "he can hire, and well fill Carnegie Hall for a one-man show of his own music."

Beyond harmony: Glanville-Hicks's interest in music with a rhythmic rather than harmonic structure surfaces in her writings as early as 1948, when she comments on the mistake of adopting vernacular music's "harmonic clichés" instead of its rhythms (G37). Most often, she equates harmonic structure with the presence of a strong bass line. Berger's music shows a commendable "Stravinskyesque bass fragmentation," she noted in 1948 (G47). While music without "harmonic bass reference," like Hindemith's unaccompanied violin sonata, might "fall apart" (but did not at the 1947 performance she reviewed, G27), in general, lack of traditional harmonic bass support was a positive attribute of new music. Danish composer Niels Bentzon, she observed in *Grove's*, is not "tied" to a "Teutonic bass foundation" but rather tends toward "spatial, rhythmic or segmentary thematic material" sustained by inherent impetus [cantilever], not by mechanical devices [arch] (G585).

Other qualities: In reviewing performers, Glanville-Hicks listened not just for correctness, integration, and organic form, but for quality of tone and expression, especially in singers (hardly surprising for an opera composer); debut artists often received a detailed technical evaluation and advice on suitable repertoire (G63, G293, G403, G631, etc.). She also listened for the quality of "spontaneity" and the control of "tension," especially rhythmic tension. Harris's *Piano Suite* had "vigor, poetry, and spontaneity" when performed by Ernest Ulmer in late 1950 (G236). Even established performers did not always meet expectations. The Paganini Quartet in 1947, though she judged them technically and interpretively correct in their playing of Beethoven, did not display the "vitality" of the content, only a feeling of "tedium" (G22). Maurice Wilk and Carlo Bussotti in 1953, on the other hand, performed Beethoven as it was meant to sound (G478), as did the Alma Trio in 1954 (G656). Some performers had performed the same music too many times, and presented a "wrapped cellophane package" without emotional involvement (G402); Lily Pons in early 1952 was "the most stupendous cellophane-wrapped product" in the "coloratura line" (G349). Sometimes she was impressed almost beyond words, by artists such as Larry Adler (G482), Marian Anderson (G455), and Andrés Segovia (G224, G368, G435).

RECOGNITION IN 1954

By 1954, at the age of forty-one, Glanville-Hicks had built a respectable work list, received a major award and the important Louisville commission, and heard her music performed by major artists with reviews by influential critics. Two important articles about her date from 1954. One is Eric Blom's article in *Grove's Dictionary* (**B37**), which, still identifying her as an Australian composer (as in his *Everyman's* article), reviews her career and names her works through *The Transposed Heads*. The other article, prepared closer to the date of publication, and evidently prepared with her collaboration, is by composer George Antheil in the *ACA Bulletin* (**B11**). (She had recently organized a performance of Antheil's *Ballet mécanique* for a Composers Forum; in a 1977 interview [**A6d**] she recalled advising him to substitute taped sounds of a jet engine for the airplane propellors that reportedly caused such chaos in the 1920s.) With Antheil's essay (in the same format as her own *ACA Bullet-in* essay on Berger the year before) is a list of her works with excerpts from reviews through the 1954 Louisville production of *The Transposed Heads*. Essay, work list, and review excerpts are still widely quoted in writings about Glanville-Hicks.

Antheil discusses her compositional principles under six general topics: "integration" of expressive aims and material means; "simplification" for increased clarity and intensity; regard for the "melody-rhythm patterns of antiquity" and "of Eastern places;" a "fusion" of oriental sound and western (harmonic) style through use of "neutral materials" as well as actual folk melody; invention of new forms rather than reliance on traditional "classic" ones; and avoidance of dissonance, especially constant "obligatory" dissonance.

The essay is apparently the first review of her work to use the phrase "woman composer." He reports that she is the only one of them he has "met" who has her "technical, mental, and spiritual stature." Antheil's remark was evidently meant to praise her, and may well have been suggested by Glanville-Hicks herself, but it is unclear which other women he had met. Many of the ACA members (and presumably *Bulletin* readers) were women and composers of stature and importance, including Bauer, Gideon, Vivian Fine, Talma, and Ballou. At any rate, while the image of Glanville-Hicks as the only woman who has ever composed music of substance is obviously inaccurate, this is the image she continued to cultivate in the press.

NEW YORK: 1955-1959

Glanville-Hicks continued to work in New York during the concert season and to leave the city when the season ended. In 1955 she hosted Indian music concerts with Yehudi Menuhin (**B405**). In mid-1955, she retreated to Germany, near Munich, inhabiting an "old boathouse" (**B77, B205**); here she completed the *Concertino Antico* (**W49**) for solo harp and string quartet, using "an ancient mode set by Flavius Josephs in A. D. 1 for harp of that time" (**G684**). She also visited Florence to investigate the work of Newell

Jenkins, a fellow Greenwich Village resident (*see* **A3b(10)**), who was editing
and recording eighteenth-century Italian instrumental music. In 1955 she
published an article on that project in the New York magazine *Hi-Fi Music at
Home* (**G679**), plus two more articles: "Opera Recordings" (**G678**) described
the recordings of the Louisville commissions, including *The Transposed
Heads* (**D21**); and " 'Willie' Has a Silver Spoon" (**G683**) discussed English
composer William Walton and his recently recorded opera *Troilus and Cressida*. In August 1955 she delivered a eulogy for *Times* critic Olin Downes,
which was broadcast on WNYC radio and later published in the *ACA Bulletin* (**G676**); she regretted that her music had never been reviewed by
Downes, but it had been, twice, in February 1953 (**B117-B118**), once favorably
and once not so favorably.

    She looked to her salary from the Composers Forum as a predictable
source of income, as her income from the *Herald Tribune* was unpredictable:
she was receiving $10 per review, but could not predict how many reviews.
Her Forum salary, however, came out of the concert budget; in early 1955, she
proposed cancelling the next concert, seeing that if she succeeded in presenting it, there might be nothing left for her salary. On this occasion and
others like it, she told Forum board members (including Thomson [**A11**],
Moore, Carleton Sprague Smith, and later John Edmunds [**A13a**]) that a man
would not tolerate such unstable and unprofessional arrangements, and
pointed out that she was as qualified as they to help pick composers, besides
carrying out board decisions. She also observed, however, that many men
who were excellent composers were also having employment problems, and
the younger composers still needed the Forum's help. In other words, she
would "fulminate" (Thomson's word), while demonstrating an "unstoppable
generosity" (**B383**). During the 1955-56 season she left the Forum job to composer Norman Dello Joio, but she returned for the 1956-57 season.

    In her own music, she continued her search for ancient sources, and
discovered the folk music of Greece. She took her direction, she has explained (**B105, B200**), from the earlier researches of Béla Bartók, who collected
Rumanian and Hungarian folk materials and used them as a basis for his
concert music--as Vaughan Williams had used English materials. Bartók told
her that folk music was more "authentic," more representative of antiquity,
as one went further "south" from eastern Europe. She listened to Bartok's
recordings in the Library of Congress, and then studied music to the south,
eventually, in the late 1950s, collecting music in several different regions of
Greece. Just as she heard in Hindu *raga* and *tala* forms the ancient roots of
European music, so in the melodic and rhythmic modes of Greek *demotic* or
folk music she heard the common ancestors of both European and Hindu
music.

    Her research was evidently prompted originally by her musical im-
pulses, not by purely antiquarian interests or an interest in musical research
for its own sake. As she had written in 1945 (on the subject, again, of Bowles),
foreign cultures exert "vital influences" when "an initial and instinctive
affinity" prompts the composer to seek them out (**G1**, p. 89). While her own
attraction to ancient Greek subjects is seen as early as the 1935 ballet *Hylas and
the Nymphs* (**W16**) and then in 1953, in the title *Three Gymnopédies,* she

continued to develop an even deeper attachment to the Greek tradition as an authentic source of physical and spiritual well-being. Her world view is the source of the title of the book she is preparing on twentieth-century music, *Apollo's House* (**G699**):   Apollo, she explains (**B346**), was the ancient Greek god of both medicine and music.

By the mid-1950s she had begun searching for a Greek subject for her next opera, and by 1955 had prepared a libretto from Thornton Wilder's *The Women of Andros*. Wilder, however, refused to grant her permission to use it (**A3**). He did not like composers setting his work, he said, unless he chose the composer, and Louise Talma was already using another of his works for her opera *The Alcestiad*.

Another work suggested itself to Glanville-Hicks, the novel *Homer's Daughter* by classical scholar and author Robert Graves, based on an earlier theory that a woman, not Homer, wrote the *Odyssey*. In the novel, set in ancient Greece, princess Nausicaa saves her father's palace from usurpers pretending to be her suitors, then instructs the court bard to revise his version of the legend of Odysseus and Penelope to sing of Penelope's heroism. Guggenheim fellowships helped support Glanville-Hicks's work on an opera named after the novel's heroine, *Nausicaa* (**W62**).

In mid-1956, as in 1955, she retreated to Europe; in Germany she completed the *Concerto Romantico* (**W51**) for viola and orchestra; the end of the score is inscribed Starnberg bei München, 17 May 1956. She also wrote a short opera, a "curtain raiser," *The Glittering Gate*, based on a play from ca. 1909 by Irish author Lord Dunsany whose work was currently attracting attention in New York. She then went to the island of Mallorca, staying in Palma, orchestrating *The Glittering Gate*, and going weekends to Deyá to work with Graves on the *Nausicaa* libretto (**A11**); he then asked his friend, writer Alastair Reid, to complete it (**B68, B179**). She returned to New York in October.

Musically, she continued to build on the innovations of her works of 1950-1954, developing a more personally expressive or "romantic" style in the third and latest phase of her work. The new approach is most evident first in the *Concerto Romantico*, both in its title and in its sound. Premiered in 1957 by violist Walter Trampler and conductor Carlos Surinach at the Metropolitan Museum of Art, on a concert she produced called New Works for Chamber Orchestra, it is orchestrated for slightly more than her usual four winds (alternate English horn and bass clarinet are added), four horns (instead of solo trumpet and horn), trombone, harp, and strings. While the concerto has the same modal-melodic structure as the *Sinfonia da Pacifica, Etruscan Concerto*, or *The Transposed Heads*, she explained (**G686**), the difference is that in those works accompaniment was largely rhythmic, while in the concerto, percussion is omitted because it would "engulf" the viola, and accompaniment is provided by "unison melodic imitation or by occasional passages of vertically-conceived harmonic blocks."

In New York she also continued to publish essays on music and musicians. In 1956 she published an article in *Hi-Fi Music at Home* (**G685**) on Edward Cole, Artists and Repertoire Director at MGM. MGM issued recordings of several of her works from the 1950s, and for each she either wrote, or assisted Cole in writing, informative liner notes: in 1956, *Sinfonia da Pacifica* and *Three Gymnopédies* (**D11/D19**, liner notes **G680**), and in 1957, *Letters from Morocco* (**D6, B72**), *Etruscan Concerto* (**D4, B71**), and *Concerto Romantico* (**D3, B70, G686**). Each set of liner notes begins by paraphrasing Antheil: "Peggy Glanville-Hicks is an exception to the rule that women composers do not measure up to the standards set in the field by men." After that unfortunate opening, however, Cole quotes the composer's own explanations, making these liner notes as reliable sources of information as her Columbia and Louisville liner notes (**G675, G677**).

In 1957 she published an essay about the operas of Rolf Liebermann in both the *ACA Bulletin* (**G687**) and the *American Record Guide* (**G688**) to counter the "panning spree" by New York reviewers of a City Center production of his *School for Wives*. Liebermann, she noted, uses several dissociated musical styles--tonal, neo-classic, atonal, French, German--as dramatic partisans, to bring new meanings (unlike Virgil Thomson's use of dissociation without posing new meaning, she added), so that the drama is posed and solved in the materials themselves. She identified several other noteworthy features of Liebermann's operas: symphonic interludes; his mastery of harmonic and metrical tensions for the "cantilever" of music's new architecture; his skill in prosody, especially recitative; and an objective approach that exhibits the timelessness of his story and subject matter. Unlike American composers, she observed, Europeans like Liebermann can hear many operas performed and thus learn the special requirements of composing for the theatre. Four years later, in 1961 (**G691**), applying that observation, she advised young American composers to travel extensively to hear European twentieth-century works. Further, she suggested that the few "real opera creators" in America could be subsidized to create a "national operatic literature of maturity and significance."

In 1957 she completed two works using ancient materials, *Musica Antiqua No. 1* (**W53**), a six-movement musical tour of South America, India, and Africa, and *Prelude and Presto for Ancient American Instruments* (**W54**), two short pieces based on South American tunes. A recording of the *Prelude and Presto* (**D8**), performed on instruments in the collection of the Andre Emmerich gallery and the American Museum of Natural History in New York, was sold at the gallery during an exhibition "Music Before Columbus" in October 1957. The *Times* reviewer (**B15**) explained that while the ancient flutes have a complete pentatonic scale, most of the other instruments make only one or two sounds, and noted that Glanville-Hicks is "fascinated by limitations."

Glanville-Hicks continued to use her skills in organizing concerts and raising funds for concert production. "Fame and widespread importance have much to do with luck and management, and not necessarily to do with quality and magnitude, when it comes to serious music," she observed in 1956 (**G683**). She made important contacts in the music world, among other composers, performers, managers, public relations experts, and sources of funding, and, as she described herself in 1958 (**B147**), she was "a good organizer because I never overlook anything or leave things to chance." People in the arts fall into two groups, she explained: those who say "if we don't do it someone else will," and those (like her) who say, "if we don't do it no one

else will." Recently in Australia she has confirmed that she had to do everything, even "lick the stamps" (B3). Two noteworthy efforts were her work on
the 1958 New York production of *The Transposed Heads* (W48b), and her
formation of The Artists Company to produce a double-bill of *The Glittering
Gate* (W52a) and Lou Harrison's *Rapunzel* in 1959.

She had wanted a New York production of *The Transposed Heads*
from the time of the 1954 Louisville premiere. The next year, in mid-1955,
James Lyons, reviewing the Louisville recording in the *American Record
Guide*, referred to a New York performance "this fall" (B228). Not that fall
but over two years later, in February 1958, the opera was presented at the
Phoenix Theatre on two successive Monday nights. Whereas the Louisville
performance had skimped on production costs--the music director, Moritz
Bomhard, had built a major part of the stage scenery himself (G678)--the New
York production was elaborate and even included authentic costumes and
props from India. Glanville-Hicks raised much of the money through the
Contemporary Music Society, Leopold Stokowski, president. A news release
(B62) under Stokowski's name, but evidently written by Glanville-Hicks,
announced in November 1957 the forthcoming production in January, and
another December release (B307) announced its postponement to February.

Publicity in February was also thorough. An enticing blurb appeared in
the *Daily News:* " 'Transposed Heads' sounds like an Alfred Hitchcock TV
show but is a new two-act opera at the Phoenix Theatre" (B396). On a more
serious note, two Sunday features on the opera were published the day before
the opening, one by Glanville-Hicks in the *New York Times* (G680) and the
other by Paul Bowles in the *Herald Tribune* (B41). Glanville-Hicks, elabo-
rating on her 1954 program notes and 1955 liner notes, titled her essay "Westward to the East" (A3) to emphasize the growing influence of Eastern cultures
on Western music and the historical shift of the world's musical focus from
ancient Greece westward to Europe, to America (from the eastern U. S. to the
western U. S.), and then to Asia; the *Times*, however, retitled the essay "A
Hindu Theme" and also cut it somewhat. Bowles, for his part, writing as
listener as well as composer and friend, explained that although one hears in
The Transposed Heads "a surprising amount of harmony present, both implied and expressed," she had suppressed "harmonic progressions and large-
scale harmonic development;" melody, not harmonic sequence, provides
"emotional directions" or cues here, and a proliferation of percussion instruments are her "figured bass."

The New York production, unlike the Louisville premiere, brought
many reviews: in the *Times* (B372), *Herald Tribune* (B212), *New York
Journal American* (B202), *New York Post* (B198), *New York World-Telegram
and Sun* (B29), *The [Greenwich] Villager* (B199), *Aufbau* (B189), and the
magazines *Opera News* (B237), *Musical America* (B249), *Musical Courier*
(B318), *New Yorker* (B338), *World Theatre* (B229), *The New Republic* (B131),
and *Musica d'oggi* (B158). Several reviewers took issue with Glanville-
Hicks's claim to have thrown out harmony and revolutionized music. Lang
reported in the *Herald Tribune* that the libretto and Hindu musical elements
were handicaps for this "able composer, with a good sense for the theater."
Glanville-Hicks found his judgment of the opera unfair, and wrote him a

scathing letter (**A3**), also taking him to task for leaving at intermission (further indication that she was no longer writing for the paper in 1958). In her next publicity brochure (**B296**) she took revenge by quoting only one of his remarks: "Frankly, I don't know how to judge this opera." In her private correspondence, a "Lang review" was any unsympathetic criticism of new music,

Only one critic, Biancolli in the *World-Telegram and Sun*, referred to gender: he was thankful for "operatic writing to compare favorably with some of the better work being done today" by her "male colleagues." Robert Evett in *The New Republic* called the opera "distinguished" in its originality, and predicted it would have "long-term significance." Glanville-Hicks asked Evett (also a composer) to write further about her work, but he replied (**A3**) that he was too busy with other projects.

Glanville-Hicks was interviewed and again stressed her uniqueness as a woman composer. One journalist (**B147**) reported that she was "probably" the only woman composer to earn a living at composing. Another (**B39**) reported that she was the first woman in recorded history to have composed and produced a full-length opera. These absurd claims, which continue to be published to this day (**B173**, **B200**, **B205**, etc.), have evidently resulted from a less than thorough knowledge of music history on the part of both composer and interviewers, combined with enthusiasm--certainly warranted--about Glanville-Hicks's music.

After *The Transposed Heads* in February, she spent six months of 1958 in Greece, from April to October (**B210**, **B298**, **A13a**). She had been commissioned to compose the ballets *The Masque of the Wild Man* (**W55**) and *Triad* (**W59**) for choreographer John Butler for the Spoleto Festival of Two Worlds, and in June 1958 she travelled to Italy to see them performed. She worked with Butler in planning *Nausicaa* (**G693**) and he was stage director for its production three years later. He was the choreographer for her next three commissioned ballets: *Saul and the Witch of Endor* (**W61**) in 1959 and *Tragic Celebration* (**W66**) in 1966, both for CBS-TV on Biblical subjects, and *A Season in Hell* (**W65**), premiered in 1967.

ATHENS: 1959-1972

From 1959 Glanville-Hicks began to consider Athens rather than New York her home port. Greece offered the silence and the time necessary for reflection and composition, and contact with Greek music, she believed, was essential. She remodeled a house on Mykonos, using local builders, local materials, and traditional techniques, and published an article about it in *Vogue* magazine (**G694**); Frank Lloyd Wright's "organic architecture" is "just old Island technique," she wrote. Still, for musical activity and intellectual stimulation, New York and European cities were indispensable: she returned to Spoleto in mid-1959 (**A13a**), then apparently spent the 1959-60 season in New York. She completed *Drama for Orchestra* (**W60**), the orchestral version of the ballet *Saul and the Witch of Endor*, in New York in November 1959 (according to the inscription at the end of the score), and it was premiered during the WNYC American music festival in February 1960 (W60a).

In 1959-1960 she finished composing *Nausicaa;* the end of the score is inscribed "N. Y. C. Apr. 30, 1960." A premiere performance at the Athens Festival in August 1960 seemed possible, but was postponed to the next year (W62a). In collaboration with local officials, and using all her organizational and fund-raising skills, she helped organize the production from her home near the ancient, restored Herod Atticus theatre where the premiere was to take place. Principal sponsor of the festival was the National Tourist Organization of Greece, itself funded, it is assumed, largely by the U. S. For additional funds Glanville-Hicks called on her American contacts, supplying advance payment for some production costs out of her own private funds when necessary (A3g).

The opera was cast with Greek-American singers, including the then almost unknown soprano Teresa Stratas in the title role; the orchestra and chorus were Greek. The principals sang in English, the chorus in Greek. The conductor was Carlos Surinach, who had conducted many of Glanville-Hicks's New York performances and most of her MGM recordings. He rehearsed the principals in New York before coming to Athens; Virgil Thomson attended a rehearsal in New York and reported on it by letter to the composer in June (A3). The *Nausicca* premiere received international press attention and acclaim, including reviews in Athens, Paris, London, Frankfurt, Belgrade, Vienna, Zagreb, Mexico City, New York, Toronto, and Melbourne. Trudy Goth, who had helped Glanville-Hicks with the publicity (according to correspondence in A3), and reviewed the performance for several publications, wrote in *Musical America* that this was probably the first time an American composer wrote, cast, rehearsed and launched her own work (B153), a statement Glanville-Hicks later confirmed (G692). Audiences were estimated variously at 3,000 (B153) to 4,800 (B338). Graves himself attended--it was his first visit to Greece, Glanville-Hicks has recalled (B205, A6d)--and photos from the premiere (G693, G696, B26) show Graves, Butler, and the composer in the audience. Review excerpts appeared in the *ACA Bulletin* (B269) and the composer published an important article on her work, "At the Source" (G693), in the Metropolitan Opera magazine *Opera News* in New York.

From her home in Greece she maintained her professional contacts in the U. S. and elsewhere: in 1961 she was awarded a Rockefeller grant for travel and research in the middle and Far East; a Fulbright fellowship to support further research in Greek music brought her to Washington, D. C. for "briefings" in January 1961 (A11), where she completed preparing the score of *Drama for Orchestra* for publication (again according to the score's inscription); in 1962 she evidently returned to India.

In 1963, she was commissioned by the San Francisco Opera, under a Ford Foundation grant, to write another opera, *Sappho* (W64, B8), based on the play by Lawrence Durell, another opera on a Greek subject and about a famous woman. The title role was written for Maria Callas as a mezzo; a photo of Durrell and the composer at work has been published (B54, B78), but *Sappho* has not been performed. At the time of its rejection by the San

Francisco Opera, in early 1964, Glanville-Hicks wrote (A3h) to director Kurt Herbert Adler explaining (though futilely) that, as in the piano-vocal score of *The Transposed Heads*, the monophonic structure makes rendition on piano inadequate to convey the variety of plush orchestral sounds. She also intended, she wrote, that singing should be almost constant, accompanying all the action, without textless orchestral interludes, for a more restless pacing than in traditional opera. She wondered whether she should have composed *Sappho* as another *Nausicaa*, a proven success, instead of progressing to a new form. More recently, she has said (A1) that *Sappho*, at Durrell's insistence, may have more beautiful, literary text than an opera libretto needs. Performances of *Sappho* elsewhere have been discussed (A3) but none has materialized so far.

In 1965 Glanville-Hicks completed *A Season in Hell* for the Harkness Ballet (W65). Her choice of plot is less understandable than in the case of *Nausicaa* or *Sappho*. Reviewing the November 1967 premiere (W62a), Winthrop Sargeant in the *New Yorker* (B337) reported that the story is "about the trouble with poets is they never get the girl." Clive Barnes in the *New York Times* (B24) was more explicit. The story, from Artur Rimbaud's *Une saison d'enfer*, involves three characters, the poet Rimbaud, his friend Verlaine, and "The Woman." Because Rimbeau despised what he saw as the materialism of women, and searched among homosexual men for a woman substitute, this "Woman," Barnes explained, is not a woman but a muse of poetry, an inspiration toward a life of art, which he eventually rejected.

Glanville-Hicks had experienced failing eyesight for several years, the result, she had told *Time* magazine at the time of the *Nausicaa* premiere (B322), of years of reading and copying music. In 1967, while in New York for the premiere of *A Season in Hell* (W65a), she was found to be suffering from a brain tumor which required surgical removal; a section of skull was replaced with a plastic version, what has come to be known as her "famous plastic skull." Although Glanville-Hicks was not able to attend the ballet, Mrs. Harkness arranged for the surgeons to do so (A3i). While the surgery greatly improved her vision, she was told that she had only five years to live, and was advised to return to Greece and enjoy the sun (B173). She returned to Athens, travelling to London several times in the next few years for more surgical procedures to "drain" the inner ear, as she wrote to Thomson in New York (A11).

In 1970, she travelled to Australia (by way of London for ear surgery enabling her to continue by plane) for the Sydney production of *The Transposed Heads* (W47c), directed by Roger Covell at the University of New South Wales. The return visit of this "Australian composer" was widely covered by the press (B54, B77, B285). Covell published an interview he had had with her in Athens earlier in the year (B101), revising, at her request, his characterization of her as an American composer three years earlier (B98). The performance was reviewed in three Sydney newspapers (B2, B32, B395). After Sydney, she travelled to Melbourne, where George Dreyfus and others presented performances of the *Concertino da Camera* (W33c, W33d), *Sonata for Recorder and Piano* (W27c), and *Sonata for Harp* (W42i). On the return to Athens she stopped in India.

RETURN TO AUSTRALIA

In the early 1970s, principally through contacts with Joyce McGrath, Arts Librarian at the State Library in Melbourne, and James Murdoch, founder of the Australia Music Centre in Sydney, she was persuaded to leave Athens and return to Australia, settling in Sydney. In 1972, Murdoch published a long article on her work in his *Australia's Contemporary Composers* (B263). Although her return was not yet definite, he noted her continuing allegiance to Australia, in spite of her American career, and her interest in non-Western music which coincided with developments among younger Australian composers. Another comprehensive review of her career through her Athens years to about 1972 appeared in 1980 in the article about her by Australian writer Elizabeth Wood in *The New Grove Dictionary* (B405), reprinted in *The New Grove Dictionary of American Music* in 1986 (B404).

In the 1970s she realized that she was to live more than five years after all, and in fact has enjoyed fairly good health, although she continues to require cortisone therapy, and in 1982 reportedly said (B120) that she expected to live only about two years more. In 1977 she was awarded a Queen's Silver Jubilee Medal (B222). The following year she organized an exhibition of music and sculpture at the Australia Music Centre; the sculptor was a friend from her Paris years, Pamela Boden, and she and six other composers contributed new music to be taped and played during the exhibit. Her piece, three minutes long, accompanied Boden's sculpture *Giraffes* and is called *Girondelle for Giraffes* (W67). Two years later, in 1980, she made a return visit to the U. S. (A12). The following year, a Melbourne newspaper announced (B300) that she was donating several scores to the State Library; the Glanville-Hicks Collection (A3) continues to grow and includes correspondence and memorabilia as well as scores.

Interviewed many times in Australia in the 1970s and 1980s, Glanville-Hicks has decried her lack of recognition and acclaim since her return; much of the recent writing about her has stressed her feeling of uniqueness as a woman composer, especially of operas, and her desire to be judged by men's standards. As she repeated in 1986 (B173), the only criterion in music is "quality," regardless of the composer's color, sex, or age. We "ladies" have to be "twice as good as the next best man to be recognized" and "will probably be paid half what he gets." But "if we start separating categories, women will automatically get into a bunch and be excluded from the main line." She has also decried the scarcity of Australian performances of music from her New York years. In fact, however, she has had many performances, noteworthy among them the January 1982 Festival of Sydney program entitled "A Salute to Peggy Glanville-Hicks." Spoken commentary by James Murdoch introduced performances by leading artists of *Profiles from China* (W32f), *Thomsoniana* (W38f), *Sonata for Piano and Percussion* (W43g), *Letters from Morocco* (W44c), and *Musica Antiqua No. 1* (W53a, apparently a premiere.

In 1983 she travelled to Bombay for the official opening of a Performing Arts Center as honored guest at a Colloquium on the East West Exchange that accompanied the opening (according to B238, B367). In 1984, she was invited to be composer-in-residence at the Cabrillo Music Festival in California, but was unable to make the trip. The festival performances included the *Sonata for Piano and Percussion* (**W43h**) and the *Etruscan Concerto*, with Keith Jarrett as soloist (**W48c**). (He apparently heard her lecture during her 1950 tour [**A11**].) In September of that year she travelled across Australia to Perth, where the Australian Broadcasting Corporation (ABC) recorded a superbly cast concert version of *The Transposed Heads* for national radio broadcast (**W46d**).

One-and-a-half years later, in March 1986, the Adelaide Festival produced *The Transposed Heads* (**W465**) and *The Glittering Gate* (**W52c**). "The most moving moment," one critic reported (**B213**), "came during the curtain calls when the frail and diminutive composer received affectionate cheers." Earlier that year she was featured on an ABC *State of the Arts* program where composer Peter Sculthorpe (b. 1929) described her as a "mother figure" to Australian music. She was apparently unimpressed, it was reported (**B200**), but Sculthorpe persisted, calling her a visionary composer. In May 1987 she was awarded an honorary doctorate by the University of Sydney, for which he wrote the citation (**B79**).

Peggy Glanville-Hicks continues to express loyalty to both America and Australia. Further, she predicts (as in **B173**) that just as the Americans were musical leaders in the mid-twentieth century, so, as world musical consciousness continues to move westward to the east, Australians and Asians will assume the lead by the time of the "apocalypse," which she expects in the year 2000. What is her favorite among her own works? she was asked in 1982 (**A1**). "It's always the one you haven't written, isn't it?" she replied.

Works and Performances

This is a chronological list according to date of composition, **W1-W70**, with date of publication listed after the title. For each year, titles are in alphabetical order. The list includes all titles mentioned in any of the work lists and other literature, and alternate dates are noted. Many of the earlier works are not included in the later, selective work lists in 1954 (**B11**), 1969 (**B297**), and 1980 (**B405**). References to items with a **D** are to entries in the "Discography," with a **G** or **B** to entries in the "Bibliography" chapters, and with an **A** to entries in "Archival Resources." Instrumentation for larger works is listed in the customary pattern of woodwinds, brasses, timpani, percussion, and strings. For example, 2.2.2.2., 4.3.2.1., timp., 3 perc. (instruments named), strings, means that the work calls for 2 flutes, 2 oboes, 2 clarinets, and 2 bassoons (alternate piccolo, English horn, bass clarinet, contrabassoon are indicated in parentheses); 4 horns, 3 trumpets, 2 trombones, and 1 tuba; timpani, 3 percussion players; and a full string section of first and second violins, violas, cellos, and double basses. The work list is followed by a publisher's directory, alphabetical list of works, and classified list of works.

BY 1931

W1   **Ireland** (Unpublished)
Choral piece.

Performance

  W1a 1931 (30? June) Melbourne, VIC. Albert Street Conservatorium Ladies' Choir. *Review:* **B244**.

BY 1932

W2   **Songs and Instrumental Pieces** (Unpublished)
See: **A9**.

Performance

W2a 1932 (2 June) Melbourne, VIC (Town Hall). *Piano Prelude* (Peggy
Glanville-Hicks, piano); *Violin Solo* (Gertrude Healy, violin); *He
Reproves the Curlew, To the Moon,* and *A Widow Bird* (Beatrice
Oakley, soprano; Peggy Glanville-Hicks, piano). *Reviews:* **B75, B76.**

1932-1933

W3 **Pastoral** (sometimes *Pastorale*) (Weintraub, 1951; 7 p.; 6 min.)
For women's chorus SSAA and clarinet or English horn.
Text by Rabindranath Tagore, "Fruit Gathering."
See: **B194, B407.** *Listed in:* **B11, B35** (says 14 p., 5 min.), **B67, B297.**

BY 1933

W4 **Meditation** (Unpublished; 12 min.)
For orchestra: 3.3.3.3., 4.3.3.0., timp., perc., harp, strings.
Listed in: **B81.**

1933

W5 **Caedmon** (Unpublished; 40 min.)
Opera in one act, three scenes.
For soloist, chorus, and orchestra.
Libretto by the composer.
Dated variously 1933 (**B36, B67**), 1934 (**B11, B132, B339**), and 1938 (**B268**).

W6 **Poem for Chorus and Orchestra** (Unpublished; 10 min.)
Text by John Fletcher.
Listed in: **B67, B132,** not **B297.**

BY 1934

W7 **Be Still You Little Leaves** (Oiseau-lyre, 1938; Broude; 3 p.; 2 min.)
Song for medium voice and piano.
Text by Mary Webb.
Sometimes dated 1931 (**B11, B67**).
Discussion: **B401.**

Performances

W7a 1982 (13 May) Champaign, IL (Memorial Room, Smith Music Hall,
University of Illinois at Urbana-Champaign). Linda Snyder, soprano;

Nancy Johnston, piano. (With: **W8b, W9a, W10a** as "Four Early Songs," **W29a, W31a, W32f, W38g**.)

W7b 1986 (13 February) Bloomington, IL (Westbrook Auditorium, Illinois Wesleyan University). Linda June Snyder and Melanie N. Williams, soprano and piano. (With: **W8c, W9b, W10b** as "Four Early Songs," **W29b, W31b, W32h, W38i**.) Concert repeated 21 March, Atlanta, GA, International Congress on Women in Music.

W 8   **Come Sleep** (Oiseau-lyre, 1938; Broude; 3 p., 2 min.)
Song for high or medium voice and piano.
Text by John Fletcher (1579).
Sometimes dated 1931 (**B11, B67**).
Discussion: **B363, B401**.

Performances

W8a 1975 (11 February), Lawrence, KS. Miriam Stewart-Green, soprano; unnamed pianist.

W8b Same as **W7a**. (With: **W7a, W9a, W10a, W29a, W31a, W32f, W38g**.)

W8c Same as **W7b**. (With: **W7b, W9b, W10b, W29b, W31b, W32h, W38i**.)

W 9   **Frolic** (Oiseau-lyre, 1938; Broude; 4 p.; 1 $1/2$ min.)
Song for high voice and piano.
Text by Æ (George Russell).
Sometimes dated 1931 (**B11, B67, B133**).
Discussion: **B363, B401**.

Performances

W9a Same as **W7a**. (With: **W7a, W8b, W10a, W29a, W31a, W32f, W32g**.)

W9b Same as **W7b**. (With: **W7b, W8c, W10b, W29b, W31b, W32h, W38i**.)

W9c 1988 (14 August) Perth, WA (His Majesty's Theatre). Mario Alafaci, tenor; Jana Kovar, piano. *Review:* **B69**.

W10 **Rest** (Oiseau-lyre, 1938; Broude; 2 min.)
Song for high voice and piano.
Text by Æ (George Russell).
Sometimes dated 1931 (**B11, B67, B133**).
Discussion: **B401**.

Performances

W10a Same as **W7a**. (With: **W7a, W8b, W9a, W29a, W31a, W32f, W38g.**)

W10b Same as **W7b**. (With: **W7b, W9b, W10b, W29b, W31b, W32h, W38i.**)

1934

W11 **Trio for Pipes: I, II** (Oiseau-lyre, 1934; 4 min.)
In: *Piper's Music* by Arthur Benjamin, Peggy Glanville-Hicks, Esther Rofe, and John Tallis, p. 6-9.
Copy in **A3, A6a**.

W12 **Sinfonietta No. 1 for Orchestra** (Unpublished; 14 min.)
Listed in: **B11, B67, B132-133, B268, B339,** not **B297.**

Premiere performance

W12a 1934 (?); London (?). Empire Orchestra; Eric Fogg, conductor (according to program notes for **W19a**).

W13 **Spanish Suite** (Unpublished)
Five movements: *Pavane, Serenade, Siesta, Fandango, Nocturne.*
Sometimes dated 1935 **(B11, B36, B67)** or 1936 **(B247).**
See: **G594**.

1935

W14 **In Midwood Silence** (Unpublished)
For soprano, oboe, string quartet.
Listed in: **B67** (as for soprano and oboe only), **B132**, not **B11, B297**.

W15 **Song in Summer** (Unpublished)
For chorus and orchestra
Text by John Fletcher
Listed in: **B67, B268** (dated 1935), not in **B11, B297**.

W16 **Hylas and the Nymphs** (Unpublished; 15 min.)
Ballet.
For flute, harp, strings, percussion.
Listed in: **B67, B268** (dated 1937 in both), **B11, B132,** not **B297**.

1936

W17 Concerto no. 1 for Piano and Orchestra (Unpublished; 20 min.)
Sometimes dated 1938 (**B36, B67**). Mentioned in program for **W19a**.

W18 The Robot
Music for an abstract cartoon film, produced in London, England.
Also called *Music for Robots* (**B36, B65**).
For orchestra.

1937

W19 Choral Suite (Oiseau-lyre, l938; miniature score, 48 p.; 20 min.)
For women's chorus SAA (soprani, alti, contralti), oboe, and strings.
Score inscribed "Paris, September 1937."
Text by John Fletcher (1579).
Contents: I. *Great God Pan;* II. *Aspatia's Song;* III. *Fair Cupid!;* IV.
Weep No More; V. *Song in the Wood.*
Recording: **D1**.

Premiere performance

W19a 1938 (20 June), movements I and V, London, England (B.B.C.
Concert Hall, Broadcasting House). International Society of Con-
temporary Music (ISCM) festival concert. Joy Boughton, oboe; The
B.B.C. Singers; Sir Adrian Boult, conductor. *Review:* **B302**.

Other performances

W19b 1971 (16 April) Melbourne, VIC. George Dreyfus Chamber
Orchestra; women members of the Tudor Choristers; David Carolane,
conductor. *Reviews:* **B305, B352**.

W19c 1987 (19 September) Adelaide, SA (Elder Hall). The Adelaide Chorus; Sarah Meagher, oboe; Graham Abbott, conductor. *Review:* **B397**.

W20 Concerto for Flute and Orchestra (Unpublished; 19 min.)
See: **B194** (specifies "small orchestra").
Listed in: **B11, B36, B67, B132-133, B204, B339**, not **B297**.

W21 Prelude and Scherzo (Unpublished)
For large orchestra.
See: **B194**.
Listed in: **B36, B67**, not **B11, B297**.

W22   String Quartet No. 1 (Unpublished)
  See: **B194.**
  Listed in: **B67, B268** (dated 1938), not **B297.**

By 1938

W23   Sinfonietta No. 2 (Unpublished)
  Mentioned in **W19a** program (June 1938).
  Listed in: **B67,** not **B11, B297.**

1938

W24   Clouds
  Music for a film produced in London, England.
  Listed in: **B67, B81,** not **B297.**

W25   Glacier
  Music for a documentary film.
  Listed in: **B67,** not **B297.**

W26   Postman's Knock   (Unpublished; 20 min.)
  Ballet after the painting "The Wedding Group" by Henri Rousseau.
  For chamber orchestra.
  Listed in: **B11, B132,** not **B297;** *sometimes dated* 1939 (**B268**) or 1940
  (**B67, B319**).

1939

W27   Sonatina for Treble [i.e., Alto] Recorder or Flute and Piano (Schott,
    1941; 4 p.; 10 min.)
  In three movements: *Animato assai; Lento recitative; Vivace.*

Performances

  W27a 1961 (25 April) Salisbury, NC (Catawba College Recital Hall). Dale
    Higbee, recorder; Lucile Epperson, piano. *See:* **B94.**

  W27b 1970 (10 July) Melbourne, VIC (Dallas Brooks Hall). "George
    Dreyfus Presents a Concert of Australian Music" assisted by the
    Australian Council for the Arts. Margaret Crawford, treble recorder;
    Rosslyn Farren-Price, piano. (With: **W33c.**) Program in **A3j**. *See:*
    B95. *Reviews:* **B305, B351.**

W27c 1970 (7 August) Melbourne, VIC (Camberwell Civic Centre). Bruce Knox, recorder; Jean Starling, piano. (With: **W33d, 42i**.) *Review:* **B350**.

W27d 1984 (23 June) Boston, MA (Alumni Lounge, Cohen Arts Center, Tufts University). American Women Composers, Inc., Conference on Women in Music. Nina Barwell, flute; Vivian Taylor, piano.

W27e 1985 (15 September) North Melbourne, VIC (Elm Street Hall). "Contemporary Chamberworks" concert of New Moods Arts Festival. (With: **W42m**.) Catherine Schieve, flute; Joan Lawrence, piano. *Review:* **B281**.

W28 Sonatina for Piano (Unpublished)
   Listed in: **B36, B67, B268**, not **B11, B297**.

1944

W29 Five Songs (Weintraub, 1952; 12 p.; 10 min.)
   Songs for mezzo-soprano voice and piano.
   Also called *Five Songs from Housman, Songs from A. E. Housman,* and *Last Poems.*
   Score inscribed "N.Y.C. 1944."
   Text: A. E. Housman
   Contents: *Mimic Heaven; He Would Not Stay; Stars; Unlucky Love;* and *Homespun Collars.*
   Reviews: **B150, B332;** *discussion:* **B401;** *see also:* **B40**.
   Recording: **D5**.

Performances

W29a 1982 (13 May) Urbana, IL (same as **W7a**). Frances Crawford, soprano; Linda Snyder, piano. (With: **W7a, W8b, W9a, W10a, W31a, W32f, W38g**.)

W29b 1986 (13 February) Bloomington, IL (same as **W7b**). (With: **W7b, W8c, W9b, W10b, W31b, W32h, W38i**.)

1945

W30 Aria Concertante (Unpublished)
   For tenor, four-part women's chorus, oboe, piano, gong
   Text by Mario Monteforte-Toledo
   Listed in: **B36, B67, B268** (+ orchestra), not **B297**.

W31 Ballade (Hargail, 1949; 8 p.; 5 min.)
Three songs for medium voice and piano.
Text: Paul Bowles
Contents: *Yet in No Sleep; How in this Garden;* and *But no! A Slow Unchanging Circle.*
Reviews: **B23, B333;** *discussion:* **B401.**

Performances

W31a 1982 (13 May) Urbana, IL (same as **W7a**). Melanie Williams, soprano; Linda Snyder, piano. (With: **W7a, W8b, W9a, W10a, W29a, W32f, W38g.**)

W31b 1986 (13 February) Bloomington, IL (same as **W7b**). (With: **W7b, W9b, W8c, W10b, W29b, W32h, W38i.**)

W32 Profiles from China (Weintraub, 1951; 8 p.; 6 min.)
Five songs for mezzo-soprano voice and piano
Also scored for tenor, piano, string quartet, and bass (Weintraub, 1951)
Text by Eunice Tietjens (1917)
Contents: *Poetics; A Lament of Scarlet Cloud; The Dream; Crepuscule;* and *The Son of Heaven.*
Reviews: **B312, B340,** quoted in **B11;** *discussion:* **B401.**

Performances:

W32a 1948 (24 October) New York City (McMillin Theater, Columbia University). Romolo de Spirito, tenor; Maro Ajemian, piano. (With: **W33b** and **W37a**.) *Reviews:* **B27, B172.**

W32b 1951 (11 April) Washington, D.C. (Howard University). Helen Thigpen, soprano; unnamed pianist. *Review:* **B168,** quoted in **B11.**

W32c 1954 (July) San Francisco, CA (San Francisco State College). Helen Thigpen, soprano; unnamed pianist. *Review:* **B51,** quoted in **B83.**

W32d 1977 (21 February) Los Angeles, CA (Bing Theater, Los Angeles County Museum of Art). Maurita Thornburgh, soprano; Nancy Fierro, piano. *Review:* **B303.**

W32e 1982 (21 January) Sydney, NSW (Town Hall foyer). "A Salute to Peggy Glanville-Hicks," Festival of Sydney cushion concert. Meg Chilcott, soprano; Anthony Fogg, piano. (With: **W38f, W43g, W44c, W53a.**) *Review:* **B4, B100.** Broadcast 1988 (30 January), according to 2MBS-FM programme guide (Sydney).

W32f 1982 (13 May) Same as **W7a**. Richard Hertel, tenor; Linda Snyder, piano. (With: **W7a, W8b, W9a, W10a, W29a, W31a, W38g**.)

W32g 1984 (12 August) Sydney, NSW (Recording Hall, Sydney Opera House). Elizabeth Campbell, mezzo-soprano; Anthony Fogg, piano. *Reviews:* **B47, B55**.

W32h 1986 (13 February) Bloomington, IL (same as **W7b**). (With: **W7b, W8c, W9b, W10b, W29b, W31b, W38i**.)

1946

W33   **Concertino da Camera** (Oiseau-lyre, 1950; 24 p.; 12 min.)
For flute, clarinet, bassoon, piano
Inscribed "P. G.-H., New York 1946"
Recording: **D2**.

Premiere performance

W33a 1948 (10 June) Amsterdam, Netherlands (Concertgebouw, Kleine Zaal). International Society for Contemporary Music festival concert. Members of the Amsterdamse Kamermuziekgezelschap. *Reviews:* **B97, B162, B195, B288, B313, B345, B365,** and **B393**; excerpts in **B11**.

Other performances

W33b 1948 (24 October) New York City (McMillin Theater, Columbia University). Carleton Sprague Smith, flute; Abram Klotzman, clarinet; David Manchester, bassoon; Maro Ajemian, piano. (With: **W32a, W37a**.) *Reviews:* **B27, B172**; excerpts in **B11**.

W33c 1970 (10 July) Melbourne, VIC (Dallas Brooks Hall). "George Dreyfus Presents A Concert of Australian Music." Margaret Crawford, flute; Pamela Spira, clarinet; George Dreyfus, bassoon; Rosslyn Farren-Price, piano. (With: **W27b**.) *See:* **B95**. *Reviews:* **B305, B351**.

W33d 1970 (7 August) Melbourne, VIC (Camberwell Civic Centre). Vernon Hill, flute; Pamela Spira, clarinet; George Dreyfus, bassoon; Rosslyn Farren-Price, piano. (With: **W27c, W42i**.) *Review:* **B350**.

W33e 1987 (4 July) Sydney, NSW (Everest Theatre, Seymour Centre, University of Sydney). Seymour Group Tenth Anniversary Concert, "Future Tense III." Seymour Group instrumental ensemble; Myer Fredman, conductor. *Reviews:* **B223, B231, B366**. Broadcast 1988 (30 January), according to 2MBS-FM programme guide (Sydney).

W33f 1989 (18 September) Melbourne, VIC (Assembly Hall). Melbourne
Spoleto Festival lunchtime chamber music concert. Prudence Davis,
Rolf Kuhlmann, Philip Miechel, and Michael Harvey, performers.

W34 **Killer-of-Enemies** (Unpublished)
Ballet
For narrator, woodwinds, percussion (4 players, according to **B319**).
Also listed in: **B67**, not **B297**.

1947

W35 **Dance Cantata** (Unpublished; 35 min.)
For tenor, narrator, speaking chorus, orchestra (2.2.2.2., 4.3.2.1., timp.,
strings).
Navaho text, arr. by Erick Hawkins.
Listed in: **B11** (without tenor), **B67**, **B81** (with solo voices), **B132** and
B339 (dated 1946 in both), not **B297**.

W36 **Sidi Amar in Winter** (Unpublished)
Three songs on texts by Paul Bowles.
Listed in: **B37**, **B67**, not **B297**.

W37 **Thirteen Ways of Looking at a Blackbird** (Weintraub, 1951; 19 p.; 10
min.)
Thirteen songs on a poem by Wallace Stevens (1923)
For medium voice and piano.
Inscribed "to Cathalene Parker."
Reviews: **B312**, **B340**; *discussion:* **B401**.

Performances

W37a 1948 (24 October) New York City (McMillian Theater, Columbia
University). Joseph Riley, tenor; Maro Ajemian, piano. (With:
W32a and **W33b**.) *Reviews:* **B27**, **B172**; excerpts in **B11**.

W37b 1951 (20 February) New York City; Times Hall. WNYC American
Music Festival, concert of music by *New York Herald Tribune* music
critics; also broadcast WNYC. Cathalene Parker, soprano; David
Allen piano. *Reviews:* **B174**, **B291**; excerpts in **B11**.

W37c 1986 (13 February) Bloomington, IL (same as **W7b**).

W37d 1986 (22 June) Sydney, NSW (Old Darlington School). Recital of
Twentieth-Century Australian songs by Opera Mode. *Review:* **B387**.

W37e 1987 (22 September) Melbourne, VIC (Melba Hall, University of Melbourne). Deborah Riedel, mezzo-soprano; Len Vorster, piano. Melbourne Spoleto Festival. *Review:* **B177.**

W37f 1988 (12 August) Perth, WA (His Majesty's Theatre). Australian Contemporary Music Concert. Anne Millar, mezzo-soprano; Jana Kovar, piano. *Reviews:* **B69, B257.**

1949

W38 Thomsoniana (ACA)
A setting of excerpts from Virgil Thomson's reviews from the columns of the *New York Herald Tribune.*
Subtitled: "A Birthday Offering to Virgil Thomson" [Thomson's birthday was November 25].
For tenor or soprano, flute, horn, piano, and string quartet.
Contents: *Stravinsky, Ansermet, Schoenberg, Satie, Clifford Curzon.*
Full score and piano reduction in **A3a.**
Reprint of full score, with program for **W38a,** in *Soundings* 14-15 (Santa Fe, NM, 1986), p. 195-223.
Discussion: **A3k.**

Performances:

W38a 1950 ("spring broadcast" mentioned in **B378**) New York City (McMillin Theater, Columbia University). Uta Graf, soprano; Carleton Sprague Smith, flute; John Barrows, horn; Leo Smit or Yara Bernette, piano; Jose Figueroa and Nicholas Berezowsky, violins; Paul Doktor, viola; Luigi Silva, cello. *Review:* **B176,** quoted in **B11, B295.**

W38b 1950 (4 August) Colorado Springs, CO. Josephine Vadala, soprano; other performers unnamed. *Reviews:* **B96, B378** quoted in **B11;** *see also:* **G208.**

W38c 1955 (1 May) Philadelphia, PA (The Settlement Music School). Unnamed performers; Arthur Cohn, conductor. *See:* **B84.**

W38d 1957 (12 May) Louisville, KY (University of Louisville). Eleventh Annual Festival of Contemporary Music. Charme Riesley, soprano; Mary Raper, piano; Conrad Crocker, flute; Dudley Howe, horn; Walter Toole and Marion Korda, violins; Edna Louis, viola; Grace Whitney, cello; Moritz Bomhard, conductor. *See:* **B86.**

W38e 1958 (1 May) Rochester, NY (Kilbourn Hall, Eastman School of Music). Twenty-Eighth Annual Eastman School Festival of American Music. Lee Dougherty, soprano; Judith Hummel, piano; Joanne Dickenson, flute; Norman Schweikert, horn; Ralph Winkler and

Jefferson Fraser, violins; John Stoll, viola; Polly Comstock, cello. *See:* **B88, B385.**

W38f 1982 (21 January) Sydney, NSW (Town Hall foyer). "A Salute to Peggy Glanville-Hicks," Festival of Sydney cushion concert. Meg Chilcott, soprano; Seymour Group chamber ensemble; Stuart Challender, conductor. (With: **W32e, W43g, W44c, W53a.**) *Review:* **B100.**

W38g 1982 (13 May) Urbana, IL (same as **W7a**). Barbara Dalheim, soprano; Nancy Johnston, piano; other instrumentalists unnamed. (With: **W7a, W8b, W9a, W10a, W29a, W31a, W32f.**)

W38h 1985 (27 June and 30 June) South Melbourne, VIC (Anthill Theatre). "Women at Work: Contemporary Music by Australian Women Composers." Jan Friedl, soprano; Anna Bailey, flute; Linda Patterson, horn; Meredith Thomas and Janet Froomes, violins; Kate Kaleski, viola; Kate Calwell, cello; Jennifer Turner, conductor. (With: *Sonata for Harp*, **W421**).

W38i 1986 (13 February) Bloomington, IL (same as **W7b**). (With: **W7b, W8c, W9b, W10b, W29b, W31b, W32h.**)

W39 Tulsa
Music for a film produced by the U.S. Department of State.
Listed in: **B67**, not **B297.**

1950

W40 Sonata for Harp, Flute, and Horn (Unpublished).
Listed in: **B38, B67** not **B297.**

W41 Tel
Music for cartoon film produced by Film Graphics, Inc.
Listed in: **B67** and **B297.**

1950-1951

W42 Sonata for Harp (Weintraub, 1953; 14 p.; 10 min.)
Contents: I. *Saeta;* 2. *Pastorale;* 3. *Rondo.*
Dedicated to Nicanor Zabaleta.
Reviews: **B219, B276, B334;** *discussion:* **G684, B21.**
Recordings: **D12-17.**

Premiere performance

W42a 1951 (February) Caracas, Venezuela (Biblioteca Nacional). Nicanor Zabaleta, harp. *Review:* **B224**, quoted in **B11**.

Other performances

W42b 1951 (23 October) Mexico D. F. *Review:* **B358**, quoted in **B11**.

W42c 1952 (10 March) New York City (Museum of Modern Art). New Music Society concert. Nicanor Zabaleta, harp. *Reviews:* **B293, 381**, quoted in **B11**.

W42d 1952 (20 March) San Juan, Puerto Rico. Nicanor Zabaleta, harp. *Review:* **B342**, quoted in **B11**.

W42e 1953 (12 May) Hamburg, Germany (Mozartsaal). Nicanor Zabaleta, harp. *Review:* **B119**.

W42f 1958 (27 January) New York City (Town Hall). Nicanor Zabaleta, harp. *Review:* **B359**, quoted in **B87**.

W42g 1958 (13 December) New York City (Carnegie Recital Hall). Susann McDonald, harp. *See:* **B89**.

W42h 1960 (13 May) Miami, FL (Beaumont Lecture Hall, University of Miami). *Saeta* [first movement] only. First Festival of American Music. Mary Spalding Sevitsky, harp. *See:* **B94**.

W42i 1970 (7 August) Melbourne, VIC (Camberwell Civic Centre). Mary Anderson, harp. (With: **W27c, W33d**.) *Review:* **B350**.

W42j 1979 (5 August) Sydney, NSW. Seymour Group's Direction 1980s series. Anthony Maydwell, harp. *Review:* **B34**.

W42k 1983 (7 May) Ann Arbor, MI, Recital Hall, University of Michigan School of Music. Op. 2 Conference on Women in Music. Lucile H. Jennings, harp.

W42l 1985 (27 June and 30 June) South Melbourne, VIC, Anthill Theatre. Mary Anderson, harp. With: **W38h**.

W42m 1985 (15 September) North Melbourne, VIC (Elm Street Hall). "Contemporary Chamberworks" concert of New Moods Arts Festival. Mary Anderson, harp. (With: **W28d**.) *Review:* **B281**.

W42n 1986 (21 March) Adelaide, SA. Adelaide Arts Festival concert. Alice Giles, harp.

W42o 1988 (15 October) London, England (Wigmore Hall). Nicanor Zabaleta (aged 81), harp.

1951

W43 **Sonata for Piano and Percussion** (ACA 1952; AMP, 1954; 24 p. score + 4 percussion parts; 10 min.)
For piano, xylophone, timp., suspended cymbal, 3 gongs, tam tam, tom tom, bass drum.
Contents: I. *Allegro*; II. *Lento sombreroso*; III. *Presto*.
Recording: **D17**.
Discussion: **G675**.

Premiere performance

W43a 1952 (6 May) New York City (Museum of Modern Art). Concert of New Music for Percussion. William Masselos, piano; Al Howard, tympani; Elden Bailey, Phil Krause, Walter Rosenberger, percussion. *Review:* **B289**, quoted in **B11, B82**.

Other performances

W43b 1953 (12 February) New York City (Town Hall). WNYC Festival of American Music concert. Maxim Schapiro, piano; percussionists of **W43a**. *Reviews:* **G425, B117, B384**, quoted in **B11, B82**.

W43c 1953 (22 March) New York City (Town Hall). Free concert by National Association of American Conductors and Composers. Performers as in **W43b**; Carlos Surinach, conductor. *See:* **G451, B290**.

W43d 1960 (15 May) Bayonne, NJ (Bayonne Jewish Community Center). "An Adventure in Sound." Paul Price Percussion Ensemble. *See:* **B94**.

W43e 1976 (15 April) Adelaide, SA. Stephen Walter or David McSkimming, piano; Richard Pusz, Denis Johnson, Greg Rush, Michael Holland, and Brenton Holmes, percussion. *Reviews:* **B248, B349**.

W43f 1981 (August) Sydney, NSW (Ervin Gallery on Observatory Hill). Synergy Percussion recital for the Seymour Group. Michael Askill, Colin Piper, Richard Miller, David Clarence, and John Clark, percussionists. *Review:* **B31**.

W43g 1982 (21 January) Sydney, NSW (Town Hall foyer). "A Salute to Peggy Glanville-Hicks," Festival of Sydney cushion concert. Colin Piper and other members of Synergy Percussion ensemble. (With:

W32e, W38f, W44c, W53a.) *Reviews:* **B4, B100**. Broadcast 1988 (30 January), according to 2MBS-FM programme guide (Sydney).

W43h 1984 (19 August) Aptos, CA (Cabrillo College Theater). Emily Wong, piano; Cabrillo Music Festival percussion ensemble. Program notes by Vincent Duckles.

1952

W44 Letters from Morocco (ACA, CFE, 1952; Peters, 1953; 63 p.; 16 min.)
For tenor and orchestra: 1.1.0.1., 0.1.0.0., timp., 3 perc. (xylophone, 3 gongs, tam tam, side drum, tom tom, bass drum), harp, strings.
Settings of excerpts from letters to the composer from Paul Bowles, in six movements.
Discussion: **B72**.
Recording: **D6**.

Premiere performance

W44a 1953 (22 February) New York City (Museum of Modern Art). American Music series sponsored by ACA and BMI. William Hess, tenor; Leopold Stokowski, conductor. *See:* **B82**. *Reviews:* **G425, B30, B107, B118, B384**; excerpts in **B11**.

Other performances

W44b 1954 (12 February) New York City (Town Hall). WNYC 15th annual Festival of American Music, also broadcast. William Hess, tenor; National Orchestral Association; Leon Barzin, conductor. *Review:* **B44, B317**.

W44c 1982 (21 January) Sydney, NSW (Town Hall foyer). "A Salute to Peggy Glanville-Hicks," Festival of Sydney cushion concert. Gerald English, tenor; Seymour Group instrumental ensemble. (With: **W32e, W38f, W43g, W53a**.) *Reviews:* **B4, B100**

W44d 1985 (22 September) Melbourne, VIC (Town Hall). Gerald English, tenor; members of the Eureka Ensemble; "Women 150" [150th anniversary of Victoria], "New Moods Arts Festival." *Review:* **B282**; *discussion:* **B144, B260**.

1952-1953

W45 Sinfonia da Pacifica (ACA, CFE, 1953 (according to **B11**); 50 p.; 16 min.)
Also called *Sinfonia Pacifica*.
Facsimile of manuscript is in **A14**.

For orchestra: 1.1.1.1., 1.1.1.0, timp., 4 perc., (3 gongs, triangle, suspended cymbal, tam tam, tom tom, timpani, bass drum, xylophone, marimba [may be played on the same instrument]), strings.
Contents: I. *Allegro*. II. *Lento tranquillo*. III. *Allegro giocoso*.
Inscribed: "S. W. Pacific, 1952. Port Antonio, Jamaica, B. W. I., 1953. P. G.-H."
Discussion: **G680**.
Recording: **D11**.

Premiere performance

W45a 1954 (25 June) Melbourne, VIC; Victorian Symphony Orchestra; Sir Bernard Heinze, conductor. Also broadcast live on AM radio station LO. *See:* **B18, B388** (refers to a "recent" Barcelona performance).

W46 **The Transposed Heads** (Piano-vocal score, Schirmer, 1953; AMP, 1958; 112 p.; 90 min.)
Copy of full score in **A10**.
Libretto by the composer after the novel by the same name by Thomas Mann (*Die vertauschten Köpfe*, 1949), English translation by Helen Lowe-Porter.
For solo soprano (Sita), tenor (Shridaman), baritone (Nanda); two speaking parts; chorus; orchestra: 1.1.1.1., 1.1.1.0., timp., 4 perc. (triangle, three gongs, suspended cymbal, tam tam, tom tom, xylophone, bass drum), harp, strings.
The first opera commissioned by The Louisville Philharmonic Society through a grant from the Rockefeller Foundation.
Also separately published, Nanda's aria "Lovesick" (AMP); *see:* **B363**.
Discussion: **G677-678, G689, B21, B41, B121, B152, B180, B182, B184, B240, B261, B279, A3c**.
Recording: **D21**.

Premiere performances

W46a 1954 (3 and 4 April) Louisville, KY; Columbia Auditorum. Produced by the Kentucky Opera Association. Monas Harlan (Shridaman); William Pickett (Nanda); Audrey Nossaman (Sita); Virginia Guernsey, wedding scene dancer; David Anderson, voice of goddess Kali; Kenneth Archer, voice of guru Kamadamana; Louisville Orchestra (Robert Whitney, Musical Director); Moritz Bomhard, conductor. *Publicity:* **B254**; *reviews:* **B135, B209, B255-256, B344**, some quoted in **B11**; *discussion:* **B388**; *see also:* **B16, A3c**.

W46b 1958 (10 and 17 February) New York City (Phoenix Theatre). Presented by the Contemporary Music Society, Inc., Chandler Cowles, producer. Loren Driscoll (Shridiman); Peter Binder (Nanda); Maria Ferriero (Sita); Raimonda Orselli, ballerina in wedding scene;

Robinson Stone, voice of guru Kamadamana; Perry Wood, voice of goddess Kali; Carlos Surinach, conductor. *Publicity:* **B62, B275, B307, B396;** *reviews:* **B29, B131, B158, B189, B198-199, B202, B212, B229, B237, B249, B318, B338, B372;** *composer interviews:* **B39, B147, B230;** *see also:* **A3d.**

Australian performances

W46c 1970 (27 June, 3 and 4 July) Sydney, NSW (Science Theatre, University of New South Wales). University of New South Wales Opera Group; Raymond Dring (Shridaman); Barry Strong (Nanda); Marilyn Richardson (Sita); orchestra ; Roger Covell, director. *Publicity and interviews:* **B54, B77, B101, B285;** *reviews:* **B2, B32, B395.** Repeated: 18 July, Mittagong (Canberra Theatre Centre, Clubbe Hall), says **B101.**

W46d 1984 (September) Perth, WA (Australian Broadcasting Corporation studios). Recorded in the presence of the composer. First broadcast on the ABC's FM network 29 November 1984. Gerald English (Shridaman); Michael Leighton-Jones (Nanda); Genty Stevens (Sita); Raymond Long, narrator; Maggie King, goddess Kali; West Australian Symphony Orchestra; Festival Chorus; David Measham, conductor. *See:* **B262, B264.**

W46e 1986 (20, 22, 23 March) Adelaide, SA. Adelaide Festival. Geoffrey Harris (Shridaman); David Brennan (Nanda); Luise Napier (Sita); Daphne Harris, voice of Kali; State Opera of South Australia; Gerald Krug, conductor; Ken Campbell-Dobbie, designer/director. (With: *The Glittering Gate,* **W52c.**) *See:* **B52-53, B106, B148;** *reviews:* **B59, B178, B206, B213, B246-247.**

1953

W47 **Three Gymnopédies** (AMP, CFE, 1953; 17 p.; 15 min.)
No. 1, *Lento tranquillo,* for oboe, harp, strings; no. 2, *Molto tranquillo alla siesta,* for harp, celeste, strings; no. 3, *Allegretto semplice,* for harp and strings.
Facsimile of manuscript in Library of Congress.
No. 1 published separately, AMP, 1957.
First page of no. 2 is printed in **B81.**
Discussion: **G594, B73, B109.**
Recordings: **D18-20.**

Performances

W47a 1959 (9 August) *Gymnopédie No. 1.* Brevard, NC (The Brevard Music Center). The Brevard Festival Orchestra; James Christian Pfohl, conductor. *See:* **B92.**

W47b 1982 (14 November) San Francisco (Herbst Theater, Civic Center). Bay Area Women's Philharmonic; Elizabeth Min, conductor. *See:* **B265**; *reviews:* **B192, B221, B308.**

W47c 1987 (28 February) San Francisco (First Congregational Church). Bay Area Women's Philharmonic; JoAnn Falletta, conductor.

1954

W48 **Etruscan Concerto** (ACA, 1954; C. F. Peters, 1985; 82 p. + parts; 16 min.) For piano solo and chamber orchestra: 1.1.1.1., 1.1.0.0., timp., 3 perc. (xylophone, tambourine, tomtom, suspended cymbal, tamtam), strings.
Also published in piano reduction of orchestra score (Peters, 1955).
The three movements, meant to evoke the Etruscan tombs of Tarquinia, bear quotations from D. H. Lawrence's *The Painted Tombs of Tarquinia* (no. 1) and *Etruscan Places* (no. 2 and 3).
Score, in composer's hand, ends with inscription "13. 7. 54 N. Y. C."
Discussion: **B71, B261, B309.**
Recording: **D4.**

Premiere performance

W48a 1956 (25 January) New York City (Grace Rainey Rogers Auditorium, Metropolitan Museum of Art). "New Works for Chamber Orchestra" concert sponsored by Music Performance Trust Fund, in collaboration with the American Composers Alliance, and the Ditson Fund of Columbia University, and arranged by Peggy Glanville-Hicks for the ACA. Carlo Bussotti, piano; chamber orchestra; Carlos Surinach, conductor. *Reviews:* **B1, B342, B389,** quoted in **B85, B390.**

Other performances

W48b 1980 (17 March) New York City (Avery Fisher Hall, Lincoln Center for the Performing Arts). Keith Jarrett, piano; Saint Paul Chamber Orchestra; Dennis Russell Davies, conductor. Program notes by Dennis D. Rooney (**B325**). *Review:* **B181.**

W48c 1984 (24 August) Aptos, CA (Cabrillo College Theater). Keith Jarrett, piano; Cabrillo Festival Orchestra; Catherine Comet, conductor. Program notes by Vincent Duckles. *See:* **B262.**

W48d 1988 (4 and 5 November) Troy, NY (4 November, Troy Savings Bank Music Hall) and Albany, NY (5 November, Palace Theatre). Penelope Thwaites, piano; Albany Symphony Orchestra; Geoffrey Simon, conductor. Program notes by David E. Gruender (**B167**). *Reviews:* **B124, B278.**

1955

W49 Concertino Antico (Unpublished; 12 min.)
For solo harp and string quartet, in three movements.
Written for Edna Phillips. Harp part revised by Nicanor Zabaleta,
according to his letter to the composer in **A3b(9)**.
Discussion: **G684**.

Premiere performances

W49a 1958 (17 January) Washington, D. C. (Coolidge Auditorium, Library
of Congress). Edna Phillips, harp; Juilliard String Quartet. *See:* **B90**.

W49b 1958 (2 February) New York City (92nd Street YM-YMHA). "Music
In Our Time" concert. *Reviews:* **B116, B193, B211**.

1956

W50 The African Story
Music for a film, *All Our Children,* produced by the United Nations.
Listed in: **B67, B297**.

W51 Concerto Romantico (C. F. Peters, 1957, rental).
For solo viola and orchestra: 1.2 (E.hn).2 (b.clar.).1., 4.0.1.0., harp,
strings.
Written for violist Walter Trampler.
Score, in composer's hand, is inscribed "Starnberg bei München
17.5.56."
Discussion: **G686, B70**.
Recording: **D3**.

Premiere performance

W51a 1957 (19 February) New York City (Grace Rainey Rogers Audi-
torium, Metropolitan Museum of Art). "New Works for Chamber
Orchestra" concert organized by Peggy Glanville-Hicks. Walter
Trampler, viola; Chamber Orchestra; Carlos Surinach, conductor.
Reviews: **B127, B175, B343**, last two quoted in **B138**.

Other performances

W51b 1984 (August) Perth, SA. Keith Crellin, viola; West Australian
Symphony Orchestra; Patrick Thomas, conductor. Recorded by the
ABC for broadcast. *See:* **B264, B402**.

W51c 1984 (?) Keith Crellin, viola; Tasmanian Symphony Orchestra; Vanco Cavdarski, conductor. Tape in **A6b**.

W51d 1989 (21 October) Geraldine Walther, viola; Bay Area Women's Philharmonic; JoAnn Falletta, conductor.

W52 **The Glittering Gate** (Franco Columbo, Belwin-Mills, 1957; rental; 108 p. score + parts; 30 min.)
Opera in one act--a "curtain raiser."
For solo tenor and bass, and orchestra: 1.1.1.1., 1.1.1.0., timp., 3 perc. (including glockenspiel), strings, electronic tape (of "unearthly laughter").
Libretto by the composer after a story by Lord Dunsany.
Composed in Munich, Germany, 1956, and orchestrated in Mallorca, Spain, 1956.
See: **B121, B261, B279, A3f.**

Premiere performance

W52a 1959 (14 May) New York City (92nd Street YM-YWHA, Kaufman Concert Hall). Robert Price, tenor (Bill); David Smith, baritone (Jim); Newell Jenkins, conductor; staged by James Price; designed by Robert Mitchell; lighting by Nicola Cernovich; produced by The Artists Company. (With: Lou Harrison, *Rapunzel*.) *See:* **B91**; *reviews:* **B58, B129, B188, B286, B301, B373.**

Australian performances

W52b 1972 (14 March) Adelaide, SA (AMP Theatre). Intimate Opera Group; Anthony Clark; Michael Lewis; Mary Handley, piano; Michael Holland, percussion. Adelaide Festival of the Arts. *See:* **B53**; *reviews:* **B45, B235, B386.**

W52c 1986 (20, 22, 23 March) Adelaide, SA. Adelaide Festival of the Arts. Graham Macfarlane, tenor (Bill); John Greene, baritone (Jim); State Opera of South Australia; Gerald Krug, conductor; Ken Campbell-Dobbie, designer/director. (With: *The Transposed Heads*, **W46e**.) *See:* **B53**; *reviews:* **B59, B106, B148, B178, B206, B246-247.**

1957

W53 **Musica Antiqua no. 1** (Unpublished; 42 p.; 18 min.)
Inscribed "N. Y. C. 1957" at end.
Copies in **A3a, A6a**.
For 2 flutes, harp, marimba, timp., 2 perc. (tam, tom tom, wood block [no. 1]; cymbal, suspended cymbal.

Contents: 1. *Prelude. From Cuxco.* 2. *Intermezzo. From Punjab.* 3. *Allegretto.* 4. *Canzonetta. From the Congo.* 5. *Andantino. From Kenya.* 6. *Presto. From Lima, Peru.*

Premiere performance

W53a 1982 (21 January) Sydney, NSW (Town Hall). "Salute to Peggy Glanville-Hicks," Festival of Sydney cushion concert. Seymour Group members. (With: **W32e, W38f, W43g, W44c**.) *Reviews:* **B4, B100.** Broadcast 1988 (30 January 1988), according to 2MBS-FM programme guide (Sydney).

W54 Prelude and Presto for Ancient American Instruments (Unpublished)
  For piccolo, flute, pan pipes, whistles (player 1); flute 2, owl, armadillo (player 2); maracas, scraper, split drum 1 and 2 (player 3); conch, drum (player 4); and handclapping.
  The Prelude is based on tunes of Lima and Cuzco, and the Presto on tunes of Ayacucho and Cuzco (tune 1) and of Lake Titicaca (tune 2).
  A copy of manuscript and recording (**D8**) is in the possession of Peter Garland, Soundings Press, Santa Fe, NM.

Performance

W54a 1957 (October) New York City (Andre Emmerich Gallery), from recording (**D8**). *Review:* **B15.**

1958

W55 The Masque of the Wild Man (CFE, 1958; 78 p.; 18 min.)
  Ballet commissioned by John Butler for the first Festival of Two Worlds at Spoleto, Italy.
  For flute, celeste, harp, piano, 2 perc., strings.
  Orchestral version titled *Tapestry for Orchestra,* **W58.**

Premiere performance

W55a 1958 (10 June) Spoleto, Italy (Caio Melisso Theatre); "Four Chamber Ballets" for the Festival of Two Worlds. Glen Tetley, Buzz Miller, Carmen de Lavallade, Charles Saint-Amant, Tina Ramirez, and Coco Ramirez, dancers; John Butler, choreographer; Rouben Ter Arutunian, sets and costumes; Robert Feist, conductor. *Publicity:* **B218, B241, A3e;** *reviews:* **B61, B136, B214, B368, B370** (quoted in **B88**), **B371.**

W56 Prelude for a Pensive Pupil (2 p., 3 min.)
  For solo piano.

Published in two collections: *New Music for Piano*, selected by Joseph Prostakoff (New York: Lawson-Gould, 1963), p. 82-83, and *Frauen Komponieren: 22 Klavierstücke des 18-20 Jahrhunderts*, ed. Eva Rieger (Mainz: B. Schott's Söhne, 1985), p. 56-57.
Copyright date 1958, by Lawson-Gould, according to Rieger.
Discussion: **B48**.
Recordings: **D8, D9**.

W57   **A Scary Time** (CFE; 2 1/2 min.)
Music for an animated film documentary on the Suez crisis.
For clarinet, violin, percussion.
See: **B225**.

W58   **Tapestry for Orchestra** (ACA; rental, Peters; 75 p. score + parts; 18 min.)
Orchestral version of *The Masque of the Wild Man* (**W55**).
For: 2 (picc.).2.2.2., 2.2.2.0., timp., perc. (cymbal, snare drum, tam tam, tambourine, xylophone, bass drum), harp, celesta, piano, strings.

W59   **Triad** (Unpublished)
Ballet music for one act of a three-act ballet (with: music by Duke Ellington, Prokofiev, and Tailleferre).
For small instrumental ensemble.
Composed for The Spoleto Festival Co.
Listed in: **B67**, not **B297**.

Premiere performance

W59a   1958 (10 June), Spoleto, Italy (Caio Melisso Theatre); "Four Chamber Ballets" for Festival of Two Worlds. Glen Tetley, Buzz Miller, Charles Saint-Amant, and Carmen de Lavallade, dancers; John Butler, choreographer; Jac Venza, set and costumes; Robert Feist, conductor. *Publicity:* **B218, A3e**; *reviews:* **B61, B214, B368, B370** (quoted in **B88**), **B371**; *photo* of Tetley and Lavallade, from premiere, in **B78**.

1959

W60   **Drama for Orchestra** (Peters, rental, 1961; 85 p.; 17 min.)
Orchestral version of *Saul and the Witch of Endor*, **W61**.
Score, in composer's hand, is inscribed at end, "N. Y. C. Nov. 5th 1959. Washington Jan. 21st 1961."
For clarinet, trumpet, piano, xylophone, timp., 3 perc. (suspended cymbal, cymbal, tam tam, snare drum), strings.

Performance

W60a 1960 (12 February) New York City (Town Hall). WNYC 21st annual American Music Festival in conjunction with the National Association for American Composers and Conductors. NAACC Festival Orchestra; Alfredo Antonini, conductor. *See:* **B93**; *reviews:* **B28, B112**.

W61   Saul and the Witch of Endor (Manuscript; rental, Peters; 85 p.; 20 min.)
Ballet commissioned by CBS TV.
For trumpet, 3 perc., (timp., xylophone, etc.), strings.
Orchestral version titled *Drama for Orchestra,* **W60**.

Performance

W61a 1959 (7 June) Choreography by John Butler. Set and Costumes by Jac Venza. "Camera Three," CBS-TV.

1959-1960

W62   Nausicaa (Manuscript of full score in **A3**; piano-vocal score, rental, Belwin-Mills; 153 p.; 120 min.)
An Opera in Three Acts [six scenes] with Prologue and Interludes.
Libretto by Robert Graves and Alastair Reid from Graves's novel *Homer's Daughter* (1954).
For solo soprano (Nausicaa), contralto (Queen Arete), three tenors (Phemius, Clytoneus, Antinous & Priest), baritone (Aethon), two basses (or bass [King Alcinous] and bass-baritone [Messenger]); chorus SATB; and orchestra (about 60 players): 2 (picc.).1.3 (b.clar).2 (c.bsn)., 2.2.1.0., perc., 2 harps, piano, strings.
Inscribed "N. Y. C., Apr 30, 1960."
Discussion: **G693, G696, B68, B121, B179;** *see also:* **B184, B261, B279, B369, A3g**.
Recording: **D7**.

Premiere performance

W62a 1961 (19, 20, and 22 August) Athens, Greece (Herodus Atticus Theatre). Athens Festival. Teresa Stratas (Nausicaa); John Modenos (Aethon); Edward Ruhl (Phemius); George Tsantikos (Clytoneus); Sophia Steffan (Arete); Spiro Malas (Alcinous); Michalis Heliotis (Antinous, Priest); George Moutsios (Eurymachus); Vassilis Koundouris (Messenger); John Butler, stage director; Andreas Nomikos, sets and costume designer; Carlos Surinach, conductor. *Publicity:* **B156, B292, B392, B311;** *reviews:* **B14, B110, B115, B151, B153-155, B157, B159-161, B163-164, B216, B238, B267, B270-273, B292, B299, B322, B357, B374, B392, B406** (many excerpted in **G696** and **B269**), **A3g**(4-5); *response:*

G692; *interview:* **B56**. Broadcast CBS Radio, 23 September 1961, "World Music Festivals" program (press release in **A3g**).

Performance of excerpt

W62b 1979 (13 March) *Duo from Act II, Scene 5.* New York City (Interart Center). Second Festival of Women's Music, first concert. Janet Steele, soprano (Nausicaa); Patrick Mason, baritone (Aethon); Michael Fardink, pianist. *Review:* **B128**.

1962

W63 Carlos Among the Candles (Unpublished)
Opera.
For one voice and instruments, according to composer's 1962 letters in **A14b**.
Unperformed
See: **B133, B279**.

1963

W64 Sappho (Manuscript; 135 min.).
Opera in three acts.
Libretto by Lawrence Durrell from his play by the same name.
For mezzo-soprano, lyric tenor, dramatic tenor, baritone, bass-baritone, bass; chorus; orchestra: 2 (picc.).2 (E.hn).2.2 (c.bsn.), 4.3.3.0., timp., perc., harp, strings.
Unperformed.
See: **B8, B121, B279, A3h**.

1965

W65 A Season in Hell (Onwin; 20 min.)
Ballet after the poem *Une saison en Enfer* by Artur Rimbaud.
Commissioned by the Harkness Ballet.
For orchestra: 2.2.2.2., 4.3.2.1., perc., strings.

Premiere performance

W65a 1967 (15 November) New York City (Broadway Theater). Harkness Ballet: Lawrence Rhodes (Rimbaud); Dennis Wayne (Verlaine); Brunilda Ruiz (Woman); choreography by John Butler; sets and costumes by Rouben Ter Arutunian; lighting by Jennifer Tipton. *Reviews:* **B24, B337**, quoted in **B78**; *photo* in **B78**.

1966

W66   Tragic Celebration (Jephthah's Daughter) (Peters, 77 p.; 19 min.)
Ballet commissioned by CBS Color TV.
For orchestra: 1.1.1.1., 0.1.0.1., timp, perc., harp, strings.

Performance

W66a   1966 (6 November) "Lamp Unto My Feet", CBS TV. Choreography
by John Butler; set by Tom John; costumes by Ann Elliot. *Photo in*
B78.

1978

W67   Girondelle for Giraffes (Manuscript in **A6a**; 3 min.)
Subtitled: "For Sculpture Show of Pamela Boden. 1978."
For flute (with piccolo), trombone, double bass (the last two "better
with jazz-pop background"), drum (deep tone), suspended cymbal
(the last two with "soft sticks--felt knobs, not wood or plastic").

Premiere performances

W67a   1978 (13 May-3 June) Sydney, NSW (Australian Music Centre, 80
George St., The Rocks). Tape of **W67** played during Boden exhibit.
See: **B5, B287**.

W67b   1978 (21 June-5 July St. Kilda, VIC (Tolarno Gallery [now United
Artists]). Tape of **W67** played during Boden exhibit. *See:* **B149, B234**.

1989--IN PROGRESS

W68   Beckett
Opera on the life of Thomas-à-Beckett.
Libretto by Wendy Beckett. *See:* **B26**.

W69   Froggyana
Piece for Indonesian frog-puppet band.

W70   Piece on Biblical text (untitled).
Commissioned by Church of England.

PUBLISHERS DIRECTORY

ACA   = American Composers Alliance: *see* CFE
AMP   = Associated Music Publishers: *see* Schirmer

Belwin   = Belwin-Mills Publishing Corp., 15800 NW 48 Ave., Miami, FL 33014
Broude   = Broude Brothers Ltd., 170 Varick St., New York, NY 10013
CFE   = Composers Facsimile Editions, now American Composers Edition Inc., 170 West 74th St., New York 10023
Colfrank = Franco Columbo, Inc.: *see* Belwin
Hargail   = Hargail Music Inc., P. O. Box 118, Saugerties, NY 12477
Peters   = C. F. Peters Corp., 373 Park Ave. S, New York, NY 10016
Onwin   = Onwin, c/o Weisberger and Frosh, 120 East 56 St., NY 10022
OL   = L'Oiseau-lyre (Lyrebird Press), Les Remparts, Monaco
Schirmer = G. Schirmer, Inc., 24 E. 22 St., New York, NY 10010. Distributed exclusively by Hal Leonard Publishing Corp., P. O. Box 13819, Milwaukee, WI 53213
Schott   = Schott & Co. Ltd., 48 Great Marlborough St., London, England
Soundings = Soundings Press (Peter Garland), P. O. Box 8319, Santa Fe, New Mexico 87504-8319
Weintraub = Weintraub Music Co. (a division of G. Schirmer, Inc.), 24 E. 22 St., New York, NY 10010

ALPHABETICAL LIST OF WORKS

The African Story **W50**
All Our Children: see *The African Story* **W50**
Ansermet: see *Thomsoniana* **W38**
Aria Concertante **W30**
Aspatia's Song: see *Choral Suite* **W19**
Ballade **W31**
Beckett **W68**
Be Still You Little Leaves **W7**
But no! A Slow Unchanging Circle: see *Five Songs* **W29**
Caedmon **W5**
Carlos Among the Candles **W63**
Choral Suite (Fletcher) **W19**; (Wright) **A9**
Clifford Curzon: see *Thomsoniana* **W38**
Clouds **W24**
Come Sleep **W8**
Concertino Antico **W49**
Concertino da Camera **W33**
Concerto for Flute and Orchestra **W20**
Concerto no. 1 for Piano and Orchestra **W17**
Concerto Romantico for Viola and Orchestra **W51**
Crepuscule: see *Profiles from China* **W32**
Dance Cantata **W35**
Drama for Orchestra **W60**
The Dream: see *Profiles from China* **W32**
Etruscan Concerto **W48**
Fair Cupid: see *Choral Suite* **W19**

Five Songs **W29**
Five Songs from Housman: see *Five Songs* **W29**
Flute Concerto: see *Concerto for Flute and Orchestra* **W20**
Flute Sonata: see *Sonata for Treble Recorder or Flute and Piano* **W27**
Froggyana **W69**
Frolic **W9**
Fruit Gathering: see *Pastoral* **W3**
Girondelle for Giraffes **W67**
Glacier **W25**
The Glittering Gate **W52**
Great God Pan: see *Choral Suite* **W19**
Gymnopédies: see *Three Gymnopédies* **W47**
Harp Sonata: see *Sonata for Harp* **W42**
He Reproves the Curlew **W2a**
He Would Not Stay: see *Five Songs* **W29**
Homespun Collars: see *Five Songs* **W29**
How in This Garden: see *Ballade* **W31**
Hylas and the Nymphs **W16**
In Midwood Silence **W14**
Ireland **W1**
Jephthah's Daughter: see *Tragic Celebration* **W66**
Killer-of-Enemies **W34**
A Lament of Scarlet Cloud: see *Profiles from China* **W32**
Last Poems: see *Five Songs* **W29**
Letters from Morocco **W45**
The Masque of the Wild Man **W55**
Meditation **W3**
Meditation for Orchestra: see *Meditation* **W3**
Mimic Heaven: see *Five Songs* **W29**
Music for Robots: see *The Robot* **W18**
Musica Antiqua no. 1 **W53**
Nausicaa **W62**
Pastoral (or Pastorale) **W5**
Piano Concerto: see *Concerto No. 1* **W17** and *Etruscan Concerto* **W48**
Piano Prelude, **W2a**. See also: *Prelude for a Pensive Pupil, W56*
Poem for Chorus and Orchestra **W6**
Poetics: see *Profiles from China* **W32**
Postman's Knock **W26**
Prelude and Scherzo **W21**
Prelude and Presto for Ancient American Instruments **W54**
Prelude for a Pensive Pupil **W56**
Profiles from China **W32**
Recorder Sonata: see *Sonata for Treble Recorder or Flute and Piano* **W27**
Recorder Trio: see *Trio for Pipes* **W11**
Rest **W10**
The Robot **W18**
Sappho **W64**
Satie: see *Thomsoniana* **W38**

Saul and the Witch of Endor   **W 61**
A Scary Time   **W 58**
Schoenberg: see *Thomsoniana*   **W 38**
A Season in Hell   **W 65**
Septet: see *Three Gymnopédies, no. 1*   **W 47**
Sheiling Song   **A 8**
Sidi Amar in Winter   **W 36**
Sinfonia da Pacifica   **W 45**
Sinfonietta for Orchestra, No. 1   **W 12**
Sinfonietta No. 2   **W 23**
The Son of Heaven: see *Profiles from China*   **W 32**
Sonata for Harp   **W 42**
Sonata for Harp, Flute, and Horn   **W 40**
Sonata for Piano and Percussion   **W 43**
Sonatina for Piano   **W 28**
Sonatina for Treble Recorder or Flute and Piano   **W 27**
Song in Summer   **W 15**
Song in the Wood: see *Choral Suite*   **W 19**
Songs of A. E. Housman: see *Five Songs*   **W 29**
Spanish Suite   **W 13**
Stars: see *Five Songs*   **W 29**
Stravinsky: see *Thomsoniana*   **W 38**
String Quartet   **W 22**
Tapestry for Orchestra   **W 58**
Tel   **W 41**
Thirteen Ways of Looking at a Blackbird   **W 37**
Thomsoniana   **W 38**
Three Gymnopédies   **W 47**
To the Moon   **W 2 a**
Tragic Celebration   **W 66**
The Transposed Heads   **W 46**
Triad   **W 59**
Trio for Pipes   **W 11**
Tulsa   **W 39**
Unlucky Love: see *Five Songs* **W 29**
Viola Concerto: see *Concerto romantico*   **W 51**
Violin Solo   **W 2 a**
Weep No More: see *Choral Suite* **W 19**
A Widow Bird   **W 2 a**
Yet in No Sleep: see *Ballade* **W 31**

CLASSIFIED LIST OF WORKS

OPERAS

Caedmon   **W 5**
The Transposed Heads   **W 46**

The Glittering Gate **W52**
Nausicaa **W62**
Carlos Among the Candles **W63**
Sappho **W64**
Beckett **W68**

BALLETS

Hylas and the Nymphs **W16**
Postman's Knock **W26**
Killer-of-Enemies **W34**
The Masque of the Wild Man **W55**
Triad **W59**
Saul and the Witch of Endor **W61**
A Season in Hell **W65**
Tragic Celebration (Jephtha's Daughter)   **W66**

ORCHESTRAL WORKS

Meditation **W4**
Sinfonietta No. 1 **W12**
Prelude and Scherzo **W21**
Sinfonietta No. 2 **W23**
Sinfonia da Pacifica **W45**
Tapestry for Orchestra **W58**
Drama for Orchestra **W60**
Tragic Celebration **W66**

CONCERTOS

Concerto no. 1 for Piano and Orchestra **W17**
Concerto for Flute and Orchestra **W20**
Etruscan Concerto **W48**
Concerto Romantico **W51**

INSTRUMENTAL CHAMBER WORKS

Instrumental Pieces **W2**
Trio for Pipes **W11**
Spanish Suite **W13**
String Quartet **W22**
Sonatina for Flute or Recorder with Piano **W27**
Sonatina for Piano **W28**
Concertino da Camera **W33**
Sonata for Harp, Flute, and Horn **W40**
Sonata for Harp **W42**
Sonata for Piano and Percussion **W43**
Three Gymnopédie(s) **W47**

Concertino Antico **W49**
Musica Antiqua No. 1 **W53**
Prelude and Presto for Ancient American Instruments **W54**
Prelude for a Pensive Pupil **W56**
Girondelle for Giraffes **W67**
Froggyana **W69**

CHORAL WORKS

Ireland **W1**
Pastorale **W3**
Poem for Chorus and Orchestra **W6**
Song in Summer **W15**
Choral Suite **W19**
Aria Concertante (also solo vocal) **W30**

SOLO VOCAL WORKS WITH PIANO

Songs **W2**
Be Still You Little Leaves **W7**
Come Sleep **W8**
Frolic **W9**
Rest **W10**
Five Songs **W29**
Ballade **W31**
Profiles from China **W32**
Thirteen Ways of Looking at a Blackbird **W37**

SOLO VOCAL WORKS WITH INSTRUMENTAL ENSEMBLE

In Midwood Silence **W14**
Aria Concertante **W30**
Dance Cantata **W35**
Thomsoniana **W38**
Letters from Morocco **W45**

MUSIC FOR FILMS

The Robot **W18**
Clouds **W24**
Glacier **W25**
Tulsa **W39**
Tel **W41**
The African Story **W50**
A Scary Time **W57**

Discography

This list is alphabetical by title and includes all commercially-produced discs, whether or not currently available. All are 33 $1/3$ rpm twelve-inch discs unless otherwise noted. Cross-references with a **W** are to "Works and Performances," with a **D** to the "Discography," with a **G** to "Bibliography by Glanville-Hicks," with a **B** to "Bibliography About Glanville-Hicks, and with an **A** to "Archival Resources."

Choral Suite (W19)

D 1   Oiseau-lyre OL-100. 1940. 78 rpm ten-inch disc.
       Female chorus, oboe, string orchestra (performers unnamed).
       Reviews: **B165, B169.**

Concertino da Camera (W33)

D2   Columbia ML 4990. 1955.
       Carlo Bussotti, piano; New York Woodwind Ensemble; Carlos
         Surinach, conductor.
       With: *Sonata for Piano and Percussion,* **D17.**
       Composer's liner notes: **G675;** *reviews:* **B46, B207.**

Concerto Romantico (W51)

D3   MGM E 3559. 1957.
       Walter Trampler, viola; MGM Orchestra; Carlos Surinach, conductor.
       Liner notes: **G686, B70;** *reviews:* **B141, B329.**

Etruscan Concerto (W48)

D4   MGM E 3557. 1956.
Carlo Bussotti, piano; MGM Orchestra; Carlos Surinach, conductor.
Liner notes: **B71**; *reviews:* **B102, B130**.

Five Songs (W29): selections

D5   Larrikan LRF 153. [ca. 1985]
Gregory Martin, baritone; Norma Williams, piano.
Performances of *Unlucky Love* and *Homespun Collars*.
In: *Australian Songs and Ballads*.

Letters from Morocco (W44)

D6   MGM E 3549. 1957.
Loren Driscoll, tenor; MGM Orchestra; Carlos Surinach, conductor.
Liner notes: **B72**; *reviews:* **B197, B250, B324**.

Nausicaa (W61): selections.

D7   Composers Recordings, Inc. CRI SD 175. 1964.
Soloists; Athens Symphony Orchestra and Chorus; Carlos Surinach,
conductor. Recorded at the Athens Festival, 1961. For complete cast
see **W62a**.
Composer's liner notes: **G696**; *reviews:* **B208, B251, A3g(7)**.

Prelude and Presto for Ancient American Instruments (W55)

D8   Recording published by Andre Emmerich Gallery, 18 East 77th Street,
New York 21, for "Music Before Columbus" exhibition. "Volume 3
in a continuing series of publications." 33 1/3 rpm seven-inch disc.
October 1957.
Performed with ancient instruments belonging to the Andre
Emmerich Gallery and the American Museum of Natural History
of New York by: Samuel Baron (pan pipe, bird-whistles, flute),
Robert Didomenica (armadillo-ocarina, owl-whistle, frog-whistle,
conch shell, flute), Elayne Jones (maracas, Teponatzli drums, bone
scraper), Herbert Harris (head drum), and Peggy Glanville-Hicks
(handclapping) Herbert Harris, conductor. Side 1 contains
commentary by Charles Collingwood, side 2 the music.

Prelude for a Pensive Pupil (W56)

D9   RCA Victor LM 7042. 1966.
      Robert Helps, piano.
      In: *New Music for the Piano. 24 Contemporary Composers.*

D10   Composers Recordings, Inc. CRI SD 288. 1972.
      Reissue of **D8.**

Sinfonia da Pacifica (W45)

D11   MGM E 3336. 1956.
      MGM Orchestra; Carlos Surinach, conductor.
      With: *Three Gymnopédies.*
      Liner notes: **G680, B73**; *reviews:* **B113, B201, B215, B324, B331, B354.**

Sonata for Harp (W42)

D12   Everest 3144 (stereo), 6144 (hi-fi). 1954
      Nicanor Zabaleta, harp.
      In: *Five Centuries of the Harp* (10 s.)

D13   Esoteric ES 523. 1954. Reissued as Counterpoint CPST 5523.
          1964/1966.
      Nicanor Zabaleta, harp.
      May be a reissue of **D12.**
      Zabaleta--Anthology of Solo Harp Music, vol. 2.
      Liner notes: **B227.**

D14   Deutsche Grammophon DG 19131 LPEM. 1964.
      Nicanor Zabaleta, harp.

D15   Classic Editions 920111-112.
      Nicanor Zabaleta, harp.

D16   *Pastoral* [second movement].
      Discourses ABK 15. 1973.
      John Marson, harp. Recorded at Theatre Projects, London, 5
          September 1972.
      Includes program notes by P. Gammond and "The Harp" by R.
          Rensch.

Sonata for Piano and Percussion (W43)

D17   Columbia ML 4990. 1955.
      Carlo Bussotti, piano; New York Percussion Group.
      With: *Concertino da Camera,* **D2.**
      Composer's liner notes: **G675**; *reviews:* **B46, B207.**

Three Gymnopédies (W47)

D18   Remington R 199 188. Two 78 rpm twelve-inch discs. 1954.
RIAS (Berlin Radio) Orchestra; Joel Perlea, conductor.
Recorded in 1953 in Berlin. Produced in cooperation with Oliver
Daniel and the American Composers Alliance.
Composer's liner notes: **G594**; *reviews:* **B109**.

D19   MGM E 3336. 1956.
MGM Chamber Orchestra; Carlos Surinach, conductor.
With: *Sinfonia da Pacifica*, **D11**.
Liner notes: **G680, B73, B109**; *reviews:* **B113, B201, B215, B324, B331,
B354**.

D20   Varèse 81046. 1979.
Reissue of **D18** on 33 1/3 rpm disc.

The Transposed Heads (W46)

D21   Louisville 545-6. 1955.
Soloists and Chorus of the Kentucky Opera Association, Moritz
Bomhard, director; Louisville Orchestra; Robert Whitney,
conductor.
Produced by the Kentucky Opera Association, 1954. For complete cast,
see **W46a**. On recording, voice of guru Kamadamana is Robert
Whitney.
Composer's liner notes: **G677**; *reviews:* **B43, B123, B207, B228**.

Bibliography By Glanville-Hicks

This chapter lists writings by Peggy Glanville-Hicks numbered **G1** to **G699** and listed chronologically by date of publication beginning in 1945. In the years when she was the most active as a critic and writer on music the material for each year is further subdivided. In the listings for each of the years 1947-1955 her *New York Herald Tribune (NYHT)* reviews are grouped together and appear in chronological order--typically she wrote from January through April and then from October through December. The *Herald Tribune* reviews, about 100-200 words long unless otherwise noted, are **G4-G27** (1947) **G30-G109** (1948), **G117-G175** (1949), **G209-256** (1950), **G257-G331** (1951), **G334-G423** (1952), **G429-G486** (1953), **G597-G662** (1954), and **G663-G674** (1955). In 1950 her *Musical America* reviews are grouped together (**G180-G208**), and in 1954 her *Grove's Dictionary* articles--first the ninety-eight American composers in alphabetical order (**G487-G584**) and then the eight Danish composers in alphabetical order (**G585-G592**).

Cross-references with a **W** are to "Works and Performances," with a **D** to the "Discography," with a **B** to "Bibliography About Glanville-Hicks," and with an **A** to "Archival Resources."

1945

G1   "Paul Bowles, American Composer." *Music and Letters* 26, no. 2 (April 1945), p. 88-96.

Bowles (at thirty-four) is one of the most interesting of the younger American composers. His wandering the world, not unusual for a writer, is unusual for a composer, since "personal presence" plays a large part in widening a composer's reputation in his own country. Bowles has lived in Spain, Mexico, Guatemala, the Sahara, and several parts of North Africa, seeking out the music of these places for his own development. Though his outward life is restless, his mental processes are ordered, mature, and original. His works subtly express contemporary American trends: concentration on melody and rhythm, elements of jazz and Latin-American music, and emphasis on winds and percussion. His music has an emotional-mystical quality, at once personal and remote, as an undercurrent beneath the austerity. Excerpts from *Roots in the Earth, Congo,* the *Spanish Songs,* and *The*

Wind Remains illustrate the article in this English periodical, and it concludes with a two-page list of his works. Ruth C. Friedberg, *American Art Song and American Poetry* (Metuchen, NJ, 1987), p. 26, 33, discussing Bowles, quotes three passages from this article.

1947

G2   "Copenhagen Festival of ISCM Shows Varied Currents in 1947 Music." *Musical Courier* 136, no. 1 (July 1947), p. 5, 24.

Long and thorough review in New York periodical covers the six main concerts, tours, and ballet, and also mentions the "semi-official" lecture recital on Indian Classical Music by Marayana Menon, delegate from India and director of the BBC Eastern Service, illustrated with recordings and her own veena. Outstanding were the three young Danish composers, Holmboe, Koppel, and Bentzon. Other composers discussed are likewise grouped by country: Sweden (Nystroem, Rosenberg, Blomdahl), Norway, (Saeverud, Valen), Italy (Negri, Pizzetti, Zecchi), France (Jolivet), England (Maconchy, Frankel), Belgium (Schmit, Absil, van de Woestyne), Holland (Escher), Hungary (Kosa), Austria (Heiller), Czechoslovakia (Novak, Kapr, Slavicky), Poland (Spisak), Switzerland (Burkhard, Martin), Spain-in Exile (Gerard), U. S. S. R. (Prokofieff), and U. S. (Copland, Sessions, Bloch).

G3   "ISCM Festival." *The Composer's News-Record*, Fall 1947, p. 4.

Article in journal of the League of Composers presents a briefer overview of the Copenhagen festival than in **G2** above. Composers represented sixteen countries. A few pieces "should claim permanent places in musical repertoires": works of Holmboe and Bentzon (Denmark; Bentzon played his own *Partita for Piano* and received an ovation for the work and for his "spectacular playing"), Slavicky (Czechoslovakia), Spisak (Poland), Negri (Italy), and Valen (Norway). As American entrants, Europeans would have preferred "works by young American-born composers" to works of Bloch and Krenek. Copy of article is in **A3**.

1947, CONTINUED: *NEW YORK*
HERALD TRIBUNE (NYHT)

G4   "Composers Forum: Ulysses Kay and Lukas Foss Works Presented." *New York Herald Tribune*, Monday, 27 October 1947, p. 15, col. 3-4.

This is apparently the first review by Glanville-Hicks to be published in the *Herald Tribune*, though there is no note of introduction or identification of the signature "P. G.-H." It does, however, occupy a prominent place at the top of the page toward the center, and it is among her longer reviews--over 500 words. The opening of the second year of the forum's revival featured Kay's "linear writing" and "wholly horizontal music." Works of Foss, including his string quartet (1947) and two songs from *The Prairie* (1942-43), showed a "synthesis" of American rhythmic and melodic elements and "an atmosphere of tranquility." His "personal idiom" has yet to be "completely stabilized" but he possesses technique. Ashley Pettis presided over the question period, though "few fruitful artistic or musical questions" arose. "Demands for a definition of the term 'invention' as applied to music became lost in irrelevancies."

G5   " 'L'Ascension': Messiaen Work Presented by the Philharmonic." *NYHT*, Monday, 3 November 1947, p. 15.

Introduced here by the San Francisco Symphony Orchestra under Pierre Monteux last April, it had its first performance by the Philharmonic-Symphony Orchestra Saturday night, Leopold Stokowski conducting. Work's subtitle "Meditation" shows Messiaen's emphasis on "mood" (four stylized moods here, in four sections) over "form." His music imparts "his experience of a state of mind and heart," not a purely musical message.

G6   "Howard Kasschau Heard at Piano in Town Hall." *NYHT*, 5 November 1947, p. 23.

First New York recital yesterday afternoon (Tuesday) is a pianist of restraint; "his careful and intelligent readings" pay "sincere tribute to the music he plays." He was good on Schumann, the "inevitable" Chopin, and Scriabin's Sonata Op. 30, but did not produce the "massive tone values" of Vivaldi"s Concerto Grosso in D minor or Franck's Prelude, Chorale, and Fugue.

G7   "Gladys Kuchta and Curtis Present Joint Recital." *NYHT*, 7 November 1947, p. 21.

Kuchta is a soprano of "considerable personality" and beauty of tone, especially in the middle part of the voice. Fauré songs were her most successful pieces, and a Granados opera aria was also beautifully sung. Charles Curtis has a pleasing tenor voice and "eminently reliable" technique; he is most at home in Schubert songs. Nathan Price was the piano accompanist.

G8   "Shura Dvorrine [Dvorine] Presents Town Hall Piano Recital." *NYHT*, Monday, 10 November 1947, p.15. Reprinted 11 November 1947, p. 25.

Young Baltimore pianist in his second New York recital has an unusually mature grip of "musical values" for a young man, above his technical efficiency. He gave a valuable restatement of the content of the "much-heard classical repertory with freshness": Haydn's *Variations in F minor*, the Bach-Busoni *Toccata in C major*, and Beethoven's *Sonata Op. 110*.

G9   "Anna Shenderoff Recital." *NYHT*, 12 November 1947, p. 23, col. 6.

Very brief review (less than 100 words) names composers and works: Bach (the *G minor Fantasia and Fugue* arranged by Liszt), Beethoven, Schumann, Chopin, Fauré, Robert Casedesus (*Three Etudes*), and Chabrier (*Bourée Fantasque*). Pianist was "not quite up to the technical and emotional demands" of her program. (Review's drop head "Force Official of Riverside Hotel to Give Safe's Combination" belongs to another news story.)

G10   "Paul Makovsky, Violinist, Gives Town Hall Recital." *NYHT*, 14 November 1947, p. 18.

Recital by "a wholly serious and highly sensitive artist" featured works of Bach, Beethoven, Ries, Wieniawski, and the accompanist, Scott Watson. Typical of his "fine musicianship" was his playing of a major modern work, the Stravinsky *Duo Concertant*, and his assigning it "a major position on his program."

G11   "Dixon's Youth Orchestra Opens Concert Series." *NYHT*, Sunday, 16 November 1947, sect. 1, p. 39, col. 7.

Dean Dixon conducted his American Youth Orchestra at the Needle Trades High School yesterday in one of his "amusing and informative" sessions. The "able conductor" presented works of Prokofiev, Brahms, and the first act of Verdi's *La Traviata*, the stage action in modern dress. Short review is around 75 words.

G12   "Jacques Abram Is Soloist With the Philharmonic." *NYHT*, 17 November 1947, p. 17.

Abram, "one of our most outstanding young pianists, performed Beethoven's 4th concerto, conducted by Muench. Also on the program, Earl George's *Introduction and Allegro* "is smoothly written in the current American idiom" but has little originality. Orchestra presented the wayward *La Valse* of Ravel, Fauré's Suite from *Pelleas and Melisande* (a good performance), and Handel's *Concerto Grosso in A minor* (uninspired).

G13   "Miss Haendl, Violinist, in Carnegie Hall Concert." Ibid.

Ida Haendel, "a violinist of romantic leanings," performed Brahms, Bach, Wieniawski, Stravinski, Bloch, and Bartok, demonstrating "general excellence" in her playing. The "somber and turbulent qualities" of the Brahms *D minor Sonata* "were sometimes emphasized a little at the expense of strict formal balance." She gave "fine" performances of Bloch's *Baal-Shem* and Bartok's *Romanian Dances*. Arthur Balsam was the accompanist.

G14   "Miss Marie Luviso in Recital." *NYHT*, 19 November 1947, p. 27, col. 1.

Dramatic soprano "did not appear to possess all the qualities that a New York recital demands." ("Review" is a forty-word announcement.)

G15   "Town Hall Cello Concert Is Given by David Soyer." *NYHT*, 22 November 1947, p. 8.

Musicianly young cellist had precision and poetic feeling. He was best in "palely romantic" works--the Huré *Sonata in F sharp minor* and Cassado's *Sonata in Ancient Spanish Style*--but did not render an authoritative performance of Bach's *Suite No. 1* for unaccompanied cello. Leopold Mitmann was at the piano.

G16   "Robert Goldsand Offers Town Hall Piano Recital." *NYHT*, Sunday, 23 November 1947, sect. 1, p. 50, col. 7-8.

First of three "programs culled entirely from modern works" covered the period 1906-1936 and included three sonatas--by Griffes ("massively impressionistic"), Hindemith (No. 2, "neatly made"), and Scriabin (No. 5)--and works of Albéniz, Prokofieff, Debussy, Chavez, and Szymanewski. It is fine to have "such definitive readings of works from the mainstream and tributaries of the modern repertory."

G17   "Miss Leslie Frick Gives Town Hall Song Recital." *NYHT*, 25 November 1947, p. 26.

Mezzo-soprano, accompanied by pianist Alderson Mowbray, performed Beethoven, Schumann, songs of Chausson, Fauré, and Duparc, Spanish songs, and a miscellany of "ballad" variety brief songs by early Americans (not named).

G18   "Composer Forums: Persichetti and Jones Works Heard in McMillin Theatre." *NYHT*, 27 November 1947, p. 39.

In the second of the Composers Forum series this year Vincent Persichetti's "attic lyricism" achieved its best expression in his *Pastoral Quintet for Winds* (1943); the gleaming and original sounds lacked close-knit design. His eleven *Poems* for piano (1939) were "dated" in the styleless "modern" manner of the 1920s, meaning an avoidance of the conventional and use of "dissonant banalities," not a positive or fresh statement. Charles Jones showed successful "wedding" of the structural aspects of neo-classicism and "certain harmonic references" of atonality.

G19   Rolf Persinger, Violist, In Times Hall Recital." *NYHT*, 1 December 1947.

Review is in clipping scrapbook in **A3b(3)** but is unsigned. Sonatas by Brahms, Ysaye, and Emil Bohnke (a "rather depressing" work receiving its first New York perform-ance) were performed, with Louis Persinger the "none-too-happy accompanist on the piano." He appeared, however, "to better advantage as assisting violinist" in a duo by Mozart and "a resilient and effective duo" (1946) by Villa-Lobos (another first New York performance).

G20   "Dorothy Eustis, Pianist, Gives Town Hall Recital." *NYHT*, 6 December 1947, p. 9.

Young pianist has the technique, "integrated with her expressive concepts," of a "first-rank artist." She played works of Mozart (an intimate and whimsical interpretation), Beethoven (introspective), Schumann (buoyant), and Brahms (two Intermezzi full of "Gothic brooding"), two pieces by Marion Bauer (first New York performances), and pieces by Samuel Barber, Ravel, and Liszt.

G21   "Kathleen Chrismann Recital: Soprano at Times Hall in French, German and English Songs." *NYHT*, 8 December 1947, p. 17.

Another unsigned review from clipping scrapbook in **A3b(3)** reports that in songs in French and German and an English folk-song group this soprano "seemed overly preoccupied with technical problems." Subsequent "items" by Strauss, Brush, Reger, and Poulenc were more stable and expressive, her voice showing to best advantage on "gentle and sensitive" songs.

G22   "Friends of Music Present Paganini Quartet Recital." *NYHT*, 8 December 1947, p. 16.

New Friends of Music presented a concert by the Paganini Quartet performing two quartets of Beethoven and, with pianist Ray Lev, Mendelssohn's Trio No. 1, Op. 49. "The playing throughout was on a high level, both technically and from the view-point of correct interpretive concepts," but "a feeling of tedium prevailed," perhaps because the players were carefully following "accepted classical interpretations" but not re-experiencing the "vitality" of the content.

G23   "Jeanne Mitchell is Heard in Debut as Violinist." *NYHT*, 10 December 1947, p. 29.

Young American violinist in New York debut presented Vieuxtemps's fourth concerto, pieces by Bach (the *Chaconne*), Milhaud, Lukas Foss, and her own charming *Andantino*. Her tone is "well balanced" but some "technical insecurities" distract her from expressivity. (*See* **G163** for a review of a later, improved recital by Mitchell.)

G24   "Gunnar Knudsen: Norwegian Violinist in U. S. Debut at Town Hall." *NYHT*, 12 December 1947, p. 24.

Grieg's third sonata is "not too well integrated formally" but this performer saved it. Also performed were pieces by Handel, Bloch, Paganini, Cassado, and some Scandanavians "seldom heard here"--Treit, Gjerstrom, and Halvorsen. Violinist has an introspective quality and an accomplished technique; his "individualized" way of playing is especially adjusted to Scandanavian music. A charming piece by accompanist Charles Haubiel was repeated.

G25   "Ivy Improta, Pianist, in Town Hall Recital." *NYHT*, 18 December 1947, p. 35.

Young pianist from Brazil performed Beethoven, Schumann, Brahms, and more recent works by "Hispanic composers" Villa-Lobos and Albéniz, and others. Pianist showed "technical ease" but lacked "stability in classic interpretations", though did well with Brahms and the modern pieces with "an improvisatory aspect."

G26   "N. A. C. C. Gives Recital Honoring Henry Hadley." *NYHT*, Sunday 21 December 1947, sect. 1, p. 34.

Concert of choral and chamber music by the National Association for American Composers and Conductors in commemoration of Hadley's birthday featured choral music of Mabel Daniels, Hermene Warlick Eichorn, Henry Hadley, Marion Bauer (only her offering "ventured far from the home base of harmonic convention"), and Dolf Swing (the conductor). Instrumental chamber music was by George Kleinsinger (a Sonatina that "bowed once to Carlos Chavez, twice to Fifty-second Street"), Samuel Barber, Halsey Stevens, Robert Russell Bennett, and Henry Hadley (his Piano Quintet, Op. 50).

G27   "Paul Bellam, Violinist, Is Heard at Town Hall." *NYHT*, 22 December 1947, p. 16.

Young violinist "of considerable taste and technical proficiency" performed a Handel sonata, Hindemith's unaccompanied sonata Op. 31, and Glazunov's A-minor Concerto. The "somewhat acid" Hindemith piece, though constructed "without harmonic bass reference" and likely to "fall apart," was convincing through fine intonation.

1948

G28   "More Contemporary Works Assayed, The ISCM Festival, Amsterdam." *Musical America* 68, no. 9 (August 1948), p. 6.

United States was better represented than last year (Copenhagen), though "Europeans have as yet only a dim idea of the amount of creative activity in America." Piston's *Sinfonietta* (given a splendid account by conductor Leonard Bernstein, with only the briefest of rehearsals) and Sessions' Second Symphony "made fine ambassadors." They also use as point of departure the "two main viewpoints still active in modern composition--the neo-classic and the atonal." Also singled out for praise are works of Elizabeth Lutyens and Humphrey Searle from

England, Raymond Chevreuille of Belgium, and Malipiero from Italy. (Review is on same page with Stuckenschmidt's review of the festival, [B365].) *See also* her *Herald Tribune* essay, **G74** below.

G29   "John Cage, '. . . a Ping, Qualified by a Thud.' " Ibid., no. 10 (September 1948), p. 5, 20.

Quote in title is Virgil Thomson's description of the sound made by a prepared piano, and Glanville-Hicks explains the technique and its notation. Cage, like many Americans before him, is fascinated with percussion, and with rhythm as the starting point for musical construction. He is also associated with the "dada" movement with noises (telephone bells, factory whistles) that Europeans take as ideology or proletarian utterance, Americans as technology or an offshoot of the percussion movement. In creating his own sounds, mechanically, free of tonal associations, he frees the creative and imaginative faculties for a new positive expression.

1948, CONTINUED: *HERALD TRIBUNE*
(JANUARY-MAY, AUGUST)

G30   "Rose Slatkovitz Gives Recital at Times Hall." *NYHT,* Saturday, 3 January 1948, p. 8, col. 4.

Violinist is "tonally inconsistent," her good left hand not matched by her bowing. Recital included works of Beethoven, Saint-Saens (B Minor Concerto), Bach, Rachmaninoff, Prokofieff, and Ravel.

G31   "Maria Safonoff Presents Recital at Carnegie Hall." *NYHT,* 5 January 1948, p. 12.

Pianist played works of Schubert, Mendelssohn, Schumann, Beethoven, Scriabin, Villa-Lobos, La Forge, Stojowski, and Kodaly. Favorable review describes her tone, manner, and "general consistency of procedure."

G32   "Miss Pobers, Soprano, In Times Hall Recital." *NYHT,* 9 January 1948, p. 18.

Groups of songs by Wolf, Duparc, Debussy, and Moussorgsky, and numbers by Barber, Casella, Ives, and Malipiero, showed finesse and good vocal technique but some problems with diction and interpretation. She was best in French and Russian.

G33   "Zimbalist in Third Recital of Series at Town Hall." *NYHT,* Sunday 11 January 1948, sect. 1, p. 51.

Violinist has an austere tone, and "tranquility and spaciousness in his musical concepts." His general style is classic with an occasional "scoop" between one note and the next that is not in character. He performed concerti of Spohr and Mendelssohn, de Beriot's *Scène de Ballet,* and the *Fantasia appassionata* of Vieuxtemps.

G34   "Dorothy Klein, Pianist, Makes New York Debut." *NYHT,* Monday, 12 January 1948, p. 10, col. 5.

Pianist is sensitive and poetic in music that suits her temperament and is within her technical grasp, and is also dramatic, but lacks some "formal stability" in longer works. Program included Brahms' Sonata in E minor, Chopin's F minor Fantasy (her best performance), Guion's *Mother Goose Suite* (17 "banal" pieces), and works of Bach and Mozart.

G35   "Chamber Music Group Heard at Carnegie Hall." *NYHT*, 17 January 1948, p. 8, col. 4.

New and old works were performed by Chamber Music Concertante: oboe (Michael Nazzi, oboist, organized the group), flute, violin, viola, cello, and piano (Helmut Baerwald is a good pianist for chamber music). Music was by Loeillet, Pergolesi, Scarlatti, Mozart, Bach, Felix White (his *The Nymph's Complaint for the Death of Her Faun* broke no new ground musically), and Britten (which "the time factor prevented this reviewer from hearing").

G36   " 'Magic Flute' Presented With Eleanor Steber." *NYHT*, 23 January 1948, p. 15, col. 3.

Eleanor Steber sang the role of Pamina for the second time (the first was 20 December), in this Mozart opera.   Mimi Benzell was Queen of the Night.

G37   "Creighton Allen Heard in Times Hall Recital." *NYHT*, 24 January 1948, p. 8, col. 8.

Pianist and composer performed his own works and those of MacDowell, Griffes, William Crowe, Beethoven, Chopin, Dohnanyi, and Liszt. His approach as a composer and pianist is "improvisatory rather than studied" and shows a lack of "real discipline, technical or aesthetic, that is a prerequisite in the creation of valid artistic productions." He draws on the harmonic clichés of vernacular music, not its rhythms--the opposite of other contemporary composers.

G38   "Goldsand Recital: Gives Second of His Series of Modern Piano Music." *NYHT*, Sunday 25 January 1948, sect. 1, p. 41, col. 3-4.

Program featured Stravinski and Copland sonatas and works of Ravel, Satie, Caturla, Villa-Lobos, Miaskowsky, and Farwell *(Navajo War Dance No. 2)*. He has "exceptional technical equipment" and usually imparts "the real content of modern works," but he "misread" the Stravinski in letting the theme dominate, rather than "thread its way" through, the "spiky, over-all texture." (Stravinski, like Virgil Thomson, has "evolved a terminology for the presentation of rhetoric" and is "frequently misinterpreted in this mood.") Goldsand's "fine sense of momentum" made for a superb performance of the Copland *Sonata*. It is one of Copland's most finely integrated works, and "the crystallization point is its emotional content, rather than the terms of its expression."

G39   "Gazarossian: Istanbul Pianist Appears in Carnegie Recital Hall." *NYHT*, 29 January 1948, p. 13.

Koharik Gazarossian, "a cultivated musician and a highly intelligent one," played works of Brahms, Schumann, Beethoven, Chopin, and Liszt, and several of her own. Here "various stylistic elements strike for supremacy," the Armenian and Middle Eastern elements, such as "rhythm and scale limitation," being incompletely assimilated (as they are assimilated in Hovhaness into the style, construction, and whole writing method).

G40 "Leonard Eisner Heard in Town Hall Recital." *NYHT*, 31 January 1948, p. 9.

Pianist of exceptional quality gave "highly individual readings" of Beethoven, Brahms, Bach, Chopin, and Debussy. His mastery of technical and interpretive questions gives conviction to what he does.

G41 "Audition Winners: Singers and Pianists Heard at Music Festival." *NYHT*, Sunday, 1 February 1948, sect. 1, p. 42.

Six state winners of National Music Festival auditions included contralto Josephine Fisher, sopranos Iris Fribrock and Eugenia Helen Ligon, tenor William Kirkpatrick, and pianists Anna Marian Stanley and Harriet Kaplan. Fisher is a "true contralto" with "a large voice as yet improperly stabilized" higher up. Kaplan, "like many of the young pianists growing up," was more at home with modern Bartok than with Handel or Chopin.

G42 "Vinaver Chorus: Pieces Based on Biblical Texts Sung at Times Hall." *NYHT*, 3 February 1948, p. 19.

Chemjo Vinaver conducted his Vinaver Chorus in pieces based on "a Biblical text, allusion, or connotation" in concert presented by the Friends of Choral Art Inc. Chorus is "extremely well trained" by this "expert conductor" and sings beautifully in works "from Vaughan Williams to the music of the synagogue." Program showed "the common bond of a modal structure and feeling," the "skeletal remains of an ancestral type."

G43 "Yehudi Menuhin: Prokofieff's Violin Sonata Included on Program." *NYHT*, 7 February 1948, p. 9.

Sonata (in its first New York performance) had some "magical passages" in first and last movements and an Andante of elegaic beauty. Menuhin's skill allows him to "sustain tensions over long varied periods even when structurally it is not quite there." His playing of contemporary works (especially "the difficult and profound unaccompanied Bartok Sonata) these last two seasons "has been of vital importance to music," both in introducing works to a wider audience and in bringing to them "a completely mature classic thought and interpretation."

G44 " 'Hansel & Gretel.' " *NYHT*, 9 February 1948, p. 10.

Metropolitan Opera Guild of New York presented Humperdinck opera at Carnegie Recital Hall with an enthusiastic cast of performers. There were one or two acting talents among the younger players, and Loys Price (as the Broommaker) seemed to have a good voice, well controlled. Frederick Vajda directed and William Sowerwine was at the piano.

G45 "The Philharmonic. Schubert Symphony in B Flat Major No. 5 Is Heard." Ibid., p. 11.

Charles Munch conducted, besides the "rarely heard" Schubert, the Saint-Saens violin Concerto, op. 6l (with Michael Rosenker as soloist), Bloch's Concerto Grosso for String Orchestra with piano, *L'Aprenti Sorcier* of Dukas. Munch's "esthetic discipline was welcome" in Saint-Saens and elsewhere, but "seemed at times to flatten out" the Schubert while "insuring stylistic and formal unity."

G46   "Composers Forum. Works of Nabokoff and Lessard." *NYHT*, 16 February 1948, p. 13.

Nicolas Nabokoff and John Lessard were the featured composers and Otto Luening the moderator (with forum organizer Ashley Pettis also on the platform). Lessard, trained in the "Boulanger-Stravinsky school of thought," still retains individuality. Some earlier piano pieces had "a melodic tranquility" but his recent *Mask* for piano shows preoccupation with "certain rhythmic and thematic desiccations." Nabokoff's piano sonata showed "an unusually effective blend of basic tonality and chromatic refractions.

G47   "The Wolff Players. Woodwind Chamber Music Is Heard at Times Hall." *NYHT*, 19 February 1948, p. 15, col. 3.

Concert included first performances of *Humoresque* by John Verrall ("tentative"), and *Quartet Sonata* by Harold Holden ("more rewarding"), as well as Arthur Berger's *Quartet in C major*, a *Quartet in F* of Everett Helm (reviewed earlier, after Composers Forum), and Hindemith's sonatas for flute and for bassoon and piano ("inventive"). Though Berger's "esthetic censorship" makes for an "austere" first impression, the quartet's charm emerged from the "spontaneity that a fluent performance brings." Elements of "Americana" in Berger's music "have been subjected to the strict process of integration in the mind's crucible which effects the transformation from a vernacular to an art expression." As his rhythmic components are contrapuntal, not a "bass accent," he starts from "Stravinskyesque bass fragmentation." Review is among her longest, over 500 words.

G48   "Chamber Music Concert Is Heard in Times Hall." *NYHT*, 21 February 1948, p. 9, col. 1.

Instrumental works by Anis Fuleihan, Douglas Moore, Elizabeth Sprague Coolidge, and Robert Sanders were performed in concert by National Association for American Composers and Conductors, along with songs by Everett Helm, John Edmunds, John Duke, Ned Rorem ("spontaneous mutuality" of text and music), and Paul Bowles (original and eloquent). Moore's "fundamentally even-beat" brand of Americana, lacking American syncopation, leans toward "European-type structures" that preserve a "bass foundation." Coolidge's Oboe Sonata, though "well played by Englebert Brenner," seemed "rather banal."

G49   "Ditson Concert. Chamber Music Program Is Heard at Columbia." *NYHT*, 23 February 1948, p. 13, col. 3

Second concert sponsored by the Alice M. Ditson Fund featured choral works of Michael Tippett and Benjamin Britten; Jacob Avshalomoff conducted the Columbia University Chorus. Britten has adroit "presentational technique (not to be confused with the organic technique of composition)," but the "initiate" sees his "almost complete absence of self-criticism and lack of aesthetic selectivity." Instrumental works were: Henry Cowell's brief and exhilarating "Suite for Wood-wind;" Arthur Berger's excellent *Quartet in C*, for winds, "already reviewed this season (**G47** above);" Richard F. Goldman's suavely written "Three Duets" for clarinet; and Nicolai Berezowsky's Brass Suite, full of nostalgia and lucidly scored.

G50   "Music Notes." Ibid., col. 8

Ingrid Rypinski, mezzo-soprano, has a fine voice and "complete mastery" of technique. Songs of Beethoven, Peter Cornelius ("all too seldom heard"), and Rachmaninoff (in English, less clear than her German), were followed by a final group of Palestinian traditional or folk songs, enriched by "her special blend of talents."

G51   "Marc D'Albert Recital.   Pianist Plays American Group With Classic Pieces at Town Hall."   *NYHT*, 24 February 1948, p. 18, col. 6.

Works of Bach, Schumann, Chopin, and Debussy and an "American group" of works by Thomson, Creston, Barber, and Griffes showed "a good deal of musicality" and a "large, full tone", with some technical "co-ordination" problems.

G52   "Elizabeth Davis Gives Recital in Times Hall."   *NYHT*, 27 February 1948, p. 20.

Recital of "considerable artistry" by a beautiful "true soprano" voice included works of Haydn, Handel, Mozart, Schumann, and Mahler and some old Swedish songs from the repertoire of Jenny Lind, which she "preluded" with a short sketch of Jenny Lind's life.

G53   "Theremin Recital.   Mrs. Lucie B. Rosen Plays Berezowsky's Passacaglia."   *NYHT*, 1 March 1948, p. 12.

Noted thereminist "has become truly adept at snatching tones from the air as it were, with her magnetic instrument," and when she "misses her point in space" she adjusts "with only the slightest of brooding glissandos." In fast passages "precision departs entirely" and a "swooping sound reminiscent of an air-raid siren is the mournful result." Berezowsky in his *Passacaglia for Theremin and Orchestra*, commissioned by the League of Composers (Carlos Salzedo played a piano arrangement of the orchestral part), used a "slow sinuous style" to avoid "the many pitfalls awaiting him." Recital included short pieces by Respighi, Satie, Roussel, and Moussorgsky.

G54   "Elmer Bernstein Makes Debut in Piano Recital."   *NYHT*, 6 March 1948, p. 9.

Young pianist performed sonatas of Beethoven and Bartok and pieces by Handel, Chopin, Liszt, Debussy, and Stefan Wolpe *(Dance in the Form of a Chaconne)*. He plays well, with musicianship, but takes some "rather moody liberties" in earlier music. He was "at home" in the Bartok sonata, with its "Balkan rhythmic forms" and "close and middle-distance tensions," and in the Wolpe *Chaconne*, which is "rugged and dissonant" but effective.

G55   "Raul Cabezas, Violinist, Is Heard in Carnegie Hall."   *NYHT*, Sunday, 7 March 1948, sect, 1, p. 45.

Violinist from Costa Rica played works of Mozart, Grieg, De Falla, Debussy, Cardona, and Sarasate, and a first New York performance of *Quatre Exquisses* by Phillippe Gaubert. He has technical skill and expressivity but some problems with intonation and tempi.

G56   "Chamber Music.   Herbert Dittler Conducts the Columbia U. Orchestra."   *NYHT*, 8 March 1948, p. 12.

Schubert's Symphony No. 6 had "an enthusiastic rendering" and Russell Sherman was an "assured and polished" soloist in Beethoven's Piano Concerto No. 5. Robert Kurka's Chamber Symphony No. 3 has intrinsically good ideas, but the "chosen instrumentation" often seemed to limit, rather than liberate, the expression, and a "beautiful melodic flow" is buried in decorative dissonance and "an unspontaneous contrapuntalism."

G57   "Philharmonic: Stokowski Leads Dello Joio's 'Concert Music.' "
       NYHT, 15 March 1948, p. 19, col. 2.

Performed yesterday (Sunday) afternoon, *Concert Music for Orchestra* (1944), a prologue plus three connected sections, shows skillful treatment and combination of various themes of differing character, and the instrumentation provides "color and sonority without sacrifice of lucidity." Stravinsky's *Pastorale* for violin solo with oboe, English horn, clarinet, and bassoon accompaniment, and works (repeated from Thursday and Friday) of Bach, Beethoven, Casadesus, and Wagner completed the program. (Review is unsigned, but is almost certainly by P. G.-H., whose signature appears at the end of the review immediately following.)

G58   "Mandelkern and Banks Heard in Joint Recital." Ibid., col. 2-3.

Rivka Mandelkern, violinist, and Violet Banks, mezzo-soprano, presented by the "Debut and Encore Concerts" series, performed violin works by Ravel, Desplanes, Mozart, Paul White ("smoothly written in somewhat tasteless impressionist terminology"), and Everett Helm ("more sophisticated"). Mandelkern has a "particularly fine bowing technicque, for which she uses her left hand." Banks's "colorful and warm" voice was best in Purcell, with insecure diction in French and German pieces.

G59   "Juana Sandoval, Pianist, Gives Town Hall Recital." *NYHT*, 18 March
       1948, p. 22, col. 4.

Argentine pianist had some technical problems that hampered "devotion to interpretive factors," especially in Brahms. Parts of Schumann's *Carnaval* were good, and the Bach-Busoni *Chaconne* showed "some sturdy finger work."

G60   "Colette Chambeau Plays Brazilian Piano Works." Ibid.

French pianist presented compositions of Jayme Ovalle, a Brazilian now attached to the Brazilian Consulate in New York. Brazilian soprano Blanca Antoni sang "delicately" a group of his songs. The shorter pieces have "charm" from its folk-elements but the longer works are "tasteless and saccharine."

G61   "Eida Turkevitch: Pianist Is Heard in Recital at the Times Hall."
       NYHT, 22 March 1948, p. 19, col. 3-4.

Works of Chopin, Liszt, Copland, and "the currently fashonable Scriabine," and "two war-horses" by Franck and Schumann demonstrated severe technical and interpretive limitations. She "might do better to scale down her activities" to "less ambitious musicality."

G62   "Haydn's 'Seven Words' Produced at Town Hall." *NYHT*, 27 March
       1948, p. 6, col. 3.

Otto Van Koppenhagen conducted and played cello and Brandon Peters was "a fine narrator." A "careful and painstaking" reading was hampered by a "general lack of expertness" and the lack of contrasts and continuity in the work itself.

G63   "Parker Recital: Soprano Includes Songs by Lockwood in Program."
NYHT, Monday, 29 March 1948, p. 10, col. 3.

Recital by Cathalene Parker, mezzo-soprano, six years after her debut, was "a colorful
program of songs" with piano, string quartet, flute, and harp. Glanville-Hicks notes
that this voice has more "color and flexibility" in the contralto range than "upward."
Though the voice is "not notable for its beauty," her diction and "general insight"
and "her unerring choice of rare and first-rate pieces" are "to be gratefully received."
[Glanville-Hicks dedicated her *Thirteen Ways of Looking at a Blackbird* to Parker,
who performed it in 1951 (**W37b**).]

G64   "Polia and Richard Give Joint Recital of Debussy." *NYHT*, Monday, 5
April 1948, p. 12, col. 4.

Mildah Polia, mezzo-soprano, and Charles Richard, pianist, presented songs (with
explanatory comments) and piano pieces from the period 1878 to 1915. Singer was at
her best in "subdued" excerpt from *Pelleas* but both performers seemed not to possess
the intelligence and sensitivity for discovering the magic in Debussy's music.

G65   " '48 Three Choirs Festival Closes With 3d Concert." *NYHT*, Monday,
12 April 1948, p. 12, col. 4.

Rutgers University Women's Chorus, United Temple Chorus of Long Island, and
the choir of Temple Emanu-el presented organ and vocal music of Scandanavia and
America last night, conducted by Karl Krueger, Douglas Moore, and Lazare
Saminsky. Composers were Moore, Finney, Saminsky, Schuman, Ben Weber, and
Jennifer Gandar.

G66   "Kathryn Ward, Soprano, Gives Times Hall Recital." *NYHT*,
Thursday, 22 April 1948, p. 17, col. 7.

Singer has natural gifts and is on her way to qualities of artistry. Works of Handel,
Mozart, Pergolesi, Schubert, Grieg, and Wolf were programmed.

G67   "Gershwin Concert. Ray Bloch and Orchestra Play in Carnegie Hall.."
NYHT, 23 April 1948, p. 17, col. 3.

B'nai B'rith Victory Lodge No. 1481 sponsored an all-Gershwin concert. Gershwin's
most unusual and personal contributions were in melody; his "vernacular clichés"
are full of "associative nostalgias." A folk-composer of the twentieth century (both
jazz and serious music), he made a "potent synthesis of current daily-life musical
elements and contemporary symphonic procedures."

G68   "Inez Bertail Sings. Recital is Benefit for French Women Deported by
Nazis." Ibid.

Concert in memory of Simone Séailles, and a benefit for L'Amicale des Deportées,
featured music of Fauré, Handel, Beethoven, Brahms, and English composers, the
French songs being especially good.

G69   "Roseville Singers Heard in Concert in Town Hall." *NYHT*, Sunday,
25 April 1948, sect. 1, p. 46.

Graydon Clark conducted music of Bach and Gluck, and some of "indifferent caliber musically." Best performances were of material with "intrinsic distinction"--David Jones's "God Is a Spirit" and the spiritual "Go Down Moses."

G70 "Composers' Forum Gives Concert at Columbia." *NYHT*, 26 April 1948, p. 14, col. 5.

Featured composers were David Van Vactor and Robert Sanders, with Carleton Sprague Smith as moderator and also flutist in Van Vactor's *Suite for Two Flutes*. Van Vactor's style in the *Duo for Two Flutes* (the "most integrated example") and other works is chromatic in the "harmonic contexts" created for "fairly diatonic" melodic lines. Sanders's work shows "a structural transformation" from "experimental romantic" to "neo-classical," still preserving the composer's own gifts of "colorful harmonic and melodic materials."

G71 "Composers Forum: Berger and Brant Works Are Given at McMillin." *NYHT*, 18 May 1948, p. 18, col. 4.

Music of Arthur Berger and Henry Brant was presented, with Aaron Copland the guest referee at Question Time. Berger's successful *Woodwind Quartet*, "already reviewed this season" [G47], and movements for string quartet show his "high sensitivity to instrumental peculiarities, so that his part writing has a kind of typecasting." This variety is not possible in the piano pieces, a *Suite* and *Bagatelles*. Brant contributed a Requiem (1934) in a lyric romantic vein, a more original *Music for an Imaginary Ballet* for piccolo, cello, and piano, and an astonishing *Concerto* for flute solo and flute orchestra.

G72 "Lewisohn Finale. Rodgers and Hammerstein Program is Heard." *NYHT*, 9 August 1948, p. 9, col. 6.

Alexander Swallow conducted and Gladys Swarthout and others, including a forty-voice choir, performed excerpts from *Allegro, Carousel, Oklahoma,* and the movie *State Fair* for a record crowd of 20,000 at Lewisohn Stadium (total season attendance is 326,000). Robert Weede's "exuberant performance" of the Soliloquy from *Carousel* scored "a particular hit.

G73 "Modern Series at Amsterdam Has Appraisal: 25 Composers From 16 Countries Represented in I. S. C. M. Festival." *NYHT*, Sunday 22 August 1948, sect. 5, p. 4, col. 3.

This is apparently Glanville-Hicks's first feature article and first by-line ("P. Glanville-Hicks") for the paper. "Holland, Poland and the United States carried off the major honors in this years festival of the International Society for Contemporary Music." Leonard Bernstein's "high-powered conducting" of Piston's *Sinfonietta* made "a personal hit" in the final concert June 13; the work was "one of the only two neo-classic pieces" at the festival [the other, which she does not name, was her *Concertino da Camera*, W33a]. Works of Rudolf Escher and Hans Henkemans represented the "puzzling" Dutch school, neither atonal nor neoclassic. From Poland came works of Artur Malawski and Andrzej Panufnik, from Spain, Julian Bautista, from Italy, Malipiero, and from England, Humphrey Searle's *Put Away the Flutes*, an "impressionist-atonal hybrid" with a "fine effect."

(SEPTEMBER-DECEMBER 1948)

G74 "Abernathy Recital. Pianist Makes His Debut Here in.Program at Town Hall." *NYHT*, 29 September 1948, p. 24, col. 2.

Extremely brief report summarizes works programmed by Hadley Abernathy and reports that the pianist lacked "both fluency and definition" and the playing "was not up to the exacting standard of a New York recital.

G75   "Leonid Hambro, Pianist, In Carnegie Hall Recital." *NYHT*, 11 October 1948, p. 15, col. 4.

Works of Mozart, Beethoven, Schubert, Bach, Bartok, Chopin, and Robert Mann displayed pianist's "many musical gifts"--delicacy of touch, an available volume of tone in his fingers, and a fine independence and control of left-hand passages. Mann's *Ten Bagatelles* are well written for the piano in "a kind of hybrid of impressionist and atonal methods."

G76   "Alan Mandel, 13, Gives Town Hall Piano Recital. *NYHT*, Sunday, 24 October 1948, sect. 1, p. 43, col. 6-8.

Playing of young pianist and composer, though limited by physical dimensions, is "full of the things that cannot be taught" such as musical awareness and "a sensitivity to music as an expressive language," giving evidence of a mature musician of distinction to come. Buxtehude *Passacaglia* and Bach *B flat Patita* and *Italian Concerto* were handled with firm assurance, clean finger work and excellent pedaling. His own *Theme and Variations, Sonata in D minor, Impromptu*, and *Toccata* indicate musicality and sense of form, though in an idiom close to the late romantics.

G77   "Ida Elkin and Israel Katz Open Series of Sonatas." *NYHT*, 1 November 1948, p. 15, col. 8

Elkn [Elkan] (piano) and Katz (violin) performed sonatas of Mozart and Beethoven, but regrettably the performers' "musical equipment is not equal to" these classics.

G78   "Ilse Sass, Pianist, Gives A Recital in Times Hall." *NYHT*, 4 November 1948, p. 22, col. 5.

Pianist "seems intelligent and musicianly" but lacks "a sense of tension." Continuity of Bach's *Chromatic Fantasia* was destroyed by "a good many liberties" in interpretation and text. Schumann's *Arabeske Op. 18*, structured around "moods," not formal periods, was better.

G79   "Rae Muscanto, Soprano, Is Heard at Town Hall." *NYHT*, Sunday, 7 November 1948, sect. 1, p. 59, col. 3.

Works of Caccini, Handel, Bach, Schubert, Fauré, Ravel, and Hindemith were presented with Martin Rich at the piano and Simeon Bellson playing the clarinet obbligato in Schubert's *Der Hirt auf dem Felsen*. A fairly small voice, not remarkable for beauty of tone, is used elegantly, with fine breath control in coloratura passages.

G80   "Recital by Helen Greco: Soprano, Assisted by Male Quartet, Is Heard at Times Hall." *NYHT*, 8 November 1948, p. 11, col. 8.

Songs and arias in Italian, German, French, and English showed "a nice voice" but "monotony of interpretation" and an absence of intimate quality in her German lieder. Male quartet accompanied her in excerpts from Haydn's *The Creation* and Verdi's *La Forza del Destino*.

G81   "Scott Watson Presents 1st N.Y. Piano Recital." *NYHT*, 9 November 1948, p. 22, col. 5-6.

Pianist played his own and various other modern works--Medtner, Prokofieff, Poulenc, Stravinsky, Sibelius, and Griffes. He has "considerable gifts and plays the work of all kinds of composers with the insight of a man who has written his own music." In his *Three Preludes on Appalachian Chorales* (premiered by the League of Composers in April), harmonic and "pianistic" accompaniments to the folk-type modal tunes stem naturally from his "melodic-harmonic integration."

G82   "Violin Recital Presented by William Yarborough." *NYHT*, 15 November 1948, p. 15.

Works of Handel, Mozart, Ravel, Clarke, and de Falla-Kreisler were heard in this debut recital, and the first performance of *Horo* by Kremenliev, "a piece in gipsy-dance Balkan style reminiscent of Enesco." Violinist has technical problems, in intonation and steadiness, and "interpretative factors went largely unattended."

G83   "Chamber Concertante Gives Y.M.H.A. Recital." *NYHT*, 16 November 1948, p. 22.

Instrumental group Chamber Music Concertante, performing Telemann, Handel, Pierné, Mozart, Roussel, and D. Scarlatti, has greatly improved in "neatness and general verve" since last season (*see* **G35**).

G84   "Jan Deman, a Pianist, Makes American Debut." *NYHT*, 18 November 1948, p. 22.

Young Dutch pianist played an all-Chopin program for "a full house of mainly Dutch speaking followers." He has "considerable interpretive delicacy" but not too extraordinary technical skill. His playing had European "thoughtfulness" to compensate for less virtuosity (dexterity, dynamic power) than the "extremely high" American standard.

G85   "Gertrude Freeze Recital: Songs by Wagner, Wolf, Schubert Included in Program." *NYHT*, 19 November 1948, p. 21.

Robust voice "seems incompletely under control" and singer lacks "the sense of detail and intimacy necessary" for Lieder.

G86   "Bowling Green Choir Is Heard at Town Hall." *NYHT*, Sunday, 21 November 1948, sect. 1, p. 51, col. 2.

Bowling Green State University A Capella Choir, conducted by Dr. James Paul Kennedy, sang with "tonality and precision." Works of Normand Lockwood, Tom Scott, and William Schuman were heard "in an Americana section of the program."

G87   "Sonata Recital Is Given By Violist and Pianist." *NYHT*, 22 November 1948, p. 18, col. 8.

Abram Loft, viola, and Alvin Bauman, piano, performed premieres of Miriam Gideon's *Sonata for Viola and Piano* and Frank Wigglesworth's *Sound Piece for Viola and Piano*; both works demonstrate "notable craftsmanship" and the "dreari-ness" of atonalism. "The 'international' idiom that has for years negated (in all but a few of its followers) an individualized expression, has apparently subdued two more talents." Sonatas of Handel (arr. Katims), Brahms (performed with erratic tempi), and Hindemith were also heard.

G88 "Bernice Kamsler: She Is Heard in Folk-Song Program at Times Hall." *NYHT*, 24 November 1948, p. 17, col. 7.

A varied program of folk and traditional songs from England, France, and Germany covered the sixteenth, eighteenth, and twentieth centuries and included a group of regional songs from America. Her distinction "does not lie in her voice" but in her use of her voice, her acting and interpreting, and her costume changes.

G89 "Composers Forum Hears Watts and Weigl Music." *NYHT*, Monday, 29 November 1948, p. 14, col. 1-2.

Wintter Watts and Karl Weigl were featured composers. Watts was out of place, as his songs are of "a 'musicale' genre that merits no serious consideration." Weigl's viola sonata was uninteresting, almost banal; his songs were well written as concerns vocal line.

G90 "Composers: National Association Presents First Concert of Season." *Ibid.*, p. 15, col. 3.

Robert Russel Bennett, NAACC president, made an opening speech and works by Roger Goeb, Henry Cowell, John Edmunds, Ernst Bacon, Ludwig Lenel, and Louise Talma were presented. Four songs by Edmunds blending "the purest elements of the middle ages and our own century, were "the most distinguished." Talma's *Four Handed Fun* for two pianos was played too heavily for the character of its themes.

G91 "Swiss-Italian Violinist Gives Brooklyn Recital." *Ibid.*, col. 4.

Giovanni Bagarotti, "young and talented," performed Handel, Franck, Sarasate, Debussy, and De Falla-Kreisler. Lowell Farr at the piano helped create "extremely good" ensemble.

G92 "Rolande Dion Is Heard In Carnegie Chamber Hall." *NYHT*, 1 December 1948, p. 21, col. 3.

Young lyric soprano from Quebec has sweet voice though unsteady on high notes. Program of Handel, Brahms, French composers (Gounod, Chausson, Fauré, Debussy, Poulenc), Sacco, Thomson, and Quilter showed "the simplicity of naiveté" rather than of "sophisticated mastery."

G93 "Juilliard Festival: Third Concert in Series of French Works Is Heard." *NYHT*, 3 December 1948, p. 23.

Works of Honegger, Messiaen, Poulenc, and Debussy were presented, and some contemporary French "gems" for recorder by Milhaud, Auric, and Pierre-Octave Ferroud. Robert Shaw, conducting Poulenc's "beautiful and calm" Mass in G, "did beautiful things with the contrasts between vocal arabesque and choral mass singing in the final movement." Messiaen's *Five Meditations* from *La Nativité du Seigneur* is mostly hypnotic "sound-spinning" with "no apparent formal pattern."

G94 "Mathilde McKinney Gives Times Hall Piano Recital." *NYHT*, 4 December 1948, p. 8, col. 3.

Her Chopin and Mozart lacked "dynamic and interpretive vitality. Theodore Strongin's *Piece for Piano* has static charm, while her own *Preludes* have "arid charm."

G95   "French Orchestra: Visitors in Final Concert at Bergen Junior College." *NYHT*, Monday, 6 December 1948, p. 13, col. 3.

Charles Munch conducted the Orchestre National de France in works of Berlioz, Piston, Ravel, Roussel, and others, demonstrating impressive mellowness, musical insight, and accuracy, through the "intelligence and sensitivity of individuals playing together." Piston's *Toccata*, however, lacked balance, perhaps because, like most American scores, this one uses the "brass core" thematically, even rhythmically, not as underpinning, while European brass sections like this one are accustomed to a "discreet, semi-submerged role." Review is rather long (about 500 words).

G96   "Eleanore Hansen Sings: Soprano Gives Varied Program at Carnegie Recital Hall." *NYHT*, 9 December 1948, p. 25, col. 7.

Program of works by Scarlatti, Monsigny, Cilea, Nin, Fauré, and de Falla demonstrated "a smallish but quite sweet lyric soprano voice" but little "technical prowess" or "interpretative variety."

G97   "Creighton Allen Recital: Pianist's Own Works on Program in Times Hall Appearance." *NYHT*, 11 December 1948, p. 9.

Recital showed "musical irresponsibility"--inaccurate and distorted readings of Haydn, and bombastic MacDowell "where austerity was due."

G98   "Nadelmann Recital: Swiss Pianist Gives Varied Program at Town Hall." *NYHT*, Sunday, 12 December 1948, sect. 1, p. 65.

Leo Nadelmann chose "standard repertory pieces" and gives "earnest and sincere consideration" to the "exact values of the music, but sometimes lacks understanding. The Schubert *Wanderer Fantasy* showed maturity and "structural continuity."

G99   "Leslie Frick, Soprano, In Recital at Fischer Hall." *NYHT*, 13 December 1948, p. 13.

Short review (about sixty words) reports that "as always, the mezzo-soprano's diction" in French, German, Spanish, and English "was quite exquisite and her technique accomplished yet unostentatious."

G100   "Everett Fritzberg, Pianist, In Carnegie Hall Recital." Ibid., col. 7.

Another short review reports that this pianist played Chopin, Mozart, Schubert, Debussy, Haubiel, and Brahms, and that "there was altogether too much banging," along with some passages of "poetic tone."

G101   "Soprano in Debut Recital: Ruth Geiger-Wolff Sings Schubert and Brahms Works at Times Hall." *NYHT*, 14 December 1948, p. 25, col. 5.

Singer seemed best in German, where excellent diction balanced lack of vocal control, but an "incessant tremolo destroys true tonality" and the voice seems to need "a far more strict form of discipline." Songs by the accompanist, Felix Wolfes, and by Rosy Geiger-Kullmann had their first performances.

G102   "Martin Kainz Recital: Tenor Is Heard in Program in Times Hall." *NYHT*, 18 December 1948, p. 8, col. 6.

Singer has "voice without artistry," a "saddening" category. Faults in projection and diction, and liberties taken in tempi, show a lack of training, more noticeable in lieder than in an aria from *Tosca*.

G103   "Trapp Family Singers: They Are Heard in Second Christmas Recital at Town Hall." *NYHT*, Monday, 20 December 1948, p. 16, col. 3.

Program was about the same as in the previous day's recital. Franz Wasner, conductor, maintains good balance and the tone is beautiful.

G104   "Joyce Robinson Heard In Recital at Times Hall." Ibid., col. 7.

Mezzo-soprano "is a singer of extraordinary charm" and her seemingly "natural" singing gives pleasure. She uses well both the contralto color and character of her lower voice and the entirely different higher parts of her range.

G105   "Composers' Forum Gives Works by Two Musicians." *NYHT*, 21 December 1948, p. 19, col. 3.

Season's second forum featured works by Bernhard Heiden and Robert Palmer. Carleton Sprague Smith played Heiden's *Suite for Flute and Piano* (1933), and here and in other works Heiden showed the influence of Hindemith, but some individuality. (Disciples of Hindemith and Vaughan Williams are apt to receive mannerism without strength.) Palmer's *Second Sonata* for piano (1948) displayed "a colorful harmonic sense" and some almost romantic singing-tone passages as well as percussive accent.

G106   "Altea Alimonda, Violinist, Is Heard in Town Hall." *NYHT*, 24 December 1948, p. 7, col. 5.

Young violinist from Brazil in debut played Beethoven, Debussy, and Villa Lobos (the *Sonata Fantasia*, "one of the composer's more integrated pieces"). She is "authoritative" with an "accomplished technique" and has a "classic" style, subordinating "the interpretative factor" to a strict formal sense. Among "women violinists she can rank as one of the distinguished."

G107   "Jaques Aritinian Presents His Debut Recital Here." *NYHT*, 29 December 1948, p. 14.

Armenian tenor has "a good, well trained voice" and does some things better than others (French songs were distorted and pedestrian). Final group of Armenian songs revealed that his "edgy timbre" comes from the harsh sound ornamenting the tranquil main tone, in the Middle and Far East singing styles.

G108   "Gerald Neikrug, Cellist, Gives Town Hall Recital." *NYHT*, 30 December 1948, p. 12.

Cellist played best the best pieces--Beethoven and Hindemith. A piece by Cassado for cello alone (like the Hindemith) lacked harmonic "underpinnings." Neikrug has a warm and full tone, though scratchy in fast passages. A "cellistic mannerism" of scooping up to high notes "seems aesthetically out of place" at times.

1949

G109   "Virgil Thomson, 'Four Saints in Three Acts.' " *Music Library Association Notes* 6, no. 2 (March 1949), p. 328-30.

Glanville-Hicks, reviewing the complete vocal score of the opera (limited edition, New York, 1948), describes Gertrude Stein's text as poetic collage. Thomson's music creates the over-all architectural form and also carries the continuity from moment to moment, infusing emotional logic into the script. The work is a classic and a high point in Thomson's own career due to his two unique attributes: the hymn-tune element in his musical esthetic, and his prosody technique (which she describes in some detail).

G110   "Virgil Thomson." *Musical Quarterly* 35, no. 2 (April 1949), p. 209-25.

The "substance" of Thomson's compositional style has its origins in America, (Missouri church music and other sounds), and his "means" come from France (Dadaism, Boulanger, dissonant neo-classicism). Significant works include: the *Sonata da Chiesa*, *Hymn Tune Symphony*, Symphony No. 2, *Four Saints in Three Acts*, *The Mother of Us All*, *The Plough that Broke the Plains*, *The River,* and the *Louisiana Story*. The article includes many musical illustrations and a two-page list of works 1919-1948 at the end. The second paragraph is quoted in Kathleen Hoover and John Cage, *Virgil Thomson: His Life and Music* (New York, 1959, p. 251, n. 26): "Thomson has a style, and a very definite one, but it is almost impossible to put one's finger on any detail of harmonic, melodic, or rhythmic procedure that it entails. It is un-idiosyncratic. The personal element lies where it most legitimately belongs--in the emotional content, the organic whole of the music rather than in its terms of expression. It is at the source that his expression is original."   John Tasker Howard (**B190**, p. 433) quotes from p. 215: "It is impossible to listen to the *Hymn Tune Symphony* without a smile, and . . . a lump in the throat."

G111   "Newly Published Works by Jolivet and Mihalovici." *Musical America* 69, no. 11 (September 1949), p. 32.

Heugel in Paris has published André Jolivet's String Quartet No. 1, a strong work built from "uninteresting" thematic material, and his *Poèmes Intimes*, which explore sensitively "the essentially exquisite French song formula." Marcel Mihalovici's Third String Quartet and a violin and piano Sonata are "admirable" but lack the "impetus, color, and beauty of the more restless, more rugged Jolivet."

G112   "Paul Bowles--'The Season of Promise.' " Ibid., 69, no. 13 (1 November 1949), p. 7, 32-33.

Two years ago Bowles left New York for North Africa. Now, as in **G1** four years earlier, Glanville-Hicks reviews several of his writings and compositions. His successes are in both the commercial and concert worlds, and his problem, in walking an "esthetic tightrope," is both material and metaphysical. Like many young artists, he is running, ideologically and geographically, from himself, from reflection and regeneration. He runs to Italy, to the Sahara, to an analyst, to personal disasters, to drink, to the nihilism of Sartre. Morocco and the Sahara, however, may be the environment in which he grows to musical maturity. There he is surrounded by music near his ideal and most dear to his heart, the ancient Afro-Hispanic music of the Andalous, "tonal in equilibrium, with an exquisite melodic development and an infinite polyrhythmic subtlety." Now forty, he has not yet found his own creative principle; the "season of promise is already unduly prolonged."

G113   "Little Orchestra Presents Series of Concerts for Children." *Cue: The Weekly Magazine of New York Living,* 18, no. 46 (12 November 1949), p. 24.

Thomas K. Scherman, conducting the Little Orchestra's "Six Saturdays at Eleven" in the 1949 season, wisely plans including puppets (in Prokofieff's *Peter and the Wolf* and de Falla's *Master Peter's Puppet Show*), dance, cartoons, a "nine-year-old lady pianist and her twin brother, a violin virtuoso," and *Hansel and Gretel* with a witch's broomstick ride.

G114   "New York at the Half-Century. Music: 1900-1950." Ibid., no. 51 (December 17, 1949), p. 38, 40.

Twilight of nineteenth-century romanticism lasted until World War I passed. The "roaring Twenties" gave us Ives's dissonances, then Ornstein, Ruggles, Cowell and "the piano-percussion boys," Varèse, and "noisy" Antheil. Around 1934, Thomson's *Four Saints in Three Acts* brought "charm and melodiousness." In past fifteen years an American style is identifiable in "mature symphonic works of Copland, Piston, Riegger, Barber, Roy Harris." Opera needs a "low-budget renaissance" in manner of City Center Company's "Blitzstein, Menotti, Britten and Kurt Weill experiments."

G115   "Any one of the four" [no heading]. *Musical America* 69, no. 15 (December 1949), p. 10.

Robert Craft conducted a "musical banquet" at Town Hall, 22 October, "too much to be adequately digested." Stravinsky's cantata *Renard* and other works opened the program. Mozart's Clarinet Concerto "fell apart a little" when Craft "lost the tension." In Falla's Harpsichord Concerto Sylvia Marlowe gave the neo-classic masterpiece "one of her finest performances." Berg's Chamber Concerto was the "closing item--a taxing one for a fresh audience, and an endurance test for a tired one."

1949, CONTINUED: *HERALD TRIBUNE*
(JANUARY-APRIL, AUGUST)

G116   "Virginia Shaw Presents Times Hall Song Recital." *NYHT,* 3 January 1949, p. 12, col. 3.

Program featured fine singing, independence of thought in choice of program, and poetic sense of arranging it. Settings of poet James Joyce by Israel Citkowitz and Herbert Hughes were most rewarding for accompaniment texture, prosody, and melodic line. Songs of Ernst Bacon were well performed; songs of John Duke, and Theodore Chanler were outstanding. Two arias from Menotti's *Medium* were also given.

G117   " 'Lucretia.' Belva Kibler and George Tozzi Heard in Britten Opera." Ibid., p. 13, col. 4.

Favorable review, longer than usual, of *Rape of Lucretia* praises the cast, the "beauti-ful" sets, and the production, which, like Britten's music, was typically English and conservative with a "decorative" surface. Britten's "musical instrumental caricature that underlines, measure by measure, the text and action" is "a legitimate theatre practice" but simply duplicates the text and can not carry it "to emotional heights inaccessible to plain speech."

G118   "John Murray: Violinist Heard at Town Hall; Introduces New Works." *NYHT*, 6 January 1949, p. 14, col. 7.

Program by John Creighton Murray included two first performances--a work by Joseph Wagner and one by Cardenas-Marti composed on a twelfth-century Mayan derivative--along with works of Bach, Beethoven, and Brahms. He is one of the "strident new players" who can play "loud, fast and accurately" but not "sweetly or expressively." Review is longer than usual--about 250 words.

G119   "Shura Dvorine: Baltimore Pianist Heard in Recital at Town Hall." *NYHT*, 10 January 1949, p. 12, col. 8.

Young pianist played a Chopin group, Schubert's *Wanderer* Fantasia, four of Virgil Thomson's *Portraits*, a piece of his own, and one by Ellis Kohs, showing real under-standing of the music in his "spontaneity." There is no schism between technique and interpretation; his playing has strength, color, sensitivity. Compared to last year [*see* G8] the playing of this "born musician" shows new concern with establishing a conscious link with his audience.

G120   "Dallas Symphony Gives Bartok Opera on Radio." Ibid., p. 13, col. 5.

Bluebeard's Castle (1911), broadcast in American premiere, has "brooding beauty" and melodic outline, with some complexities of Bartok's later style.

G121   "Florence Vitagliano Recital." *NYHT*, 12 January 1949, p. 19, col. 1.

Pianist at Carnegie Hall played heavily and inaccurately in works of Scarlatti and Beethoven. Tenderness, warmth, and abandon were conveyed in Schumann's *Davidsbuendlertaenze* but needed "more disciplined technique." Two short *Down East Sketches* of Isadore Freed, "competently written" and pianistic, had their premiere.

G122   "Eileen Borwell, Soprano, In Fischer Hall Recital." Ibid., col. 2.

South African soprano presented works for soprano and string quartet by two South African composers, Gerrit Bon and Percival Kirby, and songs of Satie, Poulenc, La-parra, Moret, and Theodore Chanler, and ends with a group of South African folk songs. She has skill, sensitivity, and "musical finesse."

G123   "Xenia Boodberg Heard In Recital at Times Hall." *NYHT*, 15 January 1949, p. 9, col. 5.

Debut of young pianist included works of Milhaud, Nin-Culmell, Sessions, and Bar-tok. She has "many qualities of sensitive musicianship" but would gain much from greater control. Milhaud's *Suite L'Automne* (a first performance) is "enchanting" and was performed with "thoughtful delicacy."

G124   "Krebs Joint Recital: Soprano and Composer-Pianist Are Heard in Times Hall." *NYHT*, 17 January 1949, p. 14, col. 8.

Mathilde Krebs, soprano, and Stanley Krebs, composer-pianist, performed "songs and piano pieces of a most banal and ostentations nature by Mr. Krebs" and pieces of Brahms, Schubert, Strauss, Duparc, Charpentier, Friedrich Niggli, and others. Miss Krebs has a steady voice in loud passages and some interpretive talent.

G125 "Gilbert Reese, Cellist, Makes Town Hall Debut." *NYHT*, 19 January 1949, p. 21, col. 3.

Young cellist from California, playing Haydn and Debussy, is "a potential virtuoso" possessing the necessary "born gifts" and control and needing only "a greater maturity."

G126 "Pro Arte Quartet Gives Recital in Y. M. H. A. Hall." *NYHT*, 21 January 1949, p. 16, col. 7.

Schubert's Quartet in G Major Op. 161, and Schoenberg's first quartet Op. 7, a "beautiful and austere quartet masterpiece" were played with brilliance and deep understanding.

G127 "Anna Steck, Hans Melzer Heard in Joint Recital." *NYHT*, 22 January 1949, p. 9, col. 2.

Soprano sang beautifully, and bass-baritone had a pleasing voice though his diction is sometimes distorted. She sang Tailleferre's *Six Chansons* which are "delicately wrought" in the exquisite modern French song style, and premieres of John Edmunds' *Four Elizabethan Songs* and three songs by Debussy. Lowell Farr was a "sensitive" accompanist.

G128 "Guido Cantelli Conducts The N. B. C. Orchestra." *NYHT*, Sunday, 23 January 1949, sect. 1, p. 47, col. 1.

Young conductor from Italy directed works of Ghedini, Casella, and Tchaikovsky with "sensitivity" and brilliance. Giorgio Ghedini's *Pezzo Concertante* contained "some sonoroties of passing beauty" but "seemed to lack integration."

G129 "Recital at Times Hall: Dorothy Berliner Commins Gives Pianoforte Program." *NYHT*, 29 January 1949, p. 9, col. 6.

Cultivated musician imparts her music message "in terms of understatement," with beautiful, when not tentative, tone. Works of Mozart, Mendelssohn, Liszt, Debussy, Fauré, and Bauer received sensitive and introspective interpretation rather than the usual "athletic" demonstration.

G130 "Dorothy Hartzell Heard: Contralto Gives Debut Recital at Carl Fischer Hall." *NYHT*, 29 January 1949, p. 8, col. 3.

She "sings extremely well" with a "controlled and beautiful" voice particularly in the "real contralto range." Arias from Wagner's *Das Rheingold, Die Walküre*, and *Tristan* she sang "easily."

G131 "Forgotten Music Society: Randolph Singers and Soloists Are Heard at Public Library." *NYHT*, 31 January 1949, p. 10, col. 2.

Third concert of the season included world premiere of an enchanting Trio for Flute, Violin, and Piano by C. P. E. Bach (with particularly sweet flute playing by Julius Baker) and vocal music by Marenzio, Monteverdi, Vert, Vecchi, Haydn, and Mozart. Randolph Singers have precision, musicality, and excellent intonation.

G132   "Composers Forum: Hovahaness and Ray Green Are Paired in Program." Ibid., p. 16, col. 6.

Concert featured a pair of opposites, "a glib man of action, Ray Green, and one of our most exquisite poets of reflection, Alan Hovhaness." Two Hovhaness works were premieres, *Saris* for violin and piano, finely played by Anahid and Maro Ajemian, is music that hovers with a kind of ecstatic stillness. Also beautiful was *Elibris* for flute and strings. Green, in his *Piano Sonatina*, a set of songs, and the *Festival Fugues*, explores the mundane world with a certain élan. In idiom he is "a kind of Fifty-seventh Street Jean Françaix," fusing metropolitan folklore with a framework part neo-classic and part blues-boogie-woogie frame.

G133   "Bonnie Douglas: Violinist, in Debut Recital, Plays Hindemith Work." *NYHT*, 3 February 1949, p. 16, col. 3.

Two "big, and difficult, works" were Hindemith's Concerto (1939) and the Brahms's Sonata No. 3 in D minor. In these and in the *Poème* of Chausson, she was "a fine artist and one whose performance pays tribute both to the music she plays and to her own interpretive powers."

G134   "Carlo Buti Is Heard: Italian 'Balladeer' Gives Concert at Carnegie Hall." *NYHT*, 5 February 1949, p. 9, col. 8.

His first New York concert appearance in ten years brought "a large audience of mainly Italian-speaking enthusiasts." Performance included comic sketches by a master of ceremonies, roller skaters, flamenco dancers, an orchestra, two more dancers, and another singer, Elaine Barrett.

G135   "American Music Festival: Choral and Piano Music." *NYHT*, 14 February 1949, p. 11, col. 2.

Broadcast over WNYC as part of the American music festival, the concert included choral works by Roy Harris, Peter Mennin, and William Bergsma. Mennin's work is "legitimate choral writing": his pieces have "real counterpoint, the color and originality of the music existing horizontally, intervals and melodic lines lying as singers like them to lie, in fluent polyphony." Two piano pieces of Virgil Thomson "livened up" the house at the end.

G136   "Ditson Concert: Works of Six Contemporary Americans Performed." *NYHT*, 16 February 1949, p. 19, col. 1.

Programmed were "a chipper neo-classic Trio by Ingolf Dahl for violin, cello and clarinet," sonatas by Adolph Weiss and Joseph Goodman, and works for chorus by Bergsma, Leon Kirchner, and Henry Brant. Bergsma's *On the Beach at Night* was more sensitively performed, and sounded "far more beautiful" than "last Sunday night" (previous review).

G137   "Three First Performances Mark Town Hall Concert." Ibid., col. 3.

Works by Gail Kubik, Celius Dougherty (*Freedom Is a Hard Fought Thing*, sung by Kenneth Spencer, bass), and Halsey Stevens (the Violin Sonata, performed by Maurice Wilk) received first performances. Also heard were Barber's Cello Sonata, Philip James's "clear, alert and beautifully written" *Suite for Woodwind Quintet*, performed by the New York Woodwind Quartet, and a piece for cello and piano by Louis Gesenway.

G138   "William Masselos: Pianist Presents Ives Sonata at Y. M. H. A. Hall." *NYHT*, 18 February 1949, p. 18, col. 7.

First complete performance of Charles Ives's "long, massive" Piano Sonata No. 1 (1902-1910) brought cheering. Masselos has "strength, insight, grace, and an astonishing technical control" mechanically and interpretively. Works of Carl Ruggles and Charles Griffes were also heard, and, perhaps the "most advanced" on the program, Dane Rudhyar's *Granites* (1929) which "it seems to me . . . achieves supremely well what André Jolivet of the Jeune France group" is seeking today. Long review (over 400 words) includes much on contemporary styles.

G139   "Edna White: Trumpet Virtuoso Is Aided by Tietjen Chorus." *NYHT*, Sunday 20 February 1949, sect. 1, p. 43, col. 3-4.

Also longer than usual, about 300 words, the review describes "one of the fanciest concerts of the season" and the first trumpet recital in Carnegie Hall. Virgil Thomson's *Concert Waltz*, a *Sonatine* by Henri Martelli, and *Procession* by Gena Branscombe were first performances. Solo works by George Enesco and Tibo Serly, and works for trumpet and chorus by Victoria, Kubik, Kodaly, and Holst were also "finely" performed.

G140   "Marc Gottlieb, Violinist, In Recital Debut Here." *NYHT*, 21 February 1949, p. 13, col. 3.

Eighteen-year-old has "considerable technical proficiency" and "a steely clarity of tone." He performed Vivaldi, Beethoven, Prokofiev, and his own *Rhapsody*.

G141   "Amelia Candwell Sings In Times Hall Recital." *NYHT*, 22 February 1949, p. 16, col. 7.

Soprano with a "clear and pure" voice and good intonation sang songs in French, English, and German. Works by Poulenc, Bruneau, Ravel, Koechlin, and Rameau--the French group--were particularly well sung, while the German songs--by Strauss, Wolf, and Loewe--lacked an "abstract intimacy."

G142   "Herma Menth, Pianist, Plays in Fischer Hall." *NYHT*, Sunday 27 February 1949, sect. 1, p. 42, col. 3-4.

Piano works by Mendelssohn, Liszt, Chopin, and others, demonstrated "volume and speed" and "a certain dramatic sense, though accuracy, both of notes and of tempi, is not an outstanding feature." She "seemed more at home among the lighter piano touches."

G143   "Irene Rosenberg at Town Hall." *NYHT*, 1 March 1949, p. 12, col. 5.

Program by "one of the most distinguished and articulate pianists" included Bach (Choral Prelude in F minor arranged by Busoni), Mozart, Brahms, Beethoven,

Profkofieff, Bergsma, and Debussy. She already possesses ":most of the qualities that
bespeak the top rank artist."

G144   "Recital by Aristo Male Quartet." *NYHT*, 2 March 1949, p. 19.

New York debuts by four young singers included solo groups (Schubert lieder and
operatic pieces) as well as quartets. Performers were: tenors Stewart McCleary and
Willard Pierce, baritone Ralph Magelssen, and bass Robert Falk.

G145   "Hovhaness at Town Hall." *NYHT*, 7 March 1949, p. 14, col. 5-6.

Alan Hovhaness conducted his own orchestral and choral works. Receiving its first
performance was *Sosi: Forest of Prophetic Sounds*, a big piece that "shows several
new Hovhaness trends, notably the combining of more than one of his thematic-
rhythmic writing methods within one work."

G146   "Antonio Iglesias, From Spain." Ibid., col. 6-7.

Young composer-pianist presented "an unusually beautiful program" of small pieces
from the Spanish piano repertoire--works of Soler, Halffter, Mompou, Rodrigo,
Molleda, Turina, Granados, Albeniz, and De Falla, but none of his own. He is "an
exquisite interpreter of what might be terms the 'sophisticated folk music' of his
country."

G147   "Thierwechter in Debut." *NYHT*, 12 March 1949, p. 7, col. 3.

Louis Thierwechter, bass-baritone, in his New York recital debut, sang "familiar
pieces" by Brahms, Mozart, Schubert, Carissimi and others. He has "assurance,
though his vocal technique is by no means infallible."

G148   "Lola Corini, Pianist." *NYHT*, 16 March 1949, p. 21, col. 2-3.

This pianist "is more mature technically" than interpretively, and thus better on
Bach, Beethoven, and Rachmaninoff (the "Corelli" Variations) than on Brahms and
Debussy.

G149   "Albert Weintraub, Violinist." *NYHT*, 21 March 1949, p. 15, col. 1.

Twenty-one-year-old in New York debut recital "appears to be a soloist of technical
stability and musical dedication" with "often a live brilliance that comes from general precision and an assimilated interpretative concept." A Vieuxtemps Concerto
showed "considerable virtuosity" but the Brahms A major Sonata, a work with "real
esthetic value" had a more convincing "interpretative feeling."

G150   "Composers Forum." Ibid.

Long review (over 400 words) of program by Robert Starer and Remi Gassmann
gives details of compositional technique and "expressive content." Both show
"mastery of their craft" but produce a "forbidding rather than endearing" effect.
Starer uses a "chromatic, evasive" style "without strong definition on either
melodic, harmonic or rhythmic planes," although his String Quartet had less of the
"effect of chaos." Gassmann sometimes, as in the *Air and Dance for Flute and Piano*
develops "certain indigenous elements" of his own style, free from the restrictions of
the "cramped diatonic system" of Hindemith, and "achieves a nice balance of ends
and means."

G151 "Robert Schrade, Pianist." *NYHT*, 28 March 1949, p. 10, col. 5.

New York debut at Town Hall revealed "a performer of some technique, taste and intelligence." César Franck's *Prelude, Chorale and Fugue* is intrinsically "somewhat purple" but Schrade's "fine" performance, accurate and restrained, with "controlled squareness," was an advantage esthetically (though a disadvantage theatrically). Last paragraph of review reports that Nicholas Farley presented "a varied program of songs" later in the evening.

G152 "Chamber Chorale." *NYHT*, Sunday 10 April 1949, sect. 1, p. 46, col. 4.

Review of about 50 words is little more than an announcement--that the New York Chamber Chorale, conducted by Thomas G. McCarthy, performed the Stabat Mater by Rossini. Names of solo singers and pianist are given, too.

G153 "Harold Border, Debut." *NYHT*, 19 April 1949, p. 17, col. 6.

Tenor offered "sensitive and intelligent singing" at Carnegie Recital Hall, in Schumann's *Dichterliebe*,"and songs of Duparc, Handel, and Massenet.

G154 "Doctors' Orchestra." *NYHT*, 22 April 1949, p. 16, col. 6-7.

Ignace Strasfogel conducted benefit concert for the Roosevelt Hospital. "The doctors played well, and had a particularly sound brass section." Miss Ania Dorfman was piano soloist in Beethoven's first Piano Concerto.

G155 "Stadium Concert Devoted to Kurt Weill Program." *NYHT*, 1 August 1949, p. 8, col. 5-6.

Maurice Abravanel conducted excerpts from *Street Scene* and *Lady in the Dark*. Soloists, two from the Metropolitan Opera, "appeared to be in fine form." The concert was terminated when "the rains came, and the 5,600 in attendance were obliged to make for shelter."

(OCTOBER-DECEMBER 1949)

G156 "N. B. C. Symphony." *NYHT*, 10 October 1949, p. 13, col. 2.

Abram Chasins' *Period Suite* in its first performance blends the formalism of the seventeenth and eighteenth centuries with modern harmonic idioms. N. B. C. Symphony Orchestra, directed by Milton Katims, gave a "neat and illuminating" performance. Also played were Bizet's Symphony in C and two Rumanian Dances by Bartok.

G157 "Youth Concerts Start: Program at Carnegie Hall Stresses Woodwind Instruments." *NYHT*, 27 October 1949, p. 23, col. 2.

Wheeler Beckett conducted New York Philharmonic-Symphony members and was "engagingly droll in his commentaries." Heard were the Allegretto from Beethoven's Symphony No. 8, Dukas's *Sorcerer's Apprentice*, Borodin's *Prince Igor* dances, and the discourses from Ravel's *Beauty and the Beast*.

G158 "Marienka Michna, Pianist." *NYHT*, 31 October 1949, p. 12, col. 8.

Works of Haydn, Schumann, and Chopin were followed by two new works, Sonatina No. 1 by Jan Cikker, a young Slovak composer, and *Characteristic Suite* by Julia Smith. The suite, in the "somewhat forbidding" twelve-tone atonal manner, uses tonal forms and organization. "One cannot help feeling, however, that the nature of form in atonality should grow from the real nature of the material rather than be borrowed from the tonalist's territory."

G159   "New Friends of Music." *NYHT*, 14 November 1949, p. 11.

Fine Arts Quartet played Brahms and Schoenberg. Leboshutz and Nemenoff gave a "scintillating, if slightly mechanized, account" of Mozart's D major Sonata for two pianos, late Sunday afternoon at Town Hall. The hall "steadily thinned" during the Schoenberg Quartet No. 3, op. 30, not because of the performance but because the work is "difficult both expressively and technically."

G160   "Dyer-Bennet Sings." *NYHT*, 14 November 1949, p. 11.

With his "perfect diction" and "unique charm," his taste, timbre of voice, and whimsy, Richard Dyer-Bennet is in the ancient tradition of the "poet-melodists" who wandered westward into Europe with the returning Crusaders. His small voice is perfectly suited to what he does with it, in a special, intimate art.

G161   "Philharmonic Presents Concert for Children." *NYHT*, Sunday 20 November 1949, sect. 1, p. 51.

Dean Dixon conducted the third movement of Haydn's Oxford Symphony, Prokofieff's Symphony no. 5, second movement, and other works. Demonstrations of musical terms were included, and "attention-gaining devices--a second violin player felt compelled to move his chair a little each time the theme appeared--had the children thoroughly alerted.

G162   "Composers Forum." *NYHT*, 21 November 1949, p. 17, col. 4-5.

Composers were Beatrice Laufer and Joseph Goodman. Only one of Laufer's songs "avoided poor prosody and harmonic cliché;" others drifted near what used to be called the "art song" category. The more recent Chamber Concerto (1948) shows the results of "considerable esthetic weeding" and the last movement contains a "real musical idea." Goodman's music, in a "bitonally-inclined neo-classic vein," shows unified "functional and expressive elements." A disciple of Hindemith, he has absorbed the principle without the mannerism of Hindemith's key-shift device; his music has a tonal center without being bound by a strict diatonicism. Virgil Thomson was moderator. (Review, unsigned, is in scrapbook in **A3**.)

G163   "Jeanne Mitchell, Violinist." Ibid., col. 6-7.

This musician has developed all kinds of qualities since her 1947 debut (**G23**). She has a larger tone and a "grasp of the shape of the composition." Performed were works of Mozart, Bach, and Glazunov, and some "small modern pieces."

G164   "Gertrude Bennett." Ibid., col. 8.

Performance "did not measure up to the general standard of New York recitalists."

G165   "Paganini Quartet." *NYHT*, 24 November 1949, p. 31.

Performance of quartets of Haydn, Beethoven, and Debussy showed delicacy, precision, and "all-around musicianly playing."

G166   "Margaret Ferguson." *NYHT*, 3 December 1949, p. 8.

Pianist in her New York debut performed music of Brahms, Schumann, Debussy, and others and showed an "erratic disregard for the music as it is written." She also had, however, "a certain delicacy in gentler passages, and a colorful tone on occasion."

G167   "Young Brazilian Pianist." *NYHT*, 5 December 1949, p. 15.

Maria Augusta Menezes de Oliva presented her debut recital in Carnegie Hall, performing Mozart, Bach, and Schumann. In spite of "overemphatic accents" and "over-acceleration," she has the qualities of a real concert pianist--"strength, variety, and a natural direct way of playing."

G168   "Bell Society Presents Carnegie Hall Concert." *NYHT*, 10 December 1949, p. 9.

Metropolitan Bell Symphony Society, an orchestra recruited from among members of the Bell System, directed by Dr. Frederic Kurzweil, performed Beethoven, Schumann, and Mendelssohn--the Violin Concerto in E minor with Miss Patricia Travers as guest soloist.

G169   "New York Wind Ensemble." *NYHT*, Sunday, 11 December 1949, sect. 1, p. 76.

The group "in amplified form" presented concert versions of Monteverdi's *Orfeo* and Stravinsky's *Mavra*. The young conductor Robert Craft, who "clearly loves the music," did not "project his ideas and intentions" clearly in the Stravinsky but gave a "buoyant" performance. The Monteverdi featured the "beautiful singing" of tenor William Hess, but "fell apart" due to the "over-tentative" piano playing of Mr. Craft and perhaps a "rehearsal shortage."

G170   "Constanza Pillori, Soprano." *NYHT*, 12 December 1949, p. 15.

Young lyric soprano in recital at Carnegie Hall presented pieces by Mozart, Puccini, Bellini, and others. With "flexibility and color" in the high middle range, the voice is perhaps more truly a clear lyric mezzo than soprano in type. Attention to diction would help her phrasing and melodic "precision."

G171   "Virginia Davis." *NYHT*, 14 December 1949, p. 23.

This "lady troubadour" with a small, beautiful lyric voice and perfect diction is a mistress of speaking and singing and "subtle degrees between the two." Traditional music of England and France was followed by some American songs which were "good technically, and expressive." (*See also* G245.)

G172   "Hadley Memorial: Composers and Conductors Give Annual Concert." *NYHT*, 21 December 1949, p. 22, col. 7-8.

National Association of American Composers and Conductors (NAACC) concert "opened with a Violin and Piano Sonata by Eusebia Simpkins Hunkins, a work that does not inspire too much confidence in the fair sex as exponents of the art of composition." A romantic Trio (1926) by Robert Sanders is unlike his later, finely crafted works. A short opera buffa *Don't We All* by Burrill Phillips performed with piano accompaniment "might be quite fun" in a more sophisticated production.

G173   "Cantelli on N. B. C." *NYHT*, 26 December 1949, p. 15, col. 7-8.

Italian conductor, "still in his twenties, is without a doubt one of the stars of the conducting firmament," with brilliance and "many deeper qualities" added since last season (*see* G128). Program included music of Handel and Bach, and Tchaikovsky's Fourth Symphony in F minor.

G174   "Brazilian Trio." *NYHT*, 30 December 1949, p. 12, col. 8.

Three Brazilian women performed trios of Beethoven, Brahms, and Lorenzo Fernandez (a first performance). Pianist Iracema Barbosa, violinist Hertha Kahn, and cellist Cecilia Zwarg have "considerable technical proficiency" but "a stony quality" that gives this new ensemble an "implacable" effect. Fernandez uses "Brazilian folk material" but in a "cheap romantic-impressionism" that does not blend with the "primitive esthetic."

G175   "After Dinner Opera." *NYHT*, 31 December 1949, p. 7, col. 1.

New group presented three short operas at the Finch College Theater, each using three singers and performed with piano accompaniment. *Savitri* by Gustav Holst is on a Hindu text. *In a Garden*, libretto by Gertrude Stein, has music by Meyer Kupferman that "filled the space that has to be occupied by sound in a way that supported and did not confuse" the text, and it made "a distinct hit." By contrast, Mark Bucci's score for *The Boor* was "a lesson in what not to do with music in the theater."

1950

G176   "Metropolitan Opera's New Manager is Learning the Ropes." *Cue: The Weekly Magazine of New York Living* 19, no. 1 (7 January 1950), p. 26.

Rudolf Bing, famous for "co-ordinating the artistic and business hazards of theatrical enterprises" and due to assume the "toughest musical-managerial job in the world" next season, is "unwilling to be critical of the present regime" or to talk about changes. The unions are a more "imposing factor" than on the Continent and in England.

G177   "Opera Made Painless." Ibid., 19, no. 3 (21 January 1950), p. 14-15.

Glanville-Hicks's copy (in A3) is marked "unauthorized rewrite!!" Only about one-quarter is left unmarked, the rest crossed out, including the title, above which she has written her intended, more positve title, "New Trends in Opera." Thomson, Blitzstein, and Menotti are "key men in the history of American opera in the past fifteen years or so" with important works by Copland, Moore, Bernard Herrman, Berezowsky, Blitzstein, and Cowell. American opera needs "adequate production facilities, for low-budget experiment."

G178   "February is the Month for the American Festival." Ibid., 19, no. 5 (4 February 1950), p. 29.

Radio station WNYC's eleventh annual American Music Festival will take over New York with "Americana in almost every shape and form, from Folk to Highbrow." Eighteen public concerts, with about forty "first performances," also broadcast, will present important new music by Foss, Kupferman, Antheil, Wilder, Nabokov, Rorem, Dello Joio, Jacobi, and Riegger.

G179   "Musical Explorers: Six Americans Who Are Changing the Musical Vocabulary." *Vogue* 116 (15 November 1950), p. 112-13, 134, 137, 139.

Cage, Hovhaness, McPhee, Bowles, Harrison, and Varèse are exploring rhythm as the basis of musical structure and form, and they recognize an affinity with Far Eastern and Middle Eastern forms (and perhaps our jazz); they do not follow the fashionable contemporary schools of thought, Parisian neo-classicism (Stravinski) and Viennese atonalism (Schoenberg). Their interests are similar to those of Messiaen and the "new Parisian atonalists," and (earlier) of Farwell, Cowell, and Antheil. "With the youthful and adventurous ears of Paris and New York turned in similar directions, the exotics may prove after all to be an *avant garde*." (Editor notes that the article is "by a distinguished music critic" who is British-born [!] and known in Europe as a composer and in the U. S. as a critic.)

1950, CONTINUED: *MUSICAL AMERICA (MA)*

G180   "Piano Score Edition Issued of Barber Vocal Work." *MA* 70, no. 1 (1 January 1950), p. 89.

Knoxville: Summer of 1915 for soprano and orchestra in piano reduction shows that with Barber "orchestral color is very much part of the formal concept." The long prose text is set well and demonstrates the "true romantic's ability" to change tempo and material without "sudden points of contrast."

G181   "New Music. Other Vocal Music." *MA* 70, no. 2 (15 January 1950), p. 90.

Works of Roger Blanchard, Francis Poulenc, and Henri Sauguet are briefly reviewed. Blanchard's *Chansons de la Louisiane* are in "an incredible patois" that may be "a bit difficult to memorize" and use folk melodies with salon accompaniment. Sauget's songs are in the "elegant" tradition established by Fauré, Debussy, Ravel, Poulenc, and Tailleferre and "like most French composers" he sets words well.

G182   "Leon Barzin Conducts Program for Children." *MA* 70, no. 3 (February 1950), p. 276.

Barzin's National Orchestral Association with other student orchestra members and an admirable young violin soloist Michael Rabin, "played well" in an ambitious program (which is published with this brief review).

G183   "Pro Arte Quartet, 92nd Street YMHA, Jan. 16." Ibid., p. 272.

Quartet from University of Wisconsin played Schoenberg's String Trio, Op. 45, an atonal, "complaining," romantic work, and quartets of Beethoven (Op. 95, with "exaggeration of the aspects of unbalance") and Schubert. Review is essentially the same as her *Herald Tribune* review of this concert (**G213**) but worded differently.

G184   "Lizabeth Pritchett, Mezzo-Soprano, Paul Doktor, Violist, Town Hall, Jan. 20." Ibid., p. 278.

Joint recital in the Debut and Encore Concerts series was "admirably balanced" in color, style, and general organization. Accompanists Otto Hertz and Artur Balsam were "excellent." Pritchett uses her "expressive voice" well, with "poetry" in the "lyric quality" of the higher voice. Doktor "has played in many premieres of contemporary masterpieces. Judgment in the unproven field is often a sign of judgment about music in general." Brahms's *Zwei Gesänge* for voice, viola, and piano had "warmth" and sensitivity to the work's "tranquil meekness."

G185   "Composers Forum, McMillin Theatre, Jan. 21." Ibid., p. 278.

Howard Swanson and Edward Cone were featured composers. Swanson's pieces each have "a stable basis" for "exquisitely free textures, arabesques, and delicate treatment of unessential notes," with "spontaneity." Cone's works seem "laboriously constructed" in a "strident" idiom.

G186   "Vladimir Horowitz, Pianist, Carnegie Hall, Jan. 23." Ibid., p. 279-80.

"Athletic" pianist's program had no intermediate plane between "mild gentleness" (as in Schumann's *Childhood Scenes)* and the "crashing volumes and high speed" of Barber's new Piano Sonata. Barber's "subject matter is often superior musically to its development and evolution."

G187   "Luigi Silva, Cellist, Times Hall, Jan. 24." Ibid., p. 280.

Cellist has "fine technique and a beautiful tone" as well as "authority" and "a gleam of humor." Carlo Bussotti accompanied. Chopin's posthumous Grand Duo Concertante on Themes from Meyerbeer's *Robert le Diable* had its first U. S. performance. The piano part alone is eloquent, as Chopin's mind dealt "brilliantly and elegantly with the disciplined and florid use of the unessential note," but the "more linear, less decorative progress of a stringed instrument seemingly hampered this process of thought."

G188   "Berl Senofsky, Violinist, Carnegie Hall, Jan. 27." *MA* 70, no. 3 (February 1950), p. 281.

Bartok's charming and exciting *Contrasts* for violin, clarinet, and piano "made a welcome variant" on the usual recital program and was splendidly performed by clarinettist Alfred Gallodoro and the brilliant, musicianly pianist, Carlo Bussotti. Violinist had "considerable distinction" throughout the program.

G189   "Robert McFerrin, Baritone, Times Hall, Jan. 29 (Debut)." Ibid., p. 282.

This "singer of more than ordinary gifts" was able to overcome his "insensitive" accompanist in works by Rameau, Schubert, and others.

G190   "Dorothy Siegfried, Mezzo-Soprano, Times Hall, Jan. 31 (Debut)." Ibid., p. 320.

Songs in Italian, French, and German lacked "well-rounded melodic line" because of poor diction. Her voice is "small but pretty" and creates an appealingly "intimate" quality.

G191   "Aurelio di Dio, Violinist, Carnegie Hall, Feb. 1." Ibid.

Violinist has "grace and charm rather than strength or virtuosity." Sonatas of
Beethoven and Franck lost "formal continuity" through faulty "sense of tempo."

G192   "Chamber Music of Our Times, Times Hall, Feb. 3." Ibid., p. 320-1.

Rolf Persinger, viola, Dorothy Parrish and Beveridge Webster, piano, and the Sagul
Trio--flutist Edith Sagul, cellist Sebe Sarser, and "really excellent pianist" Marienka
Michna--performed music of John Verrall, Bartok, Ben Weber, and Martinu. Verrall's *Sonata for Viola and Piano* is dissonant and chromatic, "of scant interest expressively or technically." Ben Weber, a "highly gifted musician," writes "twelve-
tone music, without the pedagogic tone row;" his *Fantasia Variations* for piano
("expertly played" by Webster) have variety without chaos, satisfying cadences, an
"organic" idiom, and "romantic" spirit. Martinu's Trio for Flute, Cello and Piano is
" ' the mixture as before,' as Somerset Maugham once called a pot-boiler."

G193   "Chaja Goldstein, Singing Mime, Times Hall, Feb. 4 (Debut)." Ibid., p.
321.

Her singing in Yiddish and Hebrew was "rather touching" and her dancing
"extremely affecting." Her art "hovered somewhere between" comedy and tragedy,
and though the music would scarcely merit notice, she had an intense "sincerity"
indispensable to art.

G194   "Seymour Mandel, Baritone, Times Hall, Feb. 5." Ibid., p. 322.

Review is like her review of this concert for the *Herald Tribune* (**G218** below),
though differently worded and titled.

G195   "Early Music Foundation, Town Hall, Feb. 11." Ibid., p. 324.

Review is like her review of this concert for the *Herald Tribune* (**G219** below),
though differently worded and titled.

G196   Angela Chope, Soprano, Times Hall, Feb. 14 (Debut)." *MA* 70, no. 4 (15
March 1950), p. 18, 20.

Young soprano presented songs of Beethoven, Brahms, and Wolf, some of them
"not well written for the voice." Brahms received "considerable sensitivity of
interpretation," especially in the rich, true middle voice; a "slow tremolo" made
pitch unclear in the higher voice.

G197   "American Music Festival, Times Hall, Feb. 16." Ibid., p. 20.

Concert broadcast by WNYC featured violinist Joseph Fuchs, pianist Leo Smit in
Copland's Violin Sonata and Berger's Duo. The New York Woodwind Ensemble
premiered William Presser's little *March for Woodwinds* and played pieces by
Hindemith and Persichetti. Paulist Choristers directed by Father Foley sang "ro-
mantically tinged pieces" by Sowerby, Wetzler, and Borowski. Liebling Singers
offered William Schuman's *Holiday Songs* and light songs by Griffes, Kern, and
Gershwin.

G198   "Davis Shuman, Trombonist, Town Hall, Feb. 18, 5:30." Ibid., p. 22.

Recital by "the only trombone player who regularly gives recitals in New York" included first performances of ensemble works of Roger Goeb and Robert Starer, Hindemith's Sonata, Robert Kahn's Serenade, and works of Haydn and Mozart "made over to suit the purposes of the trombone."

G199   "Nina Geverts, Violinist, Charlotte Bloecher, Soprano, Times Hall, Feb. 19, 3:00 (Debut)." Ibid.

Debut recital was by two "excellent young artists," winners of the Debut Recital Award of the New York Madrigal Society. Bloecher, described as a lyric soprano but actually an "admirable" lyric-coloratura, sang arias of Bach and Mozart and several songs. Geverts "revealed reliable musicianship" and "considerable technical command" in the "overworked Vieuxtemps D minor Violin Concerto."

G200   "Chamber Music of Our Time, Times Hall, Feb. 24." Ibid., p. 26.

Concert (in same series as G192) featuring Bartok, Martinu, Verrall, and Ben Weber "was perhaps the most rewarding." Weber's *Concerto for Piano Solo, Cello Obbligato, and Wind Instruments*, an "abstruse" atonal work, was less spontaneous and expressive than is usual with Weber, reaffirming that "atonalism is primarily a system, not an expressive medium." Verrall's Serenade for Five Wind Instruments lacked strength but contained "graceful writing," and the performers "provided wind playing that for brightness, neat detail, and finely blended tone could scarcely be bettered." Review is longer than usual--about 300 words.

G201   "NAACC, Town Hall, Feb. 26." Ibid., p. 26, 28.

Concerts of National Association for American Composers and Conductors often maintain a "standard of sheer mediocrity." This one had several dull works and several inept ones, and Roger Goeb's Wind Quintet, dissonant and angular in style and weak in "formal unity," which was given a "neat and careful performance by the New Art Wind Quintet.

G202   "Andrés Segovia, Guitarist, Town Hall March 5." Ibid., p. 32.

Review is like her review of this concert for the *Herald Tribune* (G224 below), though differently worded and titled.

G203   "New Music Reviews. Interesting Piano Pieces By Fine, Shapero, and Harris." Ibid., p. 44.

Schirmer has published Irving Fine's *Music for Piano*, "crisp, clean, and attractively lucid." Harold Shapero's *Three Sonatas for Piano* are less attractive. Fine and Shapero are of the Boulanger school and the music is "cleansed of aesthetic references (except to the Stravinsky school of Paris)." Roy Harris's *Toccata*, published by Carl Fischer under the auspices of Sigma Alpha Iota, "in no way seems a toccata, but it is an excellent composition" with "many dramatic moments."

G204   "Barbara Custance, Pianist, Town Hall, March 22." *MA* 70, no. 5 (April 1950), p. 22.

Works of Beethoven and Brahms were performed with "real insight" though with some deficiencies of "technique." Chopin pieces, florid and less formal, "clearly did not appeal to her as much."

G205   "Scandanavian Music Given at New York Library." Ibid., p. 36.

Tii Niemela, Finnish soprano, sang works of Grieg (representing Norway) and composers of Denmark, Sweden, and Finland. Kilpinen's original and beautiful *Songs of Life and Death* show how the "peculiar quality of the Finnish language seems to impose a network of detailed inflections on the melodic line without disrupting its flow. Carleton Sprague Smith, head of the New York Public Library's music division, played flute in two chamber works.

G206 "Bracha Zefira, Contralto, Town Hall, April 6." Ibid., p. 30.

Folk and traditional music of the Middle East and a group of love songs--Yemenite, Persian, and Sephardic Jewish--arranged by contemporary Palestinian composers were accompanied by piano and by 35-piece orchestra. Her clear, straight tone, like that heard in Flamenco and Arab singing and in Persian and Northern Indian vocal styles, was "exciting, intimate, and rather wild, yet at the same time sufficiently controlled."

G207 "NAACC Concert Times Hall, April 12." *MA* 70, no. 6 (May 1950), p. 10.

Review is like her review of this concert for the *Herald Tribune* (**G234** below), though differently worded and titled.

G208 "Colorado College Presents Summer Festival Programs." Ibid., no. 10 (September 1950), p. 12.

Virgil Thomson was composer in residence this year and the festival included performances of his music, lectures by Thomson, and a performance of Glanville-Hicks's *Thomsoniana* (**W39**), as well as other contemporary music and some traditional concert music. A small photograph shows Glanville-Hicks, Persichetti, Lehmer, Kohs, Effinger, Thomson, and Antheil around a piano. *See also:* **B96** and **B378**.

1950, CONTINUED: *HERALD TRIBUNE* (JANUARY-APRIL)

G209 "Twin Pianists." *NYHT*, 9 January 1950, p. 13, col. 4-5.

Jeanne and Joan Nettleton, young debut artists from Kansas City, were "perfectly matched" in touch, style, and pacing in performing two-piano works by Brahms, Chopin, Mendelssohn, Rachmaninoff, and others.

G210 "Marion Burrough." Ibid., col. 5.

Short review--less than 100 words--summarizes this soprano's recital program and identifies her piano accompanist as George Reeves.

G211 "Vittoria de Ranieri." *NYHT*, 12 January 1950, p. 20, col. 3-4.

Young pianist in debut recital "moved with elegance and crispness" in three Scarlatti sonatas and played pieces of Debussy and Ravel "with a notable delicacy and variety," but in the Mozart A major Sonata she "lost the tensions, and thus the formal outline."

G212 "Storr-Wessel Piano Team." *NYHT*, 13 January 1950, p. 15, col. 2.

Sherman Storr and Mark Wessel, "pianists of considerable solo experience," presented a recital of arrangements (an "admittedly inartistic practice") from the works of Bach, Mozart, Beethoven, Debussy, "and even Tchaikowsky" and the Brahms-Haydn Variations. "The pair play loudly, but often without real tone."

G213 "Pro Arte Quartet." *NYHT*, 17 January 1950, p. 16, col. 8.

Quartets by Beethoven and Schubert were performed with "marked finesse." Schoenberg's String Trio Op. 45 (in its first New York performance) "contains some brilliant and magic sounds, but they are unrelated" in any way that projects readily. The work is "the ultimate in dessication" and the mood is "cold despair."

G214 "Helen Lightner." *NYHT*, 20 January 1950, p. 19, col. 7-8.

Recital program by this "beautiful and accomplished young singer" was "distinguished and highly selective without being precious." Songs of Wolf and Brahms showed "fusion" of "tone technique and interpretive sensitivity."

G215 "Rosalyn Tureck, Pianist." *NYHT*, 26 January 1950, p. 19, col. 4-5.

Recital, first in her series in commemoration of the Bach bicentennial, was a "grand achievement" within a narrow, "pure classic" range of dynamics, colors, and composing methods. She has a "magic power" to make "piano tones appear to linger at undiminished volume." (Same concert is reviewed in *Musical America* by another critic.

G216 "Carol Lee Eshak, Pianist, 12." *NYHT*, 27 January 1950, p. 16, col. 8.

Debut recital by talented pianist, "full of promise," included works of Bach, Beethoven, Brahms, Chopin, and "a contemporary group." She "is by no means a prodigy, either technically or interpretatively," but has "fine natural musicality, is intelligent, and has been well taught."

G217 "Edna Ricks Sings." *NYHT*, 30 January 1950, p. 11, col. 5.

Mezzo-soprano has "too many difficulties in the technical sphere, and in the most elementary interpretive factors," to be judged as a soloist.

G218 "Seymour Mandel, Baritone." *NYHT*, 6 February 1950, p. 12, col. 8.

Songs of Carl Loewe, Hugo Wolf, some early English composers, his accompanist Fredric Kurzweil, and others demonstrated a voice of "good color and volume" but some "instability, both tonally and interpretively." Mozart's "Non più andrai" he sang "extremely well."

G219 "Early Music Foundation." *NYHT*, 13 February 1950, p. 11, col. 4.

An all Purcell program presented by five singers and a choral and orchestral group included the anthem *Jubilate Deo*, music for viols, pieces for voice and harpsichord continuo or voice and chorus, and a dramatization of *Saul and the Witch of Endor*, a paraphrase on Samuel I: 28. Here "some effectively simple staging and costuming were rather let down by some none too steady singing."

G220 "American Music Festival." *NYHT*, 16 February 1950, p. 17, col. 4-6.

Meyer Kupferman's *Divertimento for Chamber Orchestra* shows "a fine sense of pacing and a brilliant use of the chromatic idiom without recourse to atonal theory." Alec Wilder's Concerto for Oboe and Orchestra was performed well; it is "attractive and well instrumented rather than well written, organically speaking," and sections "lean rather heavily on the Gershwin esthetic."

G221 "Brilliant Event," *NYHT*, 23 February 1950, p. 20.

Premiere of George Antheil's Sixth Symphony was "an event of brilliance" closing the American Music Festival last night. The first movement features "massive independent lines moving about at different speeds, in different keys." Two movements of Ulehla's String Quartet in E minor, also given as a premiere, "showed some able writing for the strings." Ernst Bacon's cantata *The Lord Star* and *Frescobaldiana* arranged by Giannini were also performed. Review is long, about 300 words.

G222 "Soprano in Debut." *NYHT*, 3 March 1950, p. 15, col. 7-8.

Mary Simmons in her New York debut at Town Hall sang Mozart, Schubert, Wolf, Mendelssohn, Hindemith, Ravel, Bizet, and Chanler. She "is an intelligent, sensitive, and accurate singer, and one with a real voice."

G223 "Greenwich House Students." NYHT, 6 March 1950, p. 11.

Student soloists and orchestra performed Vivaldi, Handel, Mozart, Schubert, and three pieces by director Maxwell Powers--"a long, and not too tidily-played program."

G224 "Segovia and His Guitar." Ibid.

Enthusiasts packed Town Hall to hear "the world's most famous guitarist" play mainly Bach, and some modern Spanish pieces by De Falla, Turina, Granados, and Albanez. Segovia keeps "many layers of different timbre-color" separate, and his techniques are all "at the service of an exquisite and musicianly mind."

G225 "Composers Forum." *NYHT*, 13 March 1950, p. 11, col. 4-5.

Works of Dane Rudhyar and Stefan Wolpe were presented and Samuel Barlow was "special moderator." Wolpe "usurped and hour and a half of the available concert time" for music "utterly lacking in idiomatic, structural or emotional contrasts." Rudhyar's music shows a "notable sensitivity" in the use of "chromatic dissonance." His pieces written twenty-five years ago expressed a "real artist nature."

G226 "Memorial Concert." Ibid., col. 6-7.

Zilberts Choral Society, conducted by Sholom Secunda, in a concert in memory of Zavel Zilberts, sang traditional pieces in Hebrew including some arranged by Mr. Zilberts. Traces "of the beautiful traditional music of the ancient East" were heard. A "presentation of honour" to Leonard Bernstein, who was conducting in the Hollywood Bowl that night, was received by his secretary.

G227 "Roberta Berlin." *NYHT*, 16 March 1950, p. 21.

Pianist played Bach-Busoni, Mozart, Moussorgsky, Piston, Norman Dello Joio, Prokofieff, and Chopin. She needs "greater attention to tempi and a choice of works well within her technical scope."

G228   "Philippines Violinist, 19, Gives Debut Solo Recital." *NYHT*, Sunday 19 March 1950, sect. 1, p. 46, col. 4.

Gilopez Kabayao is a "gifted" musician with the "eloquent heart" that can "place him among artists." In "a conventional violinist's program" he played virtuoso passages easily so that "style and expressive character became the point of concentration."

G229   "Claude Jean Chiasson." *NYHT*, 20 March 1950, p. 11.

This builder of, and player upon, harpsichords "plays well, with an accurate rhythm and a subtle sense of style." He presented works by Attaignant, Chambonnières, Couperin, Bach, and Arne on an instrument he built in 1948 that "can produce a massive effect of great grandeur."

G230   "Ralph Sheldon, Pianist." Ibid.

His fourth Town Hall recital was "a conventional pianist's program" of Bach, Mozart, Beethoven, and Chopin. His "highly personalized" interpretations overlay "the composer's thought" with "mannerisms and freak dynamic ideas."

G231   "Violinist in Debut." *NYHT*, 24 March 1950, p. 19.

Willard Tressel, twenty-year-old violinist from Detroit, presented "a strenuous program" at Town Hall last night, including Bach, Prokofieff, Beethoven, Wieniawski, and others. Accompanist was Carlo Bussotti, "a pianist of skill, taste and discrimination."

G232   "Syril Mosteau, Soprano." *NYHT*, 27 March 1950, p. 11, col. 6.

In technique and interpretation she "does not appear to be quite up to the high standard set by New York recitalists."

G233   "Karl Harrington, Tenor." *NYHT*, 31 March 1950, p. 19.

Young singer presented works in French, English, and Italian. His voice "is small in volume and in range, though within its circumscribed limits it has a sweet tone and a certain expressivity."

G234   "Philip James Quartet." *NYHT*, 13 April 1950, p. 23, col. 4-5.

NAACC concert "boasted a major first performance, James's Quartet for Piano, Violin, Viola and Cello." Also on the program were pieces by Parks Grant, Marion Bauer, Kent Kennan, Lokrem Johnson, and Daniel Gregory Mason. James has moved from neo-classicism to "a dissonant, angular, chromatic-romantic mood." Rhapsodic forms suit the thematic material. Bauer's Trio Sonata "is an adroit little piece."

G235   "Contralto in Debut. *NYHT*, 24 April 1950, p. 12, col. 4.

Octavia Morris, accompanied by pianist Otto Hertz and lutenist Suzanne Bloch, presented a "tasteful" program of songs of Vivaldi, Dowland, Purcell, Handel, Brahms, Vaughan Williams, Carpenter, Britten and others, and an aria by Massenet. She has beautiful tones in the lower register but uncertain pitch and a lack of rhythm or pulse sense.

(NOVEMBER-DECEMBER 1950)

G236   "Ernest Ulmer Is Heard In Debut Piano Recital." *NYHT*, 17 November 1950, p. 21, col. 1-2.

Young Nebraska pianist performed Beethoven, Schumann, Roy Harris, Fauré, and Ravel with fluency and accuracy but not with a deep understanding of the subtler values in the music. He seemed far more at home with the moderns: Harris's Piano Suite had "vigor, poetry and spontaneity."

G237   "John Charles Thomas." *NYHT*, 18 November 1950, p. 6, col. 5.

Baritone demonstrates "expertness in all phases of the vocalist's art." His choice of pieces shows "no esthetic selectivity" but may be intended to define his own personality. "Like the late George Arliss, the actor, Mr. Thomas presents a vivid depiction, not so much of the idea or character he is portraying, but of himself in the act of portrayal."

G238   "Concert for Children Given by Philharmonic." *NYHT*, Sunday 19 November 1950, sect. 1, p. 75, col. 6.

Igor Buketoff conducted the New York Philharmonic Orchestra in Rossini's *William Tell* Overture, Ravel's *Mother Goose Suite,* and Douglas Moore's "lively and melodious" new children's opera *Puss in Boots,* which "comes off completely and is a really good number to add to the category of sophisticated children's music pieces."

G239   "Composers and Conductors." *NYHT*, 20 November 1950, p. 19, col. 1.

On this NAACC concert the only "signs of life" were *A Song Cycle* (1940) by Ben Weber and Three Pieces for Piano by twenty-year-old Jack Urbont. Works by John Becker, Howard Whittaker, Richard Franko Goldman, and Louis Hamvas, were also performed. Weber "displays his vivid sense of drama against the neutral color of atonalism." Urbont has "a real gift" and fluency.

G240   "Loy van Natter, Baritone." *NYHT*, 21 November 1950, p. 22, col. 5.

Recital included works of Brahms, Schubert, Strauss, Handel, and Scarlatti, and "also a group of American and English composers." The voice is warm and flexible enough when loud, but errratic crescendi and diminuendi seem to result from "incomplete control of breathing."

G241   "Elizabeth Pesce, Soprano." *NYHT*, 25 November 1950, p. 6, col. 4-6.

Recital "of some distinction" included songs in Italian, German, French, and English, and accompanist was Willard Sektberg, "a pianist of taste and skill." This soprano's precision, interpretive control, and diction give pleasure, but her "artistry is greater than her voice."

G242   "Children's Concert: Barzin Conducts First of Series in Carnegie Hall." *NYHT*, Sunday, 26 November 1950, sect. 1, p. 79, col. 2.

With "dispatch and quality" Leon Barzin directed the National Orchestral Association, augmented by orchestral resources from the Chatham Square, Greenwich House, Hempstead High School and Music School Settlement, in pieces by Schubert, Tchaikovsky, and Wagner, plus concerto movements. In spite of gale warnings "a fairly good crowd of juvenile music enthusiasts" attended, with some mamas and papas.

G243 "Theresa Richards." *NYHT*, 27 November 1950, p. 15, col. 3.

Soprano has small but "quite pretty" voice but sings everything "in a gentle mezzo-forte." Songs by Fauré "suited her far better" than pieces by Handel and Torelli and songs of Schubert, and Schumann lacked "the introspective drama that lieder-singing requires."

G244 "Roland Hayes." Ibid, col. 5.

Beautifully balanced recital program showed the artistry of this longtime "subject of critics' eulogies." To a "heavenly" voice is added technical eloquence for a total effect of "delicate intensity."

G245 "Pianist in Debut." Ibid., col. 3-4.

Herbert Stessin performed Brahms, Chopin, and Edmund Haines. He "has a considerable grasp of the larger outlines of music" but lacks "detail, refinement, to add the glow of life inside these dramatic manifestations." He "did better with the more obvious moods of Chopin" than with Brahms, whose inner "meekness" and simplicity within the "rhetorical" outward architecture is often missed by younger players.

G246 "Hanukkah Festival." *NYHT*, 8 Dec 1950, p. 21, col. 4.

Thomas Scherman conducted the Little Orchestra Society in works by Mendelssohn, Beethoven, Bloch, and others, with soprano Regina Resnik and violinist Fredell Lack, at Carnegie Hall. Review is little more than an announcement, about 75 words long.

G247 "American Debut." Ibid., col. 5.

Andre Christiansen, young baritone from Estonia, "sings with authority" and has "warmth and color" particularly in the middle register, but was hampered by an inept accompanist. Review is about 75 words, little more than an announcement.

G248 "Bach Program." *NYHT*, 8 December 1950, p. 21, col. 4.

Third concert of the Bach Festival Series at the Y. M. H. A. Auditorium featured unaccompanied violinist Alexander Schneider. He "is an authoritative performer" and takes "highly personal" but consistent liberties with rhythm, so that "the over-all effect is one of unity."

G249 "Composers' Forum." *NYHT*, 11 December 1950, p. 21, col. 1-2.

Leonard Sarason and Aaron Bodenhorn were featured, S. L. M. Barlow presided as director, and Dr. Carleton Sprague Smith acted as special moderator. Both composers "work in a tonal vein," favor modality, and use dissonance only decoratively. Bodenhorn seemed more original, in a very expressive and unpretentious "neo-archaic manner," while Sarason's music had the "stylistic mannerisms of Hinde-mithian diatonicism" without Hindemith's strengths. Review is longer than usual, over 200 words.

G250   "New Friends." Ibid., col. 2.

Hungarian Quartet played "three fine pieces"--quartets of Haydn and David Diamond and Schubert's Octet Op. 166 (with winds). Review is longer than usual (over 200 words) and more than half is devoted to description of Diamond's style: textures of "partial dissonance" almost throughout, little contrast of consonance or of "sharper dissonance" or of "rhythmic dynamism, and "an incredible melodic grace and a curious but satisfying emotional development. It appears to be one of the newer trends to achieve quiet endings, to pass from the outer world of action to the inner world of being, and the tranquility that comes from that region."

G251   "N. B. C. Symphony." *NYHT*, 12 December 1950, p. 33, col. 6.

"Guido Cantelli conducted a brilliant program" that included new music by Milhaud and Dallapiccola for the second of eight concerts in the series. Dallapiccola has "sloughed off the husk" of Europe's musical cliques and schools of thought "and kept the precious grain from them all"--continuity devices from atonalism, atmospheric collages from impressionism, and formal charting and repose from tonality and consonance. Review is longer than usual, over 200 words.

G252   " 'Manon Lescaut.' " *NYHT*, 16 December 1950, p. 9, col. 4.

Puccini's opera was given at the Metropolitan Opera last night; "Fausto Cleva conducted a smooth performance." Licia Albanese in the title role and Kurt Baum as Des Grieux "gave authoritative performances" while Hugh Thompson, singing his first Metropolitan Lescaut "did not seem quite at home--either the role is "in the less resonant regions of his voice" or he is not yet accustomed to the character.

G253   "Myna Fremont." *NYHT*, 18 December 1950, p. 16.

Coloratura soprano "does not measure up to the New York recital level in her vocal attainments."

G254   " 'Carmen' on TV." Ibid, p. 17, col. 1-2.

Yesterday's version on Station WNBT, N. B. C., was "another effective presentation of the classic" with narrator and "technical rather than original" solutions to the formidable staging and continuity problems.

G255   "Majorcan Chorus." *NYHT*, 20 December 1950, p. 22, col. 5.

The Coro Hispanico de Majorca, thirteen singers conducted by "the extremely self-effacing, but able musician Juan Maria Thomas," includes in its performance "many special effects such as the plucking, pizzicato sounds of guitars, and the booming sound of distant bells." Particularly charming were a work by Manuel de Falla and "some Majorcan songs in the Moorish manner by the conductor."

G256   "Village Opera." *NYHT*, 28 December 1950, p. 15, col. 8.

The five-year-old group presented Humperdinck's *Hansel and Gretel* with "some really excellent singers" and actors, and demonstrated "all round quality and liveliness."

1951: *HERALD TRIBUNE*
(JANUARY-APRIL)

G257   "Cello and Piano." *NYHT*, 6 January 1951, p. 7, col. 4.

Nikolai and Joanna Graudan, performing C. P. E. Bach, Bloch, Beethoven, Schumann, and Chopin, "are clearly exquisite musicians, their work showing a quality in ensemble that is rare indeed in a virtuoso era."

G258   "Virginia Davis Sings. *NYHT*, 8 January 1951, p. 10, col. 7.

Debut recital entitled "Portraits in Song" was of high class "folk" repertoire and demonstrated "her power to 'put across' her material" more than "specifically vocal attainment, though her diction is very good." (*See also* **G171**.)

G259   "Carmen Berendsen, Violinist." Ibid., col. 8.

Young Estonian in New York debut recital "is an outstanding artist and virtuoso" who has concertized widely in Europe. Works of Handel and Bach were followed by sonatas of Brahms and Franck where "the beauty and flow of the melodic line seemed at times almost verbal in its definition and eloquence."

G260   "Keith MacDonald." *NYHT*, 11 January 1951, p. 14, col. 3-4.

Young pianist dealt better with the "glittering mathematical magic" of Bartók's *Out of Doors* suite than with works of Beethoven, Chopin, and Mozart that require handling "the inner world of the heart." He has "a certain musicality" and "considerable technical skill" but lacks spontaneity.

G261   "Budapest Quartet." *NYHT*, 12 January 1951, p. 13, col. 1-2.

Quartets by Mozart, Beethoven, and Piston showed the group's "purity in interpretation" which gave exquisite results in Mozart. For Piston's Third Quartet the players were perhaps inappropriately "anchored within the zone of understatement, and adjusted to the dynamics of classicism rather than to those of modernism."

G262   "Catherine Heaney, Coloratura." *NYHT*, 15 January 1951, p. 7, col. 4.

Assisted by pianist Carroll Hollister and flutist Milton Witgenstein, soprano sang works of Bach, Saint-Saens, Debussy, and others. She has "a real voice" but has "many things to be studied before she is in full possesion of a concert artist's equipment."

G263   "Composer's Forum." Ibid., col. 4-5.

Carl Feurstner and Claus Adam, both expert craftsmen-composers but not artists, were featured composers. Feurstner has "an interesting sense of spacial design" but writes allegros close to the "banal." Adam's Piano Sonata and *Three Songs* showed "a fine sense of form and continuity working behind the dim colors of the twelve-tone row."

G264   "Don Cossack Chorus." *NYHT*, 20 January 1951, p. 6, col. 7-8.

Serge Jaroff conducted the "expert" men's chorus in pieces by Tchaikowsky, Glinka, and other Russians in Carnegie Hall. Precise diction and an immense range of dynamics are among the group's accomplishments, along with bass tones seemingly below the threshold of hearing, and falsetto sounds above the tenors sounding like "sopranos mixed in with men's voices."

G265   "League of Composers." *NYHT*, 22 January 1951, p. 13, col. 2.

Two new works "of fair interest" were a String Quartet by Priaulx Rainier and a Septet for Brass Instruments by Roger Goeb. Rainier's work has a certain "distinction in its thematic materials and in its general musical concept" but is weak in rhythm (as British music so often is). Maxim Schapiro gave a distinguished first performance of Milhaud's new Piano Sonata. Music of Paul Nordoff and Will Hudson was also presented.

G266   "First Performances." *NYHT*, 26 January 1951, p. 12, col. 4-5.

International Society for Contemporary Music presented "first concert" [by U.S. section] with Dallapiccola's *Songs in Captivity*, masterfully scored for two pianos, two harps, and percussion, in first U. S. performance. Varèse's *Ionization* was performed twice, the second time faster and better. Krenek's fourth Piano Sonata has "much sinew and little flesh." *Three Pieces for Clarinet* of Stravinski were given a "discreet, understated interpretation" by Reginald Kell.

G267   "Program of Ballads." *NYHT*, 2 February 1951, p. 13.

Richard Carter, singer, with Gerard Silverman, guitar, presented beautiful English, Scottish, and Irish traditional melodies and American songs. "The singer clearly knows, and loves this music," but "he has no voice" and sings "consistently flat throughout."

G268   "Elliot Magaziner Recital." *NYHT*, 3 February 1951, p. 7.

Young violinist with pianist Leopold Mittman played Mozart and Berezowsky, and, with harpist Abraham Rosen, Saint-Saens' *Fantaisie for Violin and Harp*.

G269   "Composers Forum." *NYHT*, 5 February 1951, p. 11.

Marga Richter and Noel Sokoloff are both young composers "of considerable talent." Sokoloff writes in an idiom "for which there are many fine models"--lyrical, well structured, "well instrumented in a contemporary genre that hovers between impressionism and neo-romanticism." Richter is in danger of "leaning on" formulas or systems, such as "twelvetonism" and thus "submerging" a "more valuable" natural attribute, her "ability to make her own forms grow from the very nature of her materials and ideas" which is "the very essense of composition."

G270   "New Art Quartet." *NYHT*, 7 February 1951, p. 17.

New Art Wood Wind Quartet gave a "brilliantly executed program of music" by Danzi, Milhaud, and August Klughardt (nineteenth century) and first performances of works Ingolf Dahl, and Jean Françaix. Dahl has "vigor" and "a strange, high-spirited humor" and his ideas come from "the nature of wood-wind behavior and wood-wind sound." Françaix "exudes charm" and his "sphere of stylistic reference is metropolitan folklore, Paris brand."

G271   "Barbara Alan Program." *NYHT*, 12 February 1951, p. 12.

Songs in French, Italian, German, and English were presented, with Carroll Hollister, piano accompanist. Singer lacks the "inner intensity" essential to lieder's form and content.

G272 "Festival of Jewish Arts." Ibid.

Chorus of City College and members of the Dance Workshop of the Jewish Theological Seminary presented Jacob Weinberg's oratorio *Isaiah*, a massive piece for chorus, organ, trumpet, and soli. Mary Graham, soprano, provided some moments of "real music." The work contains beautiful melodic elements from "synagogue procedure," with banal, incompatible harmonization and musical setting, full of nineteenth-century mannerism.

G273 "I. S. C. M. Concert." *NYHT*, 12 February 1951, p. 12.

In this program of "music of uncompromising dissonance" Milton Babbitt's *The Widow's Lament in Springtime* was outstanding musically and shows fluent use of atonalism to "utter a poetic thought poetically." The "assorted cacophony"--by Ruggles, Feldman, Wilkinson, Cone, Perle--demonstrated various stages in the history of dissonance.

G274 "Columbia Student Composers." *NYHT*, 15 February 1951, p. 15.

Concert of WNYC American Music Festival, broadcast from MacMillin, featured music of Judith Dvorkin and Donald Keats (the "most gifted" two), and Ezra Laderman, Russell Smith, Walter Blum, Alfred Grant Goodman, Roy Travis, and Julius Epstein.

G275 "Y. M. H. A. Symphony." *NYHT*, 19 February 1951, p. 13.

Maxim Waldo conducted Leon Stein's Symphony No. 2 in E, a powerful "neo-romantic" work, leaning on no "ready-made idioms or 'schools of thought' of modernism." Leon Rudin was soloist in Spencer Hoffman's Violin Concerto No. 2. Hoffman, "too, will find his natural self if he follows the more romantic trends in his expression."

G276 "League of Composers." *NYHT*, 23 February 1951, p. 17.

Program included works of Dello Joio ("Antheil's middle-of-the-road Americana), Thomson, Harris, Mennin, Bergsma ("thought out rather than felt"), Talma (a "rather dehydrated" *Alleluia in Form of Toccata)*, and Moore (diatonic and expressive).

G277 "Columbia Band Concert." *NYHT*, 26 February 1951, p. 10.

Works of Riegger (good), Holst (best), and others were performed, including a prize-winning *Brass Octet* by Edgar J. Moore which was devoid of ideas.

G278 "Eugene Fedele, Tenor." *NYHT*, 5 March 1951, p. 11.

Recital accompanied by pianist Felix Van Dyck showed singer "at home" only in the Italian language. In English his pronunciation and singing are not good and he is not at home in German.

G279 "Composers Forum." *NYHT*, 12 March 1951, p. 14, col. 7.

William T. Ames and Herman Berlinski were featured composers, neither of them "very high in musical nourishment value: but at the same time both "independent of the ready made modern schools, neo-classicism and atonalism, each being in essence tonal." Review is average length (200 words) instead of the usual longer size of Composers Forum reviews, 300-400 words.

G280   "Clyde Ellzey, Pianist." *NYHT*, 16 March 1951, p. 19.

Young pianist from Mississippi made his New York debut playing Haydn, Schubert, Moussorgsky, Debussy, Brahms, and Kurt George Roger (first performance of two dances). He is "careful and intelligent" in his playing but is not "spontaneous" in approach; "one missed throughout the poetic nature and its ability to perceive and express nuance."

G281   "The New Music Quartet." *NYHT*, 19 March 1951, p. 13-14, col. 6-7.

Quartet performed works of Hindemith and Casella (both 1920) and Dane Rudhyar's *Tetragram* (1927), representing the "high points hit by composers in three different veins" in the early twentieth century--late romanticism, neo-classicism, and chromatic impressionism, respectively. Rudhyar's work, however, in its first performance, gives a "very different" message from impressionists like Debussy.

G282   "Una Hadley, Pianist." Ibid, col. 7.

Debut recital of a "gifted and musical young pianist of considerable distinction" included works of Bach, Scarlatti, Galuppi, Chopin, Rachmaninoff, Dohnanyi, Griffes, and others. She is "not yet quite secure" technically but has "a joyous and effortless sense of rhythm, with a fine command of tone."

G283   "Richard Korn Concert." *NYHT*, 22 March 1951, p. 22.

Korn conducted an orchestral concert at the City College of New York that included Honegger's *Serenade à Angélique* and works of Arne, Wagner, Ravel, and Charles Martin Loeffler. The singing of Martha Lipton in Loeffler's "highly perfumed" *Canticle of the Sun* was the outstanding feature of the concert.

G284   "Workmen's Circle Chorus." *NYHT*, 26 March 1951, p. 13, col. 3-4.

Lazar Weiner conducted the chorus, with soloists and members of the N. B. C. orchestra. First the Workmen's Circle Hymn was "robustly sung by the entire multitude." Several works not from the "standard repertoire" used unsuitable "diatonicism of the nineteenth century" to set "ancient Jewish music." Composers need to find an idiom and construction method that "stems directly" from the "beautiful, pastoral, instrospective elements" of their ancient material.

G285   "Frantz Opera." *NYHT*, 30 March 1951, p. 15.

Ravel's *L'Heure Espagnole* and Charles Wakefield Cadman's *A Witch of Salem* were given with piano accompaniment by the Frantz Opera Players. Some good voices and acting sustained "flow and interest."

G286   "New Music Quartet." *NYHT*, 2 April 1951, p. 14, col. 7.

Group's performances of "uncompromisingly modern" quartets of Berg (1910), Riegger (1948), and Cage (1950) as usual "penetrated to the very heart of the manner." Berg is romantic though dissonant, while Riegger is no more dissonant yet has the "expressive substance" of "our time." Cage's first Quartet is "exquisitely personal" and "opens up a new phase" in his development--composition for strings that, unlike the prepared piano, have sustaining and crescendo powers.

G287   "George Fiore." Ibid., col. 8.

Pianist played sonatas of Scarlatti and works of Mozart, Mendelssohn, Weber, Chopin, Debussy, and Smetana. Though he has frequent flashes of "real musicality," he lacks taste and judgment in phrasing, pedalling, and volume--he has an ear but no heart.

G288   "Hood College Choir." *NYHT*, 3 April 1951, p. 21.

Earle Blakeslee directed this women's chorus in "a batch of choral pieces" by Leo Sowerby, Richard Winslow, Normand Lockwood, Virgil Thomson, Irving Fine, Bartók, Hindemith, and others. Thomson's *Medea* choruses show his "tremendous gift for word values, syllables achieving "their natural declamatory dynamic and rhythm" in a "neutral, impersonal musical idiom."

G289   "Program of Sonatas." *NYHT*, 9 April 1951, p. 15, col. 5-6.

Lillian Freundlich, pianist, performed sonatas of Scarlatti, Schubert, and Ernst Bloch (1935), and works of Beethoven, Brahms, and Miriam Gideon. She has an "authoritative" approach, sensitive touch, and strong and agile hands, but lacks "poetic power." Gideon's *Piano Suite No. 3* (1951) is "expert in craftsmanship" but, using the technique of "atonal chromaticism" which "does not lend itself too easily to architectural or emotional differentiation," it "seemed lacking in color or form."

G290   " 'Pinafore' at Hunter." Ibid., col. 6.

Tom Scherman directed a "cleverly abridged version of the Gilbert and Sullivan opera" at Hunter College Stage. Members of the Little Orchestra Society in English sailor hats played orchestral accompaniments and added "choral comments."

G291   "Pianist, 17, in Recital." *NYHT*, 12 April 1951, p. 25.

Herbert Holinko, performing at the Kosciusko Foundation, was not up to the New York recitalist level.

G292   "Columbia Glee Club." *NYHT*, 13 April 1951, p. 15.

Carl A. Lambert conducted these boys in variously named smaller and larger groups, performing Renaissaince music by Gibbons, di Lasso, and Samuel Webb, works of Bartók, Vaughan Williams, and Grieg, and some "close harmony numbers."

G293   "Robert Falk at Town Hall." *NYHT*, 14 April 1951, p. 8.

Singer is best in the bass range, but sometimes lacks intensity. John Duke accompanied at the piano for his own song cycle *Five Poems by Vincent McHugh* and Leo Taubmen was pianist for the rest of the recital--music of Brahms, Vera Eakin, Celius Dougherty, and Wolf.

G294   "Contemporary Belgian Music." *NYHT*, 23 April 1951, p. 13, col. 1-2.

Most musical were the songs *Mere* by Flor Peeters, on this New York Public Library program. Raymond Chevreuille--"by far the most distinguished composer of Belgium today"--was represented along with Jongen, Souris, and Poot.

G295 "Louise Hodge Bills." *NYHT*, 28 April 1951, p. 6, col. 7.

Violinist's recital was in aid of Food Relief for India and included works of Lalo, Bach, Handel, and others. She "has a truly beautiful tone" and accurate intonation and "many of the qualities that go to make a first-rate virtuoso."

G296 "Harpsichordist." *NYHT*, 30 April 1951.

Elizabeth Lang, not previously heard in New York, played works by Bach, Scarlatti, Bartok, and Rameau. Though touch and tone "are supposedly unvariable" on the instrument, she brought variety and "light and shade" to the music in this "notably fine" recital.

(OCTOBER-DECEMBER 1951)

G297 "NBC TV Opera Theater." *NYHT*, 6 October 1951, p. 8, col. 4.

Production of *Pagliacci* by Leoncavallo on WNBT channel 4, the first opera of the third season, was in English with cuts and adjustments to camera technique.

G298 "Janice Mitchell, Soprano." *NYHT*, 8 October 1951, p. 10, col. 3.

Young soprano in debut recital performed pieces by Handel, Verdi, Wolf, and Saint-Saens, and some pieces in English (by Bax, Delius, Duke, Malaby). Like many other singers she chose, instead of "real songs" in English, some "ballad-type clap trap." Her voice is pure and well trained but she lacks "innate sense of the music she sings."

G299 "Young Violinist in Debut." *NYHT*, 15 October 1951, p. 15, col. 1.

Ten-and-a-half year old Charles Castleman is "a born violinist and a sensitive musician." One fears exploitation, however, in the difficult transition from prodigy to mature virtuoso.

G300 "Juilliard Quartet." *NYHT*, 16 October 1951, p. 17, col. 1.

First in a series of Mozart recitals featured the quartets in E-flat major, A major, and C major.

G301 "Recital at Library." *NYHT*, 22 October 1951, p. 11, col. 5.

Lonny Epstein played Mozart, Haydn, and Clementi at the New York Public Library on a replica of Mozart's own piano by the famous Anton Walter.

G302 "Wheeler Beckett Orchestra." *NYHT*, 25 October 1951, p. 21, col. 8.

Children's concert in Carnegie Hall under the auspices of the New York Youth Concert Association featured works of Beethoven, Mozart, Grieg, Beckett's own *Cinderella Fantasy,* and *The Tales from the Vienna Woods* by "the earlier of the Strauss boys."

G303   "Victoria Rebollo." *NYHT*, 27 October 1951, p. 9, col. 6.

Soprano's debut recital in Carnegie Recital Hall featured songs in English, French, Spanish, and Italian. Ann Chenee was the "able accompanist" on the piano.

G304   "A New Pinkerton." *NYHT*, 29 October 1951, p. 13, col. 1.

Wesley Dalton, young lyric tenor, made a promising debut in *Madame Butterfly*.

G305   "Pianist, 14, in Debut." Ibid., col. 1-2.

Jaques Voois made his New York debut as a soloist at Carnegie Recital Hall.

G306   "Works by Lazare Saminsky." *NYHT*, 30 October 1951, p. 19, col. 7-8.

Saminsky "is a kind of brightly colored musical chameleon" in his evoking of a "period style or manner," his use of "straight" traditional tunes, and, "when he was doing neither of these things," his "Scriabo-Straussian chromaticism."

G307   "Brooklyn Academy." *NYHT*, 31 October 1951, p. 14, col. 7-8.

Victoria de los Angeles presented the first recital in the Major Concert Series, singing Monteverdi, Scarlatti, Handel, Schumann, Gounod, Ravel, and Fauré. In a "strange interpretation" Schumann's "Ich grolle nicht" was performed as a recitative and aria, with pianissimo sections and more dramatic ones.

G308   "All-Bach Recital." *NYHT*, 1 November 1951, p. 24, col. 1-2.

Pianist Rosalyn Tureck at the Y. M. H. A. Hall last night is a "sheer joy to listen to." Tureck's temperament and Bach's austerity make a "unique emotional-mental fusion" that is near the "heart of the matter with Bach."

G309   "Iturbis at Carnegie Hall." *NYHT*, 3 November 1951, p. 7, col. 6..

Amparo and her brother Jose performed Mozart, Debussy, Milhaud's *Scaramouche*, Gershwin's *Rhapsody in Blue*, and "some lively-sounding South Americans" (whom she names).

G310   "Composers Program." *NYHT*, 5 November 1951, p. 13, col. 3-8 (top) and p. 15, col. 1.

NAACC in first concert of season presented works of Bernard Heiden (a sonata whose "papa" is Hindemith and grand-papa Brahms), Charles Griffes, Sol. Berkowitz, André Singer, and Jack Beeson--"the most musical and imaginative talent."

G311   "Laurel Harley Sings." *NYHT*, 7 November 1951, p. 22, col. 6.

Debut at Town Hall was accompanied by Sergius Kagen, a "musician and pianist of distinction."

G312   "Frieda Hempel in Recital." *NYHT*, 8 November 1951, p. 17, col. 3-4.

Long famous and justly famous soprano sang Strattner, Handel, Scarlatti, Bach, and Lieder by Saint-Saens and Brahms at Town Hall for an enthusiastic audience. The voice has lost some of its "roundness" but the artistry is "thoroughly intact."

G313   "Yvonne Chalfonte." *NYHT,* 12 November 1951, p. 15, col. 3.

French lyric soprano presented a "curious" recitation-recital at Carnegie Hall Saturday night.

G314   "Christos Vrionides." Ibid.

Vrionides, conductor at the Greek Cathedral in Brooklyn, directed his "Byzantine singers" at Carnegie Recital Hall in his own and others' music, modern and ancient. His own compositions are in an "ancient, pure and powerful" traditional idiom.

G315   "Merces Silva-Telles, Pianist." *NYHT,* 13 November 1951, p. 19, col. 3-4.

Young Brazilian pianist at Town Hall recital is a brilliant pianist and an "erratic musician" who depends more on natural aptitude than on study and discipline.

G316   "Maria Montino." *NYHT,* 17 November 1951, p. 6, col. 6.

Dramatic soprano has a large and lovely voice and is a "really impressive young singer." New York debut at Town Hall featured Mozart, Schubert, Fauré, Debussy, and Grieg sung in Norwegian.

G317   "Margaret Quist." *NYHT,* 19 November 1951, p. 13, col. 4.

Singer at Carl Fischer Hall Saturday night has the dark-colored voice of a "real contralto." Piano accompanist was Albert Wiggins and she sang two of his songs. In stricter, more demanding Lieder of Wolf, Mahler, and Strauss she did not quite possess "the training and vocal discipline required."

G318   "Walter Hautzig." *NYHT,* 22 November 1951, p. 31, col. 7.

The "able pianist and responsible musician" heard at the Y. M. H. A. Auditorium was good on Brahms and Handel but not so good on Poulenc.

G319   "Isabel Chatfield, Soprano." *NYHT,* 24 November 1951, p. 10, col. 4.

With George Reeves, accompanist, she presented a taxing program, some of it "beyond her powers, though no doubt she may at an earlier period in her career have sung it beautifully."

G320   "Composers Forum." NYHT, 26 November 1951, p. 13, col. 3-4.

Featured composers were Theodore Strongin and Jack Beeson, and Virgil Thomson was moderator. In his songs and chamber pieces Strongin uses "small moving detail" to sustain a "meditative, almost static emotional continuum." Beeson's music has "considerably more dynamic punch." Like "all young composers" he has fun using plenty of dissonance--for accent and color "and, one suspects, just a little for its own sake" as in a "wrong-note-cult march" that ends his fifth Piano Sonata.

G321   "Herman Arminsky." Ibid., col. 6-7.

Pianoforte recitalist at Town Hall yesterday has a good general idea of Beethoven and Brahms but does not "meet expert concert standards."

G322   "Anna Russell" NYHT, 28 November 1951, p. 21, col. 5.

A capacity audience at Town Hall "rocked and shouted with laughter." Only "tremendously thorough musical training in all directions can make humour of this calibre."

G323   "Ray Lev." *NYHT*, 1 December 1951, p. 6, col. 4-5.

On a formidable program, this "lady of the piano" performed five new works for "enthusiasts in large numbers" at Carnegie Hall. She has "reformed" her "tendency to bang" but there are still inaccuracies--though her "technical prowess" is often impressive. A Suite by Herman Berlinski supposedly uses Hindu rhythms but its metrical pulses are the antithesis of "never-the-same-way-twice" Hindu "metre."

G324   "Mort Freeman." *NYHT*, Sunday, 2 December 1951, sect. 1, p. 87, col. 3.

Recital of folk songs and music evolved around folk material at Town Hall Saturday night showed singer at his best in Yiddish and Israeli pieces and with Bartok's *Three Hungarian Folk Songs*. Yiddish songs had inappropriate accompaniments with "nineteenth-century harmonic clichés"--it is "hard to find good accompaniments"--but the Songs of New Israel had superior accompaniments.

G325   "New Friends." *NYHT*, 3 December 1951, p. 14, col. 4.

Singer Erna Berger, last-minute substitute for the ill Claudio Arrau, presented a beautiful recital in Town Hall Sunday afternoon.

G326   "Eldin Burton." *NYHT*, 4 December 1951, p. 23, col. 6.

As a composer, Burton has "no esthetic stability" but uses a mixture of idioms "from Wagner, through Debussy to Eric Coates and Chaminade." Review of average length (about 130 words) names the performers, including Burton as pianist.

G327   "Joyce Flissler, Violinist." *NYHT*, 5 December 1951, p. 22, col. 8.

With David Garvey at piano, a "superb recital" shows that this Naumberg Award winner upholds the standards set by previous winners.

G328   "New Folk Singers." *NYHT*, 10 December 1951, p. 20, col. 6.

Balladeers--the new team of Marais and Miranda--at Town Hall Sunday night have lots of folk pieces of South African, African Bantu, and Flemish origin "fresh" to the ears of New Yorkers. Marais who also plays guitar provides "esthetically pleasing" arrangements. Miranda's "cute" style suggests that the concert hall is beoming "geared" toward T. V. as the New York theatre became geared toward Hollywood.

G329   "Ilona Kabos, Pianist." *NYHT*, 15 December 1951, p. 7, col. 5.

Town Hall recital was "in the grand manner as known in Europe" rather than in the spectacular "electric" style of Americans, and gives the effect of "maturity, responsibility and stability." Kabos has insight and "very commanding technical attainment."

G330   "Nicki Galpeer, Soprano." *NYHT*, 17 December 1951, p. 14, col. 5-6.

Town Hall recital, with pianist Arpad Sandor, featured German, French, and American songs and some by Latin-Americans (Mignone, Ginastera, and Guarnieri). Singer has a good voice, "well-trained," but she tends to cut up phrases.

G331   "Mount Holyoke Glee Club." *NYHT*, 19 December 1951, p. 22, col. 5.

A "distinguished program" of Christmas pieces in Town Hall, in aid of the scholarship fund of the Mount Holyoke Club of New York, featured a large choir of "excellently disciplined" voices and was "highly enjoyable."

1952

G332   Liner notes for *Zabaleta--Anthology of Solo Harp Music*, vol. 1: "XVI Century Spanish Masters; Contemporary French and Spanish." Esoteric ES 509 (1952). Twelve-inch 33 1/3 rpm disc. Nicanor Zabaleta, harp.

All pieces on this disk were written expressly for harp. Earlier music (by Mudarra, Narvaez, Cabezon) has "organic strength and design" and "denotes a high culture in art music at a very early period in Spain." Contemporary pieces by Spaniards (Pittaluga, Halffter) and two French composers deliberately writing in the Spanish genre (Caplet, Tournier) also have organic strength, and "national" style without trite, superficial "nationalism." Zabaleta displays "taste, judgement and power" in his playing and scholarship alike.

G333   "The Composers' Forum." *American Composers Alliance Bulletin* 2, no. 2 (1952), p. 6-7.

Miss Jean Tennyson's generous three-year grant beginning Fall 1951 has revived the Composers' Forum, founded by Ashley Pettis and now one of New York's oldest-- and liveliest--composers' organizations. Other financial assistance continues from Columbia University (an annual grant from the Alice M. Ditson Fund and use of McMillin Theatre) and the New York Public Library (office and secretarial facilities, through music director Carleton Sprague Smith). Now composers and performers can be paid a fee, composers outside New York are included, and sessions are tape recorded for broadcast. An active "reading committee" searches out the "young, talented, and untried."

1952, CONTINUED: *HERALD TRIBUNE* (JANUARY-APRIL)

G334   "David Tudor, Pianist, at Cherry Lane Theater." *NYHT*, Wednesday, 2 January 1952, p. 15, col. 1.

Works of four "intrepid explorers in the aural stratosphere" were presented: Boulez's Second Piano Sonata, Cage's *Music of Changes*, prepared piano pieces by

Christian Wolff, and *Intersection No. 2* for ordinary piano by Morton Feldman. Wolff and Feldman expound "complex metrical and spatial theories." Cage's scores create "the real impression of real poetry." Boulez is one of the "deadly deliberate" European "dissonanteers" who lack the American "joie de vivre" to transcend unrelenting dissonance. Review of Boulez is quoted by Peyser, **B304**.

G335   " 'Pique Dame': Tchaikovsky Opera Presented by N. B. C. Television." *NYHT*, 4 January 1952, p. 15, col. 1.

The Queen of Spades was broadcast at 11 o'clock last night (Thursday) with "adroit" cutting and a narrator. Much of the opera is in recitative style, there are few "real vocal opportunities, " and the libretto is of "poor literary quality."

G336   "Paul Bellam." *NYHT*, Monday, 7 January 1952, p. 16, col. 2-3.

Young violinist has an "unusually beautiful tone" but lacks "real potency." He was joined by Arpad Sandor, pianist, and Joseph Tekuda, cellist.

G337   "Clarinet Concerto." *NYHT*, 9 January 1952, p. 15, col. 3-5.

Herbert Tichman, clarinetist, and Ruth Budnevish, pianist, in a joint recital, with George Kutzen, cellist, featured a "big piece," the New York premiere of Hindemith's Concerto for Clarinet. It is a "constructed" work with no thematic ideas. In her solos the pianist had technique but "lacks a sense of musical continuity."

G338   "Pianist in Debut." *NYHT*, 10 January 1952, p. 17, col. 3.

Guy Lasson, young French pianist, is very musical in the romantic manner, with "stable expressive depth," but lacks "the technical streamlining that abounds among young Americans."

G339   "Richard Farrell, Pianist, Gives a Town Hall Recital." *NYHT*, Sunday 13 January 1952, sect. 1, p. 55, col. 1.

Young New Zealand pianist is conscientious, introspective, and understated "in comparison to the general style of New York performances." He lacks dramatization and needs "greater attention to these projection factors."

G340   "American Composers." *NYHT*, 14 January 1952, p. 12, col. 5-6.

Third NAACC concert of season included Luening's Cello Sonata, Harold Tripps' Piano Sonata performed by Vera Brodsky, and works of David Van Vactor, Henry Holden Huss, and Joseph Goodman. The only music of "special interest" was that of Goodman ("neo-classic") and Luening (an "original" esthetic and tonal blend).

G341   " 'Freischuetz' " *NYHT*, 19 January 1952, p. 9, col. 4.

Performance of von Weber opera in English at Cooper Union without orchestra and scenery was rather colorless. "The full house did hear, however, some good singing."

G342   "Kailasam Recital: Young Hindu Woman Violinist Is Heard at Town Hall." *NYHT*, Sunday 20 January 1952, sect. 1, p. 51, col. 2-3.

Olive Kailasam, billed as "prodigy Hindu violinist" played Paganini and other "Occidental repertoire" with the timbre and pitch effect of a Hindu instrumental ensemble.

G343   "Hack Driver in Recital." *NYHT*, 21 January 1952, p. 11, col. 2.

Barkev Vartanyan, baritone, sang to a full house in Carnegie Recital Hall. He has a magnificent natural voice and "a real musicality," but much needs to be done to discipline these assets "into the sophisticated category."

G344   "Kirkpatrick on Harpsichord." *NYHT*, 23 January 1952, p. 19, col. 4.

A lovely program by Ralph Kirkpatrick at Town Hall showed "Baroque grandeur, miniature in volume." He played Bach and Scarlatti, plus Mozart on a Challis reproduction of "the Mozart piano."

G345   "Town Hall Recital." *NYHT*, 24 January 1952, p. 16, col. 5.

Esther Fernandez, pianist, and Richard Sharetts, bass-baritone, winners of the Town Hall Award, are both "real winners" in every sense. The pianist was not adequate to make works of Brahms "duos, for matched artistry." As a soloist, her performance of Brahms lacked tenderness and "the more poetic qualities, though she was better on Bach and Beethoven. Sharetts also sang works of Arne, Cavalli, and Bach.

G346   "Myra Hess at Carnegie Hall." *NYHT*, Sunday 27 January 1952, sect. 1, p. 16, col. 2.

A lovely program revealed the pianist's greatness. Brahms's F minor Sonata was the high point for "this writer," where Hess moved from knowledge of music as a language, to wisdom, and to its inner essence.

G347   "Prandelli and Valentino Sing New Roles in 'Manon.' " *NYHT*, 28 January 1952, p. 10, col. 6.

Frank Valentino was only moderately convincing as Manon's cousin, and Prandelli sang beautifully, in Saturday night's performance at the Met.

G348   "Nelly Peerine, Coloratura." *NYHT*, 28 January 1952, p. 11, col. 7-8.

Billed as a coloratura soprano, she has the coloratura--very high notes, bright and clear--without the soprano part, the lower voice. With pianist George Reeves and flutist Samuel Baron the three gave a "lively" performance of Paul Creston's *Dance Variations*.

G349   "Lily Pons in Recital." *NYHT*, 31 January 1952, p. 15, col. 1.

The audience packed Carnegie Hall to hear "the most stupendous cellophane-wrapped product" in the "coloratura line." She has great virtuosity, shown in repertoire like the "Bell Song" of Delibes, but maybe lacks subtlety of color and feeling in the middle register. As Virgil Thomson said of "Heifetz' similar glossy virtuosity--'one might as well expect tenderness from an ocelot.' "

G350   "Helen Lightner Recital." *NYHT*, 1 February 1952, p. 13, col. 5.

Third Town Hall recital featured distinguished repertoire--Bach and Lully opera excerpts, Mahler, Joaquin Nin, Ginastera, Obradors, and others. Berg's *Vier Lieder, Op. 2*, and *Die Nachtigall* were "good to hear." Dello Joio's *Cycle of Love Songs--*music "from our countryside"--in New York premiere performance was "unrewarding" due to "inept" prosody and lack of unity between words and melody. Singer is good, with a personal style, although a wide and slow vibrato obscures the pitch

G351   "Records: Some New LPs." *NYHT*, Sunday 3 February 1952, sect. 4, p. 9, col. 1-2.

In her second Sunday column with a byline "P. Glanville-Hicks" (the others are G74 and G444) she describes music of four composers: Cowell's "inimitable" perform-ances of his own piano music (Circle Records), music of Villa-Lobos (Columbia) and Bohuslav Martinu (Urania), and Bartók's *Music for Strings, Celesta and Percussion* Columbia).

G352   "New Friends." *NYHT*, 4 February 1952, col. 4.

Hungarian String Quartet at New Friends of Music concert performed two Beethoven quartets and one by Walter Piston. Group is "impeccable" in technique and interpretation, but lacks "real volume and tone," pulsation and depth. Piston is "a real master" among American composers in his integration of "personal and abstract" musical elements--classic architecture and romantic lyricism.

G353   "Brana Fredericks." Ibid., col. 4-5.

Sixteen-year-old coloratura soprano "displayed remarkable accuracy, pose and musicality." The voice is not beautiful but her "youthful zest" is touching and there is "quite a lively intelligence" behind her interpretations.

G354   "Pianist From Berlin." Ibid., col. 5.

Lily Dumont, who performed Bach, Mozart, and Chopin in her New York debut, "should surely be heard again" for her "lucid and poetic readings."

G355   "William Dorn Debut." *NYHT*, 6 February 1952, p. 15, col. 4-5.

Young pianist, native of Missouri, in New York debut at Town Hall last night was "not very illuminating" but was forceful and fast.

G356   "Margaret Rederer Recital." *NYHT*, 9 February 1952, p. 7, col. 5.

Pianist performed Bach, Beethoven, Schubert, and Bartok. She has technique but is prosaic and lacks nuance and emotion.

G357   "Bernac and Poulenc." *NYHT*, 11 February 1952, p. 13, col. 3.

Pierre Bernac, baritone, sang to a packed house with composer Francis Poulenc as "partner artist at the piano." Songs by Ravel, Poulenc, Duparc, and Mompou were heard, as well as Barber's new "truly beautiful" cycle *Mélodies Passagères*, dedicated to these performers.

G358   "Jan Oines, Tenor." Ibid., col. 4.

Young Norwegian performed songs by composers of Norway, Ragnar Althen, Hugo Alfven, and Grieg, as well as pieces by Richard Strauss, Brahms, Schubert, Wagner, de Falla, Mascagni, and others. He "is clearly a fine musician" but "the music did not flow"--it was "dragging" and gave a "feeling of monotony."

G359   "Music Festival." *NYHT,* 14 February 1952, p. 15, col. 7-8.

Under this heading are two reviews of broadcast American Music Festival concerts. A concert from the Third Street Music School Settlement offered works of five faculty members and *Farewell to a Hero* by George Kleinsinger, a "big flashy piece for solo chorus and orchestra" that was good for the occasion but might not "make the grade into more sophisticated, more fastidious musical circles." The other concert, from the New York Public Library, offered works by Theodore Strongin and John Tasker Howard, who also acted as moderator. Strongin's *Quintet for Oboe and Strings* is "delicate" and "Mediterranean in style rather than hailing from any of the heavily promoted modern schools of thought."

G360   "Puccini on TV." *NYHT,* 15 February 1952, p. 13, col. 4

Il Tabarro (The Cloak) on N. B. C. "was perhaps the most successful yet of the Televsion Opera performances"--a "tight little story," a wonderfully "melodious" score, very fine singing and acting, and good direction under Peter Herman Adler.

G361   "Met Presents 'Carmen': 2 Sing Roles First Time." *NYHT,* 19 February 1952, p. 17, col. 5.

Mario del Monaco as Don Jose in Bizet's opera was "very much on the stiff side" and sometimes off pitch, though he has a good voice. Norman Scott as Zuniga seemed suitably "efficient without being distinguished." Rise Stevens, continuing as Carmen, "seems weakest tonally" in the general range of this particular role.

G362   "Giovanni Bagarotti, Violinist." *NYHT,* 21 February 1952, p. 14, col. 1-2.

Third recital of "less frequently performed pieces" presented three more Mozart violin concerti, part of Bagarotti's efforts to extend New York concert offerings beyond the "all too familiar" solo viruoso repertory.

G363   "Air Force Band at Carnegie." Ibid., col. 2.

United States Air Force Symphony Orchestra and Band played a "popular-style concert" as part of the WNYC American Music Festival. The conductor, Col. George S. Howard, channels "the youthful high spirits of the boys" into a disciplined form. Guest conductor Herman Neuman directed George Antheil's breezy *McKonkey's Ferry.*

G364   "Suzanne Bloch." *NYHT,* 25 February 1952, p. 11, col. 1.

Singer and keyboard performer, assisted by ten performers, presented music of the Renaissance (lute songs, music for virginals and recorders) and Baroque (a Trio Sonata by Quantz). Her voice lacks "legato or continuous sound between the words" and has no projection, but she is "expert" upon the virginals.

G365   "Weill Memorial." Ibid.

Kurt Weill Memorial Concert featured a "colorful galaxy of singers" giving "excellent" performances of songs and excerpts from Weill's works of the Berlin, Paris, and New York periods. Broadway's "techniques are often ten years ahead of the times" and its "esthetic is invariably fifteen years behind." The "young" can learn "the trade" from Weill, "one of the great craftsmen of theater music," if they can replace his "zombie content."

G366   "Lea Bach, Harpist." *NYHT*, 26 February 1952, p. 22, col. 7.

Spanish-born harpist played solo works and arrangements of Granados, Mompou, Albeniz, Mozart, Bach, Beethoven, and others. A general "lack of precision" was evident, and the performer's failure to damp one harmony before passing to another resulted in "a blur of overhung misplaced resonance."

G367   "Shirley Trepel." *NYHT*, 28 February 1952, p. 13, col. 8.

Cellist's recital featured works of Grieg, Bach, Jean Baptiste Breval, Schumann, Martinu, and Paradis. She has a "pretty tone" but has technical problems. Accompanist Carlo Bussotti brought to the Grieg Sonata "tension, formal control, and the sense of romantic excitement."

G368   "Segovia and Guitar." *NYHT*, 3 March 1952, p. 12, col. 6-7.

The "incredible" guitarist gave one of his "rare" recitals, performing Handel, Bach, Granados, and Albeniz, and first performances in New York of works of Villa Lobos ("colorful and exotic") and Paganini ("out of place esthetically speaking"). "His is an unbelievable combination of technique and temperament."

G369   "League of Composers." *NYHT*, 4 March 1952, p. 14, col. 6.

Valley Music Press sponsored concert representing eight composers--Imbrie, Finney, Donovan, Ellwell, Duke, Porter, Weigel, and Etler. John Duke's *White in the Moon* and *Twentieth Century* were outstanding among the songs and in fact "the most subtle music" programmed. Quincey Porter's *Suite for Viola Alone* received a "ladylike rendering" but adds to the "all-too-slim" viola repertory.

G370   "Joint Recital." *NYHT*, 6 March 1952, p. 18, col. 6-7.

Mexican singer Nestor Chayres, performing with costumed dancers and two pianists, has a "remarkable voice" that is "at once simple and wild." Accompanist Federico Kramer was "stable, varied and mature" while Emilio Osta played as though the piano keys were "red hot."

G371   "Art Music Concerts." *NYHT*, 12 March 1952, p. 19.

Beatrice Brown conducted Mozart, Bach, and Haydn--lovely and musicianly per-formances of "music of neatness and eloquence." Works of Bartok and Prokofiev provided the contemporary touch.

G372   "N. Y. Operatic Society." *NYHT*, 15 March 1952, p. 6, col. 1.

Bizet's *Carmen* in concert performance with costumes but no scenery was conducted by Dr. Theodore Feinmann. Joyce Jones as Carmen had a pretty voice in middle range but lacked fire as an actor. Nino Luciano as Don Jose is a very good singer with "arresting" stage presence and "brought the only spontaneity and vividness that the production evidenced."

G373   "Young People's Concert." Ibid., col. 1-2.

Igor Buketoff conducted vivid "post-romantic music" including Strauss' *Till Eulenspiegel* and an orchestration of Bartok's *Jack in the Box* from the *Mikrokosmos*. Perhaps program music, "accurate pictorial impression," is what these modern dissonant, romantic-impressionist idioms "do best."

G374   "Composers Forum." *NYHT*, 17 March 1952, p. 14.

Two "highly dissonant composers," Morton Feldman and Erick Itor Kahn, brought "a large crowd of avant-gardists" to McMillin Theater Saturday night. Douglas Moore was moderator. Both composers stem from the Vienna tradition, Kahn's music being atonal like Schoenberg's and Feldman's fragmented and pointillistic like Webern's. Players included pianists David Tudor and Beveridge Webster, violinist Matthew Raimondi, and soprano Uta Graf.

G375   "Mozart Orchestra." Ibid.

Robert Goldsand was "impeccable" soloist in Mozart's Piano Concerto No. 12 in A major. Robert Scholz also conducted The Mozart Orchestra in works of Haydn's Symphony No. 35 in B-flat and Albert Roussel's Sinfonietta for String Orchestra, Op. 52, "an entertaining little work which hovers somewhere between romantic impressionism and neoclassicism."

G376   "Mae Williams." *NYHT*, 18 March 1952, p. 16, col. 5-6.

Mezzo-soprano at Carnegie Hall last night sang Bach, Villa Lobos, William Grant Still, Erick J. Wolff, and several Negro Spirituals. She has a "beautiful voice, especially in its middle register and darker colors," and good control, but "not very much sense of rhythm" or inner pulse--even in the Spirituals--and she needs "a bit more abandon" as well.

G377   "City Center Opera: 'La Traviata.' " *NYHT*, 24 March 1952, p. 12, col. 6.

Saturday night's "smooth and able" performance of Verdi's opera was conducted by Frank P. Martin and featured Eva Likova as an "extraordinarily convincing" Violetta, the "disciplined and reliable" Rudolf Petrak as Alfredo, and Richard Bonelli, an expert singer and suave actor, as Giorgio Germont.

G378   "Vadim Hrenoff." Ibid., p. 13, col. 5.

Pianist performed works of Handel, Beethoven, Bartok, Schumann, Debussy, Granados, Shostakovich, and Chopin and Aaron Copland's *Passacaglia*. He was "not really up to the recital level we have come to expect in New York," although he has strength and volume and "a degree of poetry in his tonal choices."

G379   "Pianist in Recital. *NYHT*, 1 April 1952, p. 20, col. 4.

Ivan Malinoff performed Bach-Busoni, Liszt, Chopin, and Albeniz. He was musically and technically limited, "quite unequipped for his task."

G380   "Soprano and Tenor." *NYHT*, 2 April 1952, p. 22, col. 2.

Jean Bradley, soprano, and Thomas Belbas, tenor, two fine young singing talents, performed solo groups and pieces in duet. Belbas, in some Italian pieces and a group of Brahms songs, was a pleasure to listen to, though the voice is not developed to his capacity as Bradley's is.

G381 "Felice Takakjian, Pianist." *NYHT*, 7 April 1952, p. 13, col. 1-2.

Debut recital of "a really excellent pianist" featured works of Bach-Liszt, Aram Khachaturian (*Valse Caprice and Dance*, an empty little piece), Hovhaness (the well knit, joyous *Farewell to the Mountains*), Servaniziantz (Middle Eastern flavor and stylization, not from inner spirit) and Beethoven--her most impressive playing.

G382 "Young People's Concert." *NYHT*, Sunday, 13 April 1952, sect. 1, p. 36, col. 5.

Igor Buketoff conducted contemporary pieces at Carnegie Hall yesterday morning, including a prize-winning--and well-written--fantasia for violin and piano by teen-age Ralph John Jacko, well played by Michael Rabin with his mother at the piano. The young audience "can clearly take in their stride" pieces of Honegger, Copland, Prokofieff, Dello Joio, and Hindemith, and are being educated "to direct their critical and appreciative faculties at classic and modern alike"--a tough challenge to the contemporary composer "in the not too distant future, when novelty value recedes and quality alone remains."

G383 "City Center Opera: 'The Dybbuk.' " *NYHT*, 14 April 1952, p. 14, col. 3.

In last night's performance Nino Luciano sang the touching role of Channon for the first time, with unclear diction, especially in the later scenes where his voice is heard as the Dybbuk. Ralph Herbert was outstanding in his premiere as Rabbi Azrael, Mary Kreste was new to the part of the Elderly Woman, and Patricia Neway was impressive as Leah. [Composer is David Tamkin.]

G384 "Columbus Boys Choir." *NYHT*, 19 April 1952, p. 6, col. 2-3.

A "vernal freshness" characterized the fine program directed by Herbert Huffman at Carnegie Hall last night, with beautiful singing of works of Lotti, Vittoria, Leisring, Pergolesi, Bartok, Britten, and Mozart--the one-act comic opera *Bastien and Bastienne* which the little boys acted and sang in costume. Britten's *Ceremony of Carols* is the most unifed of Britten's works (if not the only unified work), his chameleon personality here anchored by specific tonal and technical limitations-- boys' voices and harp. Edna Phillips was the elegant accompanist on harp.

G385 "Composers Forum." *NYHT*, 21 April 1952, p. 25, col. 2.

Lockrem Johnson and Robert Erickson were featured composers, with Henry Cowell as "witty and whimsical" moderator. These two "really fine young composers" use "about the same degree of dissonance." Erickson moves from atonality to tonal arrival while Johnson moves from tonality "far into atonal regions." Erickson is "an abstractionist" interested in bulding, not "emotional content," while Johnson is "an opera composer" interested in "expressive message." Review is over 300 words--the usual length for Composers Forum reviews, but longer than most other reviews.

G386 "Ensemble from Chicago." Ibid.

Brief paragraph (50 words) reports that "a large audience received enthusiastically" the songs, dances, and choral numbers of the Lithuanian National Ensemble Dainava at Carnegie Hall.

G387   "Junior Night." Ibid., col. 2-3.

League of Composers presented music of seven new composers--Robert Witt, Robert David Cogan, Jacob Druckman, Raymond Wilding-White, John Strauss, William Flanagan, and Edward Herzog. Performance level was "splendid" and composers' "esthetic and technical level" was high. Further, Druckman and Flanagan had "something definitely personal to say" and Druckman's *Duo for Violin and Piano* has "its own formal design within its fragmented but coherent materials."

G388   "Sybil Yearwood." Ibid., col. 3.

Young soprano is "clearly musical" but "almost everything is wrong with her work." She sang pieces by Puccini, Bizet, Pergolesi, Schubert, and others.

G389   "Sandberg's Oratorio." *NYHT*, 23 April 1952, p. 23, col. 4-5.

Mordecai Sandberg's *Ezkerah* for eight singers and eight instrumentalist was directed by the "able" Stuart Sankey. Composer uses "quarter tones, or a twenty-four interval scale" along with "common chords and dominant sevenths of the squarest and most gauche kind" like a "modernistic resurfacing job on a dead diatonicism" rather than attempt a "synthesis" of form and material.

G390   "Brooklyn Symphony." *NYHT*, 24 April 1952, p. 20, col. 5-6.

Milton Katims conducted the Brooklyn Community Symphony Orchestra--all "good players"--in works by Franck, Enesco, and two Americans. Robert Ward's *Jubilation Overture* is a "discreet Gershwin-Copland blend" of little interest, while Scott Watson's *Appalachian Choral Preludes* is "expert, tasteful, and highly poetic" in its "esthetic concept."

G391   "Harry Zaratzian, Violist." *NYHT*, 28 April 1952, p. 10, col. 4.

The combination of "fine viola playing" and "fine music for the viola," both rare, made "an unusual concert." Milhaud's Sonata No. 1, Hindemith's Sonata Op. 11, and a new "rugged" Sonata by Krenek were followed by a charming *Scène Andalouse* by Turina. Violist's "finest playing came in the finest music, the Brahms Sonata Op. 120 No. 2, more freqently heard on the clarinet."

G392   "Harpsichord Recital." *NYHT*, p. 19, col. 5-6.

Eta Harich-Schneider performed the Goldberg Variations of J. S. Bach without cuts or intermission. There is "a slight lack of punch" in her playing, but "intelligent musicianship." The "all-Bach marathon was a little tiring on ears geared for a wider dynamic and esthetic orbit."

(OCTOBER-DECEMBER 1952)

G393   "Carlos Surinach: Catalonian Composer's Work Has Radio Premiere Here." *NYHT*, Sunday, 12 October 1952, sect. 1, p. 46, col. 6-8.

Milton Katims conducted Surinach's Symphony No. 2, broadcast on NBC. Long review (over 300 words) describes each of the three movements, built "with extraordinary spirit and freedom" and technical mastery from the "essence" of folk material. The work's "outstanding quality" is "its complete fusion of ends and means."

G394   "Rehearsal Concerts." *NYHT*, 13 October 1952, p. 13, col. 5.

Opening of "Music in the Making" concerts at Cooper Union featured new works by
Roger Goeb, John Cage, and Otto Luening, conducted by David Broekman who gave
a "sincere and thoughtful" speech. Goeb's *Concertant No. IV* for solo clarinet (David
Weber) and piano (David Tudor) was "impressive" and "entirely original." Cage's
Piano Concerto for Solo Prepared Piano, String Quartet, Woodwinds, Brass and
Percussion was "Cage at his best" and brought a "becalmed world of sound."

G395   "Baroque Music." *NYHT*, 16 October 1952, p. 28, col. 8.

Eta Harich-Schneider, "a woman of distinguished musicianship," directed and
played in ensemble with The Baroque Chamber Music Players. Works of Vivaldi,
Couperin, J. S. Bach, Quantz, and J. C. Bach were well performed. Ruth Ajootian's
"clear, lovely, boy-soprano-type voice was just right" for Couperin's *Leçon de
Tenebres*.

G396   "All-Bach Program." *NYHT*, 20 October 1952, p. 19, col. 2.

Daniel Saidenberg's Little Symphony played to a packed Y. M. H. A. Auditorium the
Brandenburg Concerti Nos. 6, 4, and, 5 with instrumental soloists, and Cantata No.
209 with Phyllis Curtin as soloist "with fine control and sense of style."

G397   "Leslie Frick." *NYHT*, 23 October 1952, p. 31, col. 3-4.

Singer presented "interesting music" of contemporary Mexican composers in a
"musicianly" interpretation. She has good Spanish diction and "discovers well the
spirit of this music--half regional, half art music in type."

G398   "Joint Recital." *NYHT*, 27 October 1952, p. 17, col. 2.

Mary d'Andrea and George Lawson (tenor) sang, with Sarah Knight a "sensitive,
dynamic, yet discreet" accompanist. Lawson's voice lacks flexibility and tone in the
"tenor altitudes," but d'Andrea is a "highly accomplished singer in every way." Her
singing was "extraordinarily lovely" in Four Neapolitan Folk Songs, transcribed by
Vittorio Giannini.

G399   "Marjorie Schloss." Ibid.

Singer is "a distinguished new exponent" of lieder singing and excelled in songs of
Wolf; her "special introspection and containment" revealed "the high degree of
integration peculiar to the lied. Jonathan Brice was the "magnificent" accompanist.

G400   "Town Hall Concert." *NYHT*, 31 October 1952, p. 23, col. 6-7.

Concert of gospel music by Roberta Martin Singers and others, with "sung and
spoken commentary" on stage and in the audience, was "midway" between a
revivalist meeting and Broadway. Musically it was "not quite suitable subject matter
for these columns."

G401   "Ivy Pouyat, Soprano." *NYHT*, 3 November 1952, p. 16, col. 5.

Singer made a "good impression" in pieces by Bach, Handel, Scarlatti, MacDowell
and others. Accompanist Margarita Grossi "somewhat neutralized" this impression
through "ineptness."

G402 "Jean Graham." *NYHT*, 6 November 1952, p. 27, col. 1-2.

Pianist presented works of Bach, Beethoven, Chopin, and Brahms. She is one of "these brilliant young talents" who "start successful touring" and then get tired, or "play the same piece too many times so that it becomes a wrapped cellophane package." Her extraordinary technique and her assurance "make the more clear the arrestment of the emotional," giving the effect of "an immense and elaborate grate in which a small fire burns."

G403 "Linda Babbitt, Soprano." *NYHT*, 7 November 1952, p. 19, col. 1.

Pieces by Haydn, Lully, Beethoven, Brahms, and Ravel demonstrated "a pretty voice" but higher notes are approached from below "rather than above the note aimed for" and thus "seem a little strained." Perhaps lower "placing of the voice might be helpful."

G404 "Boys Town Choir." *NYHT*, Sunday, 9 November 1952, sect. 1, p. 37, col. 2.

Father Flanagan's Boys Town Choir, conducted by the Rev. Francis Schmitt, sang Monteverdi, Palestrina, Barber, Brahms, Bruckner, and others, along with "traditional" songs. Group suffers from "inattention" to "metre and rhythm" and "almost everything."

G405 "Michael Field, Pianist." *NYHT*, 10 November 1952, p. 13.

Recital was well planned but not well executed. Pieces by Beethoven, Schumann, and Ravel showed "strong, swift fingers" but some inaccuracies. Schoenberg's Five Piano Pieces Op. 23 are so dissonant that they "camouflage" both the composer's "absence of creativity" and the pianist's "wrong notes." Further, dissonant music, fifty years into the twentieth century, has acquired "banality without every having acquired meaning."

G406 "Gerald Smith, Baritone, Gives Town Hall Recital." *NYHT*, 13 November 1952, p. 18, col. 8.

He leaves too much to his "natural musicality" and lacks art, intensity, and shaping of materials.

G407 "Jan Smeterlin." *NYHT*, Sunday, 16 November 1952, sect. 1, p. 67, col. 1.

Piano recital "was a re-statement of what music is all about" for a small but "enchanted" audience. Works of Haydn, Schumann, Ravel, and Chopin, were "perfection." His "interpretative mastery" of Schumann and Ravel revealed "the classic in its natural depth and dignity, the modern in its shallowness."

G408 "Toscanini Concert." Ibid., col. 2.

Arturo Toscanini conducted the NBC Symphony Orchestra in the first performance in America of Rossini's early Sonata No. 3 for Violins, Celli and Basses, which has "the incredible freshness of the very young uttering conventionalities." The Symphony No. 3 of Saint-Saens also received "the usual masterful reading" and "precision" of the "Maestro" and this orchestra.

G409   "Male Quartet." *NYHT*, 17 November 1952, p. 11, col. 2.

"The Continental-Aires" have an outstanding tenor and are "highly musical and finely drilled"

G410   "Grace Gimbel." *NYHT*, 22 November 1952, p. 10, col. 5.

Pianist in Carnegie Hall recital has a poetic quality of touch but a technique inadequate for some works--"the brisker Brahms" and Mozart.

G411   "Theodore Hines." *NYHT*, 24 November 1952, p. 20, col. 4-5.

Singer "proved himself master of many types of singing," beginning with the "coloratura style in the lower voice ranges" of Handel's "Why Do the Nations So Furiously Rage." The *Vier ernste Gesänge* of Brahms showed the "impressive color and volume range" of his voice in one of the most beautiful renderings this reviewer has heard."

G412   "William Harms." *NYHT*, 26 November 1952, p. 14, col. 1-2.

"An expert young pianist" presented a program unbalanced in quality--traditional repertoire in the first half, pieces of undistinguished "esthetic content" after intermission.

G413   "Pianist in Debut." *NYHT*, 1 December 1952, p. 19, col. 2.

Harry Fuchs has "a strong technique" and an "erratic, even petulant mood and manner" suited more to Brahms than to Mozart and Beethoven. *Four Piano Pieces, Op. 21*, of Marion Bauer had an "undistinguished" first performance.

G414   "Lois Marshall Recital." *NYHT*, 3 December 1952, p. 26, col. 5.

Naumburg winner "is one of the most superb singers this reviewer has ever heard." Program opened with songs from the "English Golden Age" and proceeded to works of Schubert, Mozart, Puccini, Falla, and Barber, demonstrating an "indescribably lovely and accurate tone" in lieder and in operatic "hugeness."

G415   "Mildah Polia Sings." *NYHT*, 5 December 1952, p. 27, col. 2.

A program entirely in French included songs by Poulenc, Hahn, Chausson, Aubert, and others. This "mature artist" comprehends the "introspective style" and chooses "slow meditative types of music" over technically "more taxing" works.

G416   "Glee Clubs." *NYHT*, 6 December 1952, p. 14, col. 3-4.

Combined Glee Clubs of New York University and Smith College created much "glee" with light popular numbers and some "fine pieces" including *Alleluia* by Randall Thompson and *Personent Hodie* by Holst.

G417   "Mario Jazzetti Recital." *NYHT*, 8 December 1952, p. 13, col. 4.

Young Italian pianist, played a second Town Hall recital of Beethoven, Chopin, and Debussy. He is "highly gifted" but "the performance is overcast by irresponsible tempi, license taken right and left in matters that are of fact, not opinion." A prodigy, he may not have looked at the music "for years" but he should.

G418 "Lee Cass, Bass-Baritone." Ibid.

Recital by "Y" Auditions Winner of 1952 at Young Men's Hebrew Association Auditorium is "as fine a bass-baritone as anyone could wish to hear." He was at ease with "the concentrated expression" of lieder and the operatic style of Verdi and Gounod.

G419 "The Composers Forum." Ibid., p. 13, col. 4, and p. 16, col. 8.

Wesley Bartlett presented three works and Timothy Cheney one, all world premieres. Otto Luening presided as moderator. Bartlett writes "in dissonant vein which he described as liberal atonalism" and the "rhythmic aspect" is "a little undeveloped." Cheney uses "pure consonance and melodic emphasis" like "a kind of twentieth-century Elizabethan" with a simplicity born of "self-searching rather than of naiveté."

G420 "Carnegie Recital Hall." *NYHT*, 13 December 1952, p. 13, col. 4.

Roland Fiore, a "fine" young conductor, directed a chamber orchestra concert with soprano Victoria Sherry, violinist Hugo Kohlberg, and flutist Milton Witgenstein assisting as "excellent" soloists. Works of Sammartini, Rossini, and Rameau were followed by Walter Piston's *Sinfonietta*--the most "substantial" of the contemporary works--and pieces by Paul Creston and Tibor Serly.

G421 "Richard Doren." *NYHT*, 15 December 1952, p. 23, col. 1.

Young pianist played Bach, Mendelssohn, Chopin, and other composers for "sympathetic listeners" who filled Carnegie Recital Hall. He does not have the technique for "a possible personal contribution" and the grownups responsible for such events should know this public appearance was premature.

G422 "Guitarist in Recital." *NYHT*, 16 December 1952, p. 24.

Haitian guitarist Franz Cassens played to an attentive audience at the Sheridan Square "Circle in the Square." He is a sensitive musician with considerable "technical prowess."

G423 "Harpsichord Quartet." *NYHT*, 17 December 1952, p. 25, col. 2.

Sylvia Marlowe at the harpsichord, with cellist Bernard Greenhouse, flutist Harold Bennett, and oboist Harry Shulman were assisted by clarinetist Wallace Shapiro, violinist Isadore Cohen, and singer Hugues Cuenod as guest soloist in Bach's Cantata No. 189, "Meine Seele." Instrumental works of Bach and Couperin, and Marlowe's "exquisite performances" of seventeenth-century pieces for solo harpsichord were also presented. "Falla's famous Concerto, which brought a closing grandeur to the concert, remains one of the greatest works of the modern vocabulary" with its simplification and richness, bespeaking "maturity and integration," and its "spare, tensely etched logic."

1953

G424 "Music in the Making at Cooper Union." *International Musician* 51, no. 9 (March 1953), p. 13, 35. Reprinted in *American Composers Alliance Bulletin* 3, no. 1 (Spring 1953), p. 8-9.

Six "Music in the Making" concerts this winter, conducted by David Broekman, have had remarkable variety: works of Cage (prepared piano and gongs played submerged under water); Kenyon Hopkins (atonal swing); the "tapesichordists," both imported (Boulez and "La Musique Concrète") and domestic (Luening, Ussachevsky); Cowell (elbows on keyboard); neo-classicism (Carter, Berger); and the leave-it-to-chance school (Feldman). There were also four "real repertory pieces for the general concert planner" by Hovhaness, Luening, Goeb, and Riegger. For the future she suggests less talking from the conductor and more from the audience, and more of the "real repertory," the solid contemporary masterpieces, whether American or European. America's "Brave New Public," insulted for years by crass underestimation, deserves the best. Article is quoted in liner notes for recording of *Tape Recorder Music* by Ussachevsky and Luening, Innovations GB 1, Phonotapes PHS 10020 (1955). *International Musician* editor S. Stephenson Smith notes that she is "at once a composer's critic, and a critic's critic. She is unbendable, and her criticism is free from any touch of coteries, even of those to which she belongs."

G425   "The WNYC American Music Festival" *Musical Courier* 147, no. 6 (15 March 1953), p. 6-7.

Fourteenth annual American Music Festival of New York's Municipal Radio Station, 12-22 February, directed by Herman Neuman, included music from universities and other schools all over the U. S. The festival always features the "glamour of many first performances," including this year two works "by your present reviewer": *Sonata for Piano and Percussion*(**W43b**), meant to open the concert and the festival "with a bang," and *Letters from Morocco* (**W44a**). *Letters* carefully eschews the "external and wearisome trappings of Asian style" (so evident in Harrison's *Canticle No. 3 for Percussion* with which it was juxtaposed), taking from the East only the structural principle of a melody-rhythm or raga-tala form.

G426   "Arthur Berger." *American Composers Alliance Bulletin* 3, no. 1 (Spring 1953), p. 2-5.

Berger's music is "one of the most successful, most delicate results" of the current American "hybridization" of the two major European techniques, atonal contrapuntal and neo-classical vertical or harmonic composition. The article, in this journal's standard format for composer articles, includes a "List of Berger Compositions" and excerpts from reviews.

G427   "Tapesichord: The Music of Whistle and Bang." *Vogue* 122 (July 1953), p. 80-81, 108.

Pierre Schaeffer started *musique concrète* around 1948, recording at "one of the noisier Paris railway terminals." Then Boulez, Hodier, Henry, and Messiaen looked for sounds beyond the possibilities of musical instruments. In New York, concrete music takes place in two places: uptown at Columbia University (Luening and Ussachevsky work with tapes of actual musical sounds), and downtown on the Bowery (Cage, after contact with Boulez, has set up a "library" of instrumental and non-instrumental sounds and noises). Concert by Luening and Ussachevsky 28 October 1952 at Museum of Modern Art was repeated, with French works, downtown at Cooper Union and received with ribaldry and interest by "the most proletarian of audiences" (*see* "Music in the Making," **G424** above). Electronic music, useful for radio programs and experimental movies, does not require, or invite, the complete concentration of the mind, but seeps in at a subconscious level. (Editorial note identifies the author as a *New York Herald Tribune* music critic for seven years, and the winner this year of a $1,000 grant from the National Institute of Arts and Letters.)

G428   "Les Six de Jazz." *American Composers Alliance Bulletin* 3, no. 3 (Autumn 1953), p. 9.

Teo Macro, Elliott Greenberg, Henry Brant (the "catalyst"), Will Hudson, Harold Gilmore, and Rayburn Wright are young musicians creating "long-haired" music that uses jazz instruments and performers in concert forms or jazz forms in concert ensembles. Jazz is "metropolitan folk-lore," a direct, almost collective expression of subconscious factors in music, and gives music "real life." A jazz tune, unlike techniques evolved from technicians, is "known to all, like the plot of a Greek drama."

1953, CONTINUED: *HERALD TRIBUNE*
(JANUARY-APRIL)

G429   "Stuart Fastovsky." *NYHT*, 5 January 1953, p. 12, col. 8.

Young violinist has considerable poetic feeling but needs work on intonation and "certain technical factors." Ravel's *Tzigane* was far off pitch in several places but had the required impetuousness and lyricism. Prokofief *Sonata* was "a bit stilted" and pianist Norman Voelcker heightened the lack of continuity. Ives *Sonata No. 2* with its "quick-change styles and moods" was well played.

G430   "Walden Quartet." *NYHT*, 12 January 1953, p. 11, col. 1.

New Friends of Music presented the Walden Quartet in two Mozart quartets and with the "great singer" William Warfield as soloist in the *Motetto da Requiem* of Alessandro Scarlatti in this "beautiful" concert. The "drama" of the Scarlatti work is "in no way dimmed by the years since it was written" and Warfield sang it "with command and eloquence."

G431   "Composers Forum." Ibid., col. 1-2.

Edward Diemente and George Rochberg, both of whom "work in a highly chromatic idiom," were featured composers. Rochberg "is already a master craftsman" with outstanding "technical ease" in infusing the twelve tone system with "more personality, expression and freedom than do most composers." Diemente's works, two of them New York premieres, were "both bright and original;" in *Jubilee* performers "welded the rather straggling development of materials into a whole."

G432   "Italian Masters." *NYHT*, 14 January 1953, p. 23, col. 4.

The Societa Corelli performed "lovely" works of Monteverdi and Vivaldi at the Brooklyn Academy of Music last night. The group of seventeen players, smoothly synchronised and blended without conductor, had a "lovely golden Italian tone." Luisa Ribacchi, mezzo-soprano, had a "fine sense of style" but was not steady or full.

G433   "Young People's Concert." *NYHT*, Sunday, 18 January 1953, sect. 1, p. 38, col. 3-4.

Igor Buketoff conducted the Philharmonic in the third in the current series Saturday morning, presenting works of Rossini and Ravel, then some "unusual instruments in usual uses"--a typewriter and revolver (Satie's *Parade*), wind machine (Strauss), hurdy gurdy (Haydn) and others.

G434   " 'Music in the Making.' " *NYHT*, 19 January 1953, p. 18, col. 3.

Robert Lawrence, Jacob Avshalomov, and Tom Scott "commentated quite heatedly." Avshalomov's *Evocations for Clarinet Solo and Chamber Orchestra* is eloquent and austere and bespeaks "a real creative gift." It has "an unusually varied and original base [bass?] structure" for music of such "melodic solidity." Kenyon Hopkins presented an exhilarating *Music for Spontaneous Dancing*. Demonstrations of "La Musique Concrète" in pieces by Pierre Boulez, Schaeffer, Henry, Messaien, and the American Tom Scott "intrigued" the "mass audience" as they had the "more special music fanciers" at their Composers Forum premiere a few weeks ago. Henry Cowell performed his *Concerto Piccolo for Piano and Orchestra* which includes his famous "musical pranks"--tone clusters, string pluckings, elbow playing on the keys.

G435 "Segovia Program." Ibid., col. 4.

The "inimitable" guitarist performed Frescobaldi, Weiss, Sor, Bach, the New York premiere of a cavatina "beautifully written for the instrument" by Alex Tansman, and other twentieth-century pieces, for a "packed" audience. At the end "encores and still more encores were called for."

G436 "Joint Recital." *NYHT*, 26 January 1953, p. 10, col. 4.

Jean Decker, soprano, and Stuart Nickolds, tenor, sang solo groups and duets in Carnegie Recital Hall on Sunday afternoon. Both are "scarcely beyond the student stage" and need revision of "many things" to reach the professional standard.

G437 "Jerome Rappaport." *NYHT*, 30 January 1953, p. 14, col. 5-6.

Pianist showed an affinity for the "Germanic tradition"--Mozart, Bach, Haydn, Hindemith--and also performed works of Robert Starer and Bartók. He has "first class technical equipment" that he places "in its true role as servant to expression," not an end in itself.

G438 "Armand Basile." *NYHT*, 11 February 1953, p. 25, col. 1.

Pianist, winner of the American Artists Award for 1952, presented a well-balanced program chosen to display thorough training and thoughtful interpretive approach--works of Scarlatti (clear, crisp) Beethoven (impressive but not moving), Chopin (fluent but without tenderness), Ravel, Debussy, and Prokofieff. Playing lacked essential quality of tension to hold an audience throughout a big work; "this quality is an emotional participation, and cannot be brought from the hands and brain."

G439 "Jan Gorbaty in Debut." *NYHT*, Sunday, 15 February 1953, sect. 1, p. 34, col. 7-8.

Distinguished young Polish pianist at Town Hall Saturday afternoon showed "an inwardness, a self-absorption that seems to separate expression from" his impressive technique. He performed Beethoven, Chopin, and the *Theme Varié in B flat minor* of the "much-neglected" Carol Czymanowsky.

G440 "Sophisticated Folk Art." *NYHT*, Monday, 16 February 1953, p. 7, col. 3-4.

Olga Coelho, richly endowed as singer and as guitarist, performed Peruvian and Columbian pieces, songs from Brazil, Argentina, and Mexico, and music of Dowland, Scarlatti, and Villa Lobos. She has brought folk art to the level of the sophisticated arts without losing its original quality.

G441   "Composers Forum."   Ibid., col. 4-5.

Composers Forum, broadcast Saturday night as part of WNYC American Music
Festival, featured orchestral works of Hunter Johnson and Jacob Avshalamov
performed by the Columbia University Orchestra, Emanuel Balahan, conductor.
Johnson's *Letter to the World,* from his 1940 ballet by the same name, has "melodic
eloquence, harmonic richness, and extraordinary rhythmic variety." *For an*
Unknown Soldier for flute and string orchestra is cool and crisp, classic in its
shapeliness and expressive content. Avshalomoff's *Sinfonietta* is more sombre and
exotic in presentation and instrumentation. The composer succeeded magnificently
in assigning the "decorative role" to the orchestration, not to the ideas and
structures; his orchestration is "completely a part of the organic and acoustic whole."

G442   " 'Tosca': Paolo Silveri Sings the Role of Scarpia at the Met." *NYHT,*
19 February 1953, p. 21

Silveri's performance "evoked cheers, bravos and long applause." Singing in this
Verdi opera was splendid throughout the "sinister dramatic characterization," and
his stage presence was histrionic yet unstereotyped. The role exploits the "varied
tonal range of his fine baritone." Other members of the cast were as before, and
Fausto Cleva conducted a "smooth and unified performance."

G443   "Mannes School Program." *NYHT,* 20 February 1953, p. 13.

Broadcast on WNYC for that radio station's annual American Music Festival, the
program included several unfamiliar works. *Music for Strings* by Karol Rathaus is a
magnificent piece, highly chromatic, with romantic freedom and linear strength.
Alexei Haieff's *Sextet* for violin, cello, flute, bassoon, trumpet, and piano has "family
resemblances" to Papa Stravinski, blended with jolly and sad moods and substances
that are purely Haieff. Bauer's *Concertino for Oboe, Clarinet, and Strings* is charming and well written and one of her best works. A touching student version of
Thomson's *Stabat Mater* gave a suitable effect of innocence without the required
sophistication to this beautiful small work.

G444   "Nine Orchestras Give Florida Its Music." *NYHT,* Sunday 22 February
1953, sect. 4, p. 5.

Yves Chardon conducts the 100 per cent professional Florida Symphony Orchestra in
Orlando, heard there Feb. 5 and 6 and in Daytona Beach. William Masselos was
"visiting soloist" in the Chopin F minor Concerto. Guest conductor Newell Jenkins,
"an American resident of Florence," led the University of Miami Orchestra in pieces
by Sammartini, Boccherini, Bellini, Rosetti, and Paisiello, some of them "recovered"
from museums and archives. Other orchestras at Fort Lauderdale, Tallahassee (attached to the university), Tampa, St. Petersburg, and Jacksonville are also active.
(This Sunday feature with by-line "P. Glanville-Hicks" is apparently her third and
last, the others being **G74** and **G351**.)

G445   "Cesare Siepi Sings Role In 'Rigoletto' at the Met." *NYHT,* 27
February 1953, p. 11, col. 8.

Role of Sparafucile had "rich-voiced singing" in this Verdi opera. The singing of
Genevieve Warner, replacing Roberta Peters as Gilda, was "both expert and moving,
in spite of a chilly metallic quality" now and then. Jan Peerce as the Duke and Paolo
Silveri as Rigoletto also gave fine performances.

G446   "Music in the Making." *NYHT,* 2 March 1953, p. 15, col. 3.

At Cooper Union, concert featured Luening's *Louisville Concerto*, that showed "undigested vernacular elements," and works of Riegger, Carter, and Broekman (who also conducted). Critics on talk panel were Paul Bowles and Robert Lawrence.

G447 "Miss Victoria, Cambetes." Ibid., col. 4.

Teresa Victoria, soprano, and Albert Cambetes, bass-baritone, acompanied by David Garvey and Alberta Masiello, respectively. Neither has a real voice to build upon but both are carefully trained.

G448 "Berenice Bramson." *NYHT*, 4 March 1953, p. 18, col. 5-6.

Soprano offered Handel, Purcell, Mozart, Milhaud, Schubert (with Alan Bramson playing clarinet obbligato), and "one or two moderns." Kilpinen has made "perhaps the greatest contribution to lieder repertory since the classic period." Accompanist Emanuel Balaban is "an aristocrat among musicians."

G449 "Margaret Hillis and Choir." *NYHT*, 13 March 1953, p. 15, col. 8.

Young conductor directed The Concert Choir last night (Thursday) in works of Bach, Carissimi, Rorem, Brahms, and some early French composers. She "can achieve any degree of sensitivity, any dynamic level, with no fuss or bother" and the singing was "exceptionally fine." Rorem "has a natural and lovely melodic gift" plus "prosodic perfection."

G450 "Rey de la Torre, Guitarist." *NYHT*, 16 March 1953, p. 19.

The young Cuban, with successes in Spain and Spanish-America is the most distinguished classic guitar virtuoso to be heard on the concert stage. He played works by Gaspar, Sanz, Robert de Visée, and others, and "he shone most brightly" in a superb group of new compositions written for him by Cuban composers.

G451 "Composers and Conductors." *NYHT*, 23 March 1953, p. 6.

"Your reviewer's" own *Sonata for Piano and Percussion* (**W43c**) was performed yesterday (Sunday) afternoon, with pieces by Robert Nagel, Hugo Kauder, Virgil Thomson, and Wallingford Riegger. Carlos Surinach conducted "with vigor and finesse."

G452 "First Sponsored Opera Written for TV Is Heard." *NYHT*, 25 March 1953, p. 25, col. 1.

NBC-TV has broadcast *The Parrot* with book by Frank Felitta and musical score for two pianos by Darrell Peter. It is more important to establish the "habit of making operas" on TV than to obtain record-breaking heights of excellence.

G453 "Puerto Rico U. Chorus." *NYHT*, 28 March 1953, p. 8, col. 7.

August Rodriguez, "a first-class musician," conducted his own music--a Kyrie and compositions emanating from "the very marrow of the bones of the chosen folk materials" of Haiti and Puerto Rico--as well as Henry Cowell's *Irishman Lilt*, William Schuman's *Te Deum*, and other works. The conducting is "precise, dynamic and alive" with perfect "sense of tension, of nuance, of esthetic mood pattern."

G454   "Joint Recital." *NYHT*, 30 March 1953, p. 18.

Vera Little, soprano, and Dorothy Taylor, violinist, with accompanists, produced "studentlike" work, not reaching the concert level that prevails in this city.

G455   "Marian Anderson." *NYHT*, 6 April 1953, p. 12, col. 4-5.

Packed house at Metropolitan Opera yesterday (Sunday) afternoon heard Handel, Schubert, a Verdi aria, and on the second half music of Howard Swanson, Roger Quilter, Benjamin Britten, and a group of Spirituals, with Franz Rupp at the piano. Swanson's *The Negro Speaks of Rivers* is substantial enough "as music" to rise to this singer's dedication and authority.

G456   "Bennington Composers." *NYHT*, 13 April 1953, p. 18, col. 8.

Works of Otto Luening, Theodore Strongin, and Beatrice McLaughlin represented various contemporary idioms--humor and fancy trombone playing (Luening), Mediterranean style and tonal melody (Strongin), and sensitive, romantic contemporary music that "has a definite expressive content and is technically quite expert" (McLaughlin). Also mentioned are Kennedy, McKinney, Wendelberg, and Blum.

G457   "George Fiore, Pianist." *NYHT*, 17 April 1953, p. 14, col. 3.

All-Chopin program by "excellent pianist" who works as an usher at the Metropolitan Opera House revealed "a sense of poetry and a poetic touch" as well as incomplete control of "technical hazards."

G458   "Swiss Works Played." *NYHT*, 20 April 1953, p. 20, col. 6.

New York Public Library concert yesterday afternoon (Sunday) featured "splendidly performed" music of Willy Burkhard, Conrad Beck, Albert Moeschinger, and Frank Martin. Burkhard and Beck are expert in the "dissonant chromatic syle" and convey a "sad romanticism." Martin, though, is jolly; his trio on Irish Folk Songs grows to "a real rhythmic form" within the style of its melodic subject matter (as Hindus "stay within the raga").

G459   " 'Rosenkavalier' At City Center." *NYHT*, 24 April 1953, p. 22, col. 3.

Three "fine vocalists" sang their roles for the first time last night (Thursday)--Edith Evans as Octavian, Delores Mari as Sophie, and Jon Crain as the singer in the first act.

G460   "Newman, Tipton At City Center." *NYHT*, 27 April 1953, p. 12, col. 8.

In *Cavalleria Rusticana* (Mascagni), Arthur Newman sang his first Alfio and in *Pagliacci* (Leoncavallo), Thomas Tipton sang his first Silvio. Newman has "strength and stability" as singer and actor; Tipton "was in every way good." Patricia Neway as Santuzza is "a splendid singer and stage personality" but her emotional "intensities" are already in "the classics" and do not have to be added, as in contemporary opera.

G461   "Sandra Strick." *NYHT*, p. 13, col. 1.

Young pianist played "nicely balanced program"--Bach, Beethoven, Brahms, Schumann, Bartok, Barber, and Debussy--in debut recital. She "has mastered much of the technical prerequisite for a professional career" but lacks perhaps the "depth and poetic sensitivity" of "a real artist's mind and heart."

(OCTOBER-DECEMBER 1953)

G462   "Pro Musica Antiqua." *NYHT*, 5 October 1953, p. 13, col. 1-2.

Noah Greenberg directed the group in music of the sixteenth and seventeenth centuries yesterday (Sunday) at the New York Public Library. "Qualities of fastidiousness, lyricism and loving precision ever evoke a timeless spirit."

G463   "Norman Carol, Violinist." *NYHT*, 6 October 1953, p. 18, col. 8.

Youthful violinist played an "exquisite recital" at Town Hall, including works of Vitali, Brahms, Wieniawski, and Schubert. Review is slightly longer than usual-- over 200 words.

G464   "Martha Schlamme." *NYHT*, 12 October 1953, p. 16, col. 3.

Balladeer from Vienna "sings many kinds of music well"--songs from Israel, Yiddish songs, Negro spirituals, and Haydn's arrangements of *Scottish Folksongs* for voice, piano, violin, and cello--but may be "swamped" by "the plethora of specialists we hear in New York."

G465   "Canadian Choir." Ibid., col. 3-4.

Large all-male chorus from Quebec Province, "L'Orphéon des Trois Rivières," is well trained and polished but lacks "legato style" and is inclined to "overphrase" and lose the larger form, in conductor Leo Carle's interpretation.

G466   "Marcella de Cray, Harpist." *NYHT*, 13 October 1953, p. 26, col. 5-6

The harp has "no major repertory from the 'box office years,' the eighteenth and nineteenth centuries," but this "extremely able young harpist" chose her program well. Scarlatti and Bach pieces (in arrangements) gave "backbone;" premiere of Marcel Tournier's *Sonatine Op. 45* gave "both cachet and some musical weight to the second part of the evening."

G467   " 'La Cenerentola' At City Center." *NYHT*, Sunday, 18 October 1953, sect. 1, p. 46, col. 5-6.

Joseph Rosenstock conducted a "streamlined" performance of the Rossini opera with "that fusion of spontaneity and rehearsed precision that is the essence of snap and sparkle in the theater." The performance, like the opera, is "without greatness" in any single element, but successful as a whole.

G468   " 'Music in the Making.' " *NYHT*, 19 October 1953, p. 19, col. 1.

Substantial review (around 300 words) describes works (all "hitherto unperformed") of Elliott Carter, Tom Scott, Rober Goeb, and Kenneth Wolf. David Broekman again conducted and Jay Harrison and Henry Simon formed the "talk-panel." Only Carter's *Prelude, Fanfare and Polka* was wholly successful; "it posed simple musical problems and solved them with spirit and distinction."

G469   "Eunice Eaton, Pianist." *NYHT*, 30 October 1953, p. 14, col. 6-8.

In her fifth Town Hall recital this young American performed a "pretentious" Piano Sonata by Howard Ferguson and works of Messiaen, Mendelssohn, Chopin, and Scarlatti. She is a "painstaking musician" but erratic tempi rob the performance of drama.

G470   "Alyne Dumas Lee." *NYHT*, 2 November 1953, p. 19, col. 3-4.

Second Town Hall recital by "a great and dedicated singer" was "one of the most lovely, finished and exciting to be heard anywhere." There was "simply nothing wrong" with her singing of *Four Serious Songs* of Brahms and four German songs by Joseph Marx. The final group in English was music of "lesser quality."

G471   "Yvette Rudin, Violinist." Ibid., col. 5.

Best was the opening *Sonata in D Major* of Handel, performed with "neatness" and a "warm tone." *Three Pieces for Violin Alone* by Eda Rapoport are "effectively written and picturesque." Beethoven's *Romance in F Major* and Leo Dubensky's *Romance* did not compliment her "personality" and expressivity.

G472   "Ida Krehm, Pianist." *NYHT*, 6 November 1953, p. 15, col. 4.

Young Canadian gave a polished performance. Her mind "seems to encompass a work in small segments" so that she was good in Scarlatti, an assemblage of carefully prepared sections, but a Scriabin sonata "fell apart" and Schumann lacked contrasts.

G473   "Little Orchestra Society." *NYHT*, 10 November 1953, p. 22, col. 8.

Group's second concert for the season featured Falla's *Master Peter's Puppets*, which the orchestra has just recorded (*see also* **G113** above). Bartok's *Music for Strings, Percussion and Celesta* Scherman has never directed so well. Robert Nagel gave a "very fine performance" as soloist in the premiere of a *Concerto for Trumpet, Strings and Percussion* by the young English composer John Addison.

G474   "Lee Cass in Debut." *NYHT*, 12 November 1953, p. 22.

Young bass-baritone (whom Glanville-Hicks reviewed on 8 December 1952, *see* **G418** above) "is a first-class artist"--a "natural singer" with training for "technical and interpretive subtlety." Recital at Town Hall yesterday (Wednesday) afternoon featured works of Lully, Mozart, Schubert, Wolf, Mahler, and Moussorgsky.

G475   "Margaret Roy." *NYHT*, 13 November 1953, p. 15, col. 5-6.

Young contralto from Buffalo "has everything"--a magnificent voice, a natural approach to interpretation and style, and "warmth, tranquility, concealed yet effective passion in her singing that alone can inhabit technical mastery making it into art." Program was a "historic panorama" of music of Robert Jones and other early English composers, Respighi, Hans Pfitzner, Stravinski, Moret, Messiaen, Milhaud, Britten.

G476   "Leonard Eisner, Pianist." *NYHT*, 16 November 1953, p. 13, col. 5-6.

Young artist in fourth Town Hall recital has "a marked dramatic sense and an enormous tone" but lacks "detail perfection." Moussorgsky's *Pictures From an Exposition* and MacDowell's Fourth Sonata had some "brilliant execution" and some "erratic" and "uneven" passages.

G477 "The Teltscheks." *NYHT*, 18 November 1953, p. 25, col. 1-2.

Duo-piano team of Herbert and Alfred Teltschek are "masters in the art of duo-pianistic precision." Music of Bach and Rachmaninof and first performances of "a not very interesting Sonata by Robert Marvel in the neo-Griffes manner, and a Toccata by Thomas Beversdorf" produced "exhilaration and satisfaction." *Variations on a Theme of Beethoven* by Saint-Saens was "beautifully laid out for the two instruments" and was "a real hit."

G478 "Maurice Wilk." *NYHT*, 20 November 1953, p. 17, col. 4.

Violinist, with Carlo Bussotti a "first class" pianist, performed Beethoven, Bach, and Luigi Dallapiccola's two *Duo Studies*--which have a "chill, prismatic atonality that is well disposed between the two instruments." Wilk "does many things well" but his "sense of pulse is not infallible." His performance of the Beethoven Sonata Op. 12 was an "ensemble" performance as the classic composers meant their pieces to sound ("not a 'top line' with obsequious 'accompaniment' as our concert routines foster").

G479 "Soloists, 14 and 15, Heard At Concert." *NYHT*, Sunday, 22 November 1953, sect. 1, p. 59, col. 3.

Wilfrid Pelletier conducted the second in a series of Young People's Concerts of the New York Philharmonic Society, producing "good-humored chaos." Soloists were Ruth Karin Dahlstrom, 15, harpist in an "ineffectual work," the Damase *Harp Concertino*, and Eric Friedman, 14, violinist in the *Rondo Capriccioso* of Saint-Saens. In the usual demonstrations of instruments the audience applauded large instruments (double bassoon, double bass) more than small ones (violins, flutes, oboes).

G480 "Emma Endres-Kountz." *NYHT*, 23 November 1953, p. 14, col. 4.

Pianist has "considerable taste and delicacy of feeling" and played works of Bach, Haydn, Brahms, and Ravel, with a few "mechanical difficulties" but "a certain classic distinction that makes her a pleasure to listen to."

G481 "Leonard Hungerford." *NYHT*, 26 November 1953, p. 30, col. 3.

The second appearance at Town Hall by this "major pianist" featured works of Schubert, Chopin, and Brahms. He has a colorful tonal palette and a velvet touch and is an "artist of understatement" whose technique is an extension of his expressive personality.

G482 "Larry Adler." *NYHT*, 9 December 1953, p. 67, col. 1.

Harmonica recital by this "true artist" and "unique virtuoso" was "a revelation" to this reviewer, hearing him for the first time. Two "first rate" pieces were written especially for him, a Suite by Milhaud and a Concerto by Arthur Benjamin.

G483 "Collegiate Chorale." *NYHT*, 16 December 1953, p. 27, col. 2.

Robert Shaw conducted "an overlong motley" of works of Gabrieli, Bach, and Handel and first performances of works of Avshalomov (*Tom O'Bedlam* on a "curiously macabre text") and Ernst Bacon both of which "seemed minimal in intrinsic musical values." Bacon's work *Five Fables with Music* acquires its interest "from extra-musi-cal stunts of various kinds." Texts by John Edmunds and Bacon "suggest a literary limbo somewhere between Aesop and the Saturday Review" and were "expertly" delivered by Edward Everett Horton "to the delight of all." While Shaw "excels with a small choir," he loses precision with these massive groups and instrumental ensembles. (*See* **B382** for Thomson's reply to Bacon's anger over this review.)

G484 "Cantata Singers." *NYHT*, 18 December 1953, p. 25, col. 6.

Alfred Mann conducted two Bach cantatas and the motet "Singet dem Herrn ein neues Lied." The choir "seemed slightly untidy and the orchestra even more so," apparently due to the conductor. Helen Boatwright, soprano soloist, and "some beautifully neat reed playing by the wood winds" made for some "smooth" sections.

G485 "2d Children's Program." *NYHT,* Sunday, 20 December 1953, sect. 1, p. 29, col. 1-2.

Wilfrid Pelletier conducted the Philharmonic Orchestra yesterday morning, opening the program with Nicolai Berezowsky's *Christmas Festival Overture.* A thirteen-year-old pianist played a movement of the Schumann Concerto, and Fay Emerson "did a simply beautiful job" as narrator in an orchestral *Story of the Nativity.*

G486 "Composers Forum." *NYHT*, 21 December 1953, p. 17, col. 4.

Wolfgang Rebner of Los Angeles and Wayne Barlow of Rochester were featured composers. David Randolph was moderator for a question period that was "unusually stimulating," due perhaps to the "tremendous contrast" between the composers. Rebner "leans toward the Werbernesque pulverization type of writing" with an extreme pointillism in his *Brass Quintet.* Barlow "handles an equal degree of dissonance" in "a legato style, deeply felt." His recent *Triptych* for string quartet shows this "emotional dominance." Review is about 400 words long.

1954: GROVE'S DICTIONARY

[*Note:* **G487** through **G584** are the American composer articles, listed alphetically, for *Grove's Dictionary of Music and Musicians,* 5th edn., ed. Eric Blom (London: Macmillan, 1954). For all articles the format is as follows: composer's dates; description ("American composer"); education; significant performances; employment history; volunteer positions (e.g., board member of composer association or other evidence of being a "good musical citizen"); comments on style (if Glanville-Hicks knows the composer's work first hand); a list of works which may be titles in a single paragraph, or a longer "Catalogue of Works" by genre; and finally, but not always, a bibliography (of only one or two titles at most). Short articles are around one-half column, medium length is one to two columns, and long articles are over two columns long, the longest being four columns (Thomson). Nineteen of these composers appeared in the *fourth edition of *Grove's* (1940), mostly in the Supplementary Volume (supp.); the remaining seventy-nine are new to the fifth edition.]

G487 "Akhron, Joseph." *Grove's Dictionary*, 5th edn. (1954), vol. 1, p. 80 [1 1/3 col.].

Akhron, 1886-1943, an American violinist and composer of Lithuanian birth, is also translator of the Rimsky-Korsakov *Manual of Harmony.* Half of the entry is a list of his works classified by genre. [*4th edn., supp., by Nathan Broder.]

G488 "Antheil, George." Ibid., p. 165-6 [1 3/4 col.].

Early works of Antheil, born 1900, are massive, dissonant, and symphonic (*Ballet mécanique,* and others), while works from about 1945 are more tranquil and more melodic-romantic in expression with new variety and depth. Ingredients of "Americana" in his style are rhythmically allied to jazz rather than to the melodic direction of folksong typical of the Copland school. [*4th edn., $1/2$ col., by Nathan Broder.]

G489   "Babbitt, Milton."   Ibid., p. 281 [$1/2$ col.].

Babbitt, born 1916, was USA section president of the ISCM in 1951-52. Short final paragraph lists his main compositions by title and date.

G490   "Barber, Samuel."   Ibid., p. 425-6 [2 $1/2$ col.].

Barber, born 1910, is a romanticist, one of the more important American styles; this more expressive manner has reappeared recently on the American scene with the passing of the "more athletic phases of neoclassicism." Barber has always possessed "technical brilliance in conventional terms" but his truly personal idiom has been longer in emerging and appears to be "an aesthetic selectivity reminiscent of Stravinsky." [*4th edn., $1/2$ col., by Reese]

G491   "Barlow, Samuel."   Ibid., p. 439 [1 col.].

Barlow, born 1892, has held offices in international arts organizations and has contributed to the League of Composers magazine *Modern Music*. Entry concludes with a "Catalogue of Works."

G492   "Barlow, Wayne."   Ibid., p. 439 [$1/3$ col.].

Barlow, born 1912, is on the Eastman School faculty; his orchestral works have been performed and broadcast. Seven "chief works" are listed.

G493   "Barrows, John, jun."   Ibid., p. 458 [$1/2$ col.].

Article on Barrows, born in California in 1913, ends with a list of thirteen "outstanding compositions." A woodwind march was performed in 1947 at the Columbia University American Music Festival.

G494   "Bauer, Marion (Eugenie)."   Ibid., p. 507 [1 col.]

American composer and writer on music, born 1887, has had orchestral works heard in New York, Syracuse, Worcester, Cleveland, Detroit, and elsewhere. Entry ends with a "Catalogue of Works."

G495   "Becker, John."   Ibid., p. 525 [$1/3$ col.].

Becker, born 1886, is Director of Music and composer in residence at Barat College of the Sacred Heart in Illinois. His Symphony no. 2 was played at the ISCM Festival in Frankfurt o/M in 1927 and his Symphony no. 3 was first performed by the New York Philharmonic. Summary of genres of other works "too numerous to be listed" is given.

G496   "Bennett, Robert Russell."   Ibid., p. 625 [$1/2$ col.].

Bennett, born 1894, American conductor and composer, has worked for various Hollywood film studios since about 1930. Entry includes names of four of his stage works and a summary of his other genres. [*4th edn., supp., by Gustave Reese.]

G497   "Berezovsky, Nicolay."   Ibid., p. 635 [1 col.].

Berezovsky, American violinist, conductor, composer of Russian birth, was born in St. Petersburg in 1900. A list of "some" of his "chief works" names twenty-five titles in chronological order, 1920-1945. [*4th edn., $3/5$ col., by Gustave Reese.]

G498   "Berger, Arthur."   Ibid., p. 640-1 [1 $1/16$ col.].

Style of this American critic and composer, born 1912, shows much "integration and assimilation" of American elements to transform them "from a vernacular into an art expression." Glanville-Hicks also finds a "Stravinsky-like disruption of the bass line," adopted for its contrapuntal rhythmic components, rather than a bass line that determines accent.

G499   "Bergsma, William."   Ibid., p. 643 [$2/3$ col.].

Style of Bergsma, born in Oakland, CA, in 1921, "still in process of stabilization, tends toward a dissonant, angular counterpoint and has an intense lyrical quality," while "the harmonic idiom is dissonant in a neutral rather than a personal way." A list of eleven major works is included.

G500   "Bernstein, Leonard."   Ibid., p. 683-684 [1 $2/3$ col.].

American conductor and composer, born in 1918, has a style resulting from his "integration" of "American rhythmic and melodic ingredients"--cowboy songs, Mexican dances, the "Negro jazz idiom" (similar to those of the earlier generation of Copland and Blitzstein). His abundance of syncopation, vitality of rhythmic buoyancy, melodic freedom, and "dissonant semi-jazz harmonic idiom" are all "stylized and disciplined into a compact and vivid expression" in which "ends and means meet in successful and happy musical solutions." Twelve "principal works" are listed.

G501   "Bingham, Seth."   Ibid., p. 712 [$2/3$ col.].

American organist and composer, born 1882, now teaching music theory at Colorado College, has had many performances of orchestral works and has written many organ works. Twenty-one of his "most important" works are named.

G502   "Bowles, Paul."   Ibid., p. 858-859 [2 $1/5$ col.].

Material on Bowles, born 1910, is mostly a list of his works. He has produced "remarkably sensitive" music for twenty stage productions and has absorbed within his own style the melodic and rhythmic "peculiarities" of Africa and Central America. In his "highly original scoring" winds and percussion predominate and strings are rarely used. He writes well for pianoforte, especially in combination with percussion instruments--marimbas, drums, gongs--and he has an "original and subtle rhythmic sense."

G503   "Brant, Henry Drefuss."   Ibid., p. 912 [$3/4$ col.].

Born in 1913 in Montreal, Brant has been an orchestrator and arranger and is teaching these commercial aspects at Columbia University. He also collects and performs on wind instruments from around the world. His "highly original orchestrations" are "effective and full of wit." Twenty-nine "chief works" are listed.

G504   "Brunswick, Mark."   Ibid., p. 985 [$1/3$ col.].

American composer and writer on music, born 1902, has chaired the National Committee for Refugee Musicians (1938-1948), been president of the U. S. section of the ISCM, and published journal articles. Six "chief works" are named.

G505   "Cage, John."   Ibid., vol. 2, p. 16-17 [1 ¹/₂ col.].

Article includes a paragraph on his style and ends with a "Catalogue of Works" that includes twenty-five "ballets in one act for solo dancer" and fifteen "other stage works." Cage, born in 1912 in California, is the inventor of the "prepared piano" which produces an effect like a "miniature gamelan or a gong and percussion ensemble." He "follows laws rather than rules" and applies the "laws of composition to utterly unprecedented material. He is "watched with interest in his own country as an experimental composer."

G506   "Carter, Elliott (Cook), jun."   Ibid., p. 97-98 [1 ²/₃ col.].

This "American critic and composer," born in 1908, is "essentially neoclassical" and shows "how the American idiom can evolve within this structural type." His music has "a distinct individuality in spite of its abstract nature." Article ends with a "Catalogue of Works" grouped by genre and dated 1933-1951.

G507   "Cazden, Norman."   Ibid., p. 133-4 [²/₃ col.].

Born 1914, Cazden was studied at Harvard (with Piston and Copland). He teaches pianoforte and theory at the Juilliard School. Eighteen "principal" titles are listed.

G508   "Chanler, Theodore Ward."   Ibid., p. 163 [1 ¹/₁₆ col.].

Chanler, born 1902, is well known as one of the most brilliant of the composer-writers on modern musical subjects, especially in *Modern Music*. His small, exquisite works are distinguished for their quality, subtlety, and technical and aesthetic excellence. Works are listed by genre, songs (13 titles) being the most numerous.

G509   "Chasins, Abram."   Ibid., p. 190-1 [¹/₂ col.].

American pianist and composer, born 1903, is best known for is radio "Master Class of the Air." His compositions for one and two pianofortes are "popular and widely known." Six works are listed. [*4th edn., supp.,²/₅ col., by Reese.]

G510   "Cohn, Arthur."   Ibid., p. 367 [³/₄ col.].

American violinist and composer, born in Philadelphia in 1910, has held several professional positions, including director of the Fleisher Collection of the Free Library. Twenty-one of his "more important works" are listed and other works are referred to in general terms.

G511   "Cowell, Henry (Dixon)."   Ibid., p. 508-9 [1 ¹/₂ col.].

Born 1897 in Menlo Park, CA, this American pianist and composer originated the term "tone cluster" (large bunches of notes hit with whole hand, fist, forearm), now part of the musical vocabulary of the U. S. A., and also uses plucking and stroking of the pianoforte strings. In 1921-32 his "extremely experimental" pianoforte music provoked scenes bordering on riots in Europe. His style has a "persistent undercurrent" of folk material; he has written in almost all the usual musical forms and has invented some. His orchestration is often brilliant and his musical style is "melodic, whimsical, and very free." Last paragraph refers to "some 500 works," and lists several titles. [*4th edn., supp., $1/2$ col., by Broder.]

G512 "Crawford (m. Seeger), Ruth." Ibid., p. 516 [$3/4$ col.].

American composer and author, 1901-1953, studied in Paris and Berlin in 1930 on a Guggenhim fellowship and in 1933 represented the U. S. A. at the ISCM. Wife of Charles Seeger, chief of the Music Division of the Pan-American Union, she collected and transcribed folk material. As music editor of *Our Singing Country* by John A. and Alan Lomax she transcribed 200 songs from field recordings. Titles of ten "chief compositions" are listed.

G513 "Cushing, Charles." Ibid., p. 565 [$2/3$ col.].

American composer, born 1905 in Oakland, CA, studied at the University of California and with Nadia Boulanger at the École Normale de Musique. His compositions, mainly chamber music, are listed in a brief "Catalogue of Works."

G514 "Dahl, Ingolf." Ibid., p. 574-5 [$1/2$ col.].

American pianist, conductor, and composer of German birth and Swiss parentage, born 1912, was a pupil of Stravinsky and works mostly in a chamber music form. Five titles are named.

G515 "Delaney, Robert Mills." Ibid., p. 647 [$2/3$ col.].

Born in Baltimore in 1903, Delaney studied at the Univeristy of Southern California and with Boulanger. He was awarded a Guggenheim fellowship in 1929 and won the 1933 Pulitzer Prize. His works, "widely performed," are listed in four categories-- choral, orchestra, violin and orchestra, and chamber.

G516 "Dello Joio, Norman." Ibid., p. 660 [1 $1/3$ col.].

American pianist, organist, and composer, born 1913, was influenced in his early works by Hindemith. Now "his own more lyrical personality" has emerged, together with impressionist tendencies in harmony and orchestration. His music is fundamentally melodic and has considerable rhythmic tension and variety. His "chief compositions" are listed under ten headings.

G517 "Diamond, David (Leo)." Ibid., p. 683-4 [2 col.].

Born in Rochester in 1915, Diamond studied with Bernard Rogers, Boulanger, Sessions, and others. He has written in many forms, showing an early and persistent trend toward the symphonic dimension. His modal sound is achieved through harmonic colouring. *Rounds for Strings* is modal and polyphonic, with a closer integration of ends and means. His expression is "personal, lyric-romantic and intense;" his technical command appears to be fully accomplished. [*4th edn., supp., $1/3$ col., by Reese.]

G518 "Donovan, Richard Frank." Ibid., p. 738 [$5/8$ col.].

American composer, born 1891 in New Haven, has written numerous works, about ten of which are listed.

G519 "Duke, John Woods." Ibid., p. 798 [$3/8$ col.].

Born 1899, Duke has been professor at Smith College since 1923. His 60-70 songs are frequently performed on recitals. Ten titles are listed.

G520   "Effinger, Cecil."   Ibid., p. 888 [1 $1/3$ col.].

Born in Colorado Springs in 1914, this American oboist and composer has an unusually large output that includes numerous transcriptions for band and for orchestra and 200 dance band arrangements in 1934-38. The classified list is "only a selection of his works."

G521   "Elkus, Albert (Israel)."   Ibid., p. 931 [$2/5$ col.].

American composer and teacher, born 1884, taught at Mills College from 1929 on and at the San Francisco Conservatory, Dominican College at San Rafael, and elsewhere. Five "principal works" are listed.

G522   "Elwell, Herbert."   Ibid., p. 936-7 [$2/3$ col.].

American teacher, critic and composer, born 1898, was head of composition and theory at the Cleveland Institute of Music until he retired to compose in 1945. Nine titles are listed.

G523   "Engel, Lehmann."   Ibid., p. 946 [$2/3$ col.].

American conductor and composer, born 1910, is "one of the best-known American wirters of incidental music for the theatre." Ten "other works of importance" are listed.

G524   "Etler, Alvin Derald."   Ibid., p. 976 [$1/3$ col.].

American composer, born 1913, is also a member of the Indianapolis Symphony Orchestra; he is on the Yale School of Music faculty and teaches privately. Eight "principal works" are listed.

G525   "Farwell, Arthur."   Ibid., vol. 3, p. 36 [1 $1/4$ col.].

American composer, 1872-1952, studied songs of American Indians and folk material of Spanish Californians. He founded the Wa-Wan Press in 1901. A "Catalogue of Works" occupies over half the entry. [*4th edn., supp., $1/8$ col., by Broder, plus as much in vol. 2 by Richard Aldrich, from 3rd edn.]

G526   "Fickenscher, Arthur."   Ibid., p. 83 [$7/16$ col.].

American composer and investigator, born 1871, studied in Munich, then from 1920-1941 headed the Music Department at the University of Virginia. In 1941 he became a full time composer. Ten works are listed. [*4th edn., supp., $5/8$ col., by Nathan Broder]

G527   "Fine, Irving."   Ibid., p. 114 [$1/2$ col.].

American conductor and composer, born 1915, studied with Boulanger and has been on the Harvard University faculty since 1940. Ten works are listed.

G528   "Finney, Ross Lee."   Ibid., p. 134-5 [$2/3$ col.].

Born 1906, Finney is on the Smith College music staff and is editor of the Smith College Music Archives. Twenty-two "outstanding works" are listed.

G529   "Foss, Lukas." Ibid., p. 454 [3/4 col.].

American pianist, conductor, and composer born in Germany in 1922 came to the U. S. A. in his teens. A prodigy, he is very much a part of the young American group. Contact with American school, especially the group around Copland, gave him tradition and stability against which to develop. Early works were chromatic, brittle, but brilliant; from about 1944 on there has been steady progress in the maturing of a very individual style and a beautiful melodic gift.

G530   "Fuller, Donald." Ibid., p. 522 [1/5 col.].

American composer, born 1919, graduated from Yale University and studied with Wagenaar, Copland, and Milhaud. A few works are listed.

G531   "Gillis, Don." Ibid., p. 643 [3/4 col.].

American trumpeter, trombonist, and composer, born 1912, writes music that aims at no subtleties and solves no aesthetic problems; he wishes it to be widely popular. Half of the entry is a list of some of his numerous works.

G532   "Goldman, Richard Franko." Ibid., p. 699 [2/3 col.].

American bandmaster and composer, born 1911, has been an ACA board member and is now on the Board of Directors of the League of Composers. Eight works are listed.

G533   "Gould, Morton." Ibid., p. 727-8 (1 1/3 col.].

American pianist, conductor, and composer, born 1913, is one of the few to move from Broadway to the concert domain (usually the move is the other way about). With Marc Blitzstein, Gould has contributed to the "process of fusion" between the popular idiom of Broadway and the standards of craftsmanship of symphonic music. Compositions are listed by genre, in about one-half column.

G534   "Griffes, Charles T." Ibid., p. 812-13 [1 1/2 col.].

American composer of German origin, 1884-1920, held teaching positions (perhaps overwork as a schoolmaster led to his early death) and composed in his leisure moments, producing some earlier American masterpieces. He heard recordings of Javanese music, and his music shows some orientalism: the Opus 9 songs are on five- and six-note scales, and he wrote a ballet in the manner of a *Noh* play. His music is "impressionistic and picturesque and highly coloured to a degree." Catalogue of works is arranged by genre. [*4th edn., 1/2 col., by Richard Aldrich, from 3rd edn.; adds. P. G.-H.]

G535   "Guion, David (Wendel Fentress)." Ibid., p. 845 [3/8 col.].

American composer, born in Texas in 1895, has composed many musical works based on musical idioms of the South West (Negro and cowboy songs) and music for a primitive African-style ballet. A teacher and choral director, he has composed choral works, many on folk material.

G536 "Haieff, Alexei." Ibid., vol. 4, p. 16-17 [1 col.].

Born in Russia in 1914, this American composer "is basically of the neo-classic school of Paris in his technical and aesthetic approach." His music has crispness, vitality, and natural attractiveness, without academicism or restriction. Several works are mentioned and four more are listed.

G537 "Hammond, Richard." Ibid., p. 36 [^{2}/$_5$ col.].

American composer of English origin, born 1896, studied at Yale University and with Nadia Boulanger in Paris. He is also an administrator (now a member of the Hollywood Bowl Association) and writer, and was American delegate to ISCM festivals at Salzburg, London, and Venice. Short paragraph names his works, including three ballets and several orchestral works.

G538 "Harman, Carter. Ibid., p. 71 [^{1}/$_2$ col.].

American critic and composer, born 1918, studied with Sessions and Luening. Last paragraph names many works, including one commissioned by the Ballet Society in 1947.

G539 "Harrison, Lou." Ibid., p. 116-17 [1 col.].

Born 1917 in Portland, Oregon, Harrison studied with Cowell, Cooper, and Schoenberg and is part of a Pacific coast group (Cowell, Cage) working with pure percussion. He selects "systems" as others select styles or idioms, writing an atonal piece, neo-classic piece, a strict medieval modal polyphonic piece, a Hindu or Balinese piece. Eleven titles are given.

G540 "Herrmann, Bernard." Ibid., p. 255 [^{7}/$_8$ col.].

American conductor and composer, born 1911, worked at CBS from 1934 and conducts rarely-performed music, old and new. Works dated 1936-1950, listed by genre, include an opera and music for seven films.

G541 "Holden, David Justin." Ibid, p. 322 [^{1}/$_3$ col.].

American composer, born 1911, also a teacher (Boston Conservatory, Holyoke College), has written *Say, Paw*, a rhapsody on Kentucky mountain tunes. Last paragraph lists several other works.

G542 "Hovhaness, Alan." Ibid., p. 386-7 [1 ^{2}/$_3$ col.].

American composer of Armenian descent, born 1911, uses a modern orchestra, preferring strings and trumpets with occasional additions of percussion, but with Asiatic (cumulative and hypnotic) rather than Western (climactic) expressive content. His music is not tonal in the key sense but usually revolves around some note or two or three notes; his structural procedure relies on melodic and rhythmic rather than harmonic elements.

G543 "Imbrie, Andrew." Ibid., p. 441-2 [^{1}/$_2$ col.]

American pianist and composer, born 1921, graduated from Princeton in 1942. He won several prizes for his music in the early 1940s; four "other works" date from 1947 and 1948.

G544   "Ives, Charles."   Ibid., p. 560 [1 $1/3$ col.].

American composer, 1874-1954, was also an organist and business man. An experimentalist as early as 1895, he is the "archetypal ancestor" of much of today's musical "Americana." Though many of his works are "without synthesis," they are full of "vigour, imagination" and many "rugged and homely" American musical elements. Catalogue of works by genre occupies one-half column. [*4th edn., supp., $7/8$ col. by Reese, adds. P. G.-H.]

G545   "James, Philip."   Ibid., p. 577 [1 $1/2$ col.].

American conductor, scholar, and composer, born 1890, is also a teacher (Columbia University, New York University). His style shows technical mastery, spontaneity, and freshness, and is not radical. Titles of his "most important works" 1913-1949 occupy three-fourths column. [*4th edn., supp., $7/8$ col., by Reese.]

G546   "Johnson, Hunter."   Ibid., p. 647 [$1/3$ col.].

American composer, born 1906 in North Carolina, spent 1933-1935 in Europe through the American Prix de Rome, and was awarded a Guggenheim fellowship in 1941. He is head of the theory department at the University of Manitoba. Last paragraph lists some of Johnson's works.

G547   "Jones, Charles."   Ibid., p. 656 [$11/12$ col.].

American composer was born in Canada in 1916. His music has been performed throughout the U. S. A. Catalogue of works by genre 1937-1948 includes nine orchestral works and six for piano.

G548   "Kay, Ulysses Simpson."   Ibid., p. 712 [$1/2$ col.].

"American (Negro) composer" born 1917 has won many prizes, including a Rosenwald fellowship in 1947-1948. Sixteen "principal works" are listed, dated 1939-1946.

G549   "Kerr, Harrison."   Ibid., p. 729 [$2/3$ col.].

American composer, born 1899, is also an "active musical citizen"--member of the editorial boards of New Music Editions and New Music Recordings, and Executive Secretary of the American Music Centre. His music is rather chromatic though not atonally so, "vivid, yet austere." A fine flow of ideas unfolds with naturalness and force within "boundaries of considerable formal strength." Sixteen "chief works" are listed, dated 1929-1945.

G550   "Kohs, Ellis."   Ibid., p. 815 [$3/5$ col.].

American composer, born 1916, has taught at the University of Middleton, CT, Stamford University, and, since 1950, at the University of Southern California. His *Concerto for Orchestra* was performed at the ISCM festival in Berkeley, 1942. Sixteen works are named, and a few more "principal works" are listed.

G551   "Lahmer, Reuel."   Ibid., vol. 5, p. 17-18 [$2/3$ col.].

Born in Ontario in 1912, this American composer studied at Cornell University and taught there 1940-41. He became Harris's assistant at Colorado College in 1948.

Choral works, orchestral works, chamber music, and music for one instrument with pianoforte are listed, dated 1939-1949.

G552   "Lessard, John Ayres." Ibid., p. 145 [1/3 col.].

American composer, born 1920, studied with Nadia Boulanger in Boston and Paris. His works are "finely constructed and tastefully stylized in the neo-classic manner" but so far show no great independence of thought within the aesthetic and technique of the "School of Paris." Seven "chief works" are listed.

G553   "Levant, Oscar." Ibid., p. 151 [1/3 col.].

American composer, born 1906, hovers "somewhere between the 'serious' and 'popular' territories." He is also a jazz band pianist and has composed film scores, a pianoforte concerto, orchestral pieces, two pianoforte sonatinas, and a string quartet.

G554   "Luening, Otto." Ibid., pp. 420-1 [1 1/2 col.].

Born in Milwaukee in 1900, this American conductor and composer studied in Munich and Zurich, returning to the U. S. A. in 1920. He held a Guggenheim fellowship in 1930, and from 1932 taught at the University of Arizona and then Bennington College. Catalogue of works lists titles by genre.

G555   "McBride, Robert (Guyn)." Ibid., p. 459 [2/3 col.].

American instrumentalist and composer, born 1911, performs on clarinet, oboe, saxophone, and pianoforte, and began teaching at Bennington College in 1935. Fifteen of his "most important" works are listed, dated 1932-1945.

G556   "McPhee, Colin." Ibid., pp. 483-4 [1 1/4 col.].

American composer, born in Montreal in 1901, composed music "more notable for its quality than for its quantity" before his sojourn in Bali in the 1930s. His *Tabuh Tabuhan* is a "synthesis of ancient and modern elements." While not a transcription of Balinese materials, it uses Balinese principles--pentatonic scale, block polyphonic structure of melody and rhythm without harmony. McPhee evolved from this "his own vivid, stylized and powerfully free form of expression." Seven "chief compositions" are named, to the 1944 *Four Iroquois Dances* for orchestra. [*4th edn., supp., 1/3 col. by Hector Charlesworth, calls him a "Canadian pianist and composer."]

G557   "Menasce, Jacques de." Ibid., p. 673 [1 col.].

"American pianist and composer of Austrian birth," born 1905, is a naturalized American citizen, active in the League of Composers. His music, not easy to classify, is "his own personal blend of the more expressive elements of several styles of the present time" and is respected for its fastidiousness and craftsmanship. In structure it is closer to impressionism than to any other "species." Emotionally and even idiomatically it is like late Bartók works in its "sombreness" and "vivid, crisp chromaticism." Twenty-two "outstanding works" are listed, dated 1934-1947.

G558   "Mennin, Peter." Ibid., p. 710 [5/6 col.].

American composer, born 1923, studied with Normand Lockwood at Oberlin College, then with Hanson and Rogers at the Eastman School. He is "one of the youngest, newest and most promising composers on the American scene." His music is not aggressively "modern" in the sense of the two well-known schools of modernism,

neo-classicism and atonalism. Rather it is neo-romantic in feeling and somewhat impressionist in approach. It is diatonic, often dissonant, flowing, and it is built on a large scale. It has a good melodic sense and is full of rhythmic interest. The rhythmic drive is "integrated and structural rather than decorative." Soon an "idiomatic maturity" should emerge that will match his technical one. Eleven of his "outstanding works" are listed, dated 1941-1947.

G559   "Menotti, Gian Carlo." Ibid., p. 710-11 [1 1/3 col.].

American composer of Italian birth, born 1911, came to the U. S. A. in 1928 on a scholarshp to the Curtis Institute. His opera *Amelia Goes to the Ball* was performed at Curtis in 1937 and later at the Metropolitan Opera and in Europe. *The Medium* was an instant success in 1946, owing to "his own well-knit libretto, an acute sense of theatre and some atmospheric music." *The Telephone* was a Broadway "hit," thereby confusing the "rather fixed minds" of the Broadway entertainment world. *The Consul* ran several weeks in London in 1950. *Amahl and the Night Visitors*, a new short opera, was televised in December 1951. Last paragraph lists several non-operatic pieces. Bibliography lists an article in *Music and Letters* on *The Consul*. [*4th edn., supp., 1/2 col., by Reese.]

G560   "Mills, Charles." Ibid., p. 781 [1 1/16 col.].

American composer, born 1914, studied with Copland, Sessions, and Harris and has won many prizes. Catalogue of works dated 1935-1949 lists titles by genre.

G561   "Moore, Douglas Stuart" Ibid., pp. 864-5 [1 2/3 col.].

American composer and author, born 1893, won the 1951 Pulitzer Prize for his opera *Giants in the Earth* and has taught at Columbia University since 1952. His style is highly melodic, with rich though unusual harmonic texture. His music has an American folk sound to it, as though he "had absorbed, digested and forgotten" the whole American folk music heritage, "or as though it had become a spring, deep underground." His music has a fresh spontaneity and romanticism and has been underestimated when "certain 'modern at all costs' groups have held the stage." His "chief compositions" 1924-1950 are listed by genre, and two books. [*4th edn., supp., 1/2 col., by Reese.]

G562   "Moross, Jerome." Ibid., p. 899 [2/3 col.].

American composer, born 1913, has done much work for the theatre, and is especially interested in discovering blends betwen the vernacular and art aesthetics, and between the opera, dance, and spoken play forms. Titles and performances are listed, then nine "other works."

G563   "Nabokov, Nikolay." Ibid., vol. 6, p. 1 [1 1/2 col.].

American composer of Russian origin, born 1903, had a ballet-oratorio produced by Diaghilev in 1920 in Paris, Berlin, and London. He came to the U. S. to lecture in 1933, became a U. S. citizen in 1939, and held a U. S. government position overseas in 1944-1947. His writings have appeared in the *New York Herald Tribune, New Republic, Atlantic Monthly, Harper's Magazine,* and the *Partisan Review.* A classified list of his "most important" compositions occupies one-half column.

G564   "Nordoff, Paul." Ibid., p. 102 [1/2 col.].

American pianist and composer, born 1901, held Guggenheim fellowships in 1933 and 1935 and won the Pulitzer Prize in 1940 for his *Piano Quintet* (1936). Ten works are listed.

G565   "Ornstein, Leo."   Ibid., p. 449 [^{2}/$_3$ col.].

American pianist and composer of Russian origin, born 1895, made his New York debut in 1911 and wrote shatteringly discordant music as part of a group of dissonant and noisy composers up to and about the 1920s. Twelve of his "principal works" are listed. [*4th edn., 1/4 col., by Warren Storey Smith.]

G566   "Palmer, Robert."   Ibid., p. 530 [^{2}/$_3$ col.].

American composer, born 1915, studied with Hanson, Rogers, Harris, and Copland. He began teaching at the University of Kansas in 1940 and then at Cornell University in 1943. Twenty-one "principal" works are listed, to 1948.

G567   "Persichetti, Vincent."   Ibid., pp. 682-3 [1 col.].

American composer, born 1915, studied with Nordoff and with Roy Harris. He began teaching at Juilliard in 1947. Twenty-one "principal works" are listed, including the prize-winning *Dance Overture*, 1942, performed at Rochester in 1944 under Hanson, the latest being the *Symphony No. 3* (1947).

G568   "Phillips, Burrill."   Ibid., p. 716 [^{3}/$_4$ col.].

Born in Omaha in 1907, this American composer studied with Hanson and Rogers, earning a B. Mus. at the Eastman School in 1932 and a Master's degree in 1933. His earlier style was programmatic, with a cultivated Americanism. Later he was quoted (by David Ewen) as saying that "no serious and honest American composer could keep the desirable Americanness out of his music if he wanted." Several works are named and seventeen others from among his "most important" works, to 1947, are listed.

G569   "Piston, Walter."   Ibid., pp. 783-4 [2 col.].

American composer and teacher, born 1894, studied music at Harvard University beginning at age 26, and in 1926 began teaching at Harvard. He is a solid craftsman and at the same time original and venturesome in his idiom; his work as both teacher and composer has had an important influence. His style is neo-classical; a tremendous contrapuntal strength gives his music volume and depth. Harmony adds "a dissonant astringency," or intensity, or lyricism, and he also uses the force of rhythmic complexity and syncopation. Catalogue of works, by genre, occupies 3/5 column.

G570   "Riegger, Wallingford."   Ibid., vol. 7, pp. 162-3 [2 col.].

American conductor and composer, born 1885, has taken his mother's family name as his first name. His early works were conservative, showing the classical inheritance and a nineteenth-century atmosphere. A transition began in the *Study in Sonority* for ten violins or any multiple of ten. Later works use Schoenberg's twelve-tone technique in an independent way, and with a "rugged rhythmic impulse" unlike Schoenberg's. Riegger's work in the theatre, particularly for dancers, was perhaps a "liberating experience" for him, as for many another composer, for, unlike the concert forms, theatre music requires "vividness and vitality of ideas and adaptability in form." Classified list of "principal works" includes titles dated 1922-1948. [4th edn., supp., 2/3 col., by Reese.]

G571   "Rogers, Bernard."   Ibid., pp. 203-4 [1 ^{1}/16 col.].

American composer, born 1895, studied at the Institute of Musical Art in New York and privately with Bloch in Cleveland. He has won many prizes for his music, including the Pulitzer Prize, a Guggenheim, and, for the opera *The Marriage of Aude*, the David Bispham Medal and an Eastman School Publication Award. His opera *The Warrior* won the Alice M. Ditson Fund Award and was produced by the Metropoli-tan Opera Company in New York. Other works named include *Invasion*, commis-sioned by the League of Composers, two works on recordings, orchestral works, a string quartet, and music for documentary films. A classified list of works follows the article's signature P. G.-H.

G572   "Rudhyar, Dane."   Ibid., pp. 325-6 [1 ^{1}/3 col.].

American composer , painter, poet, and philosopher of French descent (real name, Daniel de Chennevière) was born in Paris in 1895 and came to America in 1916. He is interested in Oriental philosophy and is "an astrologer of wide renown." In the 1920s he pioneered the dissonant style in the U. S. A. and was a founding member of the International Composers' Guild, an *avant-garde* organization of Varèse, Cowell, and others, in New York. His style is rugged, dissonant, and chromatic, showing "affinity with rather than similarity to, the late work of Skriabin." Catalogue of works dated 1914-1940 is classified as to genre.

G573   "Sanders, Robert."   Ibid., p. 400 [1 ^{1}/3 col.].

American composer, born in Chicago in 1906, has had many performances and many scholastic, administrative, and conducting posts. His earlier works are "romantic in kind and chromatic in idiom." Latterly, his work is closer to the French and neo-classic "line of thought" with concise forms, more closely knit, and a dissonant chromatic idiom. "Like many other American composers he writes extremely well for brass instruments." A classified list of compositions is included.

G574   "Schuman, William (Howard)."   Ibid., pp. 599-600 [2 ^{1}/2 col.].

American composer, born 1910, though one of the younger Americans in years, is more firmly established in his music's maturity and in public recognition than the rest of his own generation. His style has "a tremendous vigour, a great length and breadth of line and idea, and a curious intensity." A gift of writing long, flowing lines must have been inherent in Schuman, but study with Harris aided the stabilization of idiom; the two are alike in the urgency and volume of their expressive gifts and in structural invention. Schuman's idiom is melodic and rhythmic in emphasis; clashes come from bitonal melodic lines, not from chromaticism. His long themes, rhythmic and sometimes disjointed, are fused by tension over long sections. His dramatic gifts, "less accurately appraised," are evident in the ballet *Undertow* and the fourth Symphony. Classified catalogue of works occupies one column.

G575   "Sessions, Roger."   Ibid., p. 724-5 [1 ^{1}/2 col.].

Born in 1896, Sessions studied at Harvard and with Parker at Yale, and taught at Smith College and the Cleveland Institute of Music. He spent 1925-1933 in Europe; his *Symphony No. 1* was performed at the ISCM festival in Geneva in 1927. He began teaching at the University of Califonia at Berkeley in 1945. His incidental music for *The Black Maskers* (1923), performed at an ISCM festival, is still widely performed. "Sessions's works are few, for a man with his reputation." He is a good musical citizen, having served in composers' organizations and presenting the Copland-Sessions concerts. Catalogue of works lists fourteen titles. [*4th edn., supp., 4/5 col., by Reese.]

G576   "Shapero, Harold." Ibid., p. 739 [$1/2$ col.].

American composer, born 1920, received an A.B. degree from Harvard in 1941, studied with Slonimsky, Krenek, Piston, Hindemith, and Boulanger, and has had several noteworthy performances. Six chamber works are named, dated 1939-1947.

G577   "Smit, Leo (ii)." Ibid., p. 851 [$1/2$ col.].

American pianist and composer, born 1921, studied piano from age six (his Carnegie Hall debut was in 1939) and composition from age fourteen. His ballet *Virginia Sampler*, commissioned by the Ballet Russe de Monte Carlo, was first performed in New York in 1947. Other "outstanding" works are listed by genre and dated 1940-1949.

G578   "Spelman, Timothy Mather." Ibid., vol. 8, p. 4 [$1/2$ col.].

Born in Brooklyn in 1891, this American composer was educated at the Munich Conservatory. Classified list of works is included.

G579   "Thompson, Randall." Ibid., pp. 429-30 [$1/2 + 5/6$ col.].

Information from the previous edition on the education and professional life of this "American composer and educationist," born 1899, is followed by a bibliography and a catalogue of works, signed P. G.-H. ($5/6$ col.). [*4th edn., supp., $1/2$ col. by Nathan Broder.]

G580   "Thomson Virgil." Ibid., p. 432-3 [4 col.].

American critic and composer, born 25 November 1896, has developed a style featuring: hymn-like melody; condensed and diatonic harmonic structure; objective treatment of content; and brilliance and economy of orchestration. Pianoforte "portraits" of his friends show the influence of Paris in the 1920s, when composers and painters were part of the same movement. Bibliography lists only Glanville-Hicks's own 1949 *Musical Quarterly* article on Thomson (**G110**). This entry, the longest by far of her American composer entries, also discusses *The Seine at Night* and *Wheatfield at Noon*, not mentioned in her earlier article.

G581   Wagenaar, Bernard." Ibid., vol. 9, pp. 86-7 [l $1/2$ col.].

American violinist, conductor, and composer of Dutch birth, born in 1894, came to the U. S. A. in 1920 and became an American citizen in 1927. His symphonic works have been performed in New York and elsewhere conducted by Mengelberg, Tosca- nini, and others. Virgil Thomson called the *Third Symphony* (1937) "authoritative, cultured, wordly, incisive without profundity." Classified list of works occupies one-half column.

G582   Ward, Robert." Ibid., p. 178 [$1/2$ col.].

American composer, born 1917, studied pianoforte as a child, won a scholarship to the Eastman School in 1939, where he studied with Royce, Hanson, Rogers, and a graduate scholarship to Juilliard. Prizes include a Ditson award in 1944 and one from the American Academy of Arts and Letters in 1946. Several "principal works" are listed, dated 1937-1947.

G583   "Weber, Ben." Ibid., p. 222 [$1/3$ col.].

Born 1916, this American composer settled in New York in 1945 and is active in the
U. S. A. section of the ISCM. He won a $1,000 grant in 1950 from the National
Institute of Arts and Letters, and a Guggenheim fellowship for 1950-51. His
"principal compositions" are listed, dated 1939-1950.

G584 "Wigglesworth, Frank."   Ibid., p. 290 [3/4 col.].

American composer, born 1918, was educated at Bard College, Columbia University,
and Converse College (South Carolina), studying with White, Luening, and Cowell.
He has won many prizes, including the American Prix de Rome for 1951-52 and 1952-
53, and an Academy of Arts and Letters award, and is the editor of New Music
Editions and New Music Recordings. Long paragraph lists his "outstanding works"
dated 1940-1950.

[*Note:* **G585** through **G592** are articles on Danish composers in *Grove's Dictionary*, 5th edn.
Format is the same as for American composer articles.]

G585 "Bentzon, Niels Viggo." *Grove's Dictionary*, 5th edn. (1954), vol. l, p.
630-l [1 1/2 col.].

Danish composer, born 1919, he is one of Denmark's most original creators. His
music has "structural strength" like Hindemith's but is not tied to the Teutonic
"figured-bass" foundation, rather tending toward "spatial, rhythmic or segmentary
thematic material" and sustained by "inherent impetus," not by mechanical devices.

G586 "Gram, Peder." Ibid., vol. 3, p. 745 [2/3 col.].

Early works of this Danish composer, born 1881, showed his basically nordic-
romantic inspiration, later works a freshness and transparency similar to the French
school. [*4th ed., by Greville L. Knyvett; 5th ed., adds. P. G.-H.]

G587 "Høffding, Finn." Ibid., vol. 4, p. 312 [1/2 col.].

Danish composer, born 1899, wrote much music for his "music schools for the
people," also operas, symphonies, concertos, and choral music.

G588 "Holmboe, Vagn." Ibid., p. 327 (1 1/2 col.].

Danish composer, born 1909, is the most characteristically Danish of the younger
Danish composers. His music is basically tonal, with a "restricted and stylized"
musical element as in folk music, and rhythmic "exhilaration without restlessness."

G589 "Koppel, Herman D. (David)." Ibid., p. 822 [1 1/3 col.].

Danish pianist and composer, born 1908, makes highly personal use of methods of
Hindemith and (stronger) French or neo-classic school of Paris.

G590 "Schultz, Svend." Ibid., vol. 7, p. 596-7 [5/6 col.].

Danish composer, critic and conductor, born 1913, writes entertaining and optimistic
music, leaning toward expressionism and simplicity of form, not austerity.

G591 "Tarp, Svend Erik." Ibid., vol. 8, p. 311-12 [1 col.].

Danish composer, born 1908, also a teacher at Copenhagen University, became musical advisor to a "protection-of-composers'-rights organization." Article includes a classified "Catalog of Works."

G592 "Weis, Flemming." Ibid., vol. 9, p. 245 [$^3/_4$ col.).

Danish composer, born 1898, writes music with the linear texture and humour of French neo-classicism, with harmonic and chromatic details that are romantic in the tradition of Nielsen. He is also an "active musical citizen in the executive sense," as in his serving as president of the Danish section of the ISCM.

1954, CONTINUED

G593 Liner notes for Lou Harrison, *Suite for Violin, Piano, and Small Orchestra*, and Ben Weber, *Symphony on Poems of William Blake*. RCA Victor LP LM-1785. 1954.

Notes on Harrison are quoted by Oliver Daniel in liner notes for the *Suite* issued in 1957 by Composers Recordings, Inc., CRI 114, and in **B325** (1980): Formally this is "quantitative music rather than climactic, though high tension points are reached by exciting handling of the melodic curve, or by elboration, and sometimes sudden simplification of the instrumentation. Such devices take the place of the constructed climax of Western musical thought. Notes on Weber are quoted in the review of the recording by James Lyons, *American Record Guide* 20, no. 9 (May 1954), p. 326: "Atonalism is indeed the 'lost generation' style in music, and, as such, of course it has quite a following. Mr. Weber's work should appeal to all these."

G594 Liner notes for *Three Gymnopédies*. Remington R 199 188. 1954.

The *Three Gymnopédies* "have gotten loose upon the musical scene more or less by accident." They were written "on three successive Saturdays just before my departure to the Caribbean in the spring of 1953," to fill a modest and almost anonymous role as fillers for CBS radio, in response to comment by Oliver Daniel, a CBS program director. When I returned, they had been recorded, complete with one or two wrong notes in my score. The *gymnopédie* is an ancient slow dance used to instill grace in strong Greek athletes--"rather as though the "Brooklyn Dodgers, or our most illustrious ring champs, had to pass before the critical eye of George Balanchine." These three pieces were originally parts of early works--a 1934 orchestral suite written in Granada, Spain ("Spanish Suite"), and a Recorder Trio from student days in Austria.

G595 Liner Notes for *Zabaleta--Anthology of Solo Harp Music*, v. 3: "18th Century." Nicanor Zabaleta, harp. Esoteric 524. 1954. (Reissued on Counterpoint label).

Zabaleta has "some special radar for discovering the whereabouts of original harp music"--here, music by C. P. E. Bach, Beethoven, Mayer, Rosetti, and Krumpholtz. Playing shows characteristic Spanish "balance of the intellectual and emotional attributes."

G596 "Rochester Hears American Music." *Musical America* 74, no. 8 (June 1954), p. 3, 27.

The 24th annual Festival of American Music 3-10 May at the Eastman School of Music featured a high level of performance, and a wide variety of works representing the "more indigenous, more stable aspects" of American music. Howard Hanson "has rallied at Rochester these many years professors and student composers who practise sound, neutral techniques and a natural tonal idiom as a point of departure for the growth of a personal esthetic." This music may well outlast the more fashionable experiments of our time. Highly praised is Harris' Seventh Symphony. Fine esthetic selectivity was shown in Piston's Third Symphony (a master composer) and Carter's First Symphony (some problems in form--a "subject matter weak in growth potential" is subjected to mechanical development or repetition, neither of which sustains a work of this length). Also noteworthy were Donovan's *New England Chronicle* (1947), Antheil's opera *Volpone*, Owen Reed's Mexican Folk Song Symphony, and works of Thomson, Hanson, Tuthill, Bernard Rogers, and Riegger. Also performed were works of Bloom, Weed, Wayne Barlow, Hovhaness, Porter, Mennin, Will Gay Bottje, Ward, and Persichetti.

1954, CONTINUED: *HERALD TRIBUNE* (JANUARY-APRIL)

G597   " 'La Traviata' At the Met." *NYHT*, 5 January 1954, p. 19, col. 8.

Jan Peerce sang the role of Alfredo for the first time last night, with "a splendid presence" that commands attention "all the time he is onstage" but he was not in good voice. "Licia Albanese is simply lovely as Violetta" and Ettore Bastianini received ovations for his magnificent Georgio Germont, in this Verdi opera.

G598   "Robert McDowell." *NYHT*, 8 January 1954, p. 11, col. 1-2.

Debut by "exciting and highly equipped young pianist" included Sonatas of Scarlatti and Beethoven and works of Schumann and Falla. He is "a natural virtuoso" who dramatizes sudden contrasts and uses "slightly erratic rubato effects" as a personal and tasteful idiosyncracy.

G599   "3 Debuts Mark 'Figaro' at Met." *NYHT*, 11 January 1954, p. 10, col. 1.

Seasonal debuts by Eleanor Steber (Countess Almaviva), Nadine Connor ("brilliant and charming" as Susanna), and Gerhard Pechner (Don Bartolo) were part of Saturday night's "elegant and scintillating performance" of the Mozart opera conducted by Fritz Stiedry.

G600   " 'Music in the Making.' " Ibid., col. 5-6.

Another of David Broekman's forums at Cooper Union, sponsored by Local 802, presented "four more amazing pieces"--by Gunther Schuller, Dallapiccola, Schoenberg, and Henry Brant. Brant's *Millenium No. 2* for thirty brass and four busy percussionists "closed this highly dissonant program with deafening volume." Broekman has conducted forty-five new American works in the last two seasons, which he says makes "95 percent more than the three major orchestras" in New York put together.

G601   "Dutch Violin Sonatas." *NYHT*, 14 January 1954, p. 19, col. 5-6.

Arved Kurtz and Otto Hertz performed sonatas of Juriaan Andriessen (1946), Willem Pijper (1919), and Henk Badings (1932). All three works "had late romantic chromaticism as their rather gloomy esthetic climate," but the Badings sonata is best, with "integrated" chromatic idiom and romantic "vein," and had the most polished performance.

G602   "Aladar Ecsedy, Pianist." *NYHT*, 15 January 1954, p. 13, col. 1.

Young Hungarian pianist in his New York debut performed Bach, Liszt, and Chopin, but has "insufficient basic technique" to appear "before the highly critical New York audience."

G603   " 'Paris and Helen' Receives U. S. Premiere at Town Hall." *NYHT*, 16 January 1954, p. 6, col. 1-2.

American Chamber Opera Society presented an "exhilarating" production of Gluck's opera, conducted by the "brilliant" young Arnold Gamson and featuring "four superb soloists."

G604   "Boston Orchestra." *NYHT*, Sunday, 17 January 1954, sect. 1, p. 31, col. 1.

Charles Munch conducted Brahms's Haydn Variations, Haydn's D major Cello Concerto, with Paul Tortellier an "authoritative" soloist, and Saint-Saens' Symphony No. 3 in C minor. Munch emphasized the "austerity" of Brahms rather than the work's inner "purity and sweetness." The Saint-Saens work was "quite splendidly given," though it is far removed from the "classic trend" toward "selectivity and restriction." In such "sky's-the-limit" orchestrations, "esthetics disappear altogether."

G605   "Szpinalski, Violinist." *NYHT*, 18 January 1954, p. 11, col. 2.

Four first performances by George Szpinaliski, a "somewhat uneven performer" comprised a recital of sonatas of an American, Carl Bricken, the French François Serett, Grazyna Bacewicz from Poland, and the Italian Antonio Veretti. None has "particular distinction;" parts of the Bacewicz "held interest" and the Italian twelve-tone piece had ingenious "effects."

G606   "Composers' Forum." Ibid.

Featured composers were Spartaco Monello from California and Salvador Ley, a visiting Guatemalan. Monello's string quartet and other chamber music used "a highly dissonant chromaticism," at times twelve-tone, with the style's usual minimum contrasts and "unresolved suspense." Ley's idiom was "entirely tonal and with a certain Spanish or regional sound to it." A group of songs was rich in "melodic invention," with accompaniment material that was "atmospheric rather than organic to the composition."

G607   "Philharmonic Ensemble." *NYHT*, 19 January 1954, p. 18, col. 3-4.

Music for winds and solo string items--by Beethoven, Jacques Ibert, Manuel Rosenthal, and Mozart--were presented at the Hotel Plaza last night in the first private concert of the Philharmonic Chamber Ensemble. Rosenthal's early *Sonatine for Two Violins and Piano* has "a curious, acid sound" but is "extraordinarily well thought out for the instruments and the performance was fine."

G608   "Young People's Concert Given." *NYHT*, Sunday, 24 January 1954, sect. 1, p. 33, col. 5-6.

Wilfrid Pelletier conducted the Philharmonic Orchestra on Saturday morning with Deems Taylor as commentator on the history and development of the symphony. A Trumpet Overture by Arcady Dubensky was followed by excerpts from Haydn, Mozart, and Beethoven symphonies; a fourteen-year-old pianist from Venezuela, Judith Jaimes, performed the last movement of Beethoven's Piano Concerto in C minor.

G609   "Jacqueline Basinet, Soprano." *NYHT*, 26 January 1954, p. 13, col. 2.

Music of "intrinsic interest" by Schubert, Pfitzner, Strauss, Poulenc, and others displayed a "good" voice, thoroughly trained. Interpretively "a monotony" made listening rather boring. Her tone is "smooth" and "well controlled" except in faster music.

G610   "The Philharmonic." *NYHT*, 29 January 1954, p. 12, col. 6.

Concert last night was "a veritable Serkin Festival" with the "magnificent pianist" performing concertos of Mozart and Beethoven and the Strauss "Burleske." Mozart's G major (K. 453) Concerto, with "Mitropoulos' magic delicacy" and Serkin's "compelling yet understated mood," was "a rarer treat for the purists" than Beethoven's G major Concerto which was "the hit of the evening with the audience."

G611   "Lieder Singer." *NYHT*, 1 February 1954, p. 13, col. 2.

Catherine Reiner "is clearly a most cultivated musician" who knows "correct lieder singing." Technique, style, and interpretive insight are "built around a pure voice and real musicality." Her voice "would appear to have passed its prime" but her performances of songs of Schubert, Brahms, Wolf, Berg, Bartok, and Kodaly have "much to be admired."

G612   "2 'Firsts' Mark 'Rigoletto' at Met." Ibid., col. 5.

Richard Tucker sang his first Duke of the season, in "a resplendent performance," his "long phrases with imperceptible breathing" contributing a "special tension and sense of pacing" to the Verdi work as a whole. Clifford Harvuot sang his first Monterone this year. Robert Merrill as Rigoletto seemed "a little tired and out of voice" in the "long and taxing role." Alberto Erede who conducted "must surely be one of the most accomplished orchestral accompanists to be heard anywhere."

G613   " 'Cosi Fan Tutte' Sung at the Met." *NYHT*, 4 February 1954, p. 19, col. 5.

In Mozart opera, Roberta Peters was "especially fine" as actress and singer, in the role of the "witty, worldly-wise Despina" the first time this season. Also appearing for the first time were Mildred Miller, who sang well as Dorabella, and Lorenzo Alvary, who gives "a finished rendering of the mischievous Don Alfonso."

G614   "Composers Forum." *NYHT*, 8 February 1954, p. 15, col. 1-2.

Marion Bauer and Leslie Bassett presented their compositions and Oliver Daniel of CBS was moderator. Bauer's Duo for Clarinet and Oboe was "to this reviewer the richest" of her three excellent little works--a two-part piece with "personality and expressivity." Bassett, in from the University of Michigan, is "a real natural-born composer, and one of many gifts." His "precocious command of technique" is "already digested" so that his materials are "whole in the terms and forms of the works he plans. His String Quartet was snappy and free in the fast sections, deeply felt in the slow ones," and he is a highly gifted "artist-craftsman."

G615   "Concert Society." Ibid., col. 3.

Daniel Saidenberg conducted the Concert Society of New York in works of Bach, Barber, Berger, and Mozart. The performers lacked their usual "sparkle and dynamic punch." Berger's *Serenade Concertante* is "elegant and highly expressive" with "fragmented contrapuntal asides."

G616   "Anne de Ramus, Pianist." *NYHT*, 13 February 1954, p. 9, col. 4.

Young pianist in her first Town Hall recital has a consistent "lumpiness" due apparently to misplacing the "accent emphasis" of the barline, neutralizing the "down beat on the first beat of the bar." This "natural syncopation" was less noticeable in the more contemporary Roussel than in Beethoven and Chopin, and should play "more real contemporary music" and no "pure classic repertory."

G617   "Janne Janesco, Soprano." *NYHT*, 15 February 1954, p. 18, col. 4.

Young dramatic soprano from Indiana sang pieces by Handel, Scarlatti, Strauss, Brahms, Fauré, and others in debut recital. She has a "potentially powerful" voice and a "lovely poetic sense" but needs instruction for "mastery and polish."

G618   "Doris Davis Contralto." Ibid., col. 4-5.

This "sensitive and intelligent singer" sang well in "sustained" passages due to "a fine breath control"--she was at her best in songs of Brahms and Fauré--but lacked stability and flexibility in "faster moving music."

G619   "3 Premieres In 'Fledermaus.' " *NYHT*, 16 February 1954, p. 17, col. 4.

Hilde Gueden sang her first Rosalinda this year, Virginia McWatters her first Adele, and Blanche Thebom her first Prince Orlofsky, in last night's "lively performance" of the Strauss work. McWatters "gives an exhilarating account of the audacious chambermaid." Thebom "seemed to enjoy hugely" her role.

G620   "Bach Aria Group." *NYHT*, 18 February 1954, p. 24, col. 3.

Four cantatas and a group of solo arias of Bach were presented by "a splendid array of musical stars"--Jennie Tourel, guest artist, and regular members Jan Peerce, Eileen Farrell, and Norman Farrow.

G621   "American Orchestra." *NYHT*, 19 February 1954, p. 18, col. 8.

Robert Scholz conducted the American Chamber Orchestra last night (Thursday). George Grossman was soloist in a Chamber Concerto for Viola and Strings by Ellis Kohs, a work that "makes sense" and has "a beautiful poetic ending very typical of this composer's special gifts." The ensemble has extraordinary "brightness and color" and players of "equalized virtuosity."

G622   "First Performances." *NYHT*, 22 February 1954, p. 11, col. 3.

First performances of works of Ben Weber, Roger Sessions, and Andre Casanova were presented by the International Society for Contemporary Music. Sessions' Sonata for Solo Violin revealed "formidable craftsmanship" and "formidable length and acid idiom"--the sound people "are afraid modern music makes." Weber's Four Songs for Voice and Cello "took the prize for inventiveness and expressivity," atonal with "personal mood." William Masselos was soloist in Casanova's attractive Concertino for Piano and Eight Instruments; "deadlines prevented its hearing through to the end."

G623   "Plays Walton Quartet." Ibid., col. 4.

The Concert Society of New York presented the Fine Arts Quartet in a slightly dry performance of "one of William Walton's most important works," the String Quartet in A minor. Hans Hotter, bass-baritone, gave a "marvelous performance" of six songs from Schubert's *Schwanengesang*. Members of the New York Wood Wind Ensemble amplified the Fine Arts Quartet in Beethoven's Septet.

G624   "Felice Takakjian, Pianist." *NYHT,* 1 April 1954, p.19, col. 2.

Recital program included works of Beethoven, Scarlatti, Mendelssohn, Martinu, Ravel, and Khachaturian. She "has authority, and plays with a good sense of form and style."

G625   "Gertrude Rennert, Pianist." *NYHT,* 9 April 1954: 6, col. 5.

"Infant" pianist (fifteen years old) in debut performed music of Scarlatti, Mozart, Schumann, Chopin, Mendelssohn, Liszt, Debussy, and a *Novelette* by Ben Kohn, also fifteen years old. "Neither infant was prodigious" though pianist has speed and clarity.

G626   "Felice Takakjian." *NYHT,* 12 April 1954, p. 13, col. 6.

Pianist played works of Bach, Brahms, and Liszt, showing "a fine sense of dramatic tension" and, on the negative side, a lack of finger strength and fluency that blurs the detail. Alan Hovhaness directed the first performance of his Concerto for Piano and Strings No. 9, a "slight" work in which the piano is accompaniment rather than thematic material most of the way.

G627   "Swiss Music Library." *NYHT,* 13 April 1954, p. 24, col. 5.

Group directed by Marguerite Staehelin presented Swiss chamber music last night (Monday)--works of Willy Burkhard, Frank Martin (*Six Monologues* from *Jedermann* of Hofmansthal for voice and piano), Oboussier, and Franz Tischhauser (a cheerful, unpretentious *Cassation for Nine Instruments* in Parisian honky-tonk style). Martin's songs, expertly sung by Elsa Cavelti, are dramatic and have "a prosodic fastidiousness that gives great definition." Harmonically innovative accompaniments punctuate the declamatory line, without thematic or figurative patterning, maintaining "expressive tension" by the sparest of means.

G628   "Virgilio Pade Dueno." *NYHT,* 15 April 1954, p. 22, col. 5.

Young Puerto Rican pianist has considerable training and seemingly little musicality. He performed sonatas of Beethoven and Prokofieff and twelve etudes of Chopin--the best technically and expressively.

G629   "Schnabel Memorial." *NYHT,* 19 April 1954, p. 11, col. 5-6.

An austerely classical program of masterpieces by celebrities such as Dame Myra Hess (Beethoven's Opus 110 sonata) and the Juilliard Quartet (Mozart and Schnabel quartets, and Brahms's Piano Quintet, Op. 34 was presented Saturday night for the Arthur Schnabel Memorial Concert at Town Hall. Schnabel's piece sounds like "an impersonation of a great work."

G630 "NBC Symphony." Ibid., col. 7.

Milton Katims conducted a broadcast concert of Beethoven's 8th Symphony (a "scintillating performance"), Arensky's *Seven Variations on a Theme of Tchaikovsky* and Dvorak's *Carnival Overture*, as the "repertoire pieces," and the first performance of Benjamin Lees' *Profile* for orchestra. The little work makes a positive, dramatic impression without resort to "current 'originality' tactics" (indiscriminate dissonance), has "orchestrational brilliance," and shows "signs of the more rare, organic technique of the growth of materials in development."

G631 "Gayle Pierce." *NYHT*, 23 April 1954, p. 15, col. 8.

An exceptionally fine young soprano presented pieces by Handel, Mozart, and Fauré, and some seldom-heard Italian songs by Pizzetti, Respighi, and Ghedini. Accompanist Nathan Price was a bit wooden. The voice is not particularly large but "it has beautiful quality right through its range" and there were glimpses of "abandon and rapture."

G632 "Prize-Winning Composer." *NYHT*, 26 April 1954, p. 9, col. 2-3.

Ernest Bloch, Critic's Award winner in two categories for 1953, was the featured composer on NBC's 6:30 Broadcast concert yesterday afternoon (Sunday). His first and second *Concerti Grossi* (the latter the prize winner) and *Evocations* were expertly conducted by Milton Katims. The *Concerti Grossi* reflect a simplification in style, the earlier one reminiscent of Vaughan Williams (modal austerity and "jolly village green moods") and Elgar. The prize-winning second one was "the best," though the diverse elements are not quite unified: the modalism seems attached as a color or decoration rather than coming from within, from a "deep identification with modal scales and their harmonic laws." But "this work has great expressive power, great contrapuntal mastery and an orchestral expertness that is dazzling." (Quoted in **B190**, p. 395.)

G633 "Ulmer at Town Hall." *NYHT*, 27 April 1954, p. 20, col. 4.

The Partita Op. 38 by the "gifted" Danish composer Niels Viggo Bentzon is "one of the major contributions to piano literature in recent years." The composer gave it a "sensational performance" in Malmo, Sweden, at the 1947 ISCM Festival [*see* G3]. Ernest Ulmer, however, weakened, robbing the piece of its "magnificent architecture of resonances." Beethoven's Waldstein Sonata, though brilliantly played, suffered from the same lack of inner fire and dynamic tension. Ulmer was better in works of Gabrieli and Sweelinck (giving them "an arabesque elegance and tonal sweetness rare in piano recitals") and at his best in Ravel's *Gaspard de la Nuit* suite (finesse and neatness at high speeds).

(OCTOBER-DECEMBER 1954)

G634 "Selma Ajami." *NYHT*, 11 October 1954, p. 11, col. 8.

Young lyric soprano sang Mozart, Wolf, and Ravel on the first half and the "Hispanic tradition from both Old and New Worlds" in the second part of the program. She has a clear, flexible voice and "has built an artistry of considerable finesse around her available vocal assets." Songs of Ginastera were well sung, and regional songs by Maria Luisa Escobar.

G635 "Diaz and Henderson." *NYHT*, 13 October 1954, p. 23, col. 3-4.

Young singers Rosina Diaz and Stephen Henderson, tenor, "shared a program at
Carnegie Recital Hall." Henderson has a "robust and lyric" voice, not always secure
in "more florid" passages of Handel arias; he sang Schumann and Brahms well. Diaz
"has polished and refined" her vocal material. Douda Poliakine was a "dynamic and
discreet" piano accompanist.

G636   "de Paur Chorus." *NYHT*, 18 October 1954, p. 12, col. 5.

Concert under the auspices of the Brotherhood of St. Andrew, of St. Luke's and St.
James Churches opened with German, French, and English songs of the troubadour
period. *Triumvirate* of Ulysses Kay, and a *Dirge for Two Veterans* by Normand
Lockwood both "broke new ground in choral writing, the Lockwood with ease and
mastery, the Kay with more technical struggle."

G637   "American From Europe." *NYHT*, 25 October 1954, p. 9, col. 5-6.

Young pianist Thomas Brockman's "considerable success in European cities" is
understandable. Works of Schumann, Handel, Ravel, and Prokofiev showed
"strong yet poetic" interpretive concepts" and "a striking maturity of intention that is
only now and then inhibited by technical limitations."

G638   "Jules Eskin, Cellist." *NYHT*, 28 October 1954, p. 26, col. 4.

Young winner of last year's Naumburg Award performed sonatas of Brahms and
Debussy and works of Bach, Boccherini, and Schumann, proving himself a
"sensitive musician, an intelligent interpreter and a considerable technician."

G639   "Composers Group." *NYHT*, 30 October 1954, p. 6, col. 5-6.

Composers Group of New York City "offered a distracting array of gaucheries, both of
the ham and 'modernistic' varieties"--works of Alfred Pike, Robert Allen, Walter
Giannini, Robert Fairfax--with some evidence of musicality. Composers do need
opportunity, but "standard is another thing again."

G640   "Edna Bockstein." *NYHT*, 1 November 1954, p. 23.

Pianist playing Bach, Brahms, and Beethoven's Sonata Op. 110 has a not entirely
reliable technique and lacks the "grander tonal gamuts" achieved through physical
strength, but makes good use of her special assets--a velvet touch and exceptional
understanding of music.

G641   "Marienka Michna." Ibid.

Pianist performed Beethoven, Debussy, Weber, and Brahms. She has long been
familiar to New York audiences but has seldom appeared to less advantage.

G642   "Master Singers." *NYHT*, 2 November 1954, p. 15.

Joseph Liebling directed this chorus in the premiere of *Three Settings of Poems by
Ogden Nash* by James Cohn. Also well sung were a Bach motet, works of Ravel,
Mendelssohn, and Poulenc, and English madrigals of the sixteenth and seventeenth
centuries.

G643   "Doris Hornburg." *NYHT*, 6 November 1954, p. 9.

Soprano singing works of Debussy, Wolf, and Purcell has a lovely natural voice but needs work on diction, on intonation in the middle register, and sometimes on breathing. Fritz Jahoda, pianist, provided "fine support."

G644   "Composers Forum." *NYHT*, 8 November 1954, p. 28, col. 2-3.

Russell Smith and Colin McPhee were featured composers, Virgil Thomson was moderator, in opening concert of the season. Carlos Surinach conducted with "insight" and Grant Johanneson was "superb" in McPhee's *Concerto for Piano with Wind Octet Accompaniment,* with the New York Wood Wind Ensemble. The concerto, "certainly one of the classics of the '20s," expounds "instrumental and acoustic originality that--though colored by the era--is highly personal, highly expert." (Description is quoted in full by Rooney, 1980 [B325].) Smith's *Anglican Mass* revealed "beautiful resonances," while his *Duo and Fugue for Winds* was "less deeply felt" but "adroitly written."

G645   "Regino de la Maza." *NYHT*, 12 November 1954, p. 15.

Guitarist in second Town Hall recital performed works of Narvaez, Sanz, and Campion he had transcribed from tablature, also works of Ronsalli, Bach, Pittaluga, Villa Lobos, de la Maza, and Granados.

G646   "Angela Pistelli." *NYHT*, 13 November 1954, p. 6.

Pianist played the Bach-Liszt Fantasy and Fugue in G minor, Brahms, Beethoven, and Debussy. Her technique and musicality were not working together.

G647   "Philharmonic." *NYHT*, 15 November 1954, p. 15.

Franco Autori conducted the Philharmonic Orchestra in works of Richard Strauss and Gossec and the first New York performance of *Suite for Strings* by Roberto Casmano, Argentinian composer; while the louder sections suffer from "lack of thematic germ," the second movement, *Adagio Elegaico,* is "a brief interlude of extraordinary beauty, its long, rhythmless lines of sound weaving like taut wires from simplicity to complexity and back to repose." Young violin virtuoso Norman Carol gave a "polished" performance of Mozart's Violin Concerto No. 5. The conductor and orchestra were "somewhat low keyed in energy and a little lacking in tension."

G648   "Larry Walz." *NYHT*, 16 November 1954, p. 26, col. 3-4.

Impressive young pianist in recital last night (Monday) plays as though music is "an eloquent language of emotional language of emotional communication that transcends words, yet is as explicit." He plays works of Beethoven, Ravel, and Debussy--classic and modern--"equally well."

G649   "Jean Wentworth Plays." *NYHT*, 17 November 1954, p. 25, col. 4.

Pianist, Naumburg winner, played "the three 'Bs' " plus Ellis Kohs' Variations on *L'Homme Armé* and Ravel's *Gaspard de la Nuit.* She is "a good little pianist" but not the "potential concert artist" that Naumburg winners usually are.

G650   "Ray Lev." *NYHT*, 20 November 1954, p. 8, col. 4-5.

Pianist in her annual recital (*see also* **G323** above) played to "a well filled house of Lev enthusiasts" as usual. She presented an unusually "lean crop" of new music-- works of Alfred Goodman, William Ahern, and Irving Mopper. Ahern's "romantic chromaticism" was only slightly better than Goodman's "rather artificial dissonances" and Mopper's "rather naive robustness."

G651 "Chamber Ensemble." *NYHT*, 22 November 1954, p. 15, col. 4-5.

Dmitri Mitropoulous directed groups of the New York Philharmonic Chamber Ensemble in the first performance of Josef Alexander's Quintet for Winds (virtuosity in an unmelodic " 'dissonance at all costs' texture") and "a colorful performance" of Milhaud's Sonata for Two Violins and Piano. Works of Shostakovich, von Weber, and Mozart completed the "endearing, intimate" program.

G652 "Myna Fremont." Ibid., col. 6.

Coloratura soprano, assisted at the piano by Arthur Kaplan, presented an "ambitious program"--operatic numbers from Handel, Mozart, Massenet, Puccini, and Charpentier, and songs of Rachmaninoff, Bizet, and others--but she "is not equipped for the challenges of the pieces she chooses."

G653 "Grete Sultan." *NYHT*, 23 November 1954, p. 20, col. 5.

Pianist played Debussy and Beethoven with "considerable" technique but "lack of fluency" and perhaps of "natural aptitude." Schoenberg's *Klavierstücke Op. 23* she played with "punch and delicacy" to reveal any contrast factors, but they "must surely be among the world's most unattractive piano pieces."

G654 "Anthony Kooiker." *NYHT*, 27 November 1954, p. 7, col. 4.

Young pianist from Iowa played debut recital featuring four contemporary American works--by Walter Piston, Howard Swanson, Frederick Werle, and John Lessard. His interpretations are "full of bright colors" and clarity, though his fingers often falter in tough technical passages. Pieces of Brahms and Debussy drew forth a "deeper mood" from "this imperfect, but interesting, young artist."

G655 "Composers Forum." *NYHT*, 29 November 1954, p. 11, col. 1.

Works of Gunther Schuller, "horn player in the Met orchestra," and Alfonso Montecino from Chile were featured and Carlos Surinach was "bilingual moderator." Schuller's idiom is "tonal dissonance" and his "cheerful" Sonata for Clarinet and Bass Clarinet is "brilliantly written for the instruments." Montecino showed Hispanic influence only in *Five Songs*, to Lorca poems, with "shapely vocal phrases that follow the Spanish prosodic pulse." His *Duo for Violin and Piano* is neo-classic with some "romantic feeling." Review is long, even for Composers Forum reviews--around 500 words.

G656 "Alma Trio." *NYHT*, 1 December 1954, p. 25, col. 2.

Adolph Baller, "superb" chamber music pianist, Maurice Wilk, violin, and Gabor Rejto, cello, in the first of their three Beethoven programs, performed two trios, the Op. 30 Violin Sonata, and the Op. 69 Cello Sonata. All three players are "magnificent exponents of the classic tradition in its purest sense," that is, the "tradition of inter-pretation" from the time the music was composed.

G657 "Bell Symphony." *NYHT*, 3 December 1954, p. 15, col. 3.

Frederic Kurzweil conducted the Bell Symphony Society in an "esthetic cocktail" of enthusiastic performances of works of Philip James and Don Gillis, Brahms'

Symphony No. 1, and solo numbers by Charpentier, Benjamin, and Donizetti sung by the "pretty soprano voice" of Angelene Collins.

G658   "Elsa Zebranska." *NYHT*, 6 December 1954, p. 22, col. 7.

Latvian diva's recital was "a distinguished musical event." Songs of Brahms were sung with "perfect diction and phrase" combined with "a luxurious tonal curve." Songs of Darzins and Kalnins brought characteristics of "regional music" and "native performing style" into the "classic framework of the pieces."

G659   "Martha Flowers." *NYHT*, 7 December 1954, p. 26, col. 3-4.

Naumburg Award-winning soprano gave "sensational performances of the many kinds of music" on her "beautifully planned" program. Bach, Schubert, Schumann, and Wolf "soared beautifully forth" and likewise her French--Debussy, Sauguet, and Ravel--and the songs in English--by Rorem, Haieff, and Britten. Here is "voice and artistry combined in perfect fusion."

G660   " 'Encore' Concert." *NYHT*, 18 December 1954, p. 9, col. 4.

Distinguished wind players performed works of Beethoven, Poulenc, and two neo-classicists, John Lessard and Arthur Berger. Lessard uses brighter colors and more marked "textural contrasts." Berger's technique is more accomplished and the components "more highly fused."

G661   "Composers' Forum." *NYHT*, 20 December 1954, p. 13, col. 3-4.

Louis Calabro and Robert Palmer were featured composers and Otto Luening was moderator. Calabro's "remarkable" Violin Sonata and Palmer's Quintet for Clarinet, Piano and Strings had "superb performances." Calabro's works "show a remarkable blending of slow and fast moods and of melodic line and fragmented materials." Palmer is "less gifted" and "more cultivated in the matters of acquired art;" his style, "basically classic and tonal, is rich in harmonic variety."

G662   "Chinese Union Concert." *NYHT*, 27 December 1954, p. 18, col. 4.

Wing-hee Wong directed the Chinese Chorus and Chinese Choral Club, merged for this event, and orchestra in excerpts from Handel's "Messiah" to a packed house at McMillin Theatre. The choir was good but the orchestra was not.

JANUARY 1955: *HERALD TRIBUNE*

G663   "Composers Forum." *NYHT*, 10 January 1955, p. 11, col. 2, and p. 12, col. 7.

Featured composers were Hugo Weisgall and James Dalgleish (recently deceased), with his friend Don Shapiro as pianist and as "sensitive deputy" in the question period. Dalgleish had "a real musical gift," somewhat unrealized. Weisgall presented one work, a twenty-minute monologue "The Stronger" for one singer and a dumb companion as dramatic foil, which made "a clever if not lasting impression."

G664   "Carol Smith." Ibid., p. 12, col. 7.

Contralto, "a very fine singer in every sense," presented songs and arias in English, French, and German. Joachim Nin-Culmell's *Tres poemas de Gil Vicente* are "gems" in a folk "mood" that use regional material "wholly assimilated" and are expressed by "a wholly modern and highly cultured musical mind."

G665 "Glenn Gould." *NYHT*, 12 January 1955, p. 19, col. 4.

Young Canadian pianist performed Orlando Gibbons, Sweelinck, and Bach, then Webern's Variations Op. 36--"dryly, exquisitely"--and Beethoven's Sonata Op. 109 "in a mood of gentle, brooding romanticism." Berg's Sonata Op. 1 had insight, delicacy, and tensile strength. Gould's strength comes from "complete integration of the component parts" of his art rather than sheer volume.

G666 "Bach Aria Group." *NYHT*, 20 January 1955, p. 17, col. 7.

William Warfield, Jan Peerce, Eileen Farrell, Carol Smith, and conductor Frank Brieff, offered fine performances of the Mass in F major and Cantatas Nos. 55 and 100. Excellent ensemblists were Maurice Wilk, supplying violin continuo, and Julius Baker, Robert Bloom, Bernard Greenhouse, and Harry Glickman.

G667 "Fredell Lack." *NYHT*, 22 January 1955, p. 6, col. 4-5.

Wonderful, highly gifted young violinist displayed beautiful tone and phrasing and a sense of ease and security in works of Mozart, Bach, Prokofieff (her most brilliant achievement), Chausson, Copland, Paganini, and a New York premiere of George Barati's "rather contrived" *Slow Dance.*.

G668 "Wind Quintet." Ibid., col. 5-6.

National Arts Club Wind Quintet, pianist Maxim Schur, and violinist Emanuel Vardi presented works of Robert Parris (containing little music), Peter Mennin (revealing "a craftsman rather than an artist"), Ingolf Dahl, and Robert MacKinnon (these "hovering between Stravinsky manneristics and a dim folk-style lyricism") on NAACC program. Most successful by far was Bernard Wagenaar's Piano Sonata, a "fine work for pianists" with a form that grows naturally from its materials.

G669 "Concert Society." *NYHT*, 24 January 1955, p. 9, col. 5.

Concert Society of New York offered performances by Lisa Della Casa in Strauss' *Four Last Songs,* and arias of Bach and Handel, the latter with accompaniment by fine flutist Carleton Sprague Smith. Joanna and Nicolai Graudan showed fine technique and balanced ensemble in sonatas for cello and piano by Beethoven and Mendelssohn.

G670 "Alexander Brailowsky." *NYHT*, 26 January 1955, p. 14, col. 5-7.

This "really grand" pianist, famous for his "extraordinary brilliance," is also thoroughly romantic in his interpretation, so that his Chopin was the high point of his program. Works of Mozart and Scarlatti were restrained, Schumann and, especially, Bartok's *Allegro barbaro* more dramatic. Pieces by Fauré and Liszt closed the program.

G671 "Alice Shapiro." *NYHT*, 28 January 1955, p. 13, col. 3.

Debut recital of accomplished young pianist featured Four Impromptus Op. 90 of Schubert, Barber's Piano Sonata Op. 26 (rather too "extroverted" for this performer), and works of Bach and Chopin--the last revealing potentialities for her future development to "a larger expressive and technical scope."

G672   "Kije the Musicist." *NYHT*, Sunday, 30 January 1955, sect. 1, p. 30, col. 2.

This pianist entertainer told stories of "disarming naiveté" and played unsophisticated "improvisatory compositions," also works of Bach and Beethoven, as illustration.

G673   "Ajemian Sisters." *NYHT*, 31 January 1955, p. 13, col. 2.

Maro and Anahid Ajemian were the soloist ensemblists on the Carl Friedberg Music Foundation concert, playing a long program of sonatas of Mozart and Beethoven, then Debussy, Ives, and Chavez. Neither pianist is virtuosic; they play the moderns best.

G674   "Saturday's Philharmonic." Ibid., col. 3-4.

Guido Cantelli conducted a Paisiello overture, Dukas' *The Sorcerer's Apprentice*, Tchaikovsky's fourth symphony (the conductor's most distinguished work), and Haydn's cello concerto Op. 101 with Laszlo Varga as soloist. Notwithstanding "squeaks and scratches here and there," Varga has a notable sense of style, and rich tone color.

1955, CONTINUED

G675   Liner notes for *Sonata for Piano and Percussion* and *Concertino da camera*, Columbia ML 4990. 1955. *See* **D2, D17**.

Sonata for Piano and Percussion demonstrates "percussion, pitched and non-pitched, as an organic entity." In this "basic" instrumental unit, piano is the "poet" and xylophone is partner, then there is "a full octave of timpani, a rack of gongs--high, medium, low and Tam--and one general percusser to attend to miscellaneous beats and accents" (suspended cymbal, tom tom, bass drum). First and last movements use "themes from the Watuzzi Africans," fragmentary and restricted in scale as suits "both the instrumental limitation and the esthetic of the work." The slow movement uses gongs for sustained resonance. The *Concertino da Camera* "is the last of my works which show traces of the Paris neo-classic schoolroom"--it "was my swan-song."

G676   "Olin Downes (1886-1955)." *American Composers Alliance Bulletin* 5, no. 1 (1955), p. 2.

Downes proclaimed the "verities of human heart and spirit above those of the mere intellect." As a critic he reacted "the way the public reacts," and he recognized musicality as the only valid quality. Away from the United States "I have always tried to read Downes and Thomson, feeling that I was satisfying both heart and mind. If I had to choose but one, then I chose Downes." She regrets that she was never reviewed by him [but she was, in **B117-118**]. (Obituary was delivered by Glanville-Hicks at the memorial service broadcast by radio station WNYC at 4 p.m., 25 August 1955.)

G677   "Program Notes [for *The Transposed Heads* recording] by the Composer." Louisville 545-6 [1955]. (*See* **D21**.)

Glanville-Hicks presents a synopsis of the story--"a miraculous blend of humour, realistic drama and metaphysical discourse." In extracting the libretto from Mann's novel, she used "a process of deletion," completing the script in the summer of 1952 aboard a freighter in the South Pacific, then composed the whole score "in one long, unbroken period of work from May to September the following summer in a remote corner of the West Indies." My aim was "to create grand opera on a chamber music scale" form and pacing come from the vocal element (just as the shape of a baroque concerto comes from the solo elaboration). The use of Hindu folk themes "required no great amendment of my own writing· method," for "I have gradually shed the harmonic dictatorship peculiar to modernists, and have evolved a melody-rhythm structure that comes very close to the musical patterns of the antique world." Weight and volume, for building tension and climax, "exist organically, in the thematic materials, rather than in their instrumentation and amplification media." Tranquility (in the first scene) comes from "long arabesque lines with small gapped intervals, and a pulseless, static type of accompaniment subject." In the dramatic Temple scene I did the opposite, using big melodic jumps and tightening the metrical structure (rather than the volume), and added "the harmonic element, reserved until here for the stress and anxiety factors inherent in dissonance, and which make their point only when used sparingly." (These program notes, reprinted in **B78**, continue to be quoted extensively in discussions of her style.)

G678   "Opera Recordings." *Hi-Fi Music at Home* 2 (May-June 1955), p. 19-21, 50.

Columbia has recorded *The Transposed Heads* (**W46a**, **D21**), first of the Louisville Opera Commissions, and will release it in May. Also in the series are operas by Richard Mohaupt, Antheil, and Liebermann. The local concert hall, a staging nightmare, "has turned out to be a perfect hall acoustically for recording purposes." Moritz Bomhard, founder and director of the Kentucky Opera Association, coaches the singers, trains the chorus, rehearses and conducts the orchestra, and (because the Rockefeller money goes mainly to the composers, not the production) he plots the staging and production, and designs, constructs, and paints the scenery. He has extraordinary "pacing sense" (fine lieder singers have the quality in miniature--an inspired moment to moment adaptability that unifies things in a stage of motion) and has adjusted pacing and tempi to the (non-visual) recording situation. A photo shows Nanda, Sita, and Shridaman in front of the enormous Kali sculpture Bomhard built; there is also a photo of Bomhard and one from Antheil's *The Wish*. (Copy in **A3** includes the author's pencilled corrections.)

G679   "Newell Jenkins' Research in Italy." Ibid., 2 (November-December 1955), p. 37, 80-83.

Jenkins, brilliant American conductor, research scholar, linguist, and catalyst, has organized recordings of "Italian Classical Symphonists" of the 17th and early 18th centuries (released under the Haydn Society's label) from Fiesole, outside Florence, where he lives. The orchestra's 21 musicians and soloists Carlo Bussotti, Antonio Abussi, and Sidney Gallesi are also presenting live concerts of these formerly lost works Jenkins has discovered and edited--music by Gossec, Hummel, Stamitz, Grétry, Brunetti, Clementi, and Cimarosa. Seven small photos show: Jenkins; Bussotti; a double bass strapped to a small Fiat; players around the "thoughtfully improvised" wine counter in the courtyard at Bellosguardo where recording took place last summer; Glanville-Hicks and Gallesi; Abussi; and musicians in rehearsal at the Villa Mercedes.

1956

G680   Explanatory notes printed with Edward Cole's liner notes for *Sinfonia Pacifica* and *Three Gymnopédies*, MGM 3336. 1956. *See* **D11, D19, B73**.

The *Sinfonia Pacifica* was sketched in summer 1952 on board a freighter in the South West Pacific, New Orleans to Australia, and completed in May 1953 "in a remote corner of the British West Indies." It is designed to demote harmony and "reassert the right of the melodic and rhythmic elements as the primary structural forces." Instead of my usual practice of having fast movements stay fast and slow movements remain slow, in the first movement "I set for myself the problem" of developing two themes simultaneously, combining "declamatory and lyric elements." The slow second movement exploits "free melodic arabesque" in flute and oboe, accompanied by "fragments suspended from the melodic line rather than existing at its base." The finale uses a theme "of Hindu origin" (used again in *The Transposed Heads*) over a "dense carpet of percussion" to illustrate "a melody-rhythm partnership." Notes for *Three Gymnopédies* are reprinted from the Remington recording issued in 1954 (**D18**, *see* **G594**). These pieces "do not seem to me to represent myself of today as does the *Sinfonia*," but perhaps in re-writing them, "having acquired some strength in these last twenty years, I now sought to regain the grace of my innocence."

G681   Liner notes for *Zabaleta--Anthology of Solo Harp Music*, vol. 4: "17th and 19th Centuries." Esoteric ES 542. 1956. (Reissued on Counterpoint, 1958.)

Some composers on this volume, which completes a recorded anthology of works written expressly for harp, may be a surprise: Spohr (husband of a well-known harpist), Parish-Alvars (harpist-composer), Dizi, Glinka, Naderman, Fernandez de Huete (harpist and author of important treatise), and others. Performances are, as always, "a sheer delight."

G682   Liner notes for Douglas Moore's *Farm Journal*, and Marion Bauer's *Suite for String Orchestra* and *Prelude and Fugue for Flute and Strings*. Composers Recordings, Inc., CRI 101. 1956.

Moore uses American moods, color, and idiom but resorts to none of the typical phraseologies of standard "Americana." Celtic-American folksong, his melodic anchorage, lies deep in the origin of his expressive impulse, not separate and acquired. The four movements create vivid moods. Bauer (d. 1955), like Dr. Moore, spent much energy "in administrative work on behalf of the profession, students and colleagues." Still, "a composer's own personal music is the finest and most important contribution he or she can make to the world of music of his day." The recording is a timely and graceful tribute to her long life as a professional teacher, critic, and composer; her works will reveal a sensitive and accomplished musician.

G683   " 'Willie' Has a Silver Spoon." *Hi-Fi Music at Home* 2 (January-February 1956), p. 24-5, 55-6.

Fame came early to William Walton, "the composer born with a silver spoon in his mouth," with *Façade* (1923), a work demonstrating his "lively sense of humour." (But he denies he pinned a kipper to a picture in the first London exhibit of surrealist paintings. "It was a red herring," he says, and the painter "said it was an improvement.") Angel has released excerpts from his first "gift to the operatic medium," *Troilus and Cressida*, completed only last year. In the late 1930s, when the Boosey and Hawks firm--aided by the British Council, the Arts Council, and other organizations--decided to promote Britten, Walton (richer and more gifted than

Britten but perhaps less clever and sophisticated) was eclipsed. Then during the war other composers had a chance. "Fame and widespread importance have much to do with luck and management, and not necessarily much to do with quality and magnitude, when it comes to serious music." His music owes no stylistic debt to anyone past or present, and his success comes from his "very romantic spirit." (Similarly, Vaughan Williams in his *Fourth (F Minor) Symphony*, the closest thing to "real organic modernism" in English music, shows a Medieval spirit rather than reaction against 19th-century tradition; in fact atonalism and neoclassicism have not influenced English composers, nor has England produced an Orff to reform music's materials.) Photos show Walton and a scene from*Troilus and Cressida*.

G684   "Writing for the Harp." *Harp News* 2 (Spring 1956), p. 2-3.

The playing of Nicanor Zabaleta "convinced me that the harp is a major solo instrument." The "curious grace" of early music down to the 18th century was eclipsed in the increased volume, dissonance, and empty virtuosity of the 19th century. Now the harp (like the chamber orchestra, harpsichord, guitar, and winds) is again valued for its "crisp, precise sounds that are at least evocative of romanticism and its decay" and allow a focus on the musical idea itself. (*See also* her liner notes for Zabaleta's recordings, G332, G595, and G681.) Composing for the harp, the most "eloquent" of the forgotten instruments and a catalyst both melodically and rhythmically in ensembles, will require conceiving the expression in terms of the instrument's natural capacities and attributes, under the guidance of a "cultivated esthetic sensibility" for which the early classic repertoire is a touchstone. Biography that follows notes that Glanville-Hicks wrote her *Sonata for Harp* (W42) for Zabaleta, that her *Concertino Antico* (W49), written last summer in Munich for Edna Phillips, uses "an ancient mode set by Flavius Josephus in A. D. 1 for harp of that time," and that she leaves shortly for Europe, where her Guggenheim project will be an opera in collaboration with Robert Graves.

G685   " 'Young King Cole.' " *Hi-Fi Music at Home* 3 (May-June 1956), p. 28, 66-7.

Edward Cole (shown in a photo), MGM's young Artists and Repertoire Director, is an "old soul" with intuitive judgment and wisdom beyond his years. He has "a hunch for hits" and a flair for miking. Only Cole was willing to record Weill's *Three Penny Opera*; other best-sellers have been works of Hovhaness, Haieff, and Surinach. An aggregate release relates works of Verrall, Blomdahl, Holmboe, Donovan, and my own *Etruscan Concerto*, heard together recently at Rainey Auditorium. Also available or to come are works of Bartok, Satie, Poulenc, and Schoenberg. Conductors include the young Izler Solomon and Carlos Surinach, and performers include William Masselos, Beveridge Webster, the Ajemian sisters, and the Hamburg Philharmonic. Cole works for "a very marked degree of presence," or for separation and clarity over "the fluorescent effects of our canned music era."

1957

G686   "Background note" printed with Edward Cole's liner notes for *Concerto Romantico*, MGM E 3559. 1957. *See* D3, B70.

While my sudden re-inclusion of non-dissonant harmony plus the title "Romantico" have been interpreted as "a wanton and irresponsible return to the 19th century," the concerto is in fact like my other recent works in its modal-melodic structure. The difference is that here accompaniment is not rhythmic or orchestrated in percussion (which would engulf the viola), but rather "unison melodic imitation" and occasionally "vertically-conceived harmonic blocks," which would allow a piano version (a practical alternative to full orchestra) of some volume and body. The concerto

embodies the romantic "spirit" (not just 19th-century romanticism) in that "the
personal expressive urge is allowed to dominate the picture."

G687   "Some Reflections on Opera: Rolf Liebermann, Man of the Theatre."
American Composers Alliance Bulletin 6, no. 4 (1957), p. 12-15, 22.

To counter the "panning spree" by New York reviewers of City Center productions of
Liebermann's opera *School for Wives* (and operas of Orff, Von Einem, and Egk),
Glanville-Hicks assesses the works of this "born opera composer" and "man of the
theatre" from Switzerland whose achievements are recognized in Europe if not in
New York. Liebermann uses several musical styles (tonal, neo-classic, atonal,
French, German) as dramatic partisans; the drama is posed and solved in the
materials themselves. (Dissociation of materials from familiar contexts, and new
juxtapositions, bring new meanings in his operas, whereas Virgil Thomson's operas
use dissociation without posing a new meaning.) Also noteworthy in Liebermann's
works are: symphonic interludes that paraphrase and develop operatic subject
matter; his mastery of harmonic and metrical tensions for the "cantilever" of
music's new architecture; his skill in prosody, especially recitative; and an objective
approach that exhibits the timelessness of his story and subject matter. LePage (B217)
quotes this essay.

G688   "A Minority Report on Rolf Liebermann." *American Record Guide*
23, no. 10 (July 1957), p. 151-3.

Essay is almost the same as the previous essay (G687). Added is a review of the
Louisville recording of Liebermann's *School for Wives*.

1958

G689   "A Hindu Theme." *New York Times*, Sunday, 9 February 1958, sect. 2,
p. 7.

In this essay published the day before the New York premiere of *The Transposed
Heads* she explains her use of materials from India, expanding on her program notes
for the recording of the Louisville premiere (G677 above). "Any parallel between my
music and certain Oriental types lies more in an abstract principle than in the use of
specific detail, and was arrived at as much from reflection on the dilemma of
Western music as on the music of the East." More specifically, "a distrust of
composition 'systems' precipitated some years ago a searching re-examination of
music's first principles," and "a conviction grew that melody and rhythm are our
basic, perennial expressive and structural factors; that in harmony, the vertical
concept, we have come to an impasse." In this opera, based on a "timeless" and
"timely" story, the vocal melodic lines "carry the whole form and pacing of the
work," and rhythmic control (not harmonic and orchestral weight, nor even
"literary development") functions as "crisis builder." Her correspondence with Ross
Parmenter of the *Times* (in A3) indicates that the title was changed from "Westward
to the East" and the article was cut somewhat.

G690   "Technique and Inspiration." *Juilliard Review* 5 (Spring 1958), p. 3-11.

This essay contains the clearest statement of Glanville-Hicks's aesthetics. The
"composer-artist" has two areas of awareness: "technique" (including materials and
analytical factors) and "inspiration" (including expression and instinctive factors).
Only after a "journey inward" requiring "silence and time" can the composer
integrate the "emerged" and "submerged" sources and *synthesize* them into an
organic form. LePage (B217) quotes this essay at length.

1961

G691   "U.S. Opera Composers Produce and Talk." *The Music Magazine and Musical Courier* 163, no. 11 (October 1961), p. 7-8, 48.

In interview with five composers of "melodic" music (the others are Dello Joio, Giannini, Moore, and Ward), Glanville-Hicks, as in the article on Liebermann (G687-688 above), advises young U.S. composers to travel extensively to hear European twentieth-century repertoires and suggests that subsidizing the few "real opera creators" could create a "national operatic literature of maturity and significance."

G692   "Letters to the Editor: Adjustment." *Musical America* 81 (December 1961), p. 4.

To refute some statements in the magazine's review of *Nausicaa*, she explains that: this was not John Butler's first opera, and she, not the artistic director, cast the work.

G693   "At the Source." *Opera News* 26 (16 December 1961), p. 8-13.

The composition and production of *Nausicaa* (W62) followed a kind of artistic journey to the source of the river, both in musical idioms and in forms." Glanville-Hicks reviews: her long search for "first principles" in ancient and modern Greek folk music and theater concepts; the evolution of the "melody-rhythm structure" in her music; her adaption of modern twelve-tone procedure to archaic modes for dramatic vocal effects; her work with novelist and scholar Robert Graves; and her association with choreographer John Butler in realizing the "whole concept" of the opera.   Accompanying photos are of *Nausicaa* production, of Glanville-Hicks, and of Graves, Glanville-Hicks, and Butler in the audience.

1963

G694   "My Beautiful Greek House--Handmade for $2,000." *Vogue* 141 (1 April 1963), p. 14, 35-6, 52.

In converting a Mykonos birdhouse (a "grey little ruin" discovered after a search of some 36 islands) into a dwelling, Glanville-Hicks let "the dovecote aesthetic dominate the whole structure rather as a symphony will be coloured by the nature of its main theme." Local builders--carpenters, blacksmiths, weavers, well diggers--used local materials and traditional techniques. Frank Lloyd Wright's "organic architecture," is "just old Island technique" on Mykonos. The house-warming party has become something of a legend.

1964

G695   "Maria Callas, Oracle of the Opera." *Greek Heritage, The American Quarterly of Greek Culture*, 1 (1964), no. 3, p. 120-4.

Callas has first place among opera singers because of her "Greekness"--the fusion of ends and means, of Dionysian expressive content with Apollonian formal proportion. Although in "our Western afternoon" (of a Grecian morning) artistic personality has become split, so that intellectual and emotional forms are divorced, great artists speak from the "magnetic center" of this thinking-feeling duality. Strong inner poise gives Callas great versatility--she sings soprano roles and mezzo-soprano roles (Glanville-Hicks was composing *Sappho* for Callas as a mezzo), heroines and villains. Her recording of Puccini's *Butterfly* conducted by Herbert van Karajan (originally Karayannis, from Macedonia) is outstanding. Cherubini's *Medea* established her (three photos from La Scala and Covent Garden productions accompany this article), and 1961 *Medea* at Epidaurus showed unique singing and stage action.

G696   "A Note on the [*Nausicaa*] Libretto and the Music." Liner notes for Composers Recordings, Inc., CRI 175. 1964.

A booklet accompanying the recording of the opera (**D7**) contains: Glanville-Hicks's program notes from the 1961 Athens performance (**W62a**), with a synopsis of the story and brief notes on eight leading singers, the conductor, director, and designer (all probably written by her as well); the complete libretto; and excerpts from reviews of the premiere (**B14, B115, B151, B164, B238, B270, B322, B357**). The libretto was started in 1956 with Robert Graves on Mallorca, completed in New York in fall 1957, and revised the following summer as the music took shape. Composing followed two years of research in Greek music, in New York and Washington, and six months in the Aegean and Athens (Academy of Athens, Institut Français, and other sources). Ancient modes and meters are still used by rural singers and performers in Greece today. Though these abstract musical elements are common to Yugoslavia, Turkey, Persia, and India (in India the system used has been handed down in unbroken tradition), the Greek folk idiom has a flavour peculiarly its own, "evocative of the Greek temperament and of the light that floods the Grecian sea and landscape."

1966

G697   "Music: How It's Built." *Vogue* 147 (1 March 1966), p. 200-1, 207-8, 210.

"Organic form" in music, like organic form in the architecture of Frank Lloyd Wright, comes from the nature of the materials themselves. The twentieth century has brought new materials, and new uses of old materials. Increasing dissonance, as in the atonal system, only "camouflages" outworn tonality, like "an old building fashionably resurfaced." Dissonant complexity will be supplanted by the "melody-rhythm structure," just as the old European "arch" forms have been supplanted by Wright's "cantilever."

1984

G698   "Paul Bowles." Preface to *Paul Bowles: Selected Songs* Santa Fe, NM: Soundings Press, 1984, p. 4-5.

In a new brief essay for this edition, Glanville-Hicks returns to the subject of **G1** (1945). Bowles is a brilliant master of the setting of words to music, his own melodic and rhythmic writing colored by ethnic musics of Mexico, Morocco, and many other areas. Rare are such "ravishing melodies" as "the tiny, exquisite song *David*" in this present collection.

1989

G699   In progress: "Apollo's House." Book on twentieth-century music.

For planned contents, *see:* **B56** (1961) and **B120, B346, A1** (more recent).

Bibliography About Glanville-Hicks

This bibliography lists writings about Glanville-Hicks, in alphabetical order. Cross-references with a **W** are to "Works and Performances," with a **D** to the "Discography," with a **G** to "Bibliography by Glanville-Hicks," and with an **A** to "Archival Resources."

B1   A. H. "Five New Works for Chamber Orchestra." *Musical America* 76 (1 February 1956), p. 21.

>   Reviewer hears in premiere performance of the *Etruscan Concerto* (**W48a**) that: "The lady seeks to amuse with sunny tunes and simple, sophisticated harmonies. Her designs have the clarity of etchings, and her scoring the deft precision of water colors." Soloist was Italian pianist Carlo Bussotti, for whom the concerto was written.

B2   Ahern, David. "Australian Opera Has Premiere." *Daily Telegraph* (Sydney), 29 June 1970, 11.

>   *The Transposed Heads* (**W46c**), by an Australian composer, comes within the definition of traditional opera or music theatre. While the opera lacks personality, it "worked well enough." The vocal writing is above average, while the orchestration sounds like musical comedy. Best singing was from Sita, Nanda was satisfactory, Shridaman ineffective, and Kali almost inaudible.

B3   Amadio, Nadine. "About Music." *24 Hours*, 9, no. 1 (February 1984), p. 20-1.

>   Feature article in magazine of the Australian Broadcasting Corp. reviews Glanville-Hicks's training and career (in America "they handed me a career and fame and fortune on a platter"), her marriage, *Nausicaa* in Athens, her 1967 brain surgery and plastic skull (she was given five years to live then), and her coming "back home" to Australia (no one notices, she says). She talks about 20th-century music and composers. "Britten is really a 19th-century composer with a cautious overlay of dissonance for re-upholstery. He's like an old brownstone house with a modern glass front tacked on." Her music is rarely performed in Australia, exceptions being performances in 1970 and 1982. "We all know that being a composer means that right up to the end you have to lick the stamps yourself as well as everything else. This time someone else will have to knock on the doors."

B4 _____. "Salute to Composer." *Sunday Telegraph* (Sydney), 24 January 1982, p. 131.

Glanville-Hicks, now 70 [69], was present at concert devoted to her works. Highlight was the beautiful and evocative song cycle *Letters from Morocco* (**W44c**), superbly sung by Gerald English. Her "strong, magnetic music" emphasizes melody and rhythm. It contains a unique synthesis of Asian music, which she has championed all her life, and "a subtle French flavor," possibly from her studies with Boulanger. She has amazing communication and insight as a vocal writer. (Clipping is in **A7**.)

B5 _____. "A Sculpture Music First to be Staged at The Rocks." *Australian Financial Review*, 12 May 1978, p. 8.

Glanville-Hicks's *Girondelle for Giraffes* (**W67a**) is part of "Seven Sculpture Compositions" to be presented by the Australia Music Centre starting tomorrow. The sculptures, by Pamela Boden, are impressively large, giving them immediacy, and are made of wood, giving an organic feeling. James Murdoch, Centre director, describes the music by Don Banks for *The Magician's Castle*, by Ross Edwards for *Rocking Horses*, by Glanville-Hicks for *Giraffes* (a "witty" piece with trombone, piccolo, and percussion evoking feelings of distance), by David Gulpilil for *Horses Fleeing*, by Peter Sculthorpe for *Gambol*, by Lou Harrison for *Mountain Torrent*, and by Vincent Plush for *Estuary*. (Clipping is in **A6c**.)

B6 American Music Center Library. *Catalogue of Choral and Vocal Works*, comp. by Judith Greenberg Finelli. New York: American Music Center, 1975.

Listed in Cohen (**B67**), this catalog lists four works with publishers and vocal designations. [None of the works is now available from the American Music Center.]

B7 Ammer, Christine. *Unsung: A History of Women in American Music*. Westport, CT: Greenwood Press, 1980. P. 175-7.

Ammer reviews Glanville-Hicks's life and works to 1978 (**W67**), in the chapter on American women "Opera Composers and Conductors." Sources are **B11**, **B190**, **B297**, **B377**, and a letter from the composer of 1 June 1978 that describes the *Girondelle for Giraffes*, **W67**.

B8 "An American Opera is in Preparation." *New York Times*, 21 March, 1963, p. 8, col. 2.

San Francisco Opera has commissioned an American composer, Peggy Glanville-Hicks, to write a score for *Sappho* (**W64**), says Kurt Herbert Adler, general director, who has obtained funding from the Ford Foundation. Yehudi Menuhin brought him the libretto last fall, and he likes its "beautiful use of the English language." He will consider the opera for a world premiere. The composer "has retreated to a Greek island" and "is supposed to send parts of the score by September." (Associated Press announcement, dateline San Francisco, also appeared in several other newspapers; the original typescript of the press release is in **A3h**.)

B9 Anderson, E. Ruth. *Contemporary American Composers: A Biographical Dictionary*. 2nd ed. Boston: G. K. Hall, 1982. P. 196-7.

Anderson presents a biographical sketch and list of works. More works are listed than in the first edition, 1976 (p. 163), although the composer had composed only one more.

B10   Andreis, Josip, ed. *Muzicka enciklopedija*. Zagreb: Izdanje i Naklada Leksikografskog Zavoda Fnrj, 1958. P. 687.

Very brief biography of this "australiski kompozitor i kriticar" is followed by list of about half her works, classified by genre, with instrumentation and date.

B11   Antheil, George. "Peggy Glanville-Hicks." *American Composers Alliance Bulletin* 4, no. 1 (1954), p. 2-9.

Major article published by fellow ACA member at the height of Glanville-Hicks's first intensely productive phase (and quoted heavily and repeatedly ever since) includes a list of works (p. 7-9) through the Louisville production of *The Transposed Heads* (W46a) grouped by genre with durations, publishers, performances, and review excerpts (the established format for composer articles in this periodical). Antheil has "met" no other women composer with the "technical, mental, and spiritual stature" of Glanville-Hicks, and he presents, and comments on, her own explanations of her compositional principles: (1) "integration" of expressive aims and material means; (2) "simplification" for increased clarity and intensity; (3) regard for the "melody-rhythm patterns of antiquity" and "of Eastern places"; (4) a "fusion" of oriental sound and western (harmonic) style through use of "neutral materials" as well as actual folk melody; (5) invention of new forms rather than reliance on traditional "classic" ones; (6) avoidance of dissonance, especially constant "obligatory" dissonance. Small photo of Glanville-Hicks is on the cover of this issue.

B12   Apel, Paul Hermann. *Music of the Americas, North and South.* New York: Vantage Press, 1958, p. 148.

Glanville-Hicks, composer of the *Sonata for Piano and Percussion* (W44), is included in a long list of "other composers of the new generation who have enriched our music literature through their ambitious works."

B13   Archer, Robin. "Herald in the Classroom." *Sydney Morning Herald,* 11 August 1983.

A small paragraph (copy is in A7) announces that a profile of Peggy Glanville-Hicks, our greatest woman composer and "the first woman composer of note the twentieth century has produced," by George Daniel was published on 26 March 1983. *See* B105 below.

B14   Arkadinos, B. *[Nausicaa review.]. I Avgi* (Athens), 27 August 1961.

Glanville-Hicks, a composer of deep musicality and spirituality, is outstanding among U. S. composers and has achieved world-wide fame. In *Nausicaa* (W62a) we could characterize as a masterpiece the first aria of the baritone (Aethon), and the melodies of the Interlude, orchestral prelude, and song of Nausicaa have exceptional beauty. (Review is quoted in English translation in B78, B269, and G687; copy of typescript is in A11.)

B15   Ashton, Dore. "Art: Instruments of the Past." *New York Times,* 8 October 1957, p. 39.

Glanville-Hicks's delicate *Prelude and Presto for Ancient American Instruments* (**W54a** and **D8**) for exhibition "Music Before Columbus" reflects the "vast variety of sounds and rhythms" of ancient peoples, reports this art critic. Based on ancient Indian themes from the Peruvian Andes, the pieces use instruments in the exhibition. The ancient flutes have a complete pentatonic scale, but most of the other instruments make only one or two sounds. "I am fascinated by limitations," says the composer.

B16 "Audrey Nossaman, Lead--First Louisville Opera Commission." *Pan Pipes* 47, no. 2 (January 1955), p. 24-25.

An article about Nossaman, "Sita" in the Louisville premiere of *The Transposed Heads*, **W46a**, and on the recording, **D21**, appears in the section "Gifted SAIs [Sigma Alpha Iota members] in American Music Projection" with a brief biography of Glanville-Hicks and an account of her recent activities. A photo of the opera's three lead singers appears on p. 24.

B17 Australia Music Centre, Sydney. *Catalogues of Australian Compositions. IV. Vocal and Choral Music* (1976); *V. Dramatic Music* (1977). *Catalogue of Instrumental and Chamber Music* (1976).

Listed by Cohen (**B67**), these catalogues, dating from the years of Glanville-Hicks's employment at the Australia (now *Australian*) Music Centre, list all her major works whether or not they are available at the Centre.

B18 "Australian Composer's Work Premiered." *The Age* (Melbourne), 24 June 1954, Radio Supplement, p. 1.

Item announces radio broadcast of *Sinfonia Pacifica* (**W45a**) "by Australian composer Peggy Glanville-Hicks" at 9:15 p.m., Friday, 25 June, on station LO (Australian Broadcasting Corp.). The next day *The Age* runs an advertisement listing the works to be performed "tonight" by the Victorian Symphony Orchestra, Sir Bernard Heinze, conductor.

B19 "Available Recordings of Works by Women Composers." *High Fidelity/Musical America* 23 (February 1973), p. 53.

Under Glanville-Hicks two recordings are listed, *Nausicaa* (**D7**) and *The Transposed Heads* (**D21**). Twenty-nine composers are listed in all.

B20 Avshalomov, Jacob. "Peggy Glanville-Hicks Exceptional as Woman Composer." *The Oregonian* (Portland), Sunday, 4 May 1969, sect. 2, p. 22.

Composer, now music director of Portland Junior Symphony, on leave in Europe, interviewed Glanville-Hicks in Greece. Her little white Mykonos house is snug hillside harbor, while her Athens house "is exquisitely appointed, with treasures from all parts of the world." After World War II "composers clustered in New York" were "performing each other's music, organizing concerts, writing articles and criticism," and scrambling "from Town Hall to Times Hall to Carnegie" in one night to hear contemporary works on different programs. She could not accept "12-tone dogma" and looked "eastward," as did Henry Cowell, Colin McPhee, Alan Hovhaness, and Lou Harrison. Avshalomov reviews her early training and New York career, and recalls that he got some of his best reviews in her *Herald Tribune* columns [*see* **G434**, **G441**, and **G483**.] She plans to return to Sydney next year for *The Transposed Heads* (**W46c**).

B21   Bachelder, Marilyn Meyers. "Women in Music Composition: Ruth
Crawford Seeger, Peggy Glanville-Hicks, Vivian Fine." Unpublished
Master's thesis, Eastern Michigan University, 1973. P. 60-95.

Two-page biographical sketch precedes detailed discussion, with musical examples, of
the *Sonata for Harp* (**W42**) and *The Transposed Heads* (**W46**). The sonata combines
traditional Spanish melodic elements (the *Saeta* of the first movement is an
Andalusian song type) and guitar technique with "impressionistic" harmonies for
"coloristic" harp effects. The opera, set in India, uses "melody-rhythm" elements
that have Indian counterparts--repetition of motives, five-note scales, drone-like
accompaniments, decorated melodies, resonant octave doublings, and exotic
instrumental colors. Essentially Western are the tertian and quartal harmonies, key
relationships, cadences, vocal style and timbre, and prosody.

B22   Baker, Theodore. *A Biographical Dictionary of Musicians.* 7th edn.,
rev. Nicolas Slonimsky. New York: Schirmer Books, 1984. Vol. 1, p.
839.

Article on Glanville-Hicks (she is first included in the 5th edn., 1958) presents a brief
biography, including her teachers' names, the date of her marriage to Stanley Bate,
and her work for the *Herald Tribune*. List of works by genre includes many titles,
through the early 1960s. Slonimsky describes her as a "pragmatic composer of
functional music with human connotations" who "shuns the monopolistic fashion
of mandatory dissonance, but explores attentively the resources of folk music"
(Greek, Hindu) and alludes to non-Western modalities. He reports [mistakenly] that
she ceased to compose after going blind in 1969.

B23   Barlow, Wayne. "P. Glanville-Hicks: *Ballade* (3 songs)." *Music
Library Association Notes* 7, no. 2 (March 1950), p. 313.

The first two songs of the group (**W31**) are "rather imaginative treatments in an
impressionistic method" of Bowles's poems and are recommended to singers by this
reviewer [a composer]. The third is in a "different and dissonant idiom" and "will
give the singer no end of trouble."

B24   Barnes, Clive. "Dance: Harkness's 'Season in Hell.' " *New York
Times*, 15 November 1967, p. 2.

Though he finds that the music (**W65a**) "sounds derivative and of no especially
interesting sources," Barnes's long review is favorable to the production, John
Butler's effortless and unpretentious choreography, and the dancers (there is a photo
of ballerina Brunilda Ruiz). Ballet's three characters are the poet Rimbaud, his
friend Verlaine, and "The Woman." Because Rimbeau (in his *Une saison en enfer*)
despised what he saw as the materialism of women, and searched among homosexual men for a woman substitute in men, this "Woman" is not a woman but a
muse of poetry, an inspiration toward a life of art, which he eventually rejected. In
the ballet Rimbaud is tortured on the rack of creation; figure of Verlaine and the
image of inspiration mingle with the conformist figures of the external world.
(Clipping is in **A3**.)

B25   Barret, Henry. *The Viola: Complete Guide for Teachers and Students.*
University, AL: University of Alabama Press, 1972; 2nd. edn., rev. and
enl., 1978.

The *Concerto romantico* (**W51**) is listed in the appendix "Viola Music in Print," on p.
162 in the second edition ("Compositions with Orchestra, One Solo Viola") and on p.

139 in the first edition ("Concertos, Concertinos, Compositions with Orchestra"). Publisher is given as Peters in 2nd edn., CFE in 1st edn.

B26   Barrowclough, Nikki. "Peggy Glanville-Hicks: The Unsung Hero." *Mode Australia*, November 1988, p. 101-2.

The most recent Australian interviewer finds the famous composer "living on royalties without recognition" and "writing what she says is her final opera," *Beckett*. Librettist is Sydney journalist and playwright Wendy Beckett who is also writing a biography of Glanville-Hicks. Article includes three new photos and reprints of two old ones, and reviews biographical information (plus the new revelation that her husband was homosexual).

B27   Berger, Arthur. "Composers Forum Gives First Concert of the Season." *New York Herald Tribune*, 25 October 1948, p. 13.

Review, signed A.V.B., by *Herald Tribune* colleague and composer finds the *Concertino da camera* (**W33b**) easy and delightful to listen to, well scored, and representative of the "French serenade tradition of music aiming simply and unpretentiously at charming, which it does indeed." *Profiles from China* (**W32a**) and *Thirteen Ways of Looking at a Blackbird* (**W37a**) were grateful in range and content to the singing voice. *Thirteen Ways* seems to experiment with almost that many different styles, a "healthy sign" that the composer may be "in a transitional stage of reviewing the many directions open to one today in order to give greater depth to her creative approach."   (Review is quoted in **B11**.)

B28   Bernheimer, Martin. "American Music Festival Opens at Town Hall." Ibid., 13 February 1960, p. 7.

Drama for Orchestra (**W60a**), premiered Friday afternoon, was "more successful" than the other works on the program (works of Bergsma and Diamond that were conservative, lacked inspiration, and tended to overdevelop a relatively meagre musical content) in that it "at least disclosed the virtue of theatrical urgency." (Review is signed M. B.)

B29   Biancolli, Louis. "New U.S. Opera Opens at Phoenix." *New York World-Telegram and Sun*, 11 February 1958.

After the "trivial" first two scenes, a pastiche of Anglicized and Americanized Hindu custom and color, *The Transposed Heads* (**W46b**) is impressive. In the temple scene and village wedding scene "the vocal and orchestral writing showed a power to evoke a scene and set a mood and to use exotic folk fragments without making them stand out awkwardly." Elsewhere the tameness of the orchestra seemed the work of a different composer. Let us be thankful to have had "one good hour of operatic writing to compare favorably with some of the better work being done today" by the composer's "male colleagues." Cast was good, conductor spirited, and production enhanced by authentic Indian costumes and properties. (Clipping is in **A3**.)

B30   _____. "Volume, Art Mark U. S. Compositions." Ibid., 23 February 1953, p. 7, col. 1-2.

WNYC's 14th annual American Music Festival, handsomely planned, ended brilliantly last night in program conducted by "that tireless godfather of new music, Leopold Stokowski." [Program included *Letters from Morocco* premiere, **W44a**.] The (collective) American composer now acquires technique "at home" in the U. S., is a rebel at heart, yet knows his classics and keeps a healthy foothold in the past. Review does not name any composers; Oliver Daniel quotes it in **B107** below.

B31   Blanks, Fred R. "Composers Face the Music." *Sydney Morning Herald*, 4 August 1981, p. 28.

The *Sonata for Piano and Percussion* (**W43f**) is "an engaging piece, lively in rhythm, orientally accented in melody, original in its total efect rather than in ingredients."

B32   _____. "Curious Operatic Rabbit." Ibid., 29 June 1970, p. 10.

Australian premiere of *The Transposed Heads* (**W46c**) demonstrates the specialty of the Opera Group of the University of New South Wales: "pulling pedigree rabbits out of an operatic hat." This one is an "unfamiliar, mildly curry-flavored rabbit of curiously mixed pedigree," Hindu and English. Further performances next weekend could spread a glow of amusement. Music is sophisticated and low-brow, not ashamed of catchy tunes and jolly rhythms, and the orchestra is a delight. Story does not stand up to dramatic treatment; one master-stroke of dynamic theatre [beheadings and transposing of heads] is wrapped in a cocoon of static padding and philosophizing. Production is too austere; audience would like to see Sita's ritual bath, and perhaps two papier-maché heads rolling across the stage after the beheadings. The opera also cries out for choreography to give it some spirit. (Clipping is in **A3**.)

B33   _____. "Home-made Heinze." Ibid., 30 August 1986, p. 43.

Review of Radic's biography of Sir Bernard Heinze (**B314**), perhaps the only great Australian musical pioneer whose reputation was "made in Australia," strongly supported Australian composers such as Margaret Sutherland, Dorian le Gallienne, Robert Hughes, Clive Douglas (with these four he came into argument), Peggy Glanville-Hicks, and Percy Grainger. (Review is indexed on ARTSDOC.)

B34   _____. "On the Side of the Angels." Ibid., 6 August 1979, p. 8.

Sonata for Harp (**W42j**), the oldest work on this program (1950-51), was definitely harp music on the side of the angels (rather than "devilishly difficult"). Performed in virtuoso fashion by young Sydney-trained harpist Anthony Maydwell, the sonata was a melodically-ingratiating three-movement piece of faintly spiced consonances.

B35   Block, Adrienne Fried, and Neuls-Bates, Carol, comps. and eds. *Women in American Music: A Bibliography of Music and Literature.* Westport, CT: Greenwood Press, 1979.

Writings about Glanville-Hicks are included in this annotated bibliography, and her principal works are listed in its various sections according to the work's publication date and genre, with duration, performing forces, author of text, and publisher.

B36   Blom, Eric. "Peggy Glanville-Hicks." *Everyman's Dictionary of Music*. London: Dent, 1946. 4th edn.; London: Dent, 1971. P. 204-205.

Article in 4th edition, the same in all editions, consists of a brief biography to 1939 and a list of works that includes several early works seldom mentioned in later articles.

B37   _____. "Peggy Glanville Hicks." *Grove's Dictionary of Music and Musicians*. 5th edn.; London: Macmillan; New York: St. Martin's Press, 1954. Vol. 3, p. 655-6.

Blom updates his *Everyman's* article (**B36**) to 1948, when the *Concertino da Camera* was performed at the International Society of Contemporary Music festival in Amsterdam. She is the Australian delegate at the ISCM's annual meetings and is advisor to the Australian Ministry of Information in New York. She reported on the 1947 ISCM festival in Copenhagen for the *Musical Courier*, and on the 1948 festival for the *New York Herald Tribune, Musical America,* and the Melbourne *Argus*.

B38   Boenke, Heidi M. *Flute Music by Women Composers: An Annotated Catalog*. New York: Greenwood Press, 1989. Pp. 46-7.

Six works by Glanville-Hicks are listed, with publisher, duration, and level of difficulty: the Flute Concerto (**W20**), *Concertino da Camera* (**W34**, with its recording, **D2**), *Musica Antiqua No. 1* (**W53**), *Sonata for Flute, Harp, and Horn* (**W40**), *Sonatina for Flute and Piano* (**W27**), and *Thomsoniana* (**W38**). Glanville-Hicks is identified as an arts administrator, music critic, producer, writer, and prolific composer; her teachers' names and her awards are also listed.

B39   Bolton, Whitney. "Women Lick Opera." *[Unidentified newspaper]*, 11 February 1958.

Clipping in **A3d**, labelled (incorrectly) "Richmond, Va., *News-Leader*," is an interview published the day after the New York opening of *The Transposed Heads* (**W46b**). Focus is on "the first woman in recorded history to have composed and produced a full-length opera" [the hyperbole is apparently unwitting]. She is "a wisp of a woman, soft-spoken, ingratiating, completely charming, with vast cultivation and a sense that what she has done is no real monument." Article includes a summary of the opera's simple "but rather violent" plot and musical style.

B40   Borroff, Edith. "The Fairbank Collection." *College Music Symposium* 16 (Spring 1986), p. 105-22.

Working library of soprano Janet Fairbank, collected in the 1930s and 1940s, includes a copy of Glanville-Hicks's *Five Songs* (**W29**).

B41   Bowles, Paul. "Glanville-Hicks' Opera Will Be Heard Tomorrow." *New York Herald Tribune*, Sunday, 9 February 1958, sect. 4, p. 5.

Bowles, composer, author, "expert on matters exotic," and friend and former *Herald Tribune* colleague of Glanville Hicks, published this the day before the New York premiere of *The Transposed Heads* (**W46b**)--her own article (**G689**) was in the *New York Times*. Bowles provides a synopsis (like Menotti and Blitzstein she "has devised her own libretto"). She is a "musical moralist--a revolutionary, fiercely dedicated to the battering down of the culture-bar" so that "the same basic standards of evaluation" can be used for music of "seventeenth-century Germany and twentieth-century Uganda." For her, the "universal" or "world-wide" musical principles, found when non-Western materials are "digested and synthesized" in the West, are melody supported by rhythm, not harmony. Though one hears in *The Transposed Heads* "a surprising amount of harmony present, both implied and expressed," she has suppressed "harmonic progressions and large-scale harmonic development." Melody, not harmonic sequence, provides "emotional directions" or cues here, and a proliferation of percussion instruments are her "figured bass."

B42   _____*Without Stopping.* New York: G. P. Putnam's Sons, 1972.
P. 259-60, 334.

Bowles, a New York neighbor of Glanville-Hicks in the 1940s, recalls in this
autobiography that "Peggy was a staunch admirer of certain of my musical works and
made impeccable copies of many of the unpublished ones in her clear musical
calligraphy." Later she helped him obtain funding for his recordings of Moroccan
music (letters in **A14b** are related to this project). Bowles also recalls that her
husband Stanley Bate, "a British composer in a very different tradition" (from
Glanville-Hicks and Bowles), beat her and tossed her around the apartment when he
was drunk, "which he was regularly."

B43   Briggs, John. "Commissioned Opera on LP." *New York Times,*
Sunday, 10 July 1955, sect. 2, p. 11.

The Transposed Heads, recently issued on recording (**D21**) while "not without
interest" as a musical score, "does not come to life" as opera. [*See* **B228** for a response
to this judgment.] Except for tenor (Shridaman), singers perform "capably."
(Clipping is in **A13c**.)

B44   _____. "WNYC Music Fete Offers 3 Works. Ibid., 13 February
1954, p. 11, col. 8.

Letters from Morocco (**W44b**) in concert of works by three 1953 recipients of $1,000
grants from National Institute of Arts and Letters (other two are Goeb and
Lopatnikoff) raises question whether the Institute's name should be linked with a
work that glorifies the sensations induced by narcotics, specifically hashish [in fourth
song]. With or without hashish, the text is "pretentious hokum" and one is annoyed
that Glanville-Hicks has wasted her considerable gifts for lyric invention and
ingenious instrumentation on such trivia.

B45   Brisbane, Katharine. "Conmen and Suckers in a Garden of Delights."
The Australian, 18 March 1972, p. 16.

Patchy review of Adelaide Festival performance of *The Glittering Gate,* (**W52b**)
comments that plot shows the influence of [actually, from 1909, it predates] the
"clownish despair of Samuel Beckett and is a bit out of fashion now but is most
charmingly done."

B46   Broder, Nathan. "Columbia's Modern American Music Series."
Musical Quarterly 16 (1955), p. 551, 554.

Recording ML4990, containing the *Concertino da camera* and *Sonata for Piano and
Percussion* (**D2/D17**), is one of nine discs of 24 works by 15 living composers; "very
high level" performances are superbly recorded. The music shows no international
language, but rather "remarkable variety": the Schoenberg-Stravinsky-Hindemith-
Bartók constellation is not a useful classification system here, nor the chronological,
nor the vague "conservative, conservative-advanced, advanced" division. The
Concertino is "neat, lightweight, Poulenc-ish," and "yearns for a few good tunes."
The *Sonata* is more experimental, using percussion to return to pitch and tonality
(according to the composer's notes), but its "musical values are thin."

B47   Brown, Patricia. "A Program of Australiana from Two Fine Artists."
Sydney Morning Herald, 17 August 1984, p. 10.

Profiles from China (**W32g**), in a group of Asian-influenced songs on program of 20th-century Australian songs, though employing a different approach to word setting from other works, enjoyed a similar juxtaposing of the dramatic with the refined and economical--as in the closing *Sun of Heaven*. Soprano (Campbell) sang expressively and with clear diction, using her considerable colour range to great advantage. Combined characterization with pianist (Fogg) was clear and effective; they projected the songs with welcome conviction and musical polish.

B48   Butler, Stanley. *Guide to the Best in Contemporary Piano Music, An Annotated List of Graded Solo Piano Music Published Since 1950.* 2 vols. Metuchen, NJ: Scarecrow Press, 1973. Vol. 2, p. 32.

Composition #6.52 is the *Prelude for a Pensive Pupil* (**W56**) in the Prostakoff collection, which Butler describes as "lovely neo-romantic music" in a "pensoroso" mood. Left-hand accompaniment is added-note broken triads in parallel motion. There is momentary polyharmony and some chromatic coloring.

B49   Butterworth, Neil. *A Dictionary of American Composers.* New York: Garland, 1984. P. 187-8.

Short article on Glanville-Hicks, a biography and list of works, includes the [false] statement that Glanville-Hicks is blind and no longer can compose.

B50   Callaway, Frank, and Tunley, David, eds. *Australian Composition in the Twentieth Century.* Melbourne: Oxford University Press, 1978. Pp. 227-8, 243-4.

Glanville-Hicks is identified as an expatriate, now an American citizen, whose opera *Nausicaa* (**W62a**) "was greeted with acclaim at the 1961 Athens Festival." A photo and a short discography also appear.

B51   Campbell, Alan. "San Francisco." *Musical Courier* 50, no. 2 (August 1954), p. 19.

Song cycle *Profiles from China* (**W32c**), brief but musically fascinating, was of outstanding interest. This recital by Helen Thigpen was notable for the quality of the program and the radiant splendor of her soprano voice.

B52   Campbell, Lance. "Lord Harewood Looks to '88." Adelaide *Advertiser*, 1 March 1986, p. 20.

George Henry Hubert Lascelles, seventh Earl of Harewood, is pleased that operas by Peggy Glanville-Hicks [**W46e, W52c**] are to be part of this year's Adelaide Festival. Lord Harewood, director of the Edinburgh Festival from 1961 to 1965, and his wife will attend 42 Adelaide Festival attractions in the next three weeks.

B53   Cargher, John. *Bravo! Two Hundred Years of Opera in Australia.* South Melbourne: Macmillan, 1988. Pp. 167, 212, 219.

Australian performances of *The Transposed Heads* (**W46c, W46e**) and *The Glittering Gate* (**W52b, W52c**), Athens production of *Nausicaa* (**W62a**) and opera *Sappho* (**W64**) are mentioned. Glanville-Hicks, "an expatriate Australian," has "a following in *avant-garde* circles." She is "shunned by the establishment," which is happy to claim her as Australian but fails to stage her works. She "predominated" at the Adelaide

Festival in 1986, though many considered *Glittering Gate* and *Transposed Heads* "outdated musically and obscure dramatically."

B54 _____. "Time to Get to Know a Notable Australian." *The Bulletin* (Sydney), 27 June 1970, p. 49-50.

Glanville-Hicks, another "notable Australian" who made a name overseas (article reviews her training and major works) now lives in Athens. She traveled by train across Europe to London for further treatment to make it possible to come to Sydney to see production of *The Transposed Heads* (**W46c**) at the University of New South Wales. The same sets (by Dick Evans, now of Athens) and costumes (obtained by the University from the Indian government) as in the 1958 New York production will be used. Article includes photo (from **B78**) of Glanville-Hicks with Lawrence Durrell, working on opera *Sappho*.

B55 Carmody, John. "Tryptich of Native Delights." *The National Times* (Sydney), 17 August 1984, p. 32.

Profiles from China (**W32g**) performed in Sydney Opera House recital are epigrammatic, more sophisticated than some more recent songs on the program, concise, subtle, and more appealing than songs featuring a "plethora" of notes. Elizabeth Campbell, convalescent after laryngitis, did not sing with all her usual vocal assurance.

B56 Carr, Winifred. "Opera at the Foot of the Acropolis." *Daily Telegraph and Morning Post* (London), 7 September 1961, p. 11, col. 4-6.

Glanville-Hicks, interviewed at home in Athens after *Nausicaa* premiere (**W62a**), says she would like her work "assessed fairly, alongside men's" and concludes that she is "anti-feminist." Robert Graves, also present, elaborates on the evidence that a woman wrote the *Odyssey*, the basis of the *Nausicaa* plot. She is completing a book on Western music's turn to the East. Her failing eyesight makes it increasingly difficult to write music, which must be done by hand, and she exhibits an unemotional, perhaps Eastern, "acceptance of the inevitable." (Clipping is in **A3**.)

B57 Carr-Boyd, Anne. "Australian Music 1950-1980." Australian Report for the Asian Composers Conference-Festival, Hong Kong, 4-12 March 1981. Typescript, 56 p. P. 27.

Glanville-Hicks is mentioned as one of many Australian composers living mostly abroad.

B58 Carson, Leon. "'The Glittering Gate' by Glanville Hicks." *Musical Courier* 160, no. 1 (July 1959), p. 12.

Favorable review (signed L. C.) of the New York production (**W52a**) comments that the music, "written with a skilled hand, is not over-complex." Singers were "excellently cast, vocally and otherwise, and brought zest and comedy to the action with successful results." Two burglars are outside the gate of Heaven; one uses his safe-cracking instrument to open the gate, only to find a sky full of stars.

B59 Cary, Tristram. "Nice Idea But Tired Production." *Opera Australia* 101 (May 1986), p. 15.

Tribute to "Australia's senior woman composer" in Adelaide Festival's revivals of
The Glittering Gate (**W52c**) and *The Transposed Heads* (**W46e**) was a nice idea, but
should have been done properly. Tired production was not worthy of its prominent,
top-line festival billing. The works, not quite opera, perhaps sounded trendy in the
1950s, but probably not fresh and original. The first is a pleasantly whimsical story
with "vocal and dramatic overkill." Set for the first was adequate; for the second, set
was not, and "some of the stage effects would have been sub-standard in a village
hall." The music, a melange of styles (it does not work to impose a Western
emotional framework on transcriptions of genuine Indian tunes and effects) needed
visual support and did not get it. Orchestra played well, but were not placed well,
because the Playhouse is not designed for opera. Review includes a photo from each
work. (Clipping is in **A6c**.)

B60   "A Catalogue of Works by American Composers on LP Records."
American Composers Alliance Bulletin 4, no. 3 (1955), p. 19.

Listed are the *Harp Sonata* (**D13**), *Three Gymnopédies* (**D18**), *Sonata for Piano and
Percussion* (**D17**), and *The Transposed Heads* (**D21**).

B61   Chapman, Frank. "First Spoleto Festival Major Success." *Musical
America* 77, nò. 9 (August 1958), p. 10.

Report mentions "world premieres" choreographed by John Butler for the festival:
Triad (**W59a**), *Masque of the Wild Man* (**W55a**), and two by other composers.

B62   "City Premiere for Hicks Opera." *New York Herald Tribune*, 25
November 1957, p. 17, col. 2.

First announcement of the New York production of *The Transposed Heads* (**W46b**),
is of a 13 January performance [later moved to February; *see* **B307**], a project of the
Contemporary Music Society and produced by Chandler Cowles. Though the
announcement is attributed to Leopold Stokowski, president of the society, it was
apparently written by Glanville-Hicks (the original typescript is in **A3d(5)**). A shorter
version, "Opera Due at Phoenix: 'Transposed Heads' to be Given by Contemporary
Society," appeared the same day in the *New York Times* (p. 26). (Clippings of both
are in **A13c**.)

B63   Claghorn, Charles Eugene. *Biographical Dictionary of American
Music*. West Nyack, NY: Parker, 1973. P. 174.

Short biography of Glanville-Hicks includes names of four works, the most recent
being *Nausicaa* (**W62**), premiered in 1961.

B64   Clough, G. F., and Cuming, G. J. *The World's Encyclopedia of
Recorded Music, Third Supplement 1953-1955*. London: Sedgwick and
Jackson, 1957. P. 177.

Entry lists six recordings: *Choral Suite* (but omitting mention of oboe), **D1**; *Sonata
for Harp*, **D12**; *Concertino da camera* and *Sonata for Piano and Percussion*, **D2/D17**;
Three Gymnopédies, **D18**; and *The Transposed Heads*, **D21**.

B65   Coeuroy, André. *Dictionnaire critique de la musique ancienne et
moderne*. Paris: Payot, 1956. P. 16.

Glanville-Hicks is one of nine composers listed under "Australie" and is described as a student of Nadia Boulanger, composer of *Caedmon* and *Music for Robots* (hardly her major works), and wife of English composer Stanley Bate (they had been divorced since 1949).

B66   Cohen, Aaron I. *International Discography of Women Composers.* Discographies, Number 10. Westport, CT: Greenwood Press, 1984. P. 48.

Cohen lists eleven works on fourteen recordings. Information is repeated in **B67**, 2nd edn., vol. 2 (*see* next entry).

B67   _____. "Peggy Glanville-Hicks." *International Encyclopedia of Women Composers.* New York: Bowker, 1981. 2nd edn.; New York: Books and Music, 1987. Vol. 1, p. 272-3 (biography, compositions, bibliography), and vol. 2, p. 1094-5 (discography).

Biography to ca. 1965 is mainly from BMI composer brochure 1969 (**B297**). List of compositions, by genre, combines major works to 1965 (as in **B297**) and earlier titles from Antheil (**B11**) and Blom (**B36**, **B37**). Bibliography--always strong in Cohen--lists thirty published works (including these three). The "Composer for Theatre" brochure, **B78** [1969], is incorrectly described as the Phoenix Theatre program [1958]. Material in the second edition is the same as in the first edition of the *Encyclopedia*, p. 184-5, and the *Discography*, **B66**.

B68   Cohn, Alan M. "Glanville-Hicks's *Nausicaa* and Graves." *Focus on Robert Graves* 4 (June 1974), p. 71-3.

Cohn speculates (accurately) that Alastair Reid may have collaborated with Graves and Glanville-Hicks on the *Nausicaa* libretto, based on Graves's novel *Homer's Daughter*, even though Glanville-Hicks (in **G693** and **G696**) only named Graves. The libretto was published in 1964 with the recording (**D7**), Cohn discovered, and he can now identify some unexplained Graves manuscripts as early libretto drafts.

B69   Cohn, Neville. "Voicing an Emphasis on Today." *The Australian*, 15 August 1988, p. 7.

Perth performance of *Thirteen Ways of Looking at a Blackbird* (**W37f**) was, as a feat of memory for the mezzo-soprano (Millar), a tour de force, though with some occassionally fuzzy diction. Accompanist showed a distinct gift for the contemporary idiom. *Frolic* (**W9c**) was performed in a bracket of four songs; tenor (Alafaci) "had the measure of the songs" except for some strained top notes.

B70   Cole, Edward. Liner notes for Glanville-Hicks, *Concerto Romantico*, MGM Records E 3559. 1957. *See* **D3**.

Cole presents the introductory material described in the next entry (the earliest of his four) and quotes **G686**, Glanville-Hicks's own lengthy "background note" on the *Concerto Romantico*.

B71   _____. Liner notes for Glanville-Hicks, *Etruscan Concerto*, MGM Records E 3557. 1956. *See* **D4**.

Here, in the earliest (and shortest) of his four sets of liner notes for Glanville-Hicks's MGM records (**B70-B73**), Cole, Artists and Repertoire Director at MGM, sets the pattern for the other three. He reviews her life and works, always beginning with the unfortunate sentence (which paraphrases Antheil's 1954 article, **B11**): "Peggy Glanville-Hicks is an exception to the rule that women composers do not measure up to the standards set in the field by men." On this recording he mentions her work in progress on an opera to a libretto by Robert Graves and on "an unusual set of twelve piano pieces" [apparently never published] on a friend's "astrological birth chart." Then, on all four recordings, he includes her own technical and stylistic explanations of the particular work--invaluable material available nowhere else. The *Etruscan Concerto* was written in 1954-1955 for "the brilliant young Florentine Carlo Bussotti" who performed its world premiere with conductor Carlos Surinach (**W48a**). Its "highly colored" movements evoke "the moods of the Etruscan Tombs of Tarquinia" as D. H. Lawrence describes them--and Cole quotes in full the three movements' inscriptions.

B72 _____. Liner notes for Glanville-Hicks, *Letters from Morocco*, MGM Records E 3549. 1957. *See* **D6**.

Introductory material is as described in the previous entry--minus mention of the twelve piano pieces, plus the unnamed opera's name, *Nausicaa*. Glanville-Hicks composed the six songs on letters of Paul Bowles in 1952 on board a South Pacific freighter from New Orleans to Sydney and on the homeward voyage. "They evoke in their rather stark prose-poetry the sights and sounds of the Arab world of the Western Mediterranean," Cole notes. She writes music that fits her texts metrically and seems "a natural and expressive emanation"--here the music for Moroccan pieces " 'sounds' Hispanic-Berber." She rejects the "harmonic aspect" of atonalism and neo-classicism (while she retains their "contrapuntal strength" and "formal projection," respectively), and uses instead a "modal row" (melody) with "organic percussion" (rhythm), a system she developed from careful study of "the ancient tradition of melody-rhythm composition that prevails in remnants from Kashmir to the Atlas Mountains." Her "typical orchestral scheme" is: for the melody, single woodwinds, trumpet, horn, sometimes trombone, and strings ("many or few," for "economic flexibility"), and, for the rhythm, instruments "graded from pitched to unpitched" and (quoting the composer) "from fast-moving to slow-moving sounds. Thus, Xylophone, Marimba and Tympani offer a pitched range from top to bottom; high, medium and low Gongs, plus Tam Tam, give a 'pedal' effect throughout the range; while Tom Tom and 'effects' men provide the small accents of articulation."

B73 _____. Liner notes for Glanville-Hicks, *Sinfonia da Pacifica* and *Three Gymnopédies*, MGM Records E 3336. 1956. *See:* **D11/D19**.

Cole presents his introductory material as in **B71** and then quotes **G594** and **G680**, Glanville-Hicks's lengthy "explanatory notes" about the music.

B74 Coles, Helen. "The 'Role' of Women in Western Music." Unpublished Bachelor of Arts (Hons.) Thesis, Department of Music, Monash University (Melbourne), 1972. P. 93-99 *et infra*.

Section in chapter 2 discusses the career of Glanville-Hicks as composer, critic, and concert organizer, referring the reader to a partial list of works in Appendix II, is preceded by general comments on women in the composer role (one of several roles of women in music which Coles identifies).

B75 "Complimentary Concert." *The Argus* (Melbourne), 3 June 1932, p. 8.

Friends of Miss Peggy Glanville Hicks (no hyphen), young composer and pianist, arranged a complimentary farewell concert before her departure for England. She "has a graceful musical sense" and her compositions (W2a) were pleasantly atmospheric, if lacking in any pronounced feeling for further rhythmic and thematic development. A naively named "violin solo" showed more originality than three piano preludes, the first of which showed a grasp of Debussy's idiom. Her songs showed little coordination between melodic line and piano accompaniments. She had "a sincere and conscientious attitude which promised well for her future development." The anonymous critic also comments at length on musical training and performance in Australia. (The review is about half the length of the other review of this concert, B76).

B76   "Complimentary Concert. A Talented Musician." *The Age* (Melbourne), 3 June 1932, p. 14.

Miss Glanville Hicks (no hyphen) "met with every encouragement from the friendly audience" after her clever performance of a Mozart piano concerto movement and her own compositions: a piano prelude, violin solo, and three songs (W2a). She has a purely intuitive method of composition, based on emotional spontaneity rather than conformity to theoretical routine. Her work is, therefore, original, based on "sound as a direct means of artistic expression." Fritz Hart, her teacher, was given a cheering reception after his stay abroad. The anonymous critic also comments that Australian musical talent is rewarded with prizes, but students could do more with a study of musical structure.

B77   "Composer Comes Home." *Sydney Morning Herald*, 3 July 1970, p. 16.

Interview published in the Friday "News for Women" section during Glanville-Hicks's visit to Sydney for local performance of *The Transposed Heads* (W46c) includes a recent photo. Though musical catalogs have designated her American, she proclaims herself an Australian composer. She has a Hepburn-type quality of strength and delicacy, and after twenty years in the U. S. and ten in Athens, her voice is almost unaccented. Her years in New York were at "an exciting time for music in America" but now she deplores the electronic music explosion there. Her percussion pieces like the *Sonata for Piano and Percussion* (W43) made the "maximum effect for the minimum expenditure," she says. Busy surviving in New York, she could not compose, but "sloped off each summer to a remote little boathouse in Germany," to bring what was brewing inside to the boil. (Copy of article is in A3.)

B78   "Composer for Theatre: P. Glanville-Hicks." Brochure. [1969.]

In large format (30 cm [1 ft.] sq.), the elegant brochure (a gift from the Athens Festival) includes a "Biographical Note 1969" and information on four operas (*The Transposed Heads, The Glittering Gate, Nausicaa,* and *Sappho*) and five ballets (*The Mask of the Wild Man, Saul and the Witch of Endor, Tragic Celebration,* and *A Season in Hell*), with large, handsomely reproduced photographs of performances (and for *Sappho*, unperformed, a photo of author Lawrence Durrell and the composer at work, and a photo of the title page). Also reprinted are excerpts from the composer's writings on *The Transposed Heads* (G677) and *Nausicaa* (696), and excerpts from reviews. (Copies are in A2b, A3b(8), and A6c.)

B79   "Composer Honoured." *The University of Sydney News,* 2 June 1987, p. 101.

Photo of "Australian composer" Glanville-Hicks receiving an Honorary Doctorate in Music from the Chancellor, Sir Hermann Black, at a Conferring Ceremony on 2 May 1987 is captioned with a one-sentence summary of Peter Sculthorpe's citation: "Now living in Australia again after establishing an international reputation overseas, she is perhaps best known for her music for the theatre."

B80   "Composer Plans to Attend Opera." *Sydney Morning Herald*, 24 June 1970, p. 16.

Glanville-Hicks will arrive in Sydney Saturday (28 June) from Athens by way of London for the University of New South Wales production of *The Transposed Heads* (**W46c**), to be performed also in Canberra 18 July. Born in Melbourne, she made most of her reputation in Europe and the United States. The opera, set in India, is based partly on Indian melodies and rhythms she heard while studying Indian classical and folk music in India. Costumes originally provided by the Indian government have been made available for the production.

B81   *Composers of the Americas. (Compositores de América.)* Vol. 13. Washington, D.C.: Pan-American Union, 1967. P. 53-9.

Article in Spanish and English on "Peggy Glanville-Hicks" includes a one-paragraph biography, a classified list of works with instrumentation, duration, and publisher, and a facsimile of the first page of her *Gymnopédie No. 2* (**W47**).

B82   "The Concert Hall." *American Composers Alliance Bulletin* 3, no. 1 (1953), p. 24.

Section headed "Peggy Glanville-Hicks" quotes from the three 1953 performance reviews of her *Sonata for Piano and Percussion,* **W43b**, by Downes and Thomson (**B117, B384**), and of **W43c** by Parmenter (**B290**)--all reprinted in the *ACA Bulletin* the next year (**B11**). *Letters from Morocco* (**W44a**) is listed without reviews.

B83   "Concert Hall." Ibid., 4, no. 2 (1954), p. 13.

Performance of *Profiles from China* (**W32c**) is listed, and Campbell's review is quoted (**B51**).

B84   "Concert Hall." Ibid., 5, no. 2 (1955), p. 20.

Performance of *Thomsoniana* (**W38c**) is listed, without reviews.

B85   "Concert Hall." Ibid., 5, no. 3 (1956), p. 18.

Section headed "Peggy Glanville-Hicks" quotes from two reviews of *Etruscan Concerto,* **W48a**, by Schonberg (**B342**) and Trimble (**B389**)

B86   "Concert Hall." Compiled by Donna Jean Hill. Ibid., 7, no. 1 (Fall 1957), p. 20.

Section on Glanville-Hicks lists performance of *Thomsoniana* (**W38d**).

B87   "Concert Hall." Ibid., 7, no. 4 (1958), pp. 23-4.

Section on Glanville-Hicks lists performances of: *Sonata for Harp* (**W42f**) with excerpt from an anonymous review (**B359**); *Concertino Antico* (**W49b**), with excerpts from reviews by Downes (**B116**), Hughes (**B193**), and Laderman (**B211**); and *The*

Transposed Heads (**W46b**) with excerpts from Biancolli (**B29**), Johnson (**B199**), Lang (**B212**), and Taubman (**B372**).

B88   "Concert Hall." Ibid., 8, no. 1 (1958), p. 23.

Section on Glanville-Hicks lists a performance of *Thomsoniana* (**W38e**) and premiere of *The Masque of the Wild Man* (**W55a**), with an excerpt from Taubman's review (**B370**).

B89   "Concert Hall." Ibid., 8, no. 3 (1959), p. 21.

Performance of *Sonata for Harp* (**W42g**) is listed, without reviews.

B90   "Concert Hall." Ibid., 8, no. 4 (1959), p. 26.

Premiere performance of *Concertino Antico,* **W49a**, is listed, without reviews.

B91   "Concert Hall." Ibid., 9, no. 1 (1959), p. 20.

Premiere performance of *The Glittering Gate,* **W52a**, is listed, without reviews.

B92   "Concert Hall." Ibid., 9, no. 2 (1960), p. 20.

Performance of *Gymnopédie No. 1* (**W47a**) is listed, without reviews.

B93   "Concert Hall." Ibid., 9, no. 3 (1960), p. 30.

Performance of *Drama for Orchestra* (**W60a**) is listed, without reviews.

B94   "Concert Hall." Ibid., 9, no. 4 (1961), p. 22, 25.

Performances of *Sonata for Harp* (**W42h**), *Sonatina for Treble Recorder and Piano* (**W27a**), and *Sonata for Piano and Percussion* (**W43d**) are listed, without reviews.

B95   "Concert is a Family Affair." *The Age* (Melbourne), 8 July 1970, p. 19.

Glanville-Hicks is to attend the concert 10 July of works of Hugo Alpen (1842-1915), early Australian composer, as a special guest along with Alpen relatives. Announcement appears in the "Accent" section, ed. Elaine McFarling. (Copy is in **A3**.)

B96   "Contemporary Concert Presents Variety in Style." Colorado Springs *Gazette Telegraph*, 5 August 1950, p. 7.

Review (anonymous) of *Thomsoniana* (**W38b**) at Colorado College summer music festival, quoted in Antheil, **B11**, calls the work the "biggest surprise of the evening." The parodies were "superbly" carried off and "the audience loved the work." The piece called "Schoenberg"was particularly hilarious, spoofing his awkward vocal line and using his speaking-singing style in a ridiculous context.

B97   "Contemporary Music: Amsterdam Festival." *The Times* (London), 25 June 1948, p. 6.

Report "from a correspondent" singles out the *Concertino da camera* (**W33a**) as "clever" and "equally pleasing" to works of Chevreuille (Belgium) and Høffding (Denmark). No school or tendency predominated at the ISCM festival and, except for the three mentioned, the composers seemed shipwrecked, struggling in the deep waters of doubt and disillusionment, and clinging to fragile rafts (12-tone, polytonal, polyphonic, neo-classic, expressionist) that offered no passage to a secure place.

B98   Covell, Roger. *Australia's Music: Themes of a New Society.* Melbourne: Sun Books, 1967.

Radical elements in the music of Australian composers usually result from overseas contact with influences outside their own predominantly British environment. Glanville-Hicks, though "sometimes cited as an Australian composer on the grounds of birth," must be yielded up to America where she did most of her work, composing "attractive, clear-textured music." (Glanville-Hicks objected to being categorized as an American composer, so Covell called her an Australian composer in **B101**, published three years later.)

B99   _____. "Even Sir Bernard Heinze is Fascinated by Concrete Music." *The Courier-Mail* (Brisbane), 25 October 1957, p. 2.

Heinze, the noted Melbourne conductor, told Queensland Symphony Orchestra members that Glanville-Hicks, the "Australian composer and critic," taught him about *musique concrète* (or "concrete music," "concrete" in the sense of actually) in New York in 1952. Demonstrating, he dropped a pair of scissors on the floor. "Dum da-da dum. Hm. Near enough to E flat. . . . You know, ladies and gentlemen," he said, "you could record the sound of those scissors dropping and make a composition lasting an hour . . . or hours, weeks, months, years--at least theoretically." The sound could be altered, through tapes, filters, and other devices, or one of the dums, or the two da-da's, could be used separately. Such experiments in France and America give a clue to the future development of music. (*See also* **B314** for Radic's explanation.)

B100   _____. "An Important Australian Saluted." *Sydney Morning Herald*, 22 January 1982, p. 8.

Concert, with Glanville-Hicks present, featured spoken annotations by James Murdoch and performances by highly gifted musicians, of works of this important composer, still largely unknown in Australia. Her music is clearly ordered, economical, and full of vital rhythm and shapely melody. *Profiles from China* (**W32e**) were fragrant miniatures. Words of *Thomsoniana* (**W38f**) were unintelligible, though parody of Schoenberg seemed unsympathetic, parody of Satie sympathetic. The appealing *Sonata for Piano and Percussion* (**W43g**) represents composer's interest in bringing together percussion ensembles and writing for them during her New York years. Exemplary clarity of enunciation in *Letters from Morocco* (**W44c**) and virtuosity of tenor with instrumental ensemble made the performance memorable. *Musica Antiqua No. 1* (**W53a**) uses fragments of Peruvean or Andean music. (Clippings are in **A2a, A7**.)

B101   _____. "U. S. Citizen But the Music is Australian." Ibid., 13 June 1970.

Covell, music director for the upcoming first Australian performance of *The Transposed Heads*, at the University of New South Wales, Sydney (**W46c**), interviewed Glanville-Hicks in Athens earlier in the year. (A photo of the composer in Athens accompanies the article.) She is "one of Australia's most distinguished composers and liveliest spirits" (he recants his earlier [**B98**] categorization of her as American). Covell discusses her study with Fritz Hart in Melbourne, her student years in

London and Europe, her fame in New York as composer, concert organizer, and *Herald Tribune* music critic ("as offsider to Virgil Thomson"), her contributions as "author of all the American entries" for *Grove's Dictionary* [actually she only wrote the more recent *composer* entries, **G487-584**, though overseeing the rest], her field work in India and Greece, and her attempts to marry Indian and Western materials in *The Transposed Heads*. She may come to Sydney to see the opera and visit relatives, depending on "the success of an ear operation which will make it possible for her to travel by plane." American musicians, out of affection and gratitude, helped pay for an earlier "series of major operations." The opera production will be repeated in Canberra and Mittagong.

B102 Cresswell, Anthony. "These We Like." *Oregon Journal* (Portland), 2 September 1956, p. 8C.

Etruscan Concerto (**D4**) on MGM recording 3357 is "exceptionally worthy to these ears" and shows a respect for melody not always found in modern composers. Glanville-Hicks was the guiding influence behind a concert of new works for chamber orchestra in New York last January, heard on two MGM releases. (Review is quoted in **B113**.)

B103 Crisp, Deborah, comp. *Bibliography of Australian Music: An Index to Monographs, Journal Articles and Theses.* (Australian Music Studies I.) Armidale: Australian Music Studies Project, 1982.

Three writings are listed: Glanville-Hicks's "At the Source" (**G693**), Antheil (**B11**), and Ruff (**B330**).

B104 Crotty, Joel. "A Bibliographic Study on the Resources By and About Peggy Glanville-Hicks." Unpublished Bachelor's thesis (Librarianship), Royal Melbourne Institute of Technology, 1985.

The only guide to **A3**, the Glanville-Hicks archival collection in the State Library of Victoria, this useful thesis groups bibliographical titles (published and unpublished) by musical work referred to. A copy of the thesis is housed in the manuscript collection of the library.

B105 Daniel, George. "Our Greatest Woman Composer Receives Little Recognition Here." *Sydney Morning Herald*, 26 March 1983.

Glanville-Hicks at 70, "the foremost Australian woman composer" and perhaps this century's "first woman composer of note," can look back proudly on her four operas, five ballets, nine major symphonic works, numerous chamber pieces, and film music. Vaughan Williams saw her "musical genius" and used one of her themes, which she later borrowed back for *The Transposed Heads*, the work that first brought her recognition. For rhythmic vitality she looked at the complex metres of India. For melodic vitality she chose modalism, and found materials in folksong, especially Greek folksong. The outcome of her years of study, the magnificent *Nausicaa*, brought a ten-minute standing ovation in Athens [Daniel quotes from **B357**, **G696**, and other writings]. Accompanying photo shows the composer at her 70th birthday party in December 1982. (Copies are in **A2a**, **A6c**, and **A7**.)

B106 Daniel, Jason. " 'Madness' Warm-up Gets a Cool Reception." Adelaide *Advertiser*, 18 March 1986, p. 8.

Article is part of advance publicity for the Adelaide Festival's *The Transposed Heads* (**W46e**) and *The Glittering Gate* (**W52c**).

B107   Daniel, Oliver. "Alchemy by Stokowski." *American Composers Alliance Bulletin* 3, no. 1 (Spring 1953), p. 6-7.

Letters from Morocco (**W44a**), conducted by Leopold Stokowski at the Museum of Modern Art, was the concluding concert of WNYC's 14th annual American music festival. The house was packed. Paul Bowles, author of the letters Glanville-Hicks set to music, attended. Just back from Istanbul, he "was accompanied by one Moroccan in full burnoose and Libby Holman in *purdah* by way of dark glasses, while numerous turbans and saris lent an additional dash of cosmopolitanism." Daniel also quotes from concert reviews by Biancolli, Olin Downes, and Thomson (**B30, B117, B384**). (Reviewer, Daniel, was editor of this *ACA Bulletin*.)

B108   _____. "The New Festival: Glanville-Hicks." Ibid., 5, no. 1 (1955), p. 8-9.

Two-paragraph biography identifies her as "the first woman composer to have had an opera commissioned, performed and recorded" (although noting she decries the label "woman composer"), as well as a "distinguished critic" and reciipient of several grants. Discography to 1955 lists six recordings: **D1, D2, D13, D17, D18, D21**.

B109   _____. "New Recordings." Ibid., 4, no. 2 (1954), p. 15, 18-19.

Discussing recording of *Three Gymnopédies* (**D18**) Daniel quotes Glanville-Hicks's liner notes (**G594**). Also quoted are her remarks on Arthur Berger's *Quartet in C* from **G426**.

B110   Demos, Jean M. "Athens: *Nausicaa*." *Opera* 12 (Autumn 1961), p. 63-6.

Review in English periodical credits Kimon Vourloumis, director of the Athens Festival, with the decision to mount the "difficult and controversial" *Nausicaa* (**W62a**). Controversy begins with the libretto, which exceeds the limits a poet may take with legend and results in disunity of the plot. Glanville-Hicks's articulate explanation of the music is also controversial; her discovery of the only appropriate music for drama depends on an assumed connection, "surely more mystical than scientific," between ancient and modern folk music. The music of *Nausicaa*, however, is "original, consistent and often exciting," Nausicaa's monologue being one of the very effective moments. The score features musical declamation, only rarely melodic, with consistently oriental rhythms and intervals, never lapsing into "a Western progression." Production was lavish, costumes fine but anachronistic, causing the purists some pain (Demos quotes from press release to show the "somewhat *sans-façon* manner in which matters involving non-musical scholarship were dealt with"). Principals were good, Stratas was glorious, and conductor Surinach, a distinguished composer in his own right, deserves thanks for bringing to performance this important but musically forbidding score.

B111   Deri, Otto. *Exploring Twentieth-Century Music*. New York: Holt, Rinehart and Winston, 1968. P. 85.

The *Sonata for Piano and Percussion* is one of six pieces Deri names in which percussion instruments form part of a chamber music combination.

B112   Diether, Jack. "WNYC's American Music Festival." *Musical America* 80, no. 4 (March 1960), p. 29.

Drama for Orchestra, heard in premiere performance (**W60a**), leaned heavily on the famed F, E, G-flat, F motif of Vaughan Williams' Fourth Symphony." The motif, and diminutions of the motif (as in the symphony), "gave her piece not merely a feeling of quotation, but of emotional duplication on a lower plane of intensity." (Review is signed J. D.)

B113   "Discs and Reviews 1955-1956." *American Composers Alliance Bulletin* 6, no. 3 (1957), p. 21-2.

Section headed "Peggy Glanville-Hicks" quotes reviews of the MGM recordings of the *Etruscan Concerto* (**D4**), **B102** and **B130**, and of the *Sinfonia pacifica* and *Three Gymnopédies* (**D11/D19**), **B201**, **B215**, **B324**, **B331**, and **B354**, mislabeled *Christian Science Monitor*.

B114   "Distinguished Artists at Colorado College." *Southwestern Musician* 17, no. 3 (November 1950), p. 25.

Glanville-Hicks is one of five American composers besides composer-in-residence Virgil Thomson who visited the college and were represented on a program of works written during the past year. The *Thomsoniana* (**B38b**) had its first performance (Thomson says second, in **B378**).

B115   Dounias, M. [*Nausicaa* review.] *Kathimerini* (Athens), 22 August 1961.

Nausicaa (**W62a**) has "astounding beauty and continuity" because the composer remained faithful to her chosen modes of expression. She intends, in using the melodic modes and metrical variety of Greek *demotiki* music, to show the music and dance of our people as carrying the age-old spirit.   John Butler, the production's inspired director and choreographer, contributed greatly to its success." (Review is quoted in **B269** and **G687** in English; typescript is in **A3g** and **A11**.)

B116   Downes, Edward. "Variety at 'Music in Our Time' Concert." *New York Times*, 3 February 1958, p. 26.

Two of five short paragraphs (signed E. D.) are on the *Concertino Antico* (**W49b**) which he describes as based on "gap scales" like some used in the Orient. The emphasis was on "melody and instrumental color, with a minimum of very thin texture harmony. The cool lyricism and simplicity, particularly of the middle movement, entitled 'Ritual,' was very attractive indeed."

B117   Downes, Olin. "WNYC Offers Fete of American Music." Ibid., 13 February 1953, p. 17.

Opening concert of WNYC's fourteenth annual festival began with remarks by Mayor Impellitteri (Downes quotes excerpts). Glanville-Hicks's *Sonata for Piano and Percussion* (**W43b**) is in part a study in rhythms, and in part a "sonata" in which the first movement presents certain thunderously simple chord progressions from which, in the second movement, thematic developments sprout, assemble, and culminate. (Cf. **G676**.)

B118   _____. "Stokowski Conducts Final Concert of WNYC's Annual Music Festival: Group of Contemporary Works Performed at Modern Art Museum in Wind-Up." Ibid., 23 February 1953, p. 20, col. 2-3.

Audience that packed the concert room and was cordially disposed to all and sundry applauded the "conventionally oriental settings" of *Letters from Morocco* (**W44b**). Concert was a "laboratory" program of music by the avant garde of our native composers (others were Halsey Stevens, Henry Brant, Lou Harrison, Jacob Avshalomov, and Charles Ives), whether it ever made the grade of the current repertory. One wished that most of the compositions had stayed in the laboratory, and that the composers had learned their lessons in the laboratory before they endeavoured to interest the public in their mostly callow and pretentious production. Review is mentioned in **B107**. (Cf. **G676**.)

B119   Dr. H. W.-W. "Die Harfe, virtuos gespielt." *Hamburger Anzeiger* (Germany), 13 May 1953.

Nicanor Zabaleta presented the *Sonata for Harp* in its German premiere performance (**W42e**), with other original compositions inspired by Zabaleta. Glanville-Hicks's works contain Spanish elements. (Clipping is in **A3**.)

B120   Duigan, Virginia. "Back From the Past, With an Ear to the Future." *National Times* (Australia), 4-10 April 1982, p. 34.

First encouraging signs of recognition of this composer since her return to Australia seven years ago are the recent splendid Festival of Sydney concert (*see* **B4, B100**) and a 2 1/2-hour ABC Radio program on her music and ideas. During a life in England, America, and Greece, she earned "a formidable international reputation as a composer, particularly of opera, as an influential critic and a champion of young composers and contemporary music." Now she is starting no more music, and not counting on living more than about another two years. Duigan recounts much of Glanville-Hicks's conversation--about Vaughan Williams (he "pinched" a theme of hers for his E [F?] Minor Symphony and she later stole it back for the last act of *Transposed Heads)* and other teachers, Robert Graves, Malcom Sargent, Paul Bowles, the Composers Forum, husband Stanley Bate, their uneasy marriage, their divorce, his death in 1949 [actually 1959], his music (she is setting up a foundation in America from his royalties), her brain tumor, *Nausicaa* in Athens, and her book in progress on the employment and economic situation of "the forward line" of twentieth-century composers. Much "fabulous" twentieth-century music is never heard--music by Ravel, Fauré, Chavez, Villa-Lobos.

B121   Eaton, Quaintance. *Opera Production II: A Handbook.* Minneapolis: University of Minnesota Press, 1974. P. 166-7, 205-6, 279-80, 325-6.

Information on *Nausicaa* (**W62**), *Sappho* (**W64**), *The Glittering Gate* (**W52**), and *The Transposed Heads* (**W46**) includes a description of the music of each opera and a full synopsis of the action which are available nowhere else. Also noted are: libbrettist, date and place of premiere, roles, orchestra, and publisher.

B122   Edmunds, John, and Boelzner, Gordon. *Some Twentieth Century American Composers: A Selective Bibliography.* Vol. 2. New York: The New York Public Library, 1960. P. 31-32.

Several of the 45 titles--writings by and about Glanville-Hicks and about her work--are listed in no other bibliography. (Edmunds chaired the Composers Forum board in the 1950s when she was the executive director.)

B123   Elwell, Herbert. "Opera Barriers Fall for Woman Composer." *Cleveland Plain-Dealer*, 12 June 1955, p. 56-D.

In a substantial review of *The Transposed Heads* recording (**D21**), this composer-critic refers the reader to the same issue's record column by Rena C. Holtkamp for specific details, and devotes his own column to the opera itself. Glanville-Hicks "understands the human voice" and "also understands what should happen to the English language when it is sung." She is "amazingly skillful" in building "exciting dramatic tensions" and has been "canny" in choosing a story "ideal for operatic treatment." Her music, from "antique" sources, is "strongly contemporary" in the sense of "delightfully fresh and stimulating." While women composers like Chaminade, Beach, Lili Boulanger, Leginska, and Bauer "have made a certain mark," Glanville-Hicks with her vitality and skill shows that women may perhaps soon "compete with men in large numbers." Elwell's review is quoted at length in **B78**, **B263**, and **B296**.

B124   Emery, Ron. "Albany Symphony Falls Short in Troy." *Times Union* (Albany, NY), Sunday, 6 November 1988.

Etruscan Concerto (**W48d**) sounded "light-hearted and accessible" with a "movie-music mood" and a piano part that "is difficult, but not terribly showy." The reception was "mild and polite."

B125   *Enciclopedia Salvat de la música*. Barcelona: Salvat, 1967. Vol. 2, p. 357.

Short entry (eleven lines) under "Glanville-Hicks (Peggy)" identifies her as an Australian composer who studied at the Royal College in London, with Boulanger, and with Wellesz, a resident of the U. S. from 1942, *Herald Tribune* critic from 1946 [1947?], and composer of ballets, one (!) opera and symphonic, choral, chamber, film, and vocal music.

B126   *Encyclopedie van de muziek*, ed. L. M. G. Arntezenius [et al.]. Vol. 1. Amsterdam: Elsevier, 1956. P. 600.

Short entry on Glanville-Hicks identifies her (in four lines) and summarizes her compositions (three lines).

B127   Epstein, David M. "Surinach Presents New Works." *Musical America* 77, no. 4 (March 1957), p. 27.

Review (signed D. M. E.) of *Concerto romantico* premiere (**W51a**) notes it "made a strong impression, with Walter Trampler a splendid soloist." The music is "warm in feeling" with "dark insrumental colors," and its "folkish flow" is reminiscent of "Vaughan Williams and fellow Englishmen."

B128   Ericson, Raymond A. "Music: 2d Women's Festival Begins." *New York Times*, 15 March 1979, p. 20.

Heard at "Festival II" of Women's Music at the Interart Center in New York, a duet from *Nausicaa* (**W62b**) was in Glanville-Hicks's "deceptively simplistic style, with a basis in early Greek music." Ericson praises the performers for their "whole-hearted devotion." (This review is quoted by Katherine Hoover, "The Festivals of Women's Music I-IV," in **B266**, p. 357, as an example of the "patronizing" and "lukewarm tone of reviewers" of concerts of music composed by women.)

B129   _____. "First Performances." *Musical America* 79, no. 7 (June 1959), p. 20.

Review (signed R. A. E.) finds in *The Glittering Gate* premiere (**W52a**) a "theatrically ineffectual" opera. The story is "a joke of microscopic proportions." The composer has "a gift for setting pleasantly the English language and for contriving pretty sounds for orchestra. At times, her music will even embellish the text with some witty comment, but for the most part the opera is devoid of vitality or interest."

B130 "Etruscan Concerto is Released by MGM." *Wichita Beacon*, Sunday, 26 August 1956, "Sunday" sect., p. 5.

Review quotes D. H. Lawrence's words (from the liner notes) used as inscriptions to the three movements of the *Etruscan Concerto* (**D4**) and finds the music exemplifies Glanville-Hicks's ability to "express life" through dance music. Review is quoted in **B113**.

B131 Evett, Robert. "Miss Glanville-Hicks Goes Simple." *New Republic* 138, no. 8 (24 February 1958), p. 22.

One of nine operas produced in New York in this the first real "season" of American operas, *The Transposed Heads* (**W46b**), though not a world premiere, was a grand affair. In the elegant libretto, patched together by Glanville-Hicks from Mann's book, the plot unfolds quickly and simply. The composer believes (Evett quotes from **G677** and **G689**) that her melody-rhythm principle may revolutionize Western music. The score "is one of the richest outpourings of unencumbered melody in recent years." Singers carry the melody, and dozens of exquisite tunes, once sung, are expertly woven into the fabric of the work. A heavily augmented percussion section gives the music sonority and rhythmic drive. She has not thrown out harmony, though, just thinned it and slowed it down. Hindu materials are the only "false note," giving a startlingly fake-Oriental tone to the score. "Her opera is the only new one I have seen recently that is likely to have any large or long-term significance."

B132 Ewen, David. "Peggy Glanville-Hicks." *American Composers*. New York: G. P. Putnam's Sons, 1982. P. 264-6.

Substantial biography to 1977 includes quotes from the composer on her style and method and a list of "principal works" (with some wrong dates). By the early 1950s she favored "a consonant melodic-rhythmic structure that came close to the musical patterns of the antique or Middle Eastern world" and in which harmony "had been demoted to a minor, even occasional, role." She was operated on for a brain tumor in New York in 1969 [really 1967] and her vision was partly restored, but her career as a composer was over.

B133 _____. "Peggy Glanville-Hicks 1912- ." *Composers Since 1900: A Biographical and Critical Guide*. New York: H. W. Wilson, 1969. P. 233-5.

Substantial essay (about 1500 words) on life, works, and musical style through *Tragic Celebration* (**W66** in 1966) quotes from **G689** ("A Hindu Theme"), **B11** (Antheil, the only work in the bibliography), **B123** (Elwell), **B164** (Gradenwitz), and **B374** (London *Times*), and includes list of "major works" and a small photo. Date of her marriage is given as 7 November 1938; divorce was "eight years later" [actually 1949]. "She now shares her time between New York and a house she owns on the slopes of the acropolis in Athens." (Glanville-Hicks, Bauer, and Gideon are the only women's names out of 220 composers in this volume, according to Block and Neuls-Bates, **B35** above.)

B134 _____. *The New Encyclopedia of the Opera*. New York: Hill and Wang, 1971. P. 245, 270, 697-8.

Information includes a biography, mention of *Sappho* (**W64**) in list of Ford Foundation opera subsidies, and information on *The Transposed Heads* (**W46**).

B135 "Exotic Rhythms in New Opera." *Louisville Times*, 5 April 1954, p. 18.

Review of *The Transposed Heads* premiere (**W46a**) calls it a "lucid fantasy framed in melodious music" with "considerable use of exotic rhythms and authentic Hindu music." (Review is quoted in Antheil, **B11**.)

B136 Falzoni, Giordano. "Butler e Robbins trionfano con i balletti." *Il populo* (Rome), 12 June 1958, p. 4.

Music by Glanville-Hicks for the ballet *The Masque of the Wild Man* (**W55a**), "based on a melodic-rhythmic structure that almost completely omits the harmonic element, deserves special mention." It "furnishes valid cues for a choreography echoing back to the medieval modes in an idiom genuinely based on the principles of modern dance, and contributes more than anything to eliminating the need for scenery and costumes." (Excerpts are reprinted in **B78** in English translation and **B296** in Italian.)

B137 Field, Victoria. "Ancient Greek Modes in Glanville-Hicks' *Nausicaa*." Unpublished Bachelor of Arts (Hons). thesis, Department of Music, Monash University (Melbourne), 1987.

Concise study (less than 40 pages) discusses the ancient Greek "greater perfect system" of Aristoxenus as background to demonstrating a "modal scheme" for the opera's vocal lines and the tetrachord within the opera's modal structure.

B138 "First Performances." Compiled by Donna Jean Hill. *American Composers Alliance Bulletin* 6, no. 4 (1957), p. 23.

Section on Glanville-Hicks quotes from two reviews of the *Concerto Romantico* premiere (**W51a**), by Harrison (**B175**) and Schonberg (**B343**).

B139 Fleming, Shirley. "A Wallflower Blooms." *American Record Guide* 24, no. 2 (October 1957), p. 106.

Concerto Romantico (**D3**) and works by Richter and Weber for viola (the "wallflower") on same disc were commissioned by MGM records for violist Walter Trampler (review includes his photo). *Concerto Romantico*, the most ambitious and most pleasing, demonstrates composer's "skill as an orchestrator (already demonstrated in the *Etruscan Concerto* and elsewhere)." Here she emphasizes low strings (cellos) and woodwinds, to avoid overwhelming the viola. An abundance of melody also "bows to" the viola; melodic roots are in Phrygian and Hypodorian modes, according to the composer, and harmonies suggest conventional tonality. First movement has "almost classical" development process.

B140 Frank, Paul, and Altmann, Wilhelm. *Kurzgefasstes Tonkünstler-Lexikon*. 14th ed. Wilhelmshaven: Heinrichshofen, 1974. Part II, *Ergänzungen und Erweiterungen seit 1937* [1936 is the date of the previous edition], vol. 1, p. 235.

Entry for "Glanville-Hicks, P." consists of a short biography and summary of her works: operas (four titles), ballets, orchestral works, chamber works, and film music.

B141   Frankenstein, Alfred. "Peggy Glanville-Hicks: *Concerto Romantico.*" *High Fidelity* 7, no. 12 (December 1957), p. 70, 74.

It is "fun" to compare the two definitions of the term "romantic" by the two composers represented on MGM 3559. Glanville-Hicks, who dislikes dissonance and distrusts compositional systems, says that her *Concerto Romantico* (**D3**) is romantic in its "personal, expressive usage [urge]" (*see* **G686**), while for the other composer, Ben Weber, dissonance and the 12-tone system are romantic. Her "highly felicitous and attractive" concerto takes as its point of departure the rich, autumnal color of the viola. The slow movement is especially beautiful, the whole score "notable for its melodic and coloristic invention and its skillful marshaling of all its materials." Trampler plays gorgeously, and is well seconded by conductor, orchestra, and recording engineers. (Review is quoted in **B296**.)

B142   Fraser, Jane. "Heart Frank Renouf Has Won." *The Australian* (Sydney), 28 August 1985, p. 8.

Article (indexed under Glanville-Hicks in Australian database ARTSDOC) mentions "the composer Peggy Glanville-Hicks" and soprano Joan Sutherland in the category of women "who have given expression to very rare talents."

B143   Frazier, Jane. *Women Composers: A Discography.* (Detroit Studies in Music Bibliography no. 50.) Detroit: Information Coordinators, 1983, p. 37-38.

Section on Glanville-Hicks lists nineteen recordings of twelve works.

B144   Friedl, Jan. "Lights, Mirrors and Miniatures?" *N. M. A. (New Music Articles)* 4 (1985), p. 24-6.

Essay about 1985 Eureka Ensemble concert, which included *Letters from Morocco* (**W44d**), mentions Glanville-Hicks's lifelong interest in the theatre and her teaching at the Melba Conservatorium 1935-1950 (not true). Friedl also observes that *The Transposed Heads* (**W46**) is a rare instance of a woman's being active in opera in Australia.

B145   "Frustration--David Smith as a drunk." *New York Times,* Sunday, 10 May 1959, sect. 2, p. 9.

Caption accompanies the photograph of the baritone lead in *The Glittering Gate* (**W52a**). (Clippings are in **A3** and **A13c**.)

B146   Fuzek, Rita M. *Piano Music in Collections: An Index.* Detroit: Information Coordinators, 1982. P. 163.

Glanville-Hicks's *Prelude for a Pensive Pupil* (**W56**) is published in Prostakoff's anthology, *New Music for Piano* (1963).

B147   Gallagher, Sheila. "Woman Composer Earns Living At It." *New York World Telegram and Sun,* 18 February 1958, p. 21.

Composer of *The Transposed Heads* (**W46b**) maintains that people in the arts fall into two groups: those who say "if we don't do it someone else will," and those (like her) who say, "if we don't do it no one else will." She believes that musicians must be practical. "I'm a good organizer because I never overlook anything or leave things to chance." She is a prolific composer, probably the only woman composer in this country who makes a living out of it (others, she says, "compose with one hand while they rock the cradle with the other"). Though well informed on modern trends, she uses dissonances only sparingly, reserving them for stress and anxiety factors. (Clippings are in **A3** and **A13c**.)

B148   Garrett, David.   "Neglect of Major Woman Composer to be Remedied."   *Opera Australia* no. 99 (March 1986), p. 8-9.

Preview of Adelaide Festival's *The Glittering Gate* (**W52c**) and *The Transposed Heads* (**W46e**) includes biography of the composer, information on the librettists, comments on the plots, and descriptions of the staging, using quotes from the composer, from James Murdoch (**B263**), and others. Article is followed by a detailed, scene-by-scene synopsis (apparently original, not quoting any other published synopsis) by Allison Jones. There is also a copy of the program, listing performance history, cast, and production personnel of each of the operas, and a photo from each production.

B149   Geddes, Margaret.   "Sculpture and Music a Novel Audio Visual."   *The Age* (Melbourne), 10 June 1978, p. 2.

Glanville-Hicks, interviewed before the Pamela Boden sculpture exhibit "Seven Sculptures for Seven Compositions," describes assigning the composers to the sculptures, choosing *Giraffes* for herself [*Girondelle for Giraffes,* **W67b**). Opera is the most exciting medium, a "war on three fronts"--backstage, on the stage, and in the orchestra pit--according to Vaughan Williams, but wonderful when everything combines to go right. She has worked with distinguished librettists, and hopes her favorite opera, *Nausicaa* (**W62**) can be performed in Australia.

B150   George, Earl.   "P. Glanville-Hicks: Five Songs."   *Music Library Association Notes* 10, no. 3 (June 1953), p. 497.

Five Songs on Housman texts (**W29**) use a great variety of idiomatic and effective piano figurations. Vocal lines are more rhythmic than lyrical. The composer makes the most of the "dramatic implications" of the songs, which appear in carefully planned sequence, the last song, "Homespun Collars," making a particularly successful close.

B151   Gerson, Harry.   "Une inoubliable Nausicaa."   *Le Figaro* (Paris), 22 August 1961, p. 10, col. 1-2.

"An unforgettable *Nausicaa*" (**W62a**), based on a non-Homeric *Odyssey,* astonished the Greek public which is naturally influenced by mythology. Foreigners discussed the plot less; an eminent critic called the opera an example "to be emulated if the interest of the public in the lyric theatre is to find renewal." Generally the opera was well received; the composer and the conductor received most of the applause. Teresa Stratas, who has already won a first prize at the Metropolitan Opera auditions in New York, was a revelation with her warm voice, and was admirably supported by tenor Jean Modenos. Production and costumes by Andreas Nomikos were modern for the period, but the effect succeeded. (Review is quoted in **B269** and **G696** in English; clipping is in **A3g**.)

B152   "Glanville-Hicks Opera Is Scheduled." *New York Herald Tribune,* Sunday, 8 November 1953, sect. 4, p. 7, col. 8.

Announcement of $4,000 Louisville Orchestra commission of *The Transposed Heads* (**W46**) through the Rockefeller Foundation's $4000,000 grant mentions four stage performances, two television performances, and a recording.

B153   Goth, Trudy. "Athens: 'Nausicaa' and 'Medea.' " *Musical America* 81, no. 10 (October 1961), p. 25.

Goth's reviews (**B153-155, B157**) of *Nausicaa* (**W62a**) are accurate about the preparation and they are admiring of the finished product; she also helped Glanville-Hicks persuade other reviewers to attend. *Nausicaa* premiere "evoked an immediate and happy response from the audience" of 3,000. "Traditional Greek themes are still well preserved in some parts of the country, and the consonant, melodic *Nausicaa* score captures something of their noble vigor." This was probably the first time an American composer wrote, cast, rehearsed and launched her own work. The orchestra, not first rate, had insufficient rehearsals and was often too loud, but conductor Surinach acquitted himself well. Kimon Vourloumis, artistic director, overcame "local, national, and political pressure" and also deserves the main credit for the excellent young cast. The visual element, the most completely satisfying element of the production, was designed entirely by Andreas Nomikos, a Greek designer now active in America. (Review is quoted in **B269**. Glanville-Hicks took exception to this review; *see* **G692**.)

B154   _____. "El Festival de Atenas." *Audiomúsica,* October 1961, p. 18-21.

Goth's review of the Athens Festival in a Mexico City magazine praises the *Nausicaa* production (**W62a**) and includes many photos.

B155   _____. "Nei teatri di Atene ed Epidauro rivivono gli antichi miti greci. *Musica d'oggi* 4 (September-October 1961), p. 210-11.

In this review, published in Italy, of *Nausicaa* (**W62a**) in Athens (and of Callas as Cherubini's *Medea* at Epidaurus), Goth reports that the music of *Nausicaa*, consonant and melodic, had an immediate positive response from the audience. She praises Stratas as Nausicaa (she is being called "la piccola Callas"), the male principals, the conductor, the choreographer, and the designer.

B156   _____. "The Odyssey of 'Nausicaa.' " *Pictures from Greece* 57 (October 1960), p. 28.

Pre-production publicity piece includes photos of Robert Graves and Glanville-Hicks and of Graves and Goth. (Copy in **A3g(5)**.)

B157   _____. "Old Heroines in Modern Greece." *Opera News* 26 (28 October 1961), p. 28.

Nausicaa (**W62a**) at the Herod Atticus amphitheater was a brave presentation by the Athens Festival of "what must have seemed a questionable risk"--a contemporary novelty by a relatively unknown foreigner (American composer Glanville-Hicks), with a libretto that questions the authorship of Homer's Odyssey! Courage brought success; local Greek critics, many of them also composers, conceded a near triumph. The score showed the composer's sound knowledge of traditional Greek folklore, recapturing its noble vigor, modal flavor, and uneven rhythms. Teresa Stratas made a great hit, and the rest of the largely Greek-American cast left nothing to be desired. Under Surinach the chorus and orchestra sounded far better than in *Medea* (conducted at Epidauros by Nicola Rescigno). Also deserving praise are John Butler's fluid staging and Andreas Nomikos' elegant sets and costumes.

B158   _____. "Stati Uniti: Balletti e opere nuove." *Musica d'oggi* 1 (July 1958), p. 448.

Favorable review of the New York production of *The Transposed Heads* (W46b), is included in a long paragraph on recent noteworthy musical events in the U.S. in this Italian music periodical. Principals, wedding scene dancer (in the wife's costume), an conductor were good. Goth also reports here that the director of the Venice Festival wants to produce the opera [apparently he did not do it].

B159   Gradenwitz, Peter. "Athens: New Opera and Callas 'Medea.' " *Musical Courier* 163, no. 10 (September 1961), p. 35.

Composer of *Nausicaa* (W62a), one of the two "highlights" of the Athens Festival, has studied the cultures and musics of Asia and the eastern Mediterranean region all her life, and devoted two years of research to ancient Greek lore and music. Libretto is inspired by novel *Homer's Daughter* by Robert Graves, who revived the theory of Samuel ("Erewhon") Butler that Nausicaa, who sheltered Ulysses, is the real author of the *Odyssey*. Opera's score is pervaded by ancient dance meters and heterophonic instrumentation but seems "timeless in style." First act is "longish," other two more dramatic, with some beautiful vocal writing and striking orchestration. Mr. Graves and the composer were present to acknowledge, with the participants, the warm applause of an international audience.

B160   _____. "Festspiele." *Musica* 15 (November 1961), p. 604.

Review (in German) of *Nausikaa* (W62a) presents the same material on the libretto, music, performers, and production, as B159, B161, B163, and B164.

B161   _____. "Greichenland: 'Medea' und 'Nausikaa.' " *Neue Zeitschrift für Musik* 122 (October 1961), p. 418-19.

Review (in German) of *Nausikaa* (W62a) is similar to B159-B160 and B163-B164.

B162   _____. "I. S. C. M. Festival in Amsterdam." *New York Times*, Sunday, 11 July 1948, sect. 2, p. 5, col. 1.

Festival's final chamber concert presented an "entertaining" *Concertino da camera* (W33a) by Glanville-Hicks, an Australian (there was no U. S. A. representation at Amsterdam due to grievances against the central office). The chamber music concerts were more successful than the orchestral concerts. (Review is quoted in B11.)

B163   _____. "An Old Athens Custom." Ibid., Sunday, 10 September 1961, sect. 2, p. 13.

Nausicaa (W62a), the most ambitious venture so far by the newly-revived Athens Festival of Drama and Music, was one of two festive events (the other being Callas in Cherubini's *Medea*). Glanville-Hicks has long been interested in Eastern Mediterranean and Asiatic music traditions, and wrote the opera after two years of study and six months of listening to folk singers and ancient instrumental techniques in various parts of Greece. In *Nausicaa* she attempted to re-create not only the ancient legend and lore but also the form of ancient Greek drama and the spirit of traditional Greek music. The first act seems "static," like Near Eastern music, but in the second and third acts, when the chorus has a dominant role, the music rises to dramatic heights. The opera is "extremely interesting, and in parts very beautiful." Stratas (Nausicaa) was pretty, with a warm and resonant voice, and acting often reminiscent of Callas.

B164   _____. "Eine rasende Medea in Epidauros: Uraufführung der 'Nausicaa.' " *Frankfurter Allgemeine Zeitung,* no. 201 (31 August 1961), p. 14.

Nausicaa (**W62a**) is in a way timeless, treating old, modal materials in a modern "serial" spirit. The opera has "an individuality all its own" and opens "vistas to new modern roads in ancient spirit never trodden on before." (Clipping is in **A3g** and is quoted in English translation in **B269**.)

B165   Gramophone Shop, Inc. *Record Supplement for May 1940 (Record Supplement* v. 3, no. 5), p. 5.

The *Choral Suite* (**D1**), a work that shows the Vaughan Williams influence, "has been well recorded, but the un-named chorus disappoints because of poor enunciation, despite its beautiful tone."

B166   Greene, David Mason. *Greene's Biographical Encyclopedia of Composers.* Garden City, NY: Doubleday, 1985. P. 1243.

Short article quotes Virgil Thomson (**B383**) on Glanville-Hicks, identifies her as a critic and conductor (!), and includes information on her husband and his remarriage after the divorce, her brain tumor operation in 1969, her temporary blindness and inability to compose, and her return to Australia in 1976 [really 1972] to work at the Music Center in Sydney.

B167   Gruender, David E. Program notes for *Etruscan Concerto,* Albany (NY) Symphony Orchestra, 4-5 November 1988.

The attractive *Etruscan Concerto* (**W48d**) begins with "Promenade" in which seven-beat meter "imparts a characteristic ONE-two-three ONE-two ONE-two rhythm" for a light, almost tripping quality, reinforced by the xylophone's "lopsided tune." Melody is pentatonic. The "introverted" second movement, "Meditation," is marked *Lento misterioso e tranquilo* and opens with bassoon and horn over lower strings and timpani; the solo piano seems "subdued and hesitant, almost exploratory." The final Scherzo "is full of good humor and brings the work to a high-spirited conclusion."

B168   Gunn, Glenn Dillard. "Thigpen Delights With Works of New Composers." *Times-Herald* (Washington, D.C.), 12 April 1951, p. 13.

Helen Thigpen is not only one of the great vocal artists but she also performs an unhackneyed repertoire. The first new composer introduced last night was Peggy Glanville-Hicks, whose *Profiles from China* (**W32b**) have originality and "suggest exotic colors, but by relatively simple means." Despite the difficulty for the singer, when the voice moves in different tonalities from the piano, resulting in "dissonance," they are charming songs and were beautifully set forth. (Review is quoted in **B11**.)

B169   Hall, David. *The Record Book: A Guide to the World of the Phonograph.* International edition. New York: O. Durrell, 1948. P. 609.

The *Choral Suite* recording (**D1**) "is generally good." The text is "not understood" but "the music impressed us as quite beautiful in its Anglo-French impressionistic fashion." Glanville-Hicks has been active in the cause of contemporary music both in Paris and at present here in America.

B170   Handly, Donna. "Here They Are--On A Plastic Platter: A Complete Discography of Women Composers." *Ms.* 3, no. 5 (November 1975), p. 111-14.

Handly's discography of 46 composers (follwing an essay by Patricia Ashley) includes, for Glanville-Hicks, only the two CRI recordings in print, *Nausicaa* (**D7**) and *Prelude for a Pensive Pupil* (**D10**).

B171   Hannan, Michael. *Peter Sculthorpe: His Music and Ideas 1929-1980.* St. Lucia: University of Queensland Press, 1982.

Glanville-Hicks is mentioned once as the first Australian composer performed at an International Society for Contemporary Music festival (in London in 1938), but Hannan notes that she was not representing Australia.

B172   Harman, Carter. "Composers' Forum Opens at Columbia." *New York Times,* 25 October 1948, p. 29.

The *Concertino da camera* (**W33b**) "flowed along in a light and highly workable manner reflecting a French-International style" and was the "treat of the evening" (quoted by Antheil, **B11**). *Profiles from China* (**W32a**) and *Thirteen Ways of Looking at a Blackbird* (**W37a**) were given character by their piano parts rather than by contrast of vocal line.

B173   Harris, Samela. "The Grand Lady Comes Home." Adelaide *Advertiser,* 15 March 1986, p. 14.

At 73, Glanville-Hicks "is the grand old matriarch of modern music" and "the most distinguished woman composer in the world" but is "almost unknown" in Australia. Adelaide Festival will present *The Transposed Heads* (**W46e**) and *The Glittering Gate* (**W52c**). Australia's "mixed" population and fantastic composers--so different from the 1930s when she left--delighted her when she returned in 1975. In music (she reiterates for the "zillionth" time) the only criterion is "quality," regardless of the composer's color, sex, or age. We "ladies" have to be "twice as good as the next best man to be recognised" and "will probably be paid half what he gets." But "if we start separating categories, women will automatically get into a bunch and be excluded from the main line." In the 1960s after brain tumor surgery she was told she had five years to live, but "after six years" realised "I was not about to die." Now she plans to "stick around" to the year 2000 and the "apocalypse." She composes operas and songs by declaiming the text to find its melodic line, then "fiddling at the piano" for melody and writing the orchestration at a desk. The music must be cultivated by "sitting in stillness every day." Once inspired, she writes quickly and compulsively. (Clippings are in **A5** and **A7**.)

B174   Harrison, Jay S. "American Music Festival." *New York Herald Tribune,* 21 February 1951, p. 15-16.

Reviewing performance of *Thirteen Ways of Looking at a Blackbird* (**W37b**), Glanville-Hicks's colleague notes that the piano accompaniment is "a punctuation mark given the speech of music"--a question mark or dash or abrupt end. The vocal line casts images "with liquid grace" and "a remarkable plasticity." The music has "a cutting edge which slices to the root of poetic meaning." (Antheil, **B11**, quotes this.)

B175 _____. "New Chamber Music Heard At Metropolitan Museum." Ibid., 20 February 1957, p. 21.

The *Concerto romantico* (**W51a**) is "based largely on flowing melodic episodes whose idiom is both accessible and familiar. Unlike "most viola pieces" it is not "suicidally depressing, and despite the dark colors that form a luminous backdrop for the soloist, the work gives off a healthy, even spunky sonority surface. The melodic material is "not consistently interesting" but the work "treats its solo instrument like a prince." (*ACA Bulletin*, **B138**, quotes this.)

B176 _____. [*Thomsoniana* review.] Ibid., [spring 1950?], n. p.

The *Thomsoniana* (**W38a**) are remarkable evocations of the musicians and composers Virgil Thomson was reviewing. The music is "as rich in sentiment as a hymnal and as direct and full of meaning as a pistol shot." (Review is quoted in **B11** and **B296**.)

B177 Harrison, Margaret. "300 Years of Song Given Beautiful Voice." *The Age* (Melbourne), 24 September 1987, p. 15.

Thirteen Ways of Looking at a Blackbird (**W37e**) consisted of "thirteen miniatures," exquisitely written for voice. "The clear lines and economy of material make this a little masterpiece."

B178 Harrison, Michael. "Off With the Head of this Sacred Cow." *The Australian*, 24 March 1986, p. 12.

Australian compositions, like the sacred cow, are usually praised. In *The Transposed Heads* (**W46e**) and *Glittering Gate* (**W52c**) at the Adelaide Festival, musical weaknesses outnumber the positive things. *Glittering Gate* is a little more adventurous than *The Transposed Heads*, which has recurring raga-based music but yet sounds like Coleridge-Taylor and Delius. Libretto is no help and production was static, unimaginative, sometimes ludicrous. Three principal singers were very good, but chorus sounded tired. Orchestra played well; conductor achieved good balance, even with the twelve percussion players.

B179 Hayes, Deborah. "Glanville-Hicks's *Nausicaa*, Graves, and Reid." *Focus on Robert Graves and His Contemporaries* 1, no. 9 (May 1989), p. 11-14.

Article based on unpublished correspondence in Melbourne library (**A3**) confirms Cohn's hypothesis (**B68**) and suggests that Alastair Reid was the principal librettist.

B180 Henehan, Donal. "Let's Hear It for Composer Persons." *New York Times*, Sunday, 31 August 1975, sect. 2, p. D11.

News of a forthcoming concert of music by women and of Nancy Van de Vate's organization of an International League of Women Composers prompts the author to try to think of some women and the music women have composed, which includes Glanville-Hicks and *The Transposed Heads* (**W46**), a major commission (Van de Vate is quoted) and available on record [**D21**], Henehan remembers). He also names Clara Schumann, Fanny Mendelssohn Hensel, Augusta Holmès, Ruth Crawford Seeger, Elizabeth Lutyens, Thea Musgrave, Ethel Smyth, and Amy Beach.

B181 _____. "Music: St. Paul Players." Ibid., 18 March 1980, p. C9.

Keith Jarrett, a "popular jazz musician" performing the *Etruscan Concerto* (**W48b**) at Lincoln Center with the St. Paul Chamber Orchestra, is a solid musician and facile pianist. His fingers are "equal to anything" and his "brittle tone" suited the "distinctly percussive" music. The concerto, which "had a way of reminding one of Copland" rather than Etruscan activity, was "the evening's most entertaining work."

B182 Herz, Gerhard. "Current Chronicle. United States. Louisville, Kentucky." *Musical Quarterly* 41 (January 1955), p. 79.

List of works commissioned by Louisville Orchestra includes *The Transposed Heads* (**W46**) under "Operas 1954."

B183 Hetherington, Margaret. "Peggy Glanville-Hicks--'I'm not in the least interested in yesterday.' " *24 Hours* 12, no. 11 (December 1987), p. 6-7.

Article in the program guide of the Australian Broadcasting Corp. previewing a special 90-minute program in tribute to Glanville-Hicks on Monday, 28 December, repeats biographical information published in 1970 by Covell (**B84** above) and Keavney (**B186**)--even the story about Cowell designating her no "mere" woman composer. Hetherington adds the (rather peculiar) observation that, "The fact that she happens to be a woman has never carried any weight with her, nor, it seems, with her colleagues." Glanville-Hicks, now approaching her 75th birthday, is still preoccupied with the future. Photo of Durrell and Glanville-Hicks from the 1960s (from **B78**) accompanies the article. (Clipping is in **A6c**.)

B184 Hickson, Liz. "Peggy Glanville-Hicks: Operas are Her Children." *Woman's Day* (Australia), 8 September 1986, p. 8-9.

Glanville-Hicks, "Australia's foremost composer" and "the only woman composer of note that the 20th century has produced," gambled on success as a 19-year old, arriving penniless and "still wearing her school uniform" at the Royal College of Music, earning a scholarship for her efforts. Today, interviewed over "elevenses"-- prawn chips and a glass of brandy and soda--she talks of her London days, tells stories of Vaughan Williams, Sir Thomas Beecham, her marriage ("there were no children") to English composer Stanley Bate ("brilliant" but "helpless" in practical matters), his illness and death [actually they divorced before he died], her opera *Nausicaa* (**W62**), her writing of *The Transposed Heads* (**W46**) in Jamaica (as recounted in Keavney, **B205**), her brain tumor and plastic skull, and her current work on an opera and a book. Being a wife and mother is difficult for a composer, because from late teenage years until around 30 you acquire technique, and "from 30 to 50 you're writing your major works." Article is accompanied by a large photo of the composer at her piano (it "dropped three floors when her London home was blitzed during the war"); on the music rack are copies of her *Concertino da Camera* (**W33**) and *Etruscan Concerto* (**W48**) and Sculthorpe's *Mangrove*. (Clipping is in **A2a**.)

B185 Hill, Donna Jean. "American Songs: An Introduction." *American Composers Alliance Bulletin* 7, no. 3 (1958), p. 11.

Thomsoniana (**W38**), "a delight" and deftly scored, and *Letters from Morocco* (**W44**), both published by Composers Facsimile Editions, use instruments other than piano for accompanying the voice.

B186 Hill, Richard S.   Review of *Grove's Dictionary of Music and Musicians*, 5th edn., 1954.   *Music Library Association Notes* 12 (1954/55), p. 90-92.

For the updating of American material in *Grove's Dictionary*, 5th ed., editor Eric Blom "chose a friend as his chief representative in this country." A composer and writer for the *New York Herald Tribune*, Glanville-Hicks "chose to do the composers herself, and the job she turned in strikes me as being both objective and thorough. In addition to revising a number of the earlier articles, she wrote many new ones." (*See* **G487-G584**.)

B187 Hixon, Don L., and Hennessee, Don.   *Women in Music: A Bibliography.* Metuchen, NJ: Scarecrow Press, 1975. P. 113.

For information on Glanville-Hicks the reader is referred to titles listed here as **B22**, **B36**, **B37**, **B125**, **B134**, **B245**, **B263**, **B294**, **B319**, **B336**, **B339**, **B341**, **B348**, **B375**, and **B394**.

B188 Holde, Artur.   "Peggy Glanville-Hicks: 'The Glittering Gate.' " *Aufbau* (New York City), 22 May 1959, p. 13.

Music critic of a German-language weekly newspaper in New York describes the action of the opera (**W52a**): two safecrackers use the tools of their trade to break down the door of Heaven and find only the blue, star-studded firmament. Dialogue in recitative is lightly punctuated with characteristic instrumental music, but she is unable to conjure up in the score the nonexistent humor of the text. (Copy is in **A3f**.)

B189 _____.   "The Transposed Heads, Oper von Peggy Glanville-Hicks im Phoenix Theatre." Ibid., 14 February 1958, p. 14.

The opera (**W46b**), commissioned by the Ford [actually Rockefeller] Foundation for the Louisville Orchestra, was presented here by the Contemporary Music Society under the leadership of Chandler Cowles and with the help of numerous promoters. The question is whether the work, by a composer who is gifted but ignorant of the stage, was born under a favorable star. Numerous interesting melodies, many from Indian folk music, are heard, with rhythm and percussion, a Western orchestra, and homophonic instrumentation. The composer's talent is evident in the dance scene and ensembles toward the end, but even they are too thinly set. Conductor, singers, and dancer were excellent, and the applause brought composer and performers back to the stage several times. (Copy is in **A3d**.)

B190 Howard, John Tasker.   *Our American Music, Three Hundred Years of It.* 4th rev. ed.; New York: T. Crowell, 1965. Pp. 395, 433, 516, 768.

Material on Glanville-Hicks includes a paragraph on her life and works to 1957 (p. 566). Howard also quotes her remarks on three composers: Bloch (from **G632**), Thomson (from **G110**), and Swanson ("a real creative gift, a lyric, dramatic sense that evokes its own spontaneous form."). Howard ends his book (p. 768) with her words: "American [composition] is still at the beginning of the great curve of history; and as in earlier epochs of all things the fate is in the hands of the many rather than of the few. [In such an entreprise] much that is presented must of necessity fall back into obscurity and oblivion. But it is from just this humus that later the 'big trees' come."

B191   _____, and Lyons, James. *Modern Music: A Popular Guide to Greater Musical Enjoyment*. Rev. ed.; New York: Thomas Y. Crowell, 1957. P. 124.

Glanville-Hicks is one of five composers "frequently encountered in concert halls and on recordings" who "have made exotic music their own." (The others are Hovhaness, Bowles, McPhee, and Harrison.)

B192   Huck, Bill. "Philharmonic Reclaims Women's Musical Heritage." *The Sentinel* (San Francisco), 23 November 1982, p. 8.

In program notes for *Three Gymnopédies* (W48b) Glanville-Hicks "spoke eloquently" of Greek athletes. "The music is spacious, its harmonies full of air and light, its waves of sound possess the grace she sought."

B193   Hughes, Allen. "5 Composers Tell of Works at Concert." *New York Herald Tribune*, 3 February 1958, p. 12.

In *Concertino Antico* (W49b) Glanville-Hicks "is currently foregoing conventional dissonant idioms to weave bland modal counterpoints of frankly singable melodic motives" with no "distracting overlay of harmonic complexity." The slow movement has "considerable beauty" and "a mood of extraordinary tension" that the fast movements fail to develop. (Review is signed A. H.)

B194   "In the International Festival. Recognition for Peggy Glanville Hicks." *The Australian Musical News* 27 (1 February 1938), p. 28.

Glanville-Hicks has cabelled from London to her parents in Melbourne that she will have a work performed at the festival of the International Society of Contemporary Music (ISCM) [the *Choral Suite*, W19a] and may visit them at the end of February. In 1937 she studied in Vienna, Milan, Florence, and Paris (completing the scholarship year studying with Nadia Boulanger) on a travelling scholarship. Only a "small sprinkling of Australian musicians" will know the importance of the ISCM and appreciate the performance's bearing on her future career. Her more recent works, besides the *Choral Suite* (five movements for women's voices, oboe, and strings), are: a Prelude and Scherzo for large orchestra (W21), concerto for flute and small orchestra (W20), string quartet no. 1 (W22), Pastorale for women's chorus and *cor anglais* (W3), and suite for string orchestra with oboe (W13a?).

B195   "Internationaal Muziekfeest." *Algemeen Handelsblad* (Amsterdam), 11 June 1948, p. 2.

The *Concertino da camera* (W33a) "is a very pleasant little work" within traditional style, and listeners found it "enjoyable, completely unmodern." The audience "applauded so long that the composer had to come forward to be thanked."

B196   Jablonski, Edward. "Peggy Glanville-Hicks." *The Encyclopedia of American Music*. Garden City, NY: Doubleday, 1981. Pp. 375, 591.

Article (p. 375) notes that she is hardly "American" in spite of her twenty-year stay, 1939-1959, because her musical personality was formed by 1939. Five works are named, and 1948 (probably too early) is given as the beginning year of her work with Composers Forum. List of Varèse Sarabande records (p. 591) includes *Three Gymnopédies* (D20).

B197   Jennings, Donald.   "The Newest 'New Festival.' "   *American Composers Alliance Bulletin* 9, no. 2 (1960), p. 16.

Continuing Oliver Daniels's listing of ACA members' recordings (*see* **B108**), Jennings lists *Letters from Morocco* (**D6**) and quotes from Miller's review (**B250**).

B198   Johnson, Harriett.   "Words and Music. 'The Transposed Heads' at Phoenix."   *New York Post*, 11 February 1958.

While quoting accurately from Glanville-Hicks's program notes (for **W46b**), indicating an understanding of the opera, the review is not wholly favorable. Johnson likes the wedding scene best and praises the conductor, orchestra, and authentic "East Indian sets and costumes" but comments that the composer "has not been able to fuse her [Indian] materials into a consistently persuasive amalgam." (Copies are in **A3d** and **A13c**.)

B199   Johnson, Mary Kay.   "The Transposed Heads."   *The Villager* (Greenwich Village, New York City), 13 February 1958, p. 11.

Opera (**W46b**) is compared to the composer's explanations ("I have gradually shed the harmonic dictatorship peculiar to modernists"--Johnson quotes extensively from **G689**). The music itself seems tame, not even startling. The "unusually allegorical" story can also be appreciated as narrative. Visually, the production is exciting. Review is illustrated by a photo of Maria Ferriero as Sita. (Copies are in **A3d** and **A13c**.)

B200   Johnson, Sue.   "Peggy Glanville-Hicks: A Composer of Note."   *Sydney Morning Herald*, Saturday, 19 July 1986, "Good Weekend," p. 46-8, 51.

Feature article based on recent interview reviews: her training, marriage, career as critic and composer in New York, her search for new musical resources, the brain tumour operation and the "famous plastic skull," and her recent activities in Australia-- a country much changed since she left in the 1930s. Quotes are included from a *State of the Arts* program on ABC (Australian Broadcasting Corp. network) earlier in the year. Peter Sculthorpe described her as a "mother figure" to Australian music--the only composer besides Grainger whom "we can look up to, respect and admire." She says she was part of the "unpaying aspect" of music, the "avant-garde spearhead. They don't know where they're going, they're going by intuition and they will turn up the furrows that will produce the crops of tomorrow." With those views, she says, it never occurred to her that she could find a comfortable niche in Australia, "but when you get old and retire observation becomes the activity rather than creation." Article includes a recent photo of Glanville-Hicks at home in Sydney, including most of her front room, including the well-used portable typewriter that played such a large part in her work. (Copies are in **A2a, A6c**.)

B201   Kahn, E.   "Superior Beethoven by Toscanini."   *Navy Times* 5, no. 42 (4 August 1956), p. 25.

MGM recording of the *Sinfonia Pacifica* (**D11**) brings "interesting and pleasant" music that is "among the best of the new." While the composer is known for her highly individual, experimental music, the deliberate subordination of harmony is not startling here, and there is ample melody and rhythm. (Paragraph at end of classical records column is quoted in full in **B113**.)

B202   Kastendieck, Miles.   "Bizarre Opera Curiously Naive."   *New York Journal-American*, 11 February 1958, p. 24.

The Transposed Heads (**W46b**) shows a "versatile composer who needs only a more substantial libretto." First two scenes are "hopelessly static," wedding scene is better; only the temple scene is dramatic. (Review is quoted in **B296**.)

B203   Kay, Ernest. "Peggy Glanville-Hicks." *The World's Who's Who of Women.* 2nd edn. Cambridge (England): Melrose Press, 1975. P. 438.

Article accompanied by small photo lists teachers, titles of major compositions, locations of principal critical writings, appointments, and honors.

B204   Keats, Shiela. "American Music on LP Records." *Juilliard Review* 2 (1955), p. 32-3.

Discography for Glanville-Hicks lists three recordings: *Sonata for Harp* (**D13**), *Three Gymnopédies* (**D18**), and *The Transposed Heads* (**D21**).

B205   Keavney, Kay. "The Path of a Composer." *The Australian Women's Weekly,* 29 July 1970, p. 7, 12.

Feature article based on interview during Glanville-Hicks's visit to Sydney for the University of New South Wales production of *The Transposed Heads* (**W46c**) includes a recent photo of her, photos of two of her Greek homes (Mykonos and Athens), and information on her London years, her "beautiful" and "brilliant" husband, their coming to Boston in 1940 and "accidental" settling in New York, her composing of *The Transposed Heads* in Jamaica in 1953 (Professor Theo Flynn, father of Errol, "propped me up"), her later composing outside New York (Germany, Greece), and the operas *Nausicaa* (**W62**) and *Sappho* (**W64**). Cowell on American TV once uttered the "supreme male accolade" that she was not a mere "lady composer."

B206   Knight, Roger. "Bloody Opera." *The Adelaide Review* 25 (April 1986), p. 23.

Operas at Adelaide Festival make it the "goriest Festival ever"--the ritual beheading in *Transposed Heads* (**W46d**) contributes. Double bill with *Glittering Gate* (**W52c**), done on a shoestring budget, was disappointing. *Transposed Heads* was not well directed; in spite of singers and orchestra, and the producer's informative notes with their "exalted references" to the opera's theme, it was comedy from the severing of the heads onwards--even the final conflagration. "For my money, the most touching moment of the whole evening came at its close, when the elderly and obviously frail Ms. Glanville-Hicks made her way across stage to thank the cast and receive the warm applause of the first night audience."

B207   Kupferberg, Herbert. "Records: Music for the Fourth. Columbia and Louisville Feature Americans." *New York Herald Tribune Book Review,* 3 July 1955, p. 11.

Columbia's recordings--of Glanville-Hicks's *Concertino da camera* and *Sonata for Piano and Percussion* (**D2/D17**) and nine other works by other composers, show "great adeptness, even adroitness" and also the "tension and strain" of the times. *The Transposed Heads* (**D21**), likewise tense and taut, is "the most interesting" of the Louisville series with a direct quality from the percussion instruments and "a rather derivative, if highly pleasant Orientalism."

B208   _____. "Some Lyrical Americans." *Sunday New York Herald Tribune Magazine,* 12 April 1964, p. 37.

Sound of *Nausicaa* recording (**D7**) "is often quite poor." Music shows "use of Greek idioms and folk traditions." Wide leaps in vocal lines are sometimes effective, sometimes "merely contrived. *Nausicaa* builds up to some powerful musical climaxes, but fails to maintain a consistent level of quality."

B209   Kuppenheim, Hans F. "Louisville." *Musical Courier* 149, no. 8 (15 April 1954), p. 31.

Music for *The Transposed Heads* (**W46a**) is "substantial, conservative, appealing, and easy to follow. The melodic element is predominant." Some tunes and many of the intricate rhythms are from Hindu sources, according to the comoser. The principal roles were expressively sung and acted. Moritz Bomhard's careful preparation, imaginative stage setting, and vital direction were responsible for the work's favorable reception.

B210   Kyle, Margaret Kelly. "Peggy Glanville-Hicks." *Pan Pipes* 51, no. 2 (January 1959), p. 64.

Magazine of Sigma Alpha Iota, American women's music organization, reports that Glanville-Hicks spent six months in Greece in 1958 working on *Nausicaa* (**W62**) and hopes to complete it in 1959, that *Masque of the Wild Man* (**W55**) was commissioned by John Butler for the Spoleto Festival, and that she will work for the Composers Forum through the winter.

B211   Laderman, Ezra. "Music in Our Time." *Musical America* 78, no. 4 (March 1958), pp. 26-7.

Glanville-Hicks in *Concertino Antico* (**W49b**) tries to do away with harmony and hark back to modal linear lines, but the work is completely tonal and triadic with "hints (à la Lou Harrison) of exotic lands" as her musical upbringing brings her back to France. Middle movement has "haunting beauty and fragile texture," outside movements are "banal."

B212   Lang, Paul Henry. "Opera. 'The Transposed Heads.' " *New York Herald Tribune*, 11 February 1958, p. 20, col. 5-6.

Though he likes the "visual splendor" of the authentic Indian costumes of this production (**W46b**), Lang believes Mann's libretto and Hindu musical elements were handicaps for this "able composer, with a good sense for the theater." Review is illustrated with a photo of Glanville-Hicks. (Copies are in **A3** and **A12c**.) In her subsequent composer brochures (**B78**, **B296**) she quoted only one sentence from this review: "Frankly, I do not know how to judge this opera." Letters in **A3** indicate that Lang--a historian and scholar and the paper's chief critic--left at intermission, and she thought his review to be unfair and stubbornly uninformed.

B213   Lanigan-O'Keeffe, John. "Australia: Adelaide." *Opera Canada* 27, no. 3 (1986), p. 35-36.

In international section of performance "roundup," review of Adelaide Festival notes that the State Opera of South Australia took risks on unknown works by producing *The Glittering Gate* (**W52c**) and *The Transposed Heads* (**W46e**), both by Glanville-Hicks who (according to a national telecast commentator) is Australia's most forgotten composer. The first "has a melodic score and moral point in its favor. The second, intended as a *dramma giocoso* by the composer, requires performers to · walk "the tightrope between hilarity and sincerity" and is thus difficult to produce. Director achieved much toward making both operas meaningful; principals were good; conductor was in his element for the opera shows off the orchestra--the brass shone in the Wedding Scene. "The most moving moment came during the curtain calls when the frail and diminutive composer received affectionate cheers."

B214   Laudenzi, Aulo. "Quattro balletti da camera al festival dei due mondi." *La nazione italiana*, 11 June 1958, p. 8.

La maschera dell'uomo selvaggio (**W55a**) and *Triade* (**W59a**) were part of an evening of "Four Chamber Ballets" by John Butler, a choreographer of "narrative" tendencies, at the Spoleto Festival of Two Worlds. In *Triad* three strangers each dream of their ideal woman, one adolescent, one a first love, the third a desirable woman (Carmen de Lavallade in all three roles). The variety of musical themes (by Glanville-Hicks, Prokofieff, Tailleferre, and Ellington), harmonious movements, and the play of lights all contribute to a powerful psychological atmosphere. *Mask* is the romantic myth of the "wild man" whom a brutal court mocks, not knowing the beauty of the primitive freedom in which he lives. Music and choreography contrast his freedom of expression and lack of reticence and false modesty, with the spiritual prison of the court. Intensity was weakened by a certain baroque overabundance in the costumes and choreography, and the narrow stage of the Caio Melisso somewhat hampered the extremely virtuosic dancers. A small orchestra was conducted impeccably by Robert Feist, and the entire production was warmly applauded. (Copy is in **A3d**.)

B215   Lawson, Nell. "Disc Data." *Buffalo Evening News*, 8 October 1956, no. p. 27.

Glanville-Hicks is a top-ranking composer in an art in which few women are great composers. The *Three Gymnopédies*, based on ancient Greek dance, are slow, controlled, strong and muscular, and melodic. Also on MGM 3336, the *Sinfonia Pacifica* (**D11**) "opens with a bravura rush of excitement. Rhythm and lilting melody are skillfully woven together. This young woman writes 'modern' music at its best." (Review is quoted in **B113** and **B296**.)

B216   LeGallienne, Dorian. "Greek Drama and Music in the Open Air." *The Age* (Melbourne), 9 September 1961, p. 2.

Review by an Australian composer reports that *Nausicaa* (**W62a**), which "drew packed houses" three nights, has a score of skill, taste, and lyrical beauty that relies mainly on rhythm, melody, and orchestral color but did not make him "care about the characters." Photo of the Herod Atticus (outdoor) theatre and comments on the architecure and weather of Athens ("remarkably rainless") are included. "Four cheers for any composer even remotely connected with Australia, who can get an opera successfully staged anywhere!"

B217   LePage, Jane Weiner. "Peggy Glanville-Hicks." In *Women Composers, Conductors, and Musicians of the Twentieth Century: Selected Biographies*. Vol. 2. Metuchen, NJ: Scarecrow Press, 1983. P. 142-62.

With the Louisville commission for *The Transposed Heads* (**W46**) Glanville-Hicks "was the first woman, and until recently the only woman, to have ever received a major commission from a major opera company in America." To explain this and the composer's other "trend-setting accomplishments," Le Page quotes extensively (though not entirely accurately) from writings by Glanville-Hicks (in **B72, G675, G684, G687, G689, G690, G693**) and from reviews of her music (in **B11, B123, B131, B136, B164, B228, B357, B337**). Le Page also acknowledges from the outset that Glanville-Hicks utterly disapproves of books like this "that separate the ladies from the gentlemen!" (quoting from a letter to her from Glanville-Hicks dated 25 February 1978).

B218   Lerman, Leo. "Festival of Two Worlds: Spoleto." *Mademoiselle* 47, no. 2 (June 1958), p. 116.

Glanville-Hicks is one of the composers to be represented in the John Butler Evening of Chamber Ballet. Beginning of article (p. 78-9) includes photos of Butler, artistic head of all festival dance, and designer Ter-Arutanian. *See* **W55a** and **W59a**).

B219   Lewis, Lucy. "Peggy Glanville-Hicks. Sonata for Harp." *Music Library Association Notes* 10, no. 3 (June 1953), p. 487.

New sonata (**W42**) is well worth consideration by serious harpists. Sensitive awareness of the harp idiom is evident, and careful editing and fingering [by Zabaleta]. The work is primarily melodic, given to musical ideas rather than tonal effects, and it is mildly dissonant; the chromaticism is conservative but not unnaturally restrained by fear of exceeding the harp's capabilities.

B220   "A List of American Operas." *American Composers Alliance Bulletin* 7, no. 4 (1958), p. 19.

List of operas by ACA members includes *The Transposed Heads* (**W46**) and *The Glittering Gate* (**W52**).

B221   Livingstone, Janet. "BAWP Offers Musical Gem." *Berkeley* (CA) *Gazette*, 15 November 1982, p. 9.

Reviewer only mentions hearing Glanville-Hicks's *Three Gymnopédies* (**W47b**) at the concert of the Bay Area Women's Philharmonic.

B222   Lofthouse, Andrea, comp. "Peggy Glanville-Hicks." *Who's Who of Australian Women.* Based on research by Vivienne Smith. North Ryde, NSW: Methuen Australia, 1982. P. 201.

Article on Glanville-Hicks gives the names of her parents and her schools, beginning with the Clyde School [then] in Woodend, VIC. Works include four operas and five ballets (names and dates are supplied), chamber works, and film music (not named). Also listed are: publications, recordings, other professional activities (criticism and other writing), fellowships and prizes (through the Queen's Silver Jubilee Medal in 1977), and her Sydney address.

B223   Long, Martin. "A Birthday Well Worth Celebrating." *The Australian,* 6 July 1987, p. 15.

Performed by the Seymour Group at their tenth-anniversary concert, the *Concertino da camera* (**W33e**) was "a cheerful neoclassical entertainment" by a patron of the Seymour Group.

B224   Lopez, Claudio. [*Sonata for Harp* review.] *El Nacional* (Caracas), 26 February 1951.

World premiere of a Sonata for Harp (**W42a**) by English composer P. Glanville-Hicks was performed in recital by Nicanor Zabaleta for whom it was written and to whom it is dedicated. Its three movements are in neo-classic style, with predominant clarity of conception and of ideas. The *Saeta* is faintly Spanish; the Pastoral develops a poetic, lyrical, song-like melodic line over an ostinato bass; and the very classical Rondo is treated is visibly virtuosic. The literature for harp, very generous in modern works, is proudly enriched with this work. (Review is quoted in Spanish in **B11** Antheil.)

B225   Ludewig-Verdehr, Elsa, and Raines, Jean. "Music for Clarinet by Women Composers." *The Clarinet* 8 (1981), no. 2 (Winter), p. 17, and no. 3 (Spring), p. 27.

The *Concertino da camera* (**W33**) is listed as a "mixed quartet" and *A Scary Time* (**W57**) as a "clarinet and percussion trio." Instrumentation and publishers are given.

B226   Lyons, James. "Americana from Columbia." *American Record Guide* 21, no. 12 (August 1955), p. 383-4.

Review of *Concertino da Camera* and *Sonata for Piano and Percussion* (**D11/D17**) calls Australian-born Glanville-Hicks, sometime critic for the *Herald Tribune*, "one of our most gifted young composers." The 1952 *Sonata* is "gamelanish in the McPhee manner" with "audacious" percussion writing and thematic reference to the Watuzzi Africans. The 1945 *Concertino*, more intimate, also "saucy," is more typical of her style if not her syntax, which blends "vestigial atonalism and academic neo-classicism." Picture a Viennese arguing with a Parisienne, the latter winning on wit but neither having much to say."

B227   _____. "Contemporary Music Written for Harp." Liner notes for Glanville-Hicks, *Sonata for Harp.* Counterpoint/Esoteric 523. 1954.

The *Sonata for Harp* (**D13**) was written in 1953 [actually 1950-51] as "a bow to the Spanish manner," says Glanville-Hicks. The sonata reflects the Berber culture of North Africa, which became indigenous to the Spanish manner, in the rhythm of the first movement and thematically in the third movement. As she regards the tonal security of the harp as rather fragile, she uses tonic feeling, rather than a contemporary idiom, as anchorage. His review in the *American Record Guide* 21, no. 1 (September 1954), p. 21, calls it "utterly ravishing."

B228   _____. "Glanville-Hicks: *The Transposed Heads*." *American Record Guide* 21, no. 12 (August 1955), p. 408-9.

In this opera (**D21**) "Miss Glanville-Hicks has composed, in my judgment, an entirely stageworthy work of compelling and sustained loveliness," especially in the "simply beautiful" vocal writing which is "handled with aplomb by the young singers." The composer uses *Leitmotif* technique, with a repeated main theme and an almost as frequently heard "gamelanish" theme. The New York critic [Briggs, **B43**] with a known aversion to her music who has said, on the basis of this recording, that the opera "does not come to life" may eat his words when it is produced in New York this fall. (It was not performed until 1958.)

B229   _____. "United States." *World Theatre* 7, no. 2 (Summer 1958), p. 160.

In this often-quoted review of the New York production of *The Transposed Heads* (**W46b**), published in English and French in the magazine of the UNESCO-assisted International Theatre Institute, Lyons judges the opera "devoid of all the 'magnificent' encumbrances that attach to grand opera" but still a "masterpiece" in its "directness, simplicity, eschewal of harmonic cliché." He finds, however, that this production, by a "director schooled in the Broadway tradition," cheapens the message, making a burlesque out of an "allegory of universal meaning."

B230   M. G. "Peggy Glanville-Hicks: Eine ungewohnliche Komponisten." *Sie und Er*, 1 May 1958, p. 18.

Article published in Swiss periodical after the New York premiere of *The Transposed Heads* finds Glanville-Hicks to be "an uncommon woman composer." (Copy is in A3d.)

B231   McCallum, Peter. "Composer in a Rage." *Sydney Morning Herald*, 7 July 1987, p. 18.

The *Concertino da camera* (W33e) has "a liveliness and originality not always present among the Class of 1948" [date of premiere performance]. The work, which the composer calls her swansong to the Paris neo-classic school room, is in a style not often heard at Seymour Group concerts. (Another composer, Brenton Broadstock, set poems of "rage.")

B232   McCredie, Andrew D. *Catalogue of Forty-Six Australian Composers*. Canberra, ACT: Australian Government Printing Office, 1969. P. 7

Under "Glanville-Hicks" is a short biography (six lines) and partial list of works.

B233   _____. *Musical Composition in Australia*. Canberra, ACT: Australian Government Printing Office, 1969. P. 14.

Peggy Glanville-Hicks, recognized for her contributions to music-theater, studied in London, Paris, and Vienna, then settled for extended periods in America and Greece. Her "cosmopolitan background doubtless accounts for an expert, highly eclectic language, but it has also kindled her own resources, especially in the handling of rhythms and timbres" as in *Sinfonia da Pacifica* and *Three Gymnopédies* (both 1953). Literary sophistication prompted the operas *The Transposed Heads* and *Nausicaa*.

B234   McCulloch, Allan. "Composers Lend a Hand." *The Herald* (Melbourne), 15 June 1978, p. 36.

Australian composer Peggy Gr[l]anville-Hicks has composed a musical accompaniment (W67b) for one of the seven Pamela Boden sculptures, *Giraffes*, and has inspired five other Australian composers and one American to compose music for the other six. As the recorded music is played a spotlight falls on each sculpture, so that compositions and sculptures are components of "a single piece of composite architecture.

B235   McDonnell, Justin. "Queues Languish. Why?" Adelaide *Advertiser*, 11 March 1972.

The Glittering Gate (W52b) by an "Australian composer . . . at last beginning to receive serious attention in this country," will be presented at the Adelaide Festival. These lunch-hour programmes draw audiences (and queues) that other concerts do not.

B236   MacKinnon, Debra. "Music's Grand Lady Lashes Out." *[Australian Publication, Unidentified]*, Magazine, no. 2 (26 May-2 June 1983), p. 10.

Glanville-Hicks's "career has been in the U. S." and her scores are "performed regularly and extensively" in other parts of the world but not in Australia "in the nine years I've been home" [this is inaccurate]. Australia needs new opera productions and more contemporary music programming. The public would "adore" certain twentieth-century masterpieces--symphonies of Respighi and Vaughan Williams. (Copy is in **A6d**.)

B237   Mackinnon, Douglas A. "East and West." *Opera News* 22 (3 March 1958), p. 26.

Chamber opera *The Transposed Heads* (**W46b**), premiered in New York in February, "uses many of the melodies this composer has collected in various visits to India; she has relegated harmony to a minor role. Nanda and Shridaman were "personable," Sita has a fine voice, and Surinach, conductor from Barcelona, achieved wonders under unfavorable conditions. Review describes the plot and scenery and is illustrated by a photo of Maria Ferriero (Sita). Copy is in **A3d**.

B238   Magee, Bryan. "The Halle at the Athens Festival." *The Guardian* (Manchester, England), 29 August 1961, p. 5.

Nausicaa (**W62a**) plot is "conventional" but is redeemed by the "immediately appealing" musical idiom, the splendid staging, costumes, conductor, and Stratas in the title role, and it "deserves to be heard elsewhere." Athens Festival was a "very British affair"--the Halle Orchestra and the highly-publicized opera of an Australian-born composer. Review is quoted in **B269** and **G696**; a copy is in **A3g**.

B239   "Making Music on a Koto." *Daily Telegraph* (Sydney), 3 July 1970, p. 16.

Interviewed during the run of *The Transposed Heads* at the University of New South Wales (**W46c**), Glanville-Hicks explains that the music for this "whimsical legend of India" is "subtle rather than complicated, requiring virtuoso percussion." She composes not at the piano but on a Japanese koto, "a gift from Burton Fahz, former head of the Rockefeller Foundation." The opera's "total unity" makes it one of her favorites. She last visited Australia "30 years ago" [actually 1953]. She has come this time (via London) to see her opera, visit her relatives in Melbourne, and consult with three or four Australian composers whom she regards as "musical space travellers." (A copy is in **A7**.)

B240   Mann, Thomas. *Die Briefe Thomas Manns: Registen und Register.* Ed. Hans Bürgin and Hans-Otto Mayer. 5 vols. Frankfurt a. M.: S. Fischer, 1977-1987.

Three letters to Glanville-Hicks in 1948 and 1950 granting permission to use *The Transposed Heads* for an opera (**W46**) are summarized in vol. 3 (1982), and two other letters about the opera are summarized in vol. 4.

B241   Martin, John. "Dance: Spoleto." *New York Times*, Sunday, 1 June 1958, sect. 2, p. 11.

Pre-performance publicity mentions commissioned score for *Masque of the Wild Man* (**W55**) and plans [not realized] to re-title the ballet).

B242   Matilla, Alfredo. [*Sonata for Harp* Review.] *El Mundo* (San Juan, Puerto Rico), 21 March 1952.

The interesting novelty on the program was the Puerto Rico premiere of the Sonata (dedicated to Zabalaeta) by the North American composer Glanville-Hicks. It is an enchanting work, undoubtedly very modern but without aggressive boldness. The composer possesses a very personal grace; the sonata exemplifies a classical atmosphere. (Review is quoted in Spanish in **B11**.)

B243   "Melbourne Con. of Music (Albert St.)." *The Australian Musical News* 42, no. 7 (1 January 1952), p. 9.

Glanville-Hicks has sent home news of her new compositions (**W42, W43**) and her activities as music critic.

B244   "Melbourne Music Criticized. . . . Melba Conservatorium." Ibid., 20 (1 July 1931), p. 10.

Student performance of *Ireland* (**W1a**) on a "long program" showed "good writing."

B245   Michel, François. *Encyclopédie de la musique*. Vol. 2. Paris: Fasquelle, 1959. P. 271-2.

Short article dates her move to the U.S. at 1942 and the beginning of her *Herald Tribune* criticism as 1946 (probably a year too early.)

B246   Middenway, Ralph. "Adelaide." *Opera*, 37 (July 1986), p. 821-2.

Review for this English periodical (published in London) of *The Glittering Gate* (**W52c**) and *The Transposed Heads* (**W46e**) at the Adelaide Festival is similar in content to this writer's local review (**B247**), even using many of the same phrases. He adds that the night out with the music of Glanville-Hicks was splendid, "the grand old lady herself present as a bonus," but he would have preferred to see one of her big works rather than being "merely tantalised by her aura."

B247   _____. "A Double With Flair." Adelaide *Advertiser*, 22 March 1986, p. 35.

The Glittering Gate (**W52c**) and *The Transposed Heads* (**W46e**) on Adelaide Festival double bill, while not important major works like the composer's *Nausicaa* (**W62**) and *Sappho* (**W64**), achieve her goals "with flair." (Middenway compares her career and outlook to that of another expatriate Australian, Percy Grainger, of the generation before her.) *Gate* has a slight, mad story, negligible action, economical music, and vocal writing that is not especially memorable. *Heads* has more action, demanding vocal writing, and music is "as euphonious and tension-free as any classical Indian improvisation." Both work well because the composer knows how to develop her music and dramatic ideas without distracting the audience. Designer/director for this production has given more attention to design than to dramatic ebb and flow. (A copy of the review is in **A5**.)

B248   _____. "Flutes and Drums." *The Australian*, 20 April 1976, p. 8.

Glanville-Hicks's piece [*Sonata for Piano and Percussion*, **W43e**, not named] performed at the Adelaide Festival on 15 April must be her dreariest piece. (Clipping is in **A6c**.)

B249   Milburn, Frank, Jr. "The Transposed Heads." *Musical America* 78, no. 4 (March 1958), p. 22.

First two scenes of opera (**W46b**) "drag endlessly" but "the momentum picks up with the decapitation." The music is "a curious mixture of styles that refuse to blend" and does not fit the composer's explanation that she has thrown out harmony and dissonance and relied on melody and rhythm.

B250   Miller, Philip L. "Glanville-Hicks: *Letters from Morocco.*" *American Record Guide* 25, no. 4 (December 1958), p. 244-5.

Glanville-Hicks has been much praised for her manner of setting words, and *Letters from Morocco* (**D6**) is held up as an outstanding example. The soloist's tone is hardly ingratiating.

B251   _____. "Glanville-Hicks: *"Nausicaa*--Highlights." Ibid., 30, no. 9 (May 1984), p. 844, 846.

In *Nausicaa* recording (**D7**) Glanville-Hicks weaves Greek themes in to the orchestral background, often in stark octaves. Composer says themes from various parts of Greece "feel" different to anyone familiar with the heritage, but to the casual listener they are atmospheric background. Declamation of voices over this seems to have little connection with inflections of the text, except for high notes for emphasis. Full libretto, with the omitted text in contrasing type, is fortunately supplied. Singing is "all we could ask it to be." Stratas is lovely, her performance strikingly intelligent. Others, non-Americans, sing acceptably enough but with thick accents. Original cast recording is a historical document, and *Nausicaa* is of interest as an excellent example of contemporary American opera.

B252   "Miss Peggy Glanville-Hicks." *The Australian Musical News* 21 (1 December 1931), p. 3.

Albert Street (Melbourne) Conservatorium student Glanville-Hicks was runner-up for the Clarke Scholarship. Daughter of Mr. and Mrs. E. Glanville-Hicks of "Muritai," Barker's Road, Auburn, she is a pianoforte pupil of Mr. Waldemar Seidel and a composition pupil of Mr. Fritz Hart. A photo of Glanville-Hicks accompanies the announcement.

B253   Montgomery, Merle. "We're On the Air! It's Time to Tune In!" *Music Clubs Magazine* 51, no. 5 (Summer 1972), p. 5, 12-14.

Music by Glanville-Hicks will be in the first of two thirteen-week series of radio programs to be broadcast on twenty-two stations in thirty-four states, prepared by Julia Smith, National Chairwoman of the American Women Composers division of the National Federation of Music Clubs.

B254   Mootz, William. "Glanville-Hicks Opera to Receive World Premiere Saturday Afternoon." *The Courier-Journal* (Louisville, KY), Sunday, 28 March 1954, sect. 5, p. 1.

Pre-performance publicity on *The Transposed Heads* (**W46a**) reports Kentucky Opera Association music director Moritz Bomhard's descriptions of its plot, musical style, Hindu tunes and rhythms, and orchestration. Article includes a brief biography of Glanville-Hicks and photos of Bomhard, Audrey Nossaman (Sita), and the composer.

B255 _____. "Louisville Philharmonic Presents Opera Based on Mann Novel." *Musical America* 74, no. 7 (May 1954), p. 21.

The Transposed Heads (**W46a**) "abounds in attractive melodies" and displays "the human voice to its best advantage." Glanville-Hicks, following Mann's story, has produced a libretto that sometimes, as in the first two scenes, resists dramatic treatment. The barrage of percussion instruments and Eastern scale patterns give a pleasant exotic glow.

B256 _____. " 'Transposed Heads' Given Premiere Here." *The Courier-Journal* (Louisville, KY), Sunday, 4 April 1954, sect. 1, p. 18.

The opera (**W46a**) is "melodious, attractive, and tuneful," and the three "juicy" principal roles "display the voice to extremely good advantage." The barrage of percussion instruments and Eastern scale patterns give a pleasant exotic glow. Despite occasional static passages in the libretto, the opera is a colorful piece for the lyric stage. Moritz Bomhard has given it an imaginative and visually handsome production.

B257 Morgan, Derek Moore. "Pastel View of Modern Music." *The West Australian* (Perth), 15 August 1988, p. 50.

Thirteen Ways of Looking at a Blackbird (**W37f**) represented the "older composing generation" on this program of Australian contemporary music. [*Frolic* (**W9c**), also performed, is not mentioned.]

B258 Müller von Asow, Hedwig. *Komponistinnen-Discographie*. Berlin: Internationalen Musiker-Brief-Archivs, 1962.

Three-page "discography of women composers" (listed in Stern, **B361**) includes Glanville-Hicks.

B259 Murdoch, Anna. "A Composer Without Honor in Her Own Country." *The Age* (Melbourne), 15 June 1983, p. 14.

Glanville-Hicks "describes her life as a 'period of nothingness' since returning to Australia." She left to study at the Royal College of Music, then Vienna and Paris, then left London for New York in 1941 and stayed twenty years, and became famous in America for her operas. Coming to Greece resulted from search for melodic and highly rhythmic "music of the people." The classical repertoire has become "a crashing bore"--she heard nothing else as a New York critic [not exactly accurate]. "Most audiences are bored but they don't know it yet." Accompanying photo shows her at her piano with copies of her *Concertino da Camera* (**W33**) and *Thirteen Ways of Looking at a Blackbird* (**W37**) on the music rack.

B260 _____. "A Maestra to Even the Score." Ibid., 20 September 1985, p. 83.

Conductor Helen Quach (the *maestra*) before *Letters from Morocco* performance (**W44d**) comments that Glanville-Hicks's music is "so good." Glanville-Hicks sees Australian women composers as being in the same position American women were in "decades ago." Composition has nothing to do with being male or female, and is a question only of quality. As a woman "you have to be "slightly better than your male competitors so the judges can't look you in the eye and vote you out." Australian women are in the same position American women were in decades ago, and

we "won" this battle in the States. On the topic of musical style, her teacher
Vaughan Williams "told me his music lived because of the folkloric root. He
believed all the folk songs of the world were created by women."

B261   Murdoch, James. *A Handbook of Australian Music.* Melbourne: Sun
Books, 1983. P. 55, 67-8, 110, 143.

Book includes short entries on Glanville-Hicks, the *Etruscan Concerto* (**W48**), *The
Glittering Gate* (**W52**), *Nausicca* (**W62**), and *The Transposed Heads* (**W46**).

B262   _____. " 'Heads': Pivotal Work for Glanville-Hicks." *24 Hours*
9, no. 10 (November 1984), p. 18-19.

Article in Australian Broadcasting Corporation FM program guide previewing the 29
November broadcast of *The Transposed Heads* (**W46d**), recorded in the ABC's Perth
studios in August, provides a history--of Glanville-Hicks's writing of the score in
1952 and 1953 (in Jamaica), the Louisville premiere in 1954, the New York premiere
in 1958, and the Sydney performance in 1970. The opera was "pivotal" because here
she turned her back on the avant garde of the day--she jettisoned harmony--and so
became more avant garde than they. Being a New York critic, hearing the standard
repertoire plus the lunatic fringe, helped her define her own style. The Music Board
has made funds available for a new production by the State Opera, South Australia,
in 1985 [presented at Adelaide Festival, 1986]. Glanville-Hicks, who travelled to
Perth across the Nullabor on the Indian Pacific, praises the conductor and tenor.
Also this year her Piano Concerto [*Etruscan Concerto*, **W48c**] was performed at the
Cabrillo Festival (California), but she was unable to accept an invitation to be
composer-in-residence. Article includes a 1958 photo of the composer and a more
recent photo of tenor Gerald English.

B263   _____. "Peggy Glanville-Hicks." In *Australia's Contemporary
Composers.* South Melbourne: Macmillan, 1972. P. 102-7.

The first long article on Glanville-Hicks published in Australia (Murdoch is a
prominent Australian musician thoroughly familiar with her work) notes that
Glanville-Hicks, though an American citizen, still "vehemently claims her
allegiance to Australia" and may return soon. Biography is based on Antheil article
(**B11**) with updates on Australian performances such as 1970 *The Transposed Heads*
in Sydney (**W46c**), and includes chronological list of works. "Her music, although in
general enjoying a marked success in terms of recordings and key performances, has
not been a fashionable commodity." She has created a musical style "uniquely her
own"--though "her long interest in non-western music" is now coinciding with
developments among the "young composers of Australia."

B264   _____. "Peggy Gr[l]anville-Hicks." *Arts National* 2, no. 1
(September 1984), p. 41-43.

(Misspelling is only in title.) Article in Australian arts magazine published twelve
years after the previous entry, includes a 1983 photo of Glanville-Hicks and several
photos from earlier productions of *The Transposed Heads* (**W46b**) and *Nausicaa*
(**W62a**). Discussed are recent studio recordings of *The Transposed Heads* (**W46d**) and
Concerto Romantico (**W51b**), her training in Melbourne, London, and Europe, highlights of her New York years, and the lack of major performances of her work in
Australia. She returned to Australia in 1975 at the invitation of the Australia Music
Centre [Murdoch was its founder] to head the Asian Music Studies Programme established with a grant from the Myer Foundation, which within two years had become
known as the Asian Music Information Centre. She resists being put into a women
composers' "ghetto." A woman composer has to be "a darned sight better than a

man, to be accepted," she says. "The best music of the women composers must be programmed in the normal way with all the other works."

B265   *The Musical Woman: An International Perspective, 1983.* Ed. Judith Lang Zaimont, et al. Westport, CT: Greenwood Press, 1984. P. 6, 41, 286, 315-16.

"Gazette" section lists performance of *Three Gymnopédies* (**W47b**), discography lists **D7, D10,** and **D20,** and Stewart-Green article (**B362**) discusses Glanville-Hicks's songs.

B266   *The Musical Woman: An International Perspective, II (1984-1985).* Ed. Judith Lang Zaimont, et al. New York: Greenwood Press, 1987. P. 10, 38, 344, 357, 368.

Listed for 1984-85 are: performance of *Three Gymnopédies* (**W47b**); 1985 edition of *Etruscan Concerto* (**W48**); performance of *Nausicaa* excerpts (**W62b**, with reference to Ericson review, **B128**); and performance of the *Sonata for Harp* (**W42k**).

B267   Musielak, Henryk. "Festiwal w Atenach." *Ruch Muzyczny* 6, no. 1 (1962), p. 12-13.

Report on the 1961 Athens Festival in music periodical published in Warsaw, Poland, mentions *Nausicaa* (**W62a**) and includes photos of the principals and cast.

B268   *Musikens Hvem-Hvad-Hvor: Biografier.* Copenhagen: Politikens, 1961. Vol. 1, p. 246.

Article on Glanville-Hicks gives a biographical sketch and a classified list of twenty-two of her works, with dates, through the *Etruscan Concerto,* **W48**.

B269   " 'Nausicaa': Peggy Glanville-Hicks." *American Composers Alliance Bulletin* 10, no. 2 (1962), p. 2-5.

Reviews of **W62a** are excerpted: **B14, B115, B151, B153, B164, B238, B270, B273, B322, B357, B374, B406**

B270   " 'Nausicaa' a Great Success." *Daily Post* (Athens), 22 August 1961.

Saturday night's opening performance of *Nausicaa* (**W62a**) was not the failure one would expect from a modern opera, sung by unknowns, based on ancient Greek history altered by Mr. Robert Graves. All who attended were very much impressed, primarily by the music of a real master composer. (Review "by the *Post* Theatre correspondent" is quoted in **B269** in English.)

B271   " 'Nausicaa,' A New Opera." *New York Herald Tribune,* Sunday, 10 September 1961, sect. 4, p. 8.

Two-sentence announcement of the world premiere in Athens (**W62a**) appears under a large photo of Teresa Stratas (Nausicaa) on the set in Athens. Copy is in **A13c**.)

B272   " 'Nausicaa' in Greece." *New York Times,* Sunday, 10 September 1961, sect. 2, p. 13.

This caption, for a large photo of the principal singers and part of the rest of the cast, is followed by three sentences announcing that the world premiere (**W62a**) took place at the Athens Festival. (Copy is in **A13c**.)

B273   [*Nausicaa* Review.]   *Le Messager D'Athènes*, 26 August 1961.

The opera was a great success at the Athens Festival even though it was foreign to Homer's *Odyssey*. The action fell in with ancient Greek tradition, as did decor, *mise en scène*, and somewhat gaudy costumes; dances in the form of ballet (by John Butler) gave a particular character to the production, which was "more or less dazzling." Typescript copy in French is in **A11**; review is quoted in **B269** in English translation.

B274   "New Music."   *Musical Courier* 145, no. 10 (15 May 1952), p. 30.

Five Songs (**W29**), "animated and individually harmonized," catch the "characteristics of Housman's deeply human, wryly humorous and ironic, lyrics." This is an attractive recital novelty, with thoughtful content. (Reviewer *may* be Jules Wolffers.)

B275   "New Opera Set in India."   *New York Times*, Sunday, 9 February 1958, sect. 2, p. 7.

Brief announcement of the New York premiere of *The Transposed Heads* (**W46b**) appears next to Glanville-Hicks's essay "A Hindu Theme" (**G689**), with two photos, one of conductor Carlos Surinach with the composer and the other of the three principal singers in costume.

B276   "New Publications. Harp: Sonata by P. Glanville-Hicks."   *Musical Courier* 147, no. 9 (1 May 1953), p. 34.

The sonata (**W42**) is "simply planned and sincere," and the "technical requirements are of some difficulty." (Reviewer *may* be Henry W. Levinger.)

B277   "New York World's Music Centre."   *The Listener In* (Melbourne), 2-8 August 1952, p. 21.

Glanville-Hicks, interviewed during a visit home, says she attends at least four night concerts a week plus two on Saturday and sometimes three on Sunday, and writes *Herald Tribune* reviews with "one eye on my clock." Of thirty-two "musical critics" in New York, she is the only woman. Modern music is more vital, vigorous and alive in America than anywhere else in the world. She talks of her compositions, her work with the Composers Forum, and her "honorary work" as a member of the junior council of the Museum of Modern Art, including arranging two contemporary chamber concerts the past season [*see* **W42c** and **W43a**]. She mentions a "slight bias against employing women even in America," although women are "taking their places" beside men in the arts and professions, while doing the woman's job at home too. Her advice to women who are happy at home is to stay there. (A copy is in **A3**.)

B278   Nilsson, B. A.   "Albany Symphony Gives Disappointing Concert."   *Schenectady* (NY) *Gazette*, 7 November 1988.

Etruscan Concerto (**W48d**) is "exotic with its eastern influence." The "transparent orchestration enhances the delicacy of the work. Piano soloist Penelope Thwaites concealed the "tough technical requirements of the cheerful piece." Orchestra was sometimes out of "sync" with piano, sometimes too loud. Review was reprinted in *Metroland*, a Troy, NY, weekly paper under the title "Folk Orchestration."

B279 Northouse, Cameron. *Twentieth-Century Opera in England and the U. S.* Boston: G. K. Hall, 1976.

Book gives date and place of first performance, author of text, and publisher for *Nausicaa* (**W62**), libretto by Alastair Reid, and *The Transposed Heads* (**W46**), gives all information but publisher for *The Glittering Gate* (**W52**), and lists *Sappho* (**W64**), *Caedmon* (**W5**), and *Carlos and the Candles* (**W63**) under "additional works".

B280 Null, Tom. Liner Notes for *Three Gymnopédie*. Varèse Sarabande 81046. 1978.

For this recording (**D20**) Null quotes from Glanville-Hicks's explanation of the pieces on the earlier MGM recording (**G680**) and from Antheil (**B11**), and presents a brief biography. "Besides being a unique composer, she has had a career of devoted service to music and musicians."

B281 O'Connell, Clive. "Display of Neglected Women." *The Age* (Melbourne), 17 September 1985.

Sunday night's concert of eight chamber works included Glanville-Hicks's "sonatas for flute and [for] harp" (**W27e** and **W42m**).

B282 _____. "New Moods Fine Finale." Ibid., 24 September 1985, p. 14.

Letters from Morocco (**W44d**), presented at concert at end of New Moods Arts Festival Sunday afternoon, are "atmospheric vignettes." The work was surprisingly cliché-less and not too exotic or "pseudo-Oriental/African" for these days after all. Use of percussion was deft and each movement used a melodic style light years ahead of the Hollywood version of the same textual material. Helen Quach was an impressive conductor; tenor (English) was not in top form. Small attendance, while not disastrously small, was disappointing to the organisers and performers, but everybody appeared to enjoy the concert. (A copy is in **A6c**.)

B283 Oja, Carol. *American Music Recordings: A Discography of 20th-Century U.S. Composers.* New York: Institute for Studies in American Music, 1982.

Oja gives "release date" and "delete date" (based on the Schwann catalog) for almost all of Glanville-Hicks's recordings.

B284 Olve, Nils-Göran. "Peggy Glanville-Hicks." *Sohlmans Musiklexikon.* 2nd edn. Vol. 3. Stockholm: Sohlman, 1976. P. 130.

Short article includes birth date, teachers, genres of compositions, and principal titles.

B285 "Opera Figure Arrives." *Daily Telegraph* (Sydney), 24 June 1970, p. 13.

Short press release announces that Glanville-Hicks, "Australian composer" well known in "American musical circles," will arrive in Sydney from Athens, "her permanent residence since 1959," for the Australian premiere of *The Transposed Heads* (**W46c**). (Clipping is in **A7**.)

B286   Osborne, Conrad L. "Spring in Town." *Opera News* 24 (31 October 1959), p. 26.

The Glittering Gate (**W52a**) was part of an unusually stimulating program by The Artists' Company. While the work, taken from an ironic piece by Lord Dunsany, is intended as a curtain-raiser, her ingenious orchestration and graceful handling of the voice create a mild, pleasant mood. Electronic effects [unearthly laughter] by Vladimir Ussachevsky were appropriate.

B287   O'Sullivan, Margaret. "Met as Students in Paris--Here for Exhibition." *Sun-Herald* (Sydney), 14 May 1978, p. 157.

Glanville-Hicks's *Girondelle for Giraffes* (**W67a**) was written to go with a scultpure called *Giraffes* in an exhibition of fragile wooden sculptures by her longtime friend Pamela Boden, now visiting Australia from her home near San Francisco. Six other composers contributed works as well--Don Banks, Ross Edwards, David Gulpilil, Lou Harrison, Peter Sculthorpe, and Vincent Plush. At the exhibition a spotlight moves from one sculpture to another and as it stops the recorded music written for it is played.

B288   Paap, Wouter. "Het 22ste Muziekfest der International Society for Contemporary Music Te Amsterdam." *Mens en Melodie* 3, no. 7 (1948), p. 193-8.

Reviewer in Dutch music periodical finds the composer of the *Concertino da camera* (**W33a**) "a very traditional, uncreative spirit" in spite of the work's promising piano beginning.

B289   Parmenter, Ross. "Clap Your Hands--It's Part of Music." *New York Times*, 7 May 1952, p. 31.

Sonata for Piano and Percussion (**W43b**) is "absorbing and entertaining," reminiscent of "American tropical rain forest" sounds of "crickets and tree toads." Sonata's conclusion "suggested that Samson had just brought down the temple in 'Samson and Delilah.' " (Review is quoted in **B11**.)

B290   _____. "Composers' Unit Ends Season With Concert." Ibid., 23 March 1953, p. 28.

Performance of *Sonata for Piano and Percussion* (**W43c**) at NAACC concert with a different pianist from the premiere (**W43b**, reviewed in **B289** above) made a "more telling impression". "The unusual Sonata was easily the most original and exciting work of the program." (Review is quoted in **B11**.)

B291   _____. "Music By 3 Critics Given at Concert." Ibid., 21 February 1951, p. 32.

Music by *Herald Tribune* critics Glanville-Hicks, Thomson, and Berger included *Thirteen Ways of Looking at a Blackbird* (**W37b**), the work "with the greatest beauty, and the most variety and invention." Words were indistinct, so much of the cycle's charm came from "economical but wonderfully various piano parts." (Review is quoted in **B11**.)

B292   _____. "A New Homeric Opera for Ancient Greece." Ibid.,
Sunday, 19 February 1961, sect. 2, p. 9.

Nausicaa (**W62**) has been selected by the Athens Festival (a 1955 creation of the
National Tourist Organization of Greece) for performance this summer. The opera
has a Greek theme but its composer is not Greek but "Australian-American." The
libretto prepared by Robert Graves "contends that the 'Odyssey' was written by a
woman and tells how she came to write it." Five of the principals will be singers of
Greek ancestry who have never been to Greece. An opera première "gives a festival
a certain réclame and attracts knowing and fashionable people in a way that a diet of
only standard works can not." (A copy of the announcement is in **A3g**.)

B293   _____. "Spanish Program Presented Here." Ibid., 11 March 1952,
p. 23.

Sonata for Harp performed by Zabaleta in its U.S. premiere (**W42c**) was "perhaps the
loveliest piece of the evening" with "directness of statement" and "sweetness and
simplicity." (Review is quoted in **B11**.)

B294   Pavlakis, Christopher. *The American Music Handbook.* New York:
Free Press, 1974. P. 221, 332, 450.

Information on Glanville-Hicks includes list of recordings and location of
unpublished works; she has also been a member of the Advisory Committee of the
Thoine Music Fund Grants and Fellowships in New York.

B295   "Peggy Glanville-Hicks." Brochure by Associated Music Publishers,
Inc. [1955?]

Standard AMP composer brochure contains a brief biography to 1955, which begins
with Cole's "Peggy Glanville-Hicks is an exception to the rule that women do not
measure up to the standard set by men" (*see* **B71**) and then quotes Antheil (**B11**): "I
hardly know of a composer working today who has, from every point of view, a
better technique, both in the handling of musical substances and in their instrumentation. She has evolved for herself a singular and completely personal
technique." It also has a photo and a list of works with review excerpts published
1950-55: of *Letters from Morocco* (**B376**), *The Transposed Heads* (**B123** quoted almost
in full, and **B255**), *Sonata for Piano and Percussion* (**B289**, **B384**), and *Thomsoniana*
(**B96**, **B176**, **B378**). (Copy of brochure is in **A13c**, stamped National Broadcasting
Company, Inc.)

B296   "Peggy Glanville-Hicks." Brochure. [1958.]

Brochure contains a "complete list of works"--first a list of recordings and then a
classified list of works with duration, instrumentation, and publisher--and excerpts
from "recent reviews" published 1956-58, of *The Transposed Heads* (**B29**, **B131**, **B202**,
B212, **B229**, **B396**), *The Masque of the Wild Man* (**B136**, **B370**), *Concerto Romantico*
(**B141**, **B175**, **B329**, **B343**), and *Etruscan Concerto* (**B215**, **B331**). (Copies in English and
Spanish are in **A3**.)

B297   "Peggy Glanville-Hicks." Brochure by Broadcast Music, Inc. [1969.]

Standard BMI composer brochure includes "Biographical Note 1969" and classified
"List of Works" including a discography. (Copies are in **A2b**, **A3**, and **A6c**.) Earlier
BMI brochures were apparently issued as well: an announcement in the *National*

Music Council Bulletin, 28, no. 2 (1968), reports that brochures on Glanville-Hicks and five other composers are now available for distribution.

B298   "Peggy Glanville-Hicks." *Opera News* 22, no. 19 (10 March 1958), p. 3.

Brief announcement reports that the "globe-trotting Australian-born composer" will depart shortly for Greece to work in "Athenian archives to achieve authenticity in her new opera, *Nausicaa* " also notes that *Transposed Heads* (**W46**) will soon be translated into Turkish. (A copy is in **A3**.)

B299   "Peggy Glanville-Hicks--Another Opera Premiere." *Music and Dance* 52 (September 1961), p. 7.

Article in Melbourne magazine (successor to *Australian Musical News,* **B194**, etc.) reports that the Australian-born composer and music critic, whose eyes are failing through over work, had her opera *Nausicaa* (**W62a**) premiered in Athens late last month. Views of critics ranged from "excellent" to "not so good." Some thought the libretto, by renowned Greek scholar, poet, and author Robert Graves, was undramatic. Recently, Glanville-Hicks has been Australian musical adviser to the United Nations Information Centre in New York. (A copy is in **A3**.)

B300   "Peggy's One of a Few." *The Sun News Pictorial* (Melbourne), 25 February 1981, p. 21.

Glanville-Hicks, now 68, one of the few women opera composers, and with "five major works to her credit," has donated some of her opera scores and other works to the State Library of Victoria. As a woman, she said yesterday, she had to fight twice as hard to win recognition, but can feel twice the satisfaction "because I've beaten the men to it." (Clipping is in **A7**.)

B301   Perkins, Francis D. "Two U.S. Operas in Debut at Kaufmann Concert Hall." *New York Herald Tribune,* 15 May 1959, p. 13.

Glanville-Hicks in *The Glittering Gate* (**W52a**) uses an electronic sound track to indicate unearthly laughter in her account of two burglars cracking their way through the gate to Heaven. Unearthly laughter seemed slightly too discreet. Both this score and Harrison's *Rapunzel* that followed were distinguished for their orchestral craftsmanship; Newell Jenkins provided skilled musical direction. *Glittering Gate* had an unusual scenic device in the descending beer bottles of the Dunsany play; its humor was reflected in the "clever and colorful" instrumental score but rather diluted in the "flexible and singable" vocal parts. Principals used clear enunciation and good characterization.

B302   "Personalia. . . . Australian Musicians and Their Activities." *The Australian Musical News* 29 (November 1938), p. 6.

News item quotes Edwin Evans in "the informative little magazine" *The Chesterian,* reporting on the ISCM Festival in London: "Part of a choral Suite for female voices, oboe, and strings by Peggy Glanville-Hicks was welcomed chiefly as the first appearance of an Australian composer on Festival programmes. It consists of suave settings of Elizabethan lyrics" (**W19a**).

B303   Peterson, Melody. "L. A. County Museum: Women's Works." *Hi Fidelity/Musical America* 27 (June 1977), p. MA 24-5.

Profiles from China (**W32d**), "perfect miniatures," were radiantly interpreted by soprano Maurita Thornburgh and pianist Nancy Fierro (also a research collaborator for this Los Angeles program). "The concert reminded one that the compositional art rises above and beyond characteristics of the masculine or feminine."

B304 Peyser, Joan. *Boulez*. New York: Schirmer Books, 1976. P. 84.

Quoting Glanville-Hicks's *Herald Tribune* review of Boulez's Piano Sonata and Cage's *Music of Changes*, 2 January 1952 (**G334**), Peyser identifies her (somewhat inaccurately) as "a neoclassic composer in the tradition of Thomson, her superior on the *Tribune* staff," and as a critic "in the conservative vein and therefore not partial to Cage," though celebrating him over the European avant-garde. "Thus the New York press heralded the split between the music of Boulez and Cage, between the Serialists and the Dadaists."

B305 Phillips, Linda. "Bound-up Music Noisy Nonsense." *The Sun* (Melbourne), 11 July 1970.

Concertino da camera (**W33c**) and *Sonatina for Flute and Piano* (**W27b**) were "rather charming and original in melodic content and general treatment" (unlike the work to which the review's title refers).

B306 _____. "Pleasant Evening of Local Music." Ibid., 17 April 1971.

Choral Suite (**W19b**) "mirrors" the text in music "with imagery and refinement of expression," though this is not a mature work of Glanville-Hicks.

B307 "Phoenix Opera Put Off." *New York Herald Tribune*, 26 December 1957.

The Transposed Heads (**W46b**) at the Phoenix Theatre, originally scheduled for 13 January 1958 [*see* **B62**], has been postponed to 10 February. (Typescript of press release is in **A3**; clipping is in **A13c**.)

B308 Pontzious, Richard. "Restless Crowd But Nice Music." *San Francisco Examiner*, 15 November 1982, p. B13.

Three Gymnopédies (**W47b**), "though harmonically static and contrapuntally dry, are full of splendidly Romantic melodies."

B309 Pool, Jeannie G. "America's Women Composers: Up From the Footnotes." *Music Educators Journal* 65, no. 5 (January 1979), p. 28-36.

Glanville-Hicks is mentioned on p. 33 and 35 in a section on the 1930s and 1940s as "another Boulanger student who is a well-established composer," with "three operas, *The Etruscan Concerto* for piano and orchestra, and several works for full orchestra" among her credits.

B310 _____. *Women in Music History: A Research Guide*. New York: Pool, 1977. P. 33.

Discography lists four Glanville-Hicks recordings.

B311 "Une première mondiale très attendue à Athènes, le 19 août: 'Nausicaa.' Opéra. Musique de Peggy Glanville-Hicks, sur une nouvelle de *Robert Graves..*" *Paris Match* 841 (22 July 1961), p. 9.

Pre-performance announcement of the "long-awaited world premiere" of the opera *Nausicaa* in Athens, 19 August, appears on the page of *"télégrammes"* or short news reports under "Arts," subhead "Festivals," in this French weekly pictorial magazine.

B312 Quillian, James W. "P. Glanville-Hicks. 13 Ways of Looking at a Blackbird. Profiles from China." *Repertoire: The Magazine About Music That Ought to Be Known* 1, no. 3 (January 1952), p. 158-9.

In this periodical, published in Lansing, Michigan, in his column "The New and the Good," reviewer finds that in *Thirteen Ways of Looking at a Blackbird* (**W37**) the vocal line is always grateful and the accompaniments transparent in texture. *Profiles from China* (**W33**) "contain a variety of rhythmic interest and are richly endowed harmonically." It would be interesting to see the composer turn her attention to less exotic and fragmentary poetry. (Review is quoted in **B11**.)

B313 R. N. D. "Tweede kamermuziek-concert I.S.F.C.M." *Trouw* (Amsterdam), 12 June 1948, p. 34.

Article on the ISCM Festival mentions Glanville-Hicks from Australia but does not review the *Concertino da camera* (**W33a**).

B314 Radic, Thérèse. "Australian Women in Music." *Lip* 3 (1978/79), p. 97-110.

Article by noted Melbourne writer on music mentions work of "Australian" Glanville-Hicks.

B315 _____. *Bernard Heinze.* South Melbourne: Macmillan, 1986. P. 37, 105, 183-4.

Publication of music of Glanville-Hicks and Margaret Sutherland was one way in which Louise Dyer, founder of Lyrebird Press in Paris, supported Australian music. Glanville-Hicks represented Australia at the ISCM festival in London in 1938; the BBC picked up the tab. Glanville-Hicks introduced conductor Heinze (1894-1982) to *musique concrète* in New York when she was working for the Columbia Broadcasting System experimenting in the technique (Radic's reference is to the Melbourne *Herald,* 30 November 1948; *see also* **B99** above, referring to 1952). Her explanations gave force to his opinions that new ideas like "concrete music" should come to Australia, but detractors said it is mathematical and gimmicky.

B316 Rensch, Roslyn. *The Harp: Its History, Technique and Repertoire.* New York: Praeger, 1969. P. 193.

The *Concerto [Concertino] Antiqua* (**W49**) and *Sonata for Harp* (**W42**) are listed in Appendix I, "Composers, Compositions and Recordings."

B317 RePass, Richard. "U. S. A." *Musical Times* 95 (April 1954), p. 205.

Reviewer in English periodical (in "Notes from Abroad" section) finds *Letters from Morocco* (**W44b**) are settings of "florid descriptions of Moroccan nights to a correspondingly florid, melismatic vocal line, while the accompaniment throbs with bizarre rhythms and rich instrumental effects." Glanville-Hicks is like her associate at the *Herald Tribune* Virgil Thomson in sacrificing musical design to prosody.

B318   Rice, Curtis E. "The Transposed Heads." *Musical Courier* 157, no. 5 (April 1958), p. 31.

Review (signed C. E. R.) of New York production (**W46b**) discusses problems of presenting a Hindu story to "Occidentals." Music is also occidental and harmonic, in spite of composer's claims, but had "some stirring moments, and some lovely melodies." There was no orchestra "pit" and the orchestra covered the singers.

B319   Riemann, Hugo. *Musik-Lexikon.* 12th edn., ed. Willibald Gurlitt. *Personentheil,* vol. 1. Mainz: B. Schotts Söhne, 1959, p. 632-3. *Ergänzungsbände,* ed. Carl Dahlhaus, vol. 1, 1972, p. 430.

Short article in 1972 volume adds titles, instrumentations, and dates to the nineteen works listed in 1959 volume and changes year Glanville-Hicks began to write for the *New York Herald Tribune* from 1946 to 1948 (1947 is correct). Works listed are: W5, W12, W16, W17, W20, W22, W26, W29, W31 through W35, W37, W38, W42, W48, W52, and W65.

B320   Ringo, James. "Jokes, Portraits and *Collages.*" *American Composers Alliance Bulletin* 6, no. 1 (Autumn 1956), pp. 23-4.

Printed in full is Glanville-Hicks's two-stanza poem "A Portrait of Carol Truax in the Baroque Style of the Late Gertrude Stein," a parody later to be set to music. *Collage* technique is used in *Thomsoniana* (**W38**) and *Letters from Morocco* (**W44**, partly quoted).

B321   _____. "The Lure of the Orient." Ibid., 7, no. 2 (1958), p. 11.

Glanville-Hicks, Cowell, Chou Wen-chung, Cage, Hovhaness, Harrison, McPhee, and Avshalomov use Asian musical materials, thus following in the tradition of Occidental musicians fascinated with the Orient since the Renaissance and through the 18th, 19th, and 20th centuries. *Letters from Morocco* and *Profiles from China* use Oriental procedures and materials because of the texts and word-setting, but her abstract works do, too. Her Orientalism consists of her thinning of her harmonic texture, resulting in a "graceful lightness of touch" and a refusal to stun with sheer physical weight. Listeners seeking only exotic, coloristic Orientalism are often disappointed by her music.

B322   "Robert Graves & Opera." *Time,* 1 September 1961, p. 55.

Nausicaa (**W62a**), "a fine new Glanville-Hicks work," was inspired by Greek folk themes and had an unusual librettist, Graves. In his book *Homer's Daughter,* inspired by the theory that not Homer but a woman wrote the *Odyssey,* Princess Nausicaa plots against her supposed suitors who are really planning to overthrow her father, King Alcinous, and sees them all killed. The composer has "wrapped the story in sinewy, astringent music." The orchestra was deliberately limited to 60 instruments and the vocal parts use the metric cadence of Greek folk song. She is "one of the few women who have turned a successful hand to opera." Her eyes are failing, due to years of "reading and music copying." (Review is quoted in **B269** almost in full, and a short excerpt in **G696**)

B323 Rockwell, John. *All-American Music: Composition in the Late Twentieth Century.* New York: Vintage, 1983, p. 180.

Jazz pianist Keith Jarrett (born 1945) has begun to appear as a piano soloist in works of other composers, notably in concertos by Glanville-Hicks and others, and "has won warm praise from classical critics for his efforts." (*See* **W48b-c** on his *Etruscan Concerto* performances.)

B324 Rogers, Harold. "Recordings." *Christian Science Monitor* 13 April 1956, p. 7.

One paragraph (signed "H.R.") in Boston-based national newspaper reports that *Sinfonia pacifica* and *Three Gymnopédies* (**D11/D19**) show the composer's "fine sense of form, orchestral color, and invention, especially in her Gymnopédies which in no way imitate the famous set by Satie." The U. S. has an accomplished woman composer in Peggy Glanville-Hicks, now as well known as a New York music critic. (Quote over Rogers's name in **B113** is someone else's review, **B354**.)

B325 Rooney, Dennis D. "Notes on the Program." St. Paul Chamber Orchestra Program, 17 March 1980.

Program notes quote Glanville-Hicks on three of the concert's four pieces: her own *Etruscan Concerto* (from **B71**); McPhee's *Concerto for Piano with Wind Octet Accompaniment* (from **G644**); and Harrison's *Suite for Piano, Violin and Small Orchestra* (from **G593**). As introduction, Rooney quotes Thomson (**B377**) on the similarities among those three who learned "oriental methods."

B326 Rorem, Ned. "But Yesterday Is Not Today." Liner notes for "The American Art Song From 1930 to 1960." New World Records 243. 1977. P. 2.

Glanville-Hicks is one of four women among the "eight major composers in America today" and he refers to her Bowles settings [these include *Ballade* and *Letters from Morocco*].

B327 _____. *Critical Affairs.* New York: George Braziller, 1970. P. 101.

Rorem names Glanville-Hicks among women composers who are "well-schooled first-rate musicians."

B328 _____. *Music and People.* New York: George Braziller, 1968, p. 17.

Glanville-Hicks "translated Eastern sound effects into Western jargons and then spoke those jargons with controlled formality."

B329 Roussel, Hubert. [*Concerto romantico* recording review.] *Houston* (Texas) *Post*, [1957].

Glanville-Hicks, "one of the more gifted and interesting creative musicians now at work in the country" and a "propagandist" for new music, "has written a fine and beautiful piece of music." She writes (in liner notes, **G686**) that she has "practically been read out of the party" of contemporary composers who use "dissonance as a law." She shows "the musical gumption and independence to let the aim govern the means" and her "objectors" will certainly march the same way "before long." (Review is quoted in **B296**.)

B330   Ruff, Marcia. "Peggy Glanville-Hicks." *Lip* 3 (1978-79), p. 122-3.

Third section of an article in an Australian periodical (published near Melbourne) on "Four Women Composers" reviews of the life and works of Glanville-Hicks. The other three sections are on Helen Gifford, Ann Boyd, and Ann Carr-Boyd.

B331   Rule, Gunby. "Chopin Nocturne Set in New Recording." *Knoxville* (Tennessee) *News Sentinel,* 13 May 1956, p. C-2.

Issued by MGM records, the recent *Sinfonia pacifica* and the early *Three Gymno-pédies* (**D11/D19**) by Glanville-Hicks show a "gift for melody" that sets her apart from many of her colleagues." (Review is quoted in **B113**.)

B332   Sabin, Robert. "Five Housman Poems Set." *Musical America* 72, no. 16 (15 December 1952), p. 26.

The *Five Songs* (**W29**) have transparent texture and imaginative coloration; the simplicity of the music is wholly appropriate when "lyrics" are by Housman. Glanville-Hicks has set the words carefully, although her melodic ideas are dry and at times somewhat stiffly pressed. "Mimic Heaven," has a restless "pointilliste" accompaniment. "He Would Not Stay" is admirably direct and lyric and lacks only melodic tension to be profoundly eloquent. "Stars" shows the composer's delicate ear for high treble piano sonorities and glissandos. "Unlucky Love" falls into banality; the accompaniment is saved from bathos only by its dissonance. But "Homespun Collars" is a "clever trick with an extremely difficult vocal line and a rhythmically perky piano part."

B333   _____. "Glanville-Hicks, P.: Ballade." Ibid., 70, no. 3 (February 1950), p. 334.

The three songs (**W31**) "capture the vague, almost meaningless, melancholy" of the texts. "The vocal lines are forced and too dependent on the accompaniments, but the harmony and spacing" are "highly sensitive."

B334   _____. "A Sonata for Harp by P. Glanville-Hicks." Ibid., 73, no. 6 (15 April 1953), p. 20.

The sonata (**W42**) is "tasteful, unaffected, and technically interesting to the harp player." Its elegance and "lack of pretention mask the essential poverty of the musical material."

B335   Sackville-West, Edward, and Shawe-Taylor, Desmond. *The Record Guide.* London: Collins, 1951. P. 257.

For Glanville-Hicks there is a short biography (dating her marriage 1939, not 1938) and one recording, the *Choral Suite* (**D1**).

B336   Sandved, Kjell Bloch. *The World of Music: An Illustrated Encyclopedia.* New York: Abradale Press, 1963. Vol. 2, p. 519.

Short article (17 lines) on Glanville-Hicks gives birth year, teachers, and genres and principal titles of her compositions.

B337   Sargeant, Winthrop. "Musical Events: Best Feet Forward." *New Yorker*, 25 November 1967, p. 220-1.

A Season in Hell (**W65a**) has "a score of unusual expressiveness by Peggy Glanville-Hicks." Danced by the Harkness Ballet before a sort of Milky Way backdrop with steel wires in front of it, the ballet "is a sober item indeed, about the trouble with poets is that they never get the girl." (Review is quoted in **B78** brochure.)

B338   _____. "Uneasy Lies the Head." Ibid., 22 February 1958, p. 120.

Reading about *The Transposed Heads* before the New York premiere (**W46b**), "I couldn't restrain a certain apprehensive curiosity" about the mayhem of the decapitation. But it turned out to be merely horseplay in a "metaphysical farce with overtones reminiscent of Gilbert and Sullivan." The music is easy on the ear, combining an Anglo-Celtic idiom with vaguely Oriental drumming and melody for local color but most expressive in passages sticking to "Western musical thought." Skillful lyrics would have improved on Mann's hum-drum prose. The opera lacked "musical wit and sparkle" to make it hilarious. The production, though modest, was resourceful; Hindu costumes and props made quite a splash. Principal roles were handled adequately, and the orchestra was ably conducted by Surinach.

B339   Sartori, Claudio. *Enciclopedia della musica*. Vol. 2. Milano: Ricordi, 1964. P. 323.

Short biographical article says Glanville-Hicks has withdrawn all compositions before 1945 and then includes several of them in a partial list of her works.

B340   Schaefer, Theodore. "Solo Song." *Music Library Association Notes 8*, no. 4 (September 1951), p. 751-2.

Profiles from China (**W32**) show "a greater variety of rhythmic interest in the vocal line than is usually found in songs of similar aims," and rich "harmonic color" in the accompaniments, yet the cycle seems like movie mood music. *Thirteen Ways of Looking at a Blackbird* (**W37**), an arresting series, requires an accomplished mezzo-soprano and accompanist. Songs have vocally grateful melodic structure, a feeling for prosody, accompaniments full of imagery but without extraneous notes (resulting in "crystal transparency"), and sharply contrasted moods. (Quote from review is in **B11**.)

B341   Scholes, Percy Alfred. *The Oxford Companion to Music*. 10th edn. Ed. John Owen Ward. London, New York: Oxford University Press, 1970. P. 405.

Short entry on Glanville-Hicks gives her birth year, where she studied, and the genres in which she has composed.

B342   Schonberg, Harold C. "Five Premieres." *New York Times*, 26 January 1956, p. 24.

Etruscan Concerto (**W48a**) was "clever and catchy, with a fairly conservative harmonic idiom," Italian flavor, agreeable melodic flow, and "completely idiomatic" scoring. (**B11** quotes this.)

B343 _____. "Old-Style Works by Moderns Played at Rogers Auditorium." Ibid., 20 February 1957, p. 37.

Concerto Romantico (**W51a**) "deals with simple harmonies with an orthodox tonal center, is lyric and tuneful, is structurally clear, and is right in the nineteenth century." Is this clarity and defiance of the atonalists the "new revolution?" (**B138** and **B296** quote this.)

B344 Shavin, Norman. "Glanville-Hicks Opera Has World Premiere in Louisville." *New York Herald Tribune,* Sunday, 5 April, 1954, sect. 1, p. 41, col. 1-2.

Shavin, identified as Music Editor of *The Louisville Times,* reports that *The Transposed Heads* (**W46a**) "won pleased response from music patrons for its lucid story and melodic lines." Erratic rhythms "lend authentic flavor," and xylophone, gongs, and vibraphone "add many hues to the mystic surroundings of a Hindu temple." Yet the music "lacks proper orchestral dynamics." The principals all "sang creditably in roles that made no great demands on vocal fireworks." (Clipping is in **A13c**.)

B345 Shawe-Taylor, Desmond. "New Music in Amsterdam." *The New Statesman and Nation* (London) 35, no. 903 (26 June, 1948), p. 519.

The "modest and charming" *Concertino da camera* (**W33a**) from Australia exhibited the "French element" of "clarity, lightness, concision and simplicity." Otherwise the ISCM Festival was dominated by the Teutonic tradition in decline. (**B11** Antheil quotes.)

B346 Shmith, Michael. "Harmony in the House of Apollo." *The Age* (Melbourne), 22 March 1986, Saturday extra section, p. 11.

In this interview by the paper's opera correspondent, Glanville-Hicks talks about being a "woman composer," her brain surgery twenty years earlier and "plastic skull," her study with Nadia Boulanger, her work on the *Herald Tribune,* the Greek production of *Nausicaa,* twentieth-century musical alternatives to neo-classicism and atonality, and her current plans. She is writing a book on twentieth-century music titled "Apollo's House"--Apollo is the god of music and medicine, concerned with the "wellbeing" of both spirit and body. Article includes a recent photo.

B347 "A Short List of Australian Women Composers." Compiled by the Fellowship of Australian Composers. Strathfield, NSW: The Fellowship, 1982.

Glanville-Hicks is listed as a composer of dramatic music, keyboard music, and miscellaneous genres. Brochure, listing 63 names (including four living overseas and nine deceased), was a supplement to the lecture-recital given by Margaret Brandman and Ann Carr-Boyd at the Second International Congress on Women in Music, Los Angeles, 1-4 April 1982. It is available from the Secretary of the Fellowship, P.O. Box 522, Strathfield, NSW 2135. (Copy is in **A2**.)

B348 Silbermann, Alphons. "Peggy Glanville-Hicks." *Die Musik in Geschichte und Gegenwart.* Ed. Friedrich Blume. Vol. 5. Kassel, New York: Bärenreiter, 1956. Col. 214-15.

Short article presents a paragraph of bibliography--date and place of birth, training, important performances, marriage, professional positions--followed by a list of works, classifed by genre, and a final brief paragraph on her musical style based on **B11** (Antheil). For her, melody and rhythm are the real structural elements and harmony is only a byproduct. She often uses Eastern models, and her music, though Western in its language, often has an exotic Oriental sound.

B349   Silsbury, Elizabeth. "The Good and Not So Good." *Adelaide Advertiser*, 17 April 1976, p. 22.

Sonata for Piano and Percussion (**W43e**) at the Adelaide Festival, though its pseudo-Oriental effects sound rather dated now, has many good ideas and lots of energy and vitality. It exploited the "considerable skill" of these performers. (Clipping is in **A6c**.)

B350   Sinclair, John. "Musical Tribute to a Composer." *The Herald* (Melbourne), 8 August 1970, p. 20.

Glanville-Hicks attended "recital-reception," a tribute to her attended by other composers and leaders of Melbourne's musical community. Three of her works were played in order of composition. *Sonatina for Recorder and Piano* (**W27c**) is "gay and neatly turned out." *Concertino da Camera* (**W33d**) is "equally attractive but more complex," dating from a time when Boulanger was the dominant influence on her. *Sonata for Harp* (**W42i**) is "unpretentious and beautiful."

B351   _____. "One-Stringed Muddle." Ibid., 11 July 1970, p. 18.

The *Sonatina for Treble Recorder and Piano* (**W27b**) and *Concertino da camera* (**W33c**) were "two valid and interesting works" (unlike the work to which the title of the review refers).

B352   _____. "Problems in Presenting Australian Works." Ibid., 17 April 1971.

Choral Suite (**W19b**) is "a relatively early, but significant, work, by a composer who was even then winning international recognition." The choral writing obscures the words, however, and in this performance the orchestra obscured the choir.

B353   _____. "A Woman of Music." Ibid., 10 July 1970, p. 15.

Announcement of concert introduces Glanville-Hicks, "one of the most successful women composers of serious music in the world today." Concert today will feature two early works: the *Sonatina for Treble Recorder* (**W27a**), first performed at the 1948 ISCM Festival [actually it was the *Concertino da Camera*], and the *Concertino da Camera* (**W33c**).

B354   [*Sinfonia da Pacifica* and *Three Gymnopédies* recording review.] Reprinted in **B113**: "Discs and Reviews 1955-1956," *American Composers Alliance Bulletin* 6, no. 3 (1957), pp. 21-2.

Review, labeled *Christian Science Monitor* but different from Rogers' review (**B324**) in that newspaper, explains that Glanville-Hicks emphasizes rhythm and melody over harmony, and develops two contrasting themes simultaneously rather than successively. The *Sinfonia Pacifica* is in three movements; the first has "percussive rhythms with curt melodic factors," the second is chiefly melodic, and the finale uses a "brisk" theme "of Hindu origin again played over insistent percussive rhythms." The "peaceful" *Three Gymnopédies* have slow, vagrant melodies over throbs of rhythms.

B355   Skowronski, JoAnn. *Women in American Music: A Bibliography.*
Metuchen, NJ: Scarecrow Press, 1978.

Reader is referred to five works mentioning Glanville-Hicks in this recent attempt
(but superseded by Cohen, **B67**) to document women's work in music.

B356   Smith, Julia. *Directory of American Women Composers with Selected
Music for Senior and Junior Clubs.*   Chicago: National Federation of
Music Clubs, 1970. P. 15.

Smith gives addresses (for Glanville-Hicks, c/o American Music Center), types of
works composed, and publishers.

B357   Solo. "Opera Review: *Nausicaa.*" *Variety* 234, no. 1 (30 August 1961),
p. 56.

Review of Athens production (**W62a**) concentrates on the production (Butler's
staging is "top drawer") and soloists (first rate). "A 10-minute standing ovation
greeted the world premiere," the cast of 150 winning eight curtain calls from a capacity crowd of 4800 that "represented the cream of Athens society." Minor faults are
mentioned: the 55-piece orchestra sometimes covered the singers, and Nausicaa's
first-act lament "drew snickers." (Review is quoted in **G696, B217, B269**.)

B358   [*Sonata for Harp* review] *El Nacional* (Mexico City), 23 October 1951.

Quoted in **B11** Antheil, review reports that the sonata [**W42b**] by the Australian
composer from Melbourne, around forty years old [38], "was a surprise for its
modernity in harmony".

B359   [*Sonata for Harp* review] Quoted in *American Composers Alliance
Bulletin* 7, no. 4 (1958), p. 23.

Senor Zabaleta performed the Glanville-Hicks sonata (**W42f**), an interesting and
beguiling work he introduced six years ago. It was a pleasure to hear the melodic
subtlety and variety of gentle hues in the "Pastorale" [second movement].

B360   Stanberg, Andrea K. "Australian Female Composers: A Resource
Kit." Unpublished B.M.E. Research Project, New South Wales State
Conservatorium of Music, Sydney, 1987. Pp. 13-14, 62-74.

Resource kit for classroom teachers includes good biography of Glanville-Hicks (and
ten others), excerpt from *The Transposed Heads* score (**W46**), style analysis, list of
works, and discography.

B361   Stern, Susan. *Women Composers: A Handbook.* Metuchen, NJ:
Scarecrow Press, 1978.

Author lists thirteen sources of information on Glanville-Hicks, in another (like
B187, B355) pre-Cohen (**B67**) bibliography.

B362   Stewart-Green, Miriam. "Consider These Creators." *American Music
Teacher* 25, no. 3 (January 1976), p. 9-12.

Glanville-Hicks is one of the women composers in the contemporary or modern style who have achieved "lyricism with strength through the musical language of the individual."

B363 _____. "Women Composers' Songs: An International Selective List, 1098-1980." In *The Musical Woman, An International Perspective, 1983* (**B265**), p. 315-16.

List includes *Frolic* (**W9**), *Come Sleep* (**W8**), and Nanda's aria "Lovesick" from *The Transposed Heads* (**W46**) and gives author of text, range, suitability for male or female singer, description of overall style, and publishers.

B364 _____. *Women Composers: A Checklist of Works for the Solo Voice.* Boston: G. K. Hall, 1981. P. 31, 168, 192, 223.

References to Glanville-Hicks include: a resumé of number of works in each vocal genre, with publishers and library locations; and listings of titles under cantata, song cycles, and songs with instruments.

B365 Stuckenschmidt, H. H. "Amsterdam Host to I.S.C.M." *Musical America* 68 (August 1948), p. 6.

The *Concertino da camera* (**W33a**), an independent entry from Australian-born composer P. Glanville-Hicks, reflected the weaknesses of a style which develops from the composition school of Nadia Boulanger and sometimes from a misunderstanding of Stravinsky. Review is on same page with Glanville-Hicks's own review of the Festival [**G28**]. (Copy is in **A3**.)

B366 Sykes, Jill. "Chilling Night of the Owl." *The Sun-Herald* (Sydney), 12 July 1987, p. 101.

The *Concertino da camera* (**W33e**) "bounded along with verve and personality--no need for a conductor there." (Title refers to songs by Vincent Plush on same program.)

B367 _____. "Peggy Glanville-Hicks." *APRA Journal* 2, no. 10 (1982), p. 14-15.

Article in journal of the Australasian Performing Right Association, Ltd. (and published near Sydney) is based on interview with the composer. Article surveys her "global" career and focuses on performing rights and copyright protection in an age of tape recorders and photostat copiers. One of her works [*Sonata for Harp*] has been used as a test piece in harp competitions for 20 years, she says, but the publishers have sold less than 100 copies. While Glanville-Hicks approves of recordings as a means of communicating with the general listener, she treasures the beautiful French edition of one of her compositions [*Concertino da Camera* , which has pride of place on her piano. So far, only a few of her works have been performed in Australia, but she says, "I would rather be appreciated by my colleagues than by a dubious public." Article includes a recent close-up photo of the composer.

B368 Tani, Gino. "Acclamati ieri a Spoleto i balletti da camera di John Butler." *Il messaggero* (Rome), 11 June 1958, p. 3.

Review mentions Glanville-Hicks as one of three composers of Butler's ballet tryptich *Triad* (**W59a**). Her music for *Masque of the Wild Man* (**W55a**) reflects certain musics of the thirteenth and fifteenth centuries. (Clipping is in **A3e**.)

B369 Taruskan, Richard. Review of Rzewski *Antigone-Legend* recording. *Opus* 4, no. 2 (February 1988), p. 4.

Glanville-Hicks [in *Nausicaa*, **W62**] is the composer of one of several recent "noble failures" in the "effort to recapture the incantatory magic of the music-cum-ritual of ancient Greece".

B370 Taubman, Howard. "4 Chamber Ballets by Butler Presented at Spoleto Festival." *New York Times*, 12 June 1958, p. 35.

Review by the paper's drama critic of *Triad* (**W59a**) and *Masque of the Wild Man* (**W55a**) reports that the score of *Masque*, "written in a few days, had color and rhythmic life." The dancing had "force and vitality, though stated rather broadly." *Triad*, the longest ballet, had "some touching lyrical moments" by the dancers, and a score put together from music by Prokofieff, Tailleferre, Glanville-Hicks, and Ellington.

B371 _____. "New Festival in Old Town." Ibid., Sunday, 15 June 1958, sect. 2, p. 9.

Review of Spoleto Festival of Two Worlds only mentions Glanville-Hicks as one of the "contemporary composers" represented (with Lee Holby, Valentino Bucchi, Duke Ellington, and Stanley Hollingsworth). Her ballets are not named (*see* preceding entry) but the restoration of the Teatro Caio Melisso, where they were presented, is described.

B372 _____. "Opera Premiere: Peggy Glanville-Hicks' 'Transposed Heads.' " Ibid., 11 February 1958, p. 36.

Review of New York premiere of *The Transposed Heads* (**W46b**) finds the music's orientalisms "repetitive and bare," not revolutionary as the composer believes (she says she has "gradually shed the harmonic dictatorship peculiar to modernists"--he quotes extensively from **G689**). This production's staging was "ingenious," with "delightfully evocative" costumes and props from India. Hindu folk and classical music sources, melismatic writing, many percussion instruments, and transparent "orchestral tissue" help give the music an Eastern cast (sometimes reminiscent of Slavic dance and American jazz). Two "moody, impetuous" Hindu men, in an excess of religious devotion and friendship, cut off their own heads with a huge sword. A "sensible goddess" puts things right, but a poor, blundering girl transposes the heads, fixing the husband's head on the world-be lover's body and vice-versa. (Copies are in **A3** and **A13c**.)

B373 _____. "Opera: Two Premieres, 'Glittering Gate' and "Rapunzel' at 'Y'." Ibid., 15 May 1959, p. 25.

Libretto for *The Glittering Gate* (**W52a**), based on Lord Dunsany's amusing fantasy, is not much more than a drawn-out anecdote with a mildly surprising ending. Music has melodic grace but adds nothing to the story and characters. (Review is accompanied by photo of David Smith as Jim.) (Clipping is in **A3**.)

B374   "Theme of Nausicaa Not Powerful Enough for Opera." *The Times* (London), 25 August 1961, p. 5.

Signed "from our Athens correspondent," lengthy review reports of **W62a** reports that Greek critics seemed to agree that the theme "was not powerful enough--or was not handled forcibly enough by the anonymous librettist--for operatic treatment." The audience of 4,500 was "warmly receptive" and soloists and chorus were acclaimed. Glanville-Hicks used folk song of various regions in Greece and believes that it "belongs to the common ancient classicism" of Asia the unbroken tradition of which is heard in India. (Review is quoted, along with some of the Greek critics, in **G696**, and almost in full in **B269**.

B375   Thompson, Oscar. "Peggy Glanville-Hicks." *The International Cyclopedia of Music and Musicians*. 11th edn. Ed. Bruce Bohle. New York, Toronto: Dodd, Mead; London: J. M. Dent & Sons, 1985. P. 827-8.

Brief biography and classified list of works, given as in **B297**, are repeated from the 8th through 10th edns., 1964-1975; entry is considerably briefer in the 6th and 7th edns., 1952 and 1956. (Although Hixon and Hennessee (**B187**) report that about ten percent of women musicians' names in the 9th edn were omitted from the 10th edn., Glanville-Hicks remained.)

B376   Thomson, Virgil. "American Music: Original and Exciting." *New York Herald Tribune*, 23 February 1953, p. 11.

Letters from Morocco (**W44a**) are "six longish songs for tenor and orchestra composed in frank (and often imaginative, always agreeable) evocation of North African musical ways." Texts are beautiful descriptions of Morocco culled from letters of Paul Bowles. The music, "in at least two cases, is poetically touching." The work "is scored with a sure hand, and its application of Arabic vocal melisma to English words gives pungent flavor."

B377   _____. *American Music Since 1910*. New York: Holt, Rinehart and Winston, [1971]. P. 8, 12, 88.

Glanville-Hicks "has given us practical works in the operatic format" (p. 8). Her own musical idiom from Indian, North African, and Greek elements "has proved useful in ballet and English-language opera" (p. 12). Her operas "have undeniable quality" (p. 88).

B378   _____. "Colorado Springs Cultivates String Playing and New Music." *New York Herald Tribune*, Sunday, 27 August 1950, sect. 5, p. 5.

The *Thomsoniana* (**W38b**), "heard last spring from a broadcast," are "a skit pulled off with no mean skill" but the work "has more character and musical power in it than one might expect of a good joke" and is not frivolous. (Review is quoted in **B11**.)

B379   _____. " 'Greatest Music Teacher'--At 75." *New York Times*, Sunday, 4 February 1962, sect. 6, p. 24, 33, 35. Rpt. *Music Educators' Journal* 49, no. 2 (September-October 1962), p. 42-4; *Piano Quarterly* 39 (January-March 1962), p. 16-19; and in *The Virgil Thomson Reader* (Boston, 1981), p. 389-93.

Glanville-Hicks was one of Nadia Boulanger's students in the "batch" of the 1920s and 1930s.

B380 _____. "Music." In *Quality*. Ed. Louis Kronenberger. New York: Balance House, 1967.

Thomson asserts that, given the "rarity" of women composers, they will not soon make the "harmful impact" some men (he mentions Sir Thomas Beecham) predict. "America welcomes them . . . but does not promote their works." Glanville-Hicks and others "are quality workmen who merit praise rather than unfair treatment."

B381 _____. "New Music Society." *New York Herald Tribune*, 11 March 1952, p. 14.

The "charm" of the *Sonata for Harp* (**W42c**), "like the harp itself, could have been wearing" except for the work's brevity. "In a repertory lacking music of much depth her sonata stands forth for neat poetry and elegance of statement."

B382 _____. *Selected Letters*. Ed. Tim Page and Vanessa Weeks Page. New York: Summit Books, 1988. P. 149, 272, 288.

Thomson built up a distinguished music department for the *Herald Tribune*, Glanville-Hicks being among the contributors. He writes to Ernst Bacon, 22 December 1953: "I must say that Peggy Glanville-Hicks' review [**G483**] of your choral piece (I was out of town myself) seems a little severe to me, but she did say that the audience liked it, thus attesting, as a good reporter, that the work was a success with the public. . . . I do not know how to insure artists against an unfavorable review other than by engaging only musicians to write reviews and demanding of them that they express their honest opinion in correct English." With a letter to Brazilian diplomat Margareda Guedes Nogueira, 20 September 1955, editor identifies her as the second wife of English composer and pianist Stanley Bate, whose first wife was Glanville-Hicks.

B383 _____. *Virgil Thomson*. New York: Alfred A. Knopf, 1966. P. 334, 343-5.

Glanville-Hicks, one of Thomson's "panel of music writers" for the *Herald Tribune*, was one of several composers from England who spent the war here, along with Britten, Arnell, and Stanley Bate (her husband). Bate drank and quarrelled (his wife "backed him up loyally" in his war against Britten and the musical Establishment), and eventually went back to England. Glanville-Hicks "stayed here, supporting herself by writing articles and by copying music, achieved distinction as a composer, and became a citizen." She was "thin, passionate, tireless, and insistent." She wrote for the *Herald Tribune* and for magazines, copied music, managed concerts, ran everybody's errands, went on lecture tours by bus in the Dakotas, composed documentary films for UNICEF, made musicological trips to India for the Rockefeller Foundation, and saw other people's music through the perils of recording. She wrote a great deal of music, got it published and recorded, and grew into an opera composer of marked originality. "She believed, upon some evidence, that the world was out to crush women composers." She was an indispensable colleague. "Even from Greece, where she now lives (still frugally), she continues to fulminate and to be useful. Her generosity is no more to be stopped than her scolding ways. And she remains a memorable composer."

B384 _____. "WNYC Music Festival." *New York Herald Tribune*, 13 February 1953, p. 13.

The *Sonata for Piano and Percussion* (**W43b**) was the most impressive of the "rehearings" on the program. "Its rhythmic texture is sophisticated, its orchestral color picturesque and far from crude. The slow movement is original and deeply poetic" and the other two less mysterious and stimulating though "evocative." (Review is quoted in **B11** and **B384**.)

B385   " 'Thomsoniana' Played: Peggy Glanville-Hicks' Suite Heard at Eastman Festival." *New York Times*, 2 May 1958, p. 31.

Signed by a "special correspondent" (perhaps the composer?), the article is an announcement of the performance (**W38e**) rather than a review. (Clipping is in **A13c**.)

B386   Tidemann, Harold. "Polished Singing in Operas." Adelaide *Advertiser*, 15 March 1972.

The Glittering Gate (**W52b**) in Australian premiere featured "skillful pianist Mary Handley" with percussion and two singers, performing during the lunch hour yesterday.

B387   Toop, Richard. "Opera Mode: Australian Song Recital." *Sydney Morning Herald*, 24 June 1986, p. 16.

Thirteen Ways of Looking at a Blackbird (**W37d**), Glanville-Hicks's setting of Wallace Stevens's much-set poem, did not particularly impress this reviewer [who is a musicologist at the New South Wales Conservatorium].

B388   " 'Transposed Heads,' New Opera, is Sung." *New York Times*, 4 April 1954, p. 86.

Article by a "special correspondent" (the composer?) is announcement of Louisville premiere, not a review, and refers to a recent Barcelona performance (?) of *Sinfonia da Pacifica*. (Clipping is in **A13c**.)

B389   Trimble, Lester. "New Compositions Played at Concert." *New York Herald Tribune*, 26 January 1956, p. 19.

Etruscan Concerto (**W48a**) is an ingratiating work, full of the warmth and ebullience of the Mediterranean, and "riotously rhythmic in its speedy movements. It is all very delicately exotic, and yet quite clear and Anglo-Saxon in its means." Review (signed L. T.) is quoted in **B390** below. (Clipping is in **A13c**.)

B390   Truax, Carol. "Report of ACA-Sponsored Concerts." *American Composers Alliance Bulletin* 5, no. 4 (1956), pp. 11-12.

Concert 25 January 1956 was arranged by Peggy Glanville-Hicks; *Etruscan Concerto* (**W48a**) was included on program, which is reprinted here. Two reviews are quoted at length, by Schonberg (**B342**) and Trimble (**B389**).

B391   Uglow, Jennifer S. *The International Dictionary of Women's Biography*. New York: Continuum, 1982. P. 195.

Short entry lists a few works and notes that "her instrumental music, especially of the 1950s, shows a lively concern for expanding the repertories for percussion and harp."

B392 "U.S. Opera in Greek Debut." *New York Times,* 21 August 1961, p. 23.

Announcement reports that Glanville-Hicks, "American composer," attended the *Nausicaa* premiere (**W62a**), that the opera was praised by the critics, and that "Leressa" [i.e., Teresa] Stratas, a Greek-Canadian, sang the lead role. (Copy is in **A13c**).

B393 Van Lier, Bertus. "Muziekfeest I.S.C.M., Tweede en laatste Kamermuziekavond." *Het Parool* (Amsterdam), 11 June 1948, p. 3.

The "airy" *Concertino da camera* (**W33a**) "had a striking success due to the cheerful almost exuberant character of the fast movements, which framed a poetic Adagio." It was not "modern" enough to sound at home at the festival, but it was "too playful" to question it. (**B11** quotes this in Dutch.)

B394 Vinton, John. *Dictionary of Contemporary Music.* New York: Dutton, 1974. P. 272.

Short biography is followed by a list of principal compositions and a reference to *Composers of the Americas* (**B81**) for a "list to 1967."

B395 Wagner, Eve. "Grand Opera on a Chamber Music Scale." *The Australian,* 29 June 1970, p. 6.

Glanville-Hicks's own description of *The Transposed Heads* is used as the title of this review (of **W46c**). The opera is a suitable choice for a university setting, as an "intriguing, interesting, and often entertaining experiment." There is too much material in too little space, however, and the story "lacks emotional commitment."

B396 Walker, Danton. "Broadway." *New York Daily News,* 12 February 1958.

Columnist observes that "Transposed Heads" sounds like an Alfred Hitchcock TV show but is a new two-act opera at the Phoenix Theatre (**W46b**). "It won't set the North River afire, but it's more interesting than [Barber's] 'Vanessa' " (which had played there earlier). (Clipping is in **A3**; review is quoted in **B296**.)

B397 Whittington, Stephen. "Conductor Draws Together Cohesive Performance." Adelaide *Advertiser,* 22 September 1987, p. 15.

The *Choral Suite* (**W19c**) is "well crafted and effectively scored with an elaborate concertante part for oboe." Though it is a relatively early work and shows no particularly individual compositional "voice," it should certainly find a place in the scarcely superabundant catalogue of good Australian choral music.

B398 *Who's Who in America.* 43rd edn. (1984-85). Chicago: Marquis, 1984.

Glanville-Hicks is first listed in the 38th edn. (1974-75)--about the time of her move from Athens to Sydney--and then in the 39th (1976-77), 40th (1978-79), 41st (1980-81) and 42nd (1982-83) edns.

B399 *Who's Who in Music.* New York: Hafner, 1962. P. 82.

Glanville-Hicks was a music critic on the *Herald Tribune*, her style is "non dissonant avant-garde," and her works include two Sonatinas.

B400   *Who's Who of American Women.* 7th edn. (1972-73). Chicago: Marquis, 1971.

Glanville-Hicks, "composer, music critic," is also in the 2nd edn. (1961-62), 3rd (1964-65), 4th (1966-67), and 6th (1970-71) edns. Entry includes her parents' names, Ernest and Myrtle (Bailey) Glanville-Hicks. It dates her coming to the U. S. as 1940, lists her professional activities and organizations, names her major works, performances, commissions, and awards, and refers to her writings on music.

B401   Williams, Melanie. "The Songs of Peggy Glanville-Hicks." Unpublished D.M.A.thesis [i.e., research project], University of Illinois, 1983.

In the first 142 pages, a "Brief Biography of the Composer" is followed by discussion of "The Songs and Their Poets." On the next 87 pages are reproduced the scores of 35 songs--W7-10, W29, W31, W32, W37, and W38. "In setting the works of American and British poets, the composer is able to identify herself with the intrinsic style of a text . . . so that the music seems a natural and expressive emanation." Most striking characteristics are modality and economy of means.

B402   Winstanley, Margaret. "Works of Contemporary Australian Composers to Get An Airing." *West Australian Music Maker* 2, no. 4 (July/August 1984), p. 31.

Article in program guide of Australian Broadcasting Corp. announces that violist Keith Crellin and the West Australian Symphony Orchestra, directed by Patrick Thomas, will record the *Concerto Romantico* (**W51**), along with other Australian music, on August 6. Glanville-Hicks, Australian veteran composer with a greater reputation overseas than in her own country, and one of the few women to gain an international reputation as an opera composer, will be in Perth for the occasion--and for the orchestra's recording of *The Transposed Heads* (**W46d**) in September.

B403   "Women in Music: Peggy Glanville-Hicks." *BMI, The Many Worlds of Music,* 1977, issue 4, p. 19.

Article, accompanied by photograph, uses quotes from Glanville-Hicks on her childhood piano playing and writing of music. On the development of her style from the 1940s Antheil (**B11**) is quoted on her need to develop a body of work that is deeply personal. She spent part of each year in New York City and the rest in "faraway places," and her work "reflects where she's been."

B404   Wood, Elizabeth. *The New Grove Dictionary of American Music.* Ed. H. Wiley Hitchcock and Stanley Sadie. London: Macmillan, 1986. Vol. 2, p. 227.

Article is the same as in *The New Grove*, **B405** below.

B405   _____. "Peggy Glanville-Hicks." *The New Grove Dictionary of Music and Musicians.* Ed. Stanley Sadie. London: Macmillan, 1980. Vol. 7, p. 422.

Substantial (and reliable) article--almost a full page--provides a biography to about 1972, a "selective list" of works, and a brief bibliography: **G690, B11, B98, B133 B232-233,** and **B263.** During her American years 1942 to 1959 "many of her major works were composed, and she was engaged in notable activities for the propagation of new music and the sponsorship of young composers."

B406 "The World Premiere of 'Nausicaa': A Real Triumph for the 'Young' Festival." *Athens News,* 20 August 1961.

Even if the Athens press will not accept this opera **(W62a)** to an original if audacious libretto by Robert Graves, to this international festival-minded critic and reporter, *Nausicaa* was 100 percent successful. Composer knows Greek folklore and her score recaptures some of the noble vigor of Greece. The story may be sacriligious to historians, but the idea that a woman might have written the *The Odyssey* has a certain fascination and appeal. (Review is quoted in English in **B269.**)

B407 "Young Composer's Scholarship Coveted Award for Melbourne Girl." *The Australian Musical News* 26 (1 August 1936), p. 29.

Glanville-Hicks has won her fifth scholarship at the Royal College of Music, a traveling scholarship, and will leave London in October for advanced study of composition in Budapest and Vienna. Several of her compositions were played in an Empire broadcast last year. Short article is accompanied by a current photograph of her.

B408 "Young Melbourne Composer Peggy Glanville Hicks Wins Scholarship." Ibid., 22 (1 October 1932), p. 7-8.

Glanville-Hicks, who sailed for London with her mother on 13 June, arriving 21 July, to study composition and piano at the Royal College of Music, has cabeled her family that she has won the new Carlotta Rowe Scholarship with an annual value of £85, to continue her studies. She is to study composition with Vaughan Williams and R. O. Morris and piano with Australian composer Arthur Benjamin. Many great composers and musicians (Hubert Clifford, Cyril Scott, H. A. Thomson, Arnold Bax, and others) "have commented very favourably" on her composition and her piano. She credits her Melbourne teachers Fritz Hart (composition), who is "very favoured and distinguished" in London, and Waldemar Seidel (piano). Mrs. James Dyer (*see* A3), while Acting Lady Mayoress in Melbourne, had forwarded ten of Glanville-Hicks's compositions to London in hopes of a scholarship award, but Glanville-Hicks found upon arrival that she had to enter the competition with talent from the entire United Kingdom. She began work on a choral arrangement of Tagore's "Fruit Gathering" **[W3]** .

B409 Zingel, Hans Joachim. *Harfenmusik: Verzeichnis der gedruckten und zur Zeit greifbaren Literatur für Pedalharfe.* Hofheim am Taunus: Hofmeister, 1965. P. 9.

Index of published harp music lists Glanville-Hicks's *Sonata* **(W42)** under "Soli, Originale."

B410 _____. *Lexikon der Harfe.* Laaber: Verlag Dr. Henning Müller-Buscher, 1977. P. 70.

Glanville-Hicks, born in Australia and living in America, is the composer of a *Sonata* **(W42)** that is well known.

Archival Resources

These archival materials are listed by library, in alphabetical order by location and library name (with international library sigla, as in *RISM*, in parentheses). List represents holdings as of August 1988. (Indiana University in Bloomington, listed in **B35**, no longer has any holdings.) References with a **W** are to "Works and Performances," with a **D** to the "Discography," with a **G** to "Bibliography by Glanville-Hicks," and with a **B** to "Bibliography About Glanville-Hicks."

AUSTRALIA

A1 Canberra, ACT. National Film and Sound Archive. "Peggy Glanville-Hicks," film/video tape of the composer in interview by James Murdoch, 1982, for the Australia Council, 60 minutes. (The NFSA has offices also in Melbourne and Sydney and a viewing center in Perth.) Glanville-Hicks discusses: setting up a foundation for young composers; her book in progress; return to Australia; life in Greece; Asian music and the melody-rhythm structure as a way out of the building without windows (atonalism); *Nausicaa; The Transposed Heads; The Glit-tering Gate; Sappho;* Fritz Hart; Thomas Mann, Robert Graves; Lawrence Durrell; Thornton Wilder; Greek *demotic* music; John Butler; Teresa Stratas; Marayana Menon; music of India; New York activities; Museum of Modern Art concerts; Composers Forum; the theremin recital [**G54**]; Leopold Stokowski; need for percussion players and instruments; the Royal College of Music; Constant Lambert; Vaughan Williams; Sir Adrian Boult; and Nadia Boulanger; her favorites among her own works ("It's always the one you haven't written, isn't it?"); which ones "work" the best (*The Transposed Heads, Letters from Morocco, Nausicaa);* and contemporary Australian music.

A2 Canberra, ACT. National Library of Australia (**CAnl**).

  A2a Music Section. Clipping file contains copies of Australian concert reviews and publicity.

A2b   Oral History Section. (1) Audio tape and transcript of Glanville-Hicks interviewed by Diana Ritch, 6 July 1983. Subjects covered are: her education in London, study with Wellesz, then Boulanger, the New York years (*Herald Tribune,* Composers Forum, concerts at the Museum of Modern Art, living in Greenwich Village, composing of smaller works and U. N. film music), study of Indian musics, melody and rhythm, *The Transposed Heads,* her study of Eastern musics (Bartok's tapes at the Library of Congress), life in Greece, *Nausicaa,* comparison of music with architecture (arch and cantilever), percussion as music's root and foundation, her three houses in Greece, return to Australia, demise [not true] of the Australia Music Centre, the lack of twentieth-century music performances, and the need for performances of Australian works. (2) "Peggy Glanville-Hicks," BMI brochure 1969 (**B297**).

A2c   Film (video recording), "Australian Women Composers" by Adele Sztar, 1983 (45 min.). Documentary on women composers in Australia from ca. 1900 uses their music, including *The Transposed Heads* (**D21**), as background to the narration.

A3   Melbourne, VIC. State Library of Victoria (**Msl**). Peggy Glanville-Hicks Collection. Partial inventory in **B104**.

A3a   Scores of: *Ballade,* **W31**; *Be Still You Little Leaves,* **W7**; *Choral Suite,* **W19**; *Come Sleep,* **W8**; *Concertino da Camera,* **W33** (two copies, one the "composer's copy" with her corrections, plus vocal and instrumental parts); *Concerto Romantico,* **W51**; *Etruscan Concerto,* **W48**; *Five Songs,* **W29**; *Frolic,* **W9**; *Gymnopédie No. 1,* **W48**; *Letters from Morocco,* **W44**; *Musica Antiqua No. 1,* **W53**; *Nausicaa,* **W62**; *Pastorale,* **W5**; *Profiles from China,* **W33**; *Rest,* **W10**; *Sonata for Harp,* **W42**; *Sonata for Piano and Percussion,* **W43**; *Thirteen Ways of Looking at a Blackbird,* **W37**; *Trio for Pipies,* **W11**; *Thomsoniana,* **W38**.

A3b   Miscellaneous materials, 1932-1969: (1) Poster for "Complimentary Farewell Concert to Miss Peggy Glanville-Hicks, the Young Composer-Pianiste," 2 June 1932 (*see* **W2a**). (2) Program for ISCM concert, London, 20 June 1938, including *Choral Suite* (**W19a**). (3) Clippings of her *New York Herald Tribune* reviews, 1947-54, *Musical America* reviews, 1949-50, and *Cue* articles, 1949-50. (4) Two letters from Ralph Vaughan Williams (1950, 1954). (5) Copy of "This I Believe," radio script (3'40") by Glanville-Hicks, submitted ca. June 1954 to Raymond Swing, editor, CBS. (6) "The Women of Andros," libretto by Glanville-Hicks for an opera in five scenes, typescript. (7) Correspondence from Thornton Wilder and Isobel Wilder (1955-56) denying Glanville-Hicks permission to use *The Women of Andros.* (8) Composer brochures from the 1950s and 1960s--**B78 B295, B296, B297**--and typescript drafts of material. (9) Correspondence with Leopold Stokowski (1953), Carlo Bussotti (1953), Roland Hayes (1953), Nicanor Zabaleta (1953, 1955), Colin McPhee (n.d.), Paul Bowles (1953, 1954, 1966, 1967). (10) Newspaper photos of Glanville-Hicks, Newell Jenkins, and other "distinguished villagers" who will attend Greenwich Village's "Masquerade" evening festival 12 June 1959. (11) Copy of article "H. MOYEIKH EAN APXITEK-TONIKH [Music as Architecture]," *Architectoniki [Architecture, Art, and Decoration]* 27 (May-June 1961), p. 49-51, and correspon-dence with editor about article. (12) Notification of $500 award from William and Noma Copley Foundation, June 1961, "for your past achievements in the field of music composition."

A3c   Materials on *The Transposed Heads,* **W46,** and 1954 Louisville production, **W46a:** (1) Copies of publicity and reviews. (2) Letters from Moritz Bomhard, 1954-55, 1958. (3) Libretto (by Glanville-Hicks) with pencilled corrections (copy varies somewhat from published score). (4) Bomhard's German translation of libretto. (5) Program notes by Glanville-Hicks. (6) Correspondence with Schirmer on score. (7) Correspondence and other materials concerning recording (**D21**).

A3d   Materials on *The Transposed Heads,* 1958 New York production, **W46b:** (1) Copies of publicity and reviews. (2) Correspondence 1957-1958 with Santha Rama Rau Bowers and Maryana (Mrs. Rehka) Menon concerning costumes from India. (3) Bills from Madras, India, for costumes. (4) Correspondence concerning fund-raising by Contemporary Music Society, Inc., for production: carbon copies of Glanville-Hicks's typewritten fund-raising letters to individuals (same letter, different addresses); correspondence about institutional funds (Ditson Fund, William Hale Harkness Foundation); correspondence with Leopold Stokowski (CMS president) and Ralph Backlund (secretary). (5) Typescripts of press releases, 25 November 1957 (**B62**) and 26 December 1957 (**B307**). (6) Correspondence with Ross Parmenter concerning her *New York Times* article (**G689**). (7) Reviews: of "Le Teste scambiate," *La Scala* magazine (n.d., n.p.). (8) Letter to Paul Henry Lang.

A3e   Correspondence and press clippings on 1958 Spoleto Festival, *Masque of the Wild Man,* **W55a** and *Triad,* **W59a:** (1) Copies of reviews. (2) Copy of publicity piece "Stasera al teatro Caio Melisso 'prima' dei balletti di John Butler," *Giornale del mattino,* 10 June 1958, p. 5.

A3f   Materials on *The Glittering Gate* (**W52**) and its performances (**W52a, W52b**): (1) Photocopy of letter from Lord Dunsany (author), 4 November 1927, (not to Glanville-Hicks) saying *Glittering*

Gate was his first play and the first to be produced. (2) Correspondence of Glanville-Hicks and attorney for Lord Dunsany's estate. (3) Correspondence with Oliver Daniel, on necessity to perform opera before exclusivity contract expires. (4) Correspondence with many potential contributors before 1959 New York production. (5) Copy of agreement with American Guild of Musical Artists for production (**W52a**), and other documents. (6) Copies of publicity pieces and reviews of this 1959 production and of 1972 Adelaide Festival production (**W52b**).

A3g   Materials on *Nausicaa* (**W62**), 1961 premiere (**W62a**), and recording (**D7**): (1) Correspondence with: Robert Graves, Alastair Reid, Maria Callas, John Butler, Virgil Thomson, *Nausicaa* principals, Franco Colombo, Roger Goeb, Carlos Surinach, Kimon Vourloumis, Andreas Nomikos, Trudy Goth, Oliver Daniel, Muriel Francis, Edgar Vincent, Jane Morton, Herbert Graf, Dorle Soria, Peter Gradenwitz, James Fassett, Robert Evett, Harold Schonberg, Jani Christou, Gorgo Siciliano, and others. (2) Typescript of opera synopsis (for program?). (3) BMI press release about performance, typescript, 3 pp., and 11-p. handwritten list of publications (for press release?). (4) Copies of Athens reviews and related materials, many with English translations (besides **B** listings under **W62a**): Dion Giatris," 'Nausicaa': The World Premiere of the Work of Miss P. Glanville-Hicks," *To Vima* (Athens), 22 August 1961; Spyros Melas, "A Work," *Estia*, 22 August 1961, anonymous English translation (typescript); F. Anogeianakis, " 'Nausicaa' by P. Glanville-Hicks," *Etnos* (Athens), 26 August 1961, English translation by Kate Fatourou (typescript). (5) Copies of published publicity articles and reviews (besides **B** listings): Maurice Rapin, " 'Nausicaa' sera créé au Festival d'Athènes," *Le Figaro* [n.d.]; "Teresa Triumphs," Toronto *Telegram* , 21 August 1961; "Stratas in Greece," Toronto *Globe and Mail,* 22 August 1961; "Toronto Opera Singer Big Success in Greece, *Guardian* (Guelph, Ontario), 24 August 1961; articles from Zagreb *Telegram,* 6 October 1961, and Belgrade *Borba*, 8 October 1961 (in French translation); paragraph on Butler from *Dance News*, October 1961; paragraph from *Show Business Illustrated* (n.d.), p. 11; rehearsal announcement in *Variety*, 9 August 1961; " 'Nausicaa': An American Premier in Greece." *Progress-Index* (Petersburg, VA), 20 August 1961; review in *Die Wochen-Presse*, Vienna, 2 September 1961; announcement in Vienna *Abend Zeitung*, 16 August 1961, and review, 28 August. (6) Article "Composer Facing Failing Eyesight," *Australia* [blank, 1961]. (7) Copies of published record reviews (besides **B** listings under **D7**): Ralph Jones, "The New Records," August 1964 [publication unnamed]; Thomas B. Sherman, "Music and the Arts: The Opera 'Nausicaa' by Peggy Glanville-Hicks," *St. Louis Post-Dispatch*, Sunday [n. d.], p. 5C.

A3h   Materials on *Sappho* (**W64**): Correspondence (1962-64) with Lawrence Durrell, Q. Eaton, Metropolitan Opera (Rudolf Bing's assistant), Kurt Herbert Adler, Franco Colombo.

A3i   Materials on *A Season in Hell* (**W65a**): Correspondence with Mrs. [Rebekah] Harkness, John Butler, and others; reviews and publicity.

A3j   Correspondence from the early 1970s with: Joyce McGrath, George Dreyfus, James Murdoch, Anthony Steel (Adelaide Festival), Elizabeth Wood (about *New Grove* article, **B405**), Marayana Menon, and others.

A3k   Typed transcript of interview with Glanville-Hicks by Joyce McGrath, Director, Music and Performing Arts Library of the State Library of Victoria. Recorded in Woollarha (Sydney), 24 August 1970, the day of Glanville-Hicks's departure for India and Athens, she discusses two main topics: her Composers Forum activities and how a similar project could be staged in Australia; and her *Thomsoniana* and its tendency to scandalize audiences.

A3l   Materials from the 1980s: (**1**) Audio tape of Glanville-Hicks interviewed by Mary-Lou Jelbart, 1982 (15 min.). (**2**) Audio tape of Glanville-Hicks interviewed by James Mellon (80 min.) (**3**) Program of *Etruscan Concerto* performance, **W48b**. (**4**) Program from 1985 New Moods Arts Festival concert (**W27e, W42m, W44d**). (**5**) Program from 1985 Eureka Ensemble concert (**W44d**). (**6**) Program of 1985 Melbourne exhibit, "The Work of Louise Hanson-Dyer and the Lyrebird Press," including materials from **A9**. (**7**) Program from 1986 Adelaide Festival. (**8**) Miscellaneous reviews, one with short note from Maria Prerauer, music critic of *The Australian*, 1986. (**9**) Newspaper photo of Rodney Waterman and Roger Glanville-Hicks (nephew) performing early music, 1981.

A4   Melbourne, VIC. State Library of Victoria (**Msl**) and LaTrobe Library. Bernard Heinze Collection (uncatalogued): correspondence and memorabilia relating to Glanville-Hicks.

A5   Sydney, NSW. Australia Council Library (**Sac**). Small clipping file of reviews of Australian concerts in the 1970s and 1980s.

A6   Sydney, NSW. Australian Music Centre (**Smc**). Holdings include:

A6a   Scores and parts of several works, including *Trio for Pipes* (**W11**), *Musica Antiqua No. 1* (**W53**), and *Girondelle for Giraffes* (**W67**).

A6b   Audio tape of performance of *Concerto Romantico* (**W51c**) by
Keith Crellin, viola, with Tasmanian Symphony Orchestra, Vanco
Cavdarski, conductor (n.d.).

A6c   Large clipping file of Australian and American publicity, reviews,
and brochures, including "Composer for Theatre" (**B78**) and BMI
brochure (**B297**), both 1969.

A6d   Interview by Terry Torpey, interspersed with excerpts from
recordings of her music (**D2, D3, D7, D17**) and Antheil's *Ballet
mécanique*, broadcast on 2MBS-FM Sydney, 19 September 1977
(110 min.) Glanville-Hicks discusses *The Transposed Heads*,
Robert Graves, *Nausicaa*, scale revision (pruning the diatonic
branch off the musical tree), Bartok's tapes in Library of Congress
archives, Antheil, McPhee, Hovhaness, Fritz Hart, Vaughan
Williams, and Boulanger.

A7   Sydney, NSW. Sydney Opera House. Denis Wolanski Library and
Archives of the Performing Arts (**Swl**): clipping file (including **B13**,
found nowhere else).

A8   Sydney, NSW. Unpublished interview of Glanville-Hicks by Peter
Dunbar-Hall, G. Hodge, and A. Pollak. Typescript transcription in
possession of Dunbar-Hall, Lecturer in Music Education, New South
Wales State Conservatorium of Music.

MONACO

A9   L'Oiseau-lyre Library. Private collection. Holdings include: Louise
Hanson-Dyer letters and memorabilia, including letters from Glanville-
Hicks, all undated, from Earls Court, and one of 9 August, New York
City (no year); copies of Glanville-Hicks's scores published by Éditions
de l'Oiseau-lyre or Lyrebird Press; original manuscripts for these works;
and original manuscripts of early works not published: *Sheiling Song*
(words by Fiona McLeod), *They are not long* (Ernest Dowson), *He
Reproves the Curlew* (W. B. Yeats), and *Choral Suite* (David McKee
Wright, *not* **W19**). Exhibit program in **A31(6)** lists some of the holdings.

UNITED STATES

A10 Louisville, KY. University of Louisville, School of Music Library (**Lou**):
archives contain letter from Glanville-Hicks to Robert Whitney (Music

Director, Louisville Orchestra) and copy of full score (manuscript) of *The Transposed Heads*

A11   New Haven, CT.   Yale University Music Library (**NH**).   Virgil Thomson Collection: about 100 letters from Glanville-Hicks to Thomson, 1940s to 1980s, from Reno, Alta (CA), New York, Delhi, Jamaica, Athens, and elsewhere.   There are also copies of two letters to her from Thomson. (There is some confusion of her materials with those of Mr. Granville Hicks of Grafton, NY, an English professor.)

A12   New York City.   Carl Haverlin Collection/BMI Archives.   Broadcast Music, Inc., 320 West Fifty-seventh Street, New York 10019.   Collection contains letters and autograph manuscripts of Glanville-Hicks, as listed in D. W. Krummel, *Bibliographical Handbook of American Music* (Urbana, IL, 1987), #1040.

A13   New York City.   New York Public Library (**NYp**).

   A13a   Correspondence file contains letters--one in ISCM file, one in Ross Lee Finney, about 85 in Composers Forum file: to Finney, other composers, Carleton Sprague Smith, other board members.

   A13b   Iconographic file contains photographs of Glanville-Hicks.

   A13c   Clipping file.   File contains performance reviews and publicity releases to 1958.

A14   Washington, D.C.   Library of Congress.   Music Division (**Wc**).

   A14a   Arnold Schoenberg Collection: contains one letter with multiple signatures (one of them Glanville-Hicks's).

   A14b   Old Correspondence Collection: contains thirteen letters by Glanville-Hicks, to Richard Hill, Harold Spivacke, dated 1954, 1956, 1957, 1958, 1962, about Bowles's Moroccan recordings, possibility of *Carlos Among the Candles* (**W63**) performance, *Nausicaa* recording, *Concerto Romantico* recording.   Also one 1972 from Australia, requesting Bowles's recordings for the Australia Music Centre.

Index

This index lists authors, book and periodical titles, composers, performers, titles of Glanville-Hicks's compositions and longer articles, and other significant categories. References to the "Biography" are indicated by the actual page number; items located in the other chapters are identified with the relevant mnemonic (**W, D, G, B, A**) and catalog number.

Perle, G273
Perlea, Joel, D18, D20
Persichetti, 22, G18, G197, G208, G567, G596
Persinger, Louis, G19
Persinger, Rolf, G19, G192
Pesce, Elizabeth, G241
Peter, Darrel, G452
Peters, Brandon, G63
Peters, Roberta, G445, G613
Peterson, Melody, B303
Petrak, Rudolf, G377
Pettis, Ashley, G333
Peyser, Joan, B304
Pfitzner, Hans, G475, G609
Pfohl, James Christian, W47a
Phillips, Burrill, G172, G568
Phillips, Edna, W49, W49a, G384, G684
Phillips, Linda, B305-306
Phoenix Theatre, 28, B307
Piano Concerto: see *Concerto No. 1,* W17, and *Etruscan Concerto,* W48
Piano Prelude, W2a, B75-76
Piano Quarterly, B379
Pickett, William, W46a
Pictures from Greece, B156
Pierce, Gayle, G631
Pierce, Willard, G144
Pierné, G83
Pijper, Willem, G601
Pike, Alfred, G639
Pillori, Constanza, G170
Piper, Colin, W43g
Pistelli, Angella, G646
Piston, Walter, 7, 19-20, G28, G73, G95, G114, G227, G352, G420, G569, G576, G596, G654
Pittaluga, G332, G644
Pizzetti, G2, G631
Plush, B5, B366, B388
Pobers, Miss, G32
Poem for Chorus and Orchestra, W6
Poetics: see *Profiles from China,* W32
Polia, Mildah, G64, G415
Poliakine, Douda, G635
Politikens (Copenhagen), B268
Pons, Lily, 23, G349
Pontzious, Richard, B308
Pool, Jeannie G., B309-310
Poot, G294
Populo, Il, B136
Porter, Quincy, G369, G596
Postman's Knock, The, W26
Poulenc, G21, G82, G92-93, G122, G141, G181, G318, G357, G415, G609, G642, G660, G685
Pouyat, Ivy, G401
Powers, Maxwell, G223
Prandelli, G347
Prelude and Presto for Ancient American Instruments, 27, W54, D8
Prelude and Scherzo, W21
Prelude for a Pensive Pupil, W56, D9-10

Prerauer, A31
Presser, William, G197
Price, James, W52a
Price, Loys, G44
Price, Nathan, G7, G631
Price, Robert, W52a
Price, Paul (Percussion Ensemble), W43d
Pritchett, Lizabeth, G184
Pro Arte Quartet, G126, G183
Pro Musica Antiqua, G462
Profiles from China, 7, 12, 32, W32, B4, B27, B47, B51, B55, B100, B168, B172, B303, B312, B340, B401, A3a
"Program Notes [for The Transposed Heads] by the Composer," G668, A3c(5)
Progress-Index (Petersburg, VA), A3g
Prokofiev, G2, G11, G16, G30, G42, G81, G114, G140, G143, G161, G227, G231, G371, G382, G429, G438, G628, G637, G667
Prostakoff, Joseph, W56
Puccini, G170, G252, G304, G360, G388, G414, G652, G695
Puerto Rico University Chorus, G453
Purcell, G58, G219, G235, G448, G643
Pusz, Richard, W43e

Q

Quantz, G364, G395
Quillian, James W., B312
Quilter, Roger, G92, G455
Quist, Margaret, G317

R

R. A. E.: see Ericson, Raymond A.
RIAS Orchestra, D18, D20
R. N. D.: see *Trouw*
Rabin, Michael, G182, G382
Rachmaninoff, G30, G50, G148, G209, G282, G477, G652
Radic, Thérèse, B314-315
Raimondi, Matthew, G374
Raines, Jean, B225
Rainier, Priaulx, 11, G265
Rameau, G141, G189, G296, G420
Ramirez, Coco & Tina, W55a
Ramus, Anne de, G616
Randolph, David, G486
Randolph Singers, G131
Ranieri, Vittoria de, G211
Raper, Mary, W38d
Rapin, Maurice, A3g
Rapoport, Eda, G471
Rappaport, Jerome, G437
Rathaus, Karol, G443
Rau (Bowers), Santha Rama, A3d
Ravel, G20, G30, G38, G58, G79, G82, G95, G141, G157, G211, G222, G236, G238, G285, G307, G357, G403, G405, G407, G429, G433, G438, G480, G624, G633-634, G637, G642, G648-649, G659, B120
Rebner, Wolfgang, G486

Slonimsky, Nicolas, G576, B22
Smetana, G287
Smeterlin, Jan, G406
Smit, Leo, W38a, G197, G577
Smith College Glee Club, G416
Smith, Carol, G664, G666
Smith, Carleton Sprague, 12, W33b, W38a,
   G70, G105, G205, G249, G333, G669, A13a
Smith, David, W52a
Smith, Gerald, G406
Smith, Julia, 11, 22, G158, B254, B356
Smith, Russell, G274, G644
Smith, S. Stephenson, G424
Snyder, Linda, W7a-b, W29a-b, W32f,
   W32h, W37c, W38i
Societá Corelli, G432
Sohlmans Musiklexikon, B286
Sokoloff, Noel, G269
Soler, G146
Solo (Variety critic), B357
Solomon, Izler, G685
"Some Reflections on Opera: Rolf
   Lieberman, Man of the Theatre," G687
Son of Heaven, The: see Profiles from
   China, W32
Sonata for Harp, 12, 15, W42, D12-16, G675,
   B21, B34, B76, B89, B94, B119, B219, B224,
   B227, B281, B293, B342, B350, B358-359,
   B381, A3a
Sonata for Harp, Flute, and Horn, 6, W40
Sonata for Piano and Percussion, 12-16, 20,
   33, W43, D17, G425, G451, G666, B4, B31,
   B46, B94, B100, B117, B207, B248, B289-
   290, B349, B384, A3a
Sonatina for Piano, W38
Sonatina for Treble Recorder or Flute and
   Piano, W27, B94-95, B281, B305, B350-351
Song in Summer, W15
Song in the Wood: see Choral Suite, W19
Songs of A. E. Housman: see Five Songs,
   W29
Sor, G435
Soria, Dorle, A3g(1)
Souris, G294
Southwestern Musician, B114
Sowerby, Leo, G197, G288
Sowerwine, William, G44
Soyer, David, G15
Spanish Suite, W13, G594
Spelman, Timothy Mather, G578
Spencer, Kenneth, G137
Spira, Pamela, W33c
Spirito, Romolo de, W32a
Spisak, Michel, G2, G3
Spivacke, Harold, A14b
Spohr, G33, G672
Spoleto Festival, 29, W55, W55a, W59,
   W59a, A3e
Staehelin, Marguerite, G627
Stamitz, G670
Stanberg, Andrea K., B360
Stanley, Anna Marian, G41

Starer, Robert, G150, G198, G437
Stars: see Five Songs, W29
State Library of Victoria (Melbourne), 21,
   31, B300, A3, A4
State of the Arts (ABC), 33, B200
State Opera of SA, W46e, W52c
Steber, Eleanor, G36, G599
Steck, Anna, G127
Steel, Anthony, A3j
Steele, Janet, W62b
Stein, Gertrude, G109, G175, B320
Stein, Leon, G275
Stern, Susan, B361
Stessin, Herbert, G245
Stevens, Genty, W46d
Stevens, Halsey, G26, G137
Stevens, Rise, G361
Stevens, Wallace, W7
Stewart-Green, Miriam, B362-364
Stiedry, Fritz, G599
Still, William Grant, G376
Stojowski, G31
Stokowski, 16, 28, W44a, G5, G57, B30,
   B107, B384, A1, A3b, A3dd
Stoll, John, W38e
Stone, Robinson, W46b
Storr-Wessel piano team, G212
Strasfogel, Ignace, G154
Stratas, Teresa, 30, W62, A1
Strattner, G312
Strauss, Johann, G302, G619
Strauss, John, G387
Strauss, Richard, G21, G124, G141, G240,
   G317, G358, G373, G433, G459, G609-610,
   G647, G669
Stravinsky, 9, 20, 23, G10, G13, G38, G47,
   G58, G82, G115-116, G169, G179, G266,
   G443, G475, G490, G498, G514, B46
Stravinsky: see Thomsoniana, W38
Strick, Sandra, G461
String Quartet, W22
Strong, Barry, W46c
Strongin, Theodore M., 8, G94, G320, G359,
   G456
Stuckenschmidt, H. H., 7, B365
Sultan, Grete, G646
Sun News Pictorial, B300
Sun, The (Melbourne), B305-306
Sun-Herald (Sydney), B287, B366
Sunday Telegraph (Sydney), B4
Surinach, 26, 30, W46b, W48a, W51a,
   W62a, D2-4, D6-7, D11, D19, G393, G451,
   G644, G655, G676, B71, A3g
Swallow, Alexander, G72
Swanson, Howard, G185, G455, G654
Swarthout, Gladys, G72
Sweelinck, G633, G665
Swing, Raymond, A3b(5)
Sydney Morning Herald, B13, B31-34, B47,
   B77, B80, B100, B105, B200, B231, B387
Sydney Opera House Library, A7
Sykes, Jill, B366-367

About the Author

DEBORAH HAYES is Associate Professor of Music History at the University of Colorado in Boulder. She has written about men and women composers and their music from the eighteenth century to the present in Europe and the United States for the *Journal of the American Musicological Society, Current Musicology, American Music,* and the *College Music Symposium.*

**Recent Titles in
Bio-Bibliographies in Music**

Vincent Persichetti: A Bio-Bibliography
Donald L. Patterson and Janet L. Patterson

Robert Ward: A Bio-Bibliography
Kenneth Kreitner

William Walton: A Bio-Bibliography
Carolyn J. Smith

Albert Roussel: A Bio-Bibliography
Robert Follet

Anthony Milner: A Bio-Bibliography
James Siddons

Edward Burlingame Hill: A Bio-Bibliography
Linda L. Tyler

Alexander Tcherepnin: A Bio-Bibliography
Enrique Alberto Arias

Ernst Krenek: A Bio-Bibliography
Garrett H. Bowles, compiler

Ned Rorem: A Bio-Bibliography
Arlys L. McDonald

Richard Rodney Bennett: A Bio-Bibliography
Steward R. Craggs, compiler

Radie Britain: A Bio-Bibliography
Walter B. Bailey and Nancy Gisbrecht Bailey

Frank Martin: A Bio-Bibliography
Charles W. King, compiler